MW01028699

Two Scholarly Friends

To Karen and Bob Riegel
with love and best wishes,

Mary Crow Anderson

February 5, 1998

Two Scholarly Friends

Yates Snowden–John Bennett Correspondence, 1902–1932

Edited by
Mary Crow Anderson

Published by the University of South Carolina Press
in cooperation with the Caroline McKissick Dial
South Caroliniana Library Endowment Fund and the
South Caroliniana Society

Library of Congress Cataloging-in-Publication Data

Snowden, Yates, 1858–1933.
    Two scholarly friends : Yates Snowden–John Bennett correspondence,
1902–1932 / edited by Mary Crow Anderson.
        p.   cm.
    "In cooperation with the Caroline McKissick Dial South
Caroliniana Library Endowment Fund, and the South Caroliniana
Society."
    Includes bibliographical references and index.
    ISBN 0-87249-961-8 (hard cover : acid-free)
    1. South Carolina—Intellectual life—20th century. 2. American
literature—South Carolina—History and criticism. 3. Arts,
American—South Carolina. 4. Arts, Modern—20th century—South
Carolina. 5. Snowden, Yates, 1858–1933—Correspondence.
6. Bennett, John, 1865–1956—Correspondence.   I. Bennett, John,
1865–1956. II. Anderson, Mary Crow, 1922-   . III. Title.
F274.S63   1993
975.5'04—dc20   93–14054

To Orin, Innis, and Dick

Contents

research; early Charleston suffragette movement; Flora MacDonald; Bennett's recorded songs.

Work on legends; *Master Skylark* on stage; World War I; art and Lewis R. Mignot; unveiling in State House of marble tablet to Snowden's mother; Gullah stories by Ambrose Gonzales.

Gullah origins and usage; World War I; translations by J. A. Symonds and G. H. Sass; Gonzales's *Laguerre.*

Work on *Madame Margot;* Smythe nicknames; scarlet fever at Christmas; Hampton anecdote; Sams and Gonzales's Gullah glossary; D. J. McCord house; Confederate ladies; J. F. J. Caldwell's poem; literary figures; formation of South Carolina Poetry Society.

Acclaim for *Master Skylark* and *The Treasure of Peyre Gaillard;* picture of Louisa Cheves McCord for a University publication; Snowden's commencement address on William H. Trescot, James D. B. DeBow, John McCrady, and Paul H. Hayne; publication of *Madame Margot* and its reception.

Sunday *State* "Writers and Books" page; *Madame Margot* reviews; Jane Bennett's engagement; a Civil War love story; Rowland Rugeley's burlesque translation of *Dido and Aeneas;* early South Carolina writings; the MacDowell Colony and work with DuBose Heyward and Hervey Allen; Salt Sulphur Springs memories; Heyward and Allen's *Carolina Chansons;* Gonzales's *Black Border.*

Last English licenser of books; Billy Sunday's reference to Col. Alfred Rhett; Arthur Hugh Clough and

Charleston; William Rose Benet and Henry Seidel
Canby and "The Abbot of Derry"; *Apothecaries' Hall;*
Hervey Allen's reaction to a Snowden article; Orient
and Jane's wedding.

G. A. Wauchope's anthology; 1782 London account
of Isaac Hayne's execution; criticism of the McCord
family; Bennett's new project; Basil Gildersleeve and
Charleston; F. P. Gaines's reference to *Madame
Margot;* Huguenot Church's Coligny medallion unveiling; tribute to Gonzales and Heyward; *Southern
Review* authors; silhouette of flying-horse.

Revolutionary War Captain John McCord and his
mother; Francis Asbury's *Journal;* Governor and Mrs.
Thomas Worthington of Ohio; family news; Confederate General Isaac Ridgeway Trimble; Bennett's account of scene with Major Smythe at time of his
request to marry Susan; "The Magnificat of the Hills";
works of Dr. Joseph B. Ladd in eighteenth century.

Vagrant Verse; tribute to Elizabeth O'Neill Verner;
Simons, Stoney, and Lapham book on Charleston
architecture; W. W. Ball's move to *News & Courier;*
Julien Green's *Mont-Cinère;* Salt Sulphur Springs and
"Magnificat"; contemporary Charleston writers.

Bennett's election to Phi Beta Kappa; memories of a
traveling band; Poetry Society Year Book; Dr. Robert Wilson's *Half-Forgotten By-Ways;* Bennett's *Pigtail of Ah Lee Ben Loo;* Romeo and Juliet silhouette;
Snowden's pamphlet jest.

Bennett's Northern and Southern kinsmen; Bennett's
first grandchild, Anne Wells; Martha Laurens
Ramsay's book; news of young Jack Bennett and

friends; Eliza Crawley Murden's book; Snowden and Fitz McMaster's automobile wreck; artist Alfred Hutty.

Preface

Yates Snowden and John Bennett, who wrote the letters which appear in *Two Scholarly Friends,* were literary men who belonged to an elitist group of educators, authors, and artists. They were both allied to patrician families in the state; they were far from wealthy, but not as poor as many other citizens of South Carolina, the Lowcountry as well as the Upcountry. In a state which remained primarily agricultural but in which the textile industry was growing fast, they did not face the daily problems of the average South Carolinian. For many farmers or mill workers, just to make enough to stay alive was a daily challenge.

From 1902 to 1932 was a time when South Carolina was poor monetarily but rich in tradition. The state had not yet emerged from the effects of the Civil War and the aftermath of Reconstruction.

During the first ten years of the correspondence, under the presidencies of William McKinley, Theodore Roosevelt, and William Howard Taft, South Carolina was represented in the United States Senate by bitter rivals, Benjamin Tillman and John L. McLaurin. When Ellison D. Smith defeated McLaurin, South Carolina had two so-called "farmer advocates" in Washington. Governors of the state at this time were Duncan C. Heyward, a former rice planter, followed by Martin F. Ansel, a prohibitionist. Quietly they helped bring about changes, such as abolishing the Dispensary system and providing for public high schools. Then Coleman L. Blease became governor.

In the next ten years, when the presidents were Woodrow Wilson and Warren G. Harding, Tillman and Smith remained South Carolina's senators until Tillman's death in 1918. N. B. Dial won the election to replace Tillman, but in turn was defeated by former governor Coleman Blease. Richard I. Manning, who succeeded Blease as governor, led the state through World War I, persuading the legislature to make progressive changes in areas such as education and child labor laws. Robert A. Cooper, becoming governor in 1919, also worked for reforms.

The last ten years of the correspondence covered a period with Harding, Calvin Coolidge, and Herbert Hoover, as presidents, and ended soon after Franklin D. Roosevelt's election in 1932. "Coley"

Blease, until he was defeated by James F. Byrnes in 1930, and "Cotton Ed" Smith were the senators for South Carolina. Thomas G. McLeod, John G. Richards, and I. C. Blackwood served as governors. It was an era of growing electric power, highway expansion, school improvements, and the awakening of cultural arts in the state. The whole country, however, was by 1929 in the throes of an economic depression as deep as South Carolina's had been for so long.

Snowden was a Charlestonian through and through and remained so all his life. Born two years before the War Between the States and an eyewitness to the burning of Columbia during his childhood, he remained forever an unreconstructed Rebel. Perhaps his best-known poem is "A Carolina Bourbon," a tribute to another of similar heritage and beliefs. Sometimes an irascible critic, authoritatively certain that the values of the past were best, Snowden nonetheless became a well-beloved professor, often quoted and now remembered by the University in a dormitory named for him, not far from where he once lived on campus. At his death in 1933, a student guard of honor stood watch over the body, which lay in state in the Carolina library before the funeral.

Born in Chillicothe, Ohio, one month after General Robert E. Lee's surrender at the Appomattox courthouse, John Bennett continued throughout his life an inveterate Yankee. When he came to South Carolina in the late 1890s, he was already a recognized novelist. A few years later, he became allied with a patrician Southern family through marriage. His Yankee upbringing gave him a different point of view from that of his professor friend. In one letter Bennett tells Snowden that while growing up he "used to say, with a boy's honest fervor, 'Thank God Grant won!'" He never completely relinquished his Northern sentiments, but he tempered his ideas in his search for both strengths and weaknesses of any side of a situation. When Bennett made his home in Charleston, he not only continued with his writing career, but also began helping others achieve success in the fields of literature and art.

The friendship which developed between the Southerner and the Northerner lasted more than thirty years and resulted in a correspondence that dealt primarily with intellectual interests, rather than with the state's economic and political problems. The social events mentioned were usually those of literary, educational, or cultural arts groups. Above all, the two were involved in the preservation of knowledge and the creation of new art and literature.

In the 1960s I had studied the works of both men while preparing my doctoral dissertation, "The Huguenot in the South Carolina Novel," Snowden for the traits of the French Protestants to whom he referred in poems and articles and Bennett for his novel *The Treasure of Peyre Gaillard.* When the correspondence of the two was made available to me at the South Caroliniana Library, I was delighted.

In approaching the presentation of these letters of two scholarly friends for publication, I first copied them faithfully, exactly as they were written. Besides those in the collection given to the South Caroliniana Library by John Bennett many years ago, a few were found in Charleston in the South Carolina Historical Society archives. Once the transcriptions were finished, annotations added, introductions written to each chapter, and the first and last chapters completed, the size of the volume was immense. It was decided that a selection from the correspondence must be made.

The letters chosen for this book are those which show the men's primary interests and at the same time reveal the personalities of two very different friends. From their first meeting, in spite of, or perhaps because of, their differences, these two former newspapermen enjoyed corresponding with each other. Subjects discussed at length were research about the Revolutionary and Civil Wars, literature, music, art, and Gullah. Both delighted in unearthing facts hidden or glossed over by previous historians, Bennett for proposed novels and Snowden for his classes.

Because of the fiasco of the South Carolina history that bears his name, although not written by him, Snowden has been considered a poor historian by those not knowing the circumstances of the publication. Having signed an agreement to help with a history of the state, he later found to his embarrassment that it was only his name that was wanted for reaching possible financial contributors, and the resulting volumes were a disaster. Although documented in other Snowden papers, the experience was so painful to him that it was nowhere mentioned in his letters to Bennett.

Living in Charleston was sometimes difficult for Bennett because of social obligations and other demands on his time. In some letters he joked about not wanting his wife to have to support him, although royalties from earlier books continued to arrive regularly. He yearned to leave a worthwhile legacy of fine books, each different in subject matter and style. Like many creative artists, Bennett suffered when his book in progress did not develop as quickly as he would have liked. Yet he distrusted easy composition, rewriting again and again to achieve the exact tone he wanted.

In music and art, their tastes differed. Snowden knew little about either, although he was greatly interested in both, accumulating an art collection and serving as the first president of the Columbia Art Association. Bennett had not only been an artist, but also a member of a travelling band before becoming a writer of novels. Through the years he continued to play his guitar, write songs, teach drawing, and send his friends Christmas silhouettes.

In literature, the two friends' tastes often differed radically. Snowden liked only poems with well-defined rhyme schemes. He disliked certain verses written by Bennett, which showed modern influence in style. Snowden approved heartily of the work with the melodies of blacks done by Bennett and his wife Susan. Snowden praised the important research and publications of Bennett on the distinctive Lowcountry language, Gullah. Nevertheless, while commending the style of Bennett's *Madame Margot*, he did not praise its subject matter. Snowden was unable to accept blacks as heroes or heroines in literature. Although in this correspondence he made no allusion to his distaste for Julia Peterkin's 1928 Pulitzer prize-winning novel, *Scarlet Sister Mary*, or to her other fine stories, Snowden did comment on DuBose Heyward's work. He wrote favorably of Heyward's poetry, yet he scorned *Porgy*. Bennett, a close friend and mentor of Heyward, recognized the young author's genius in both the novel and poetry; and he joyfully lauded Heyward on occasion after occasion.

The Yates Snowden–John Bennett letters are important because of the two friends who wrote them. The influence of Bennett and Snowden has been great in the intellectual life of twentieth-century South Carolina. Snowden, perhaps the most colorful history professor that ever taught in the state, was a forever-rebel Southerner, quick of wit and temper, who believed that Charleston was the "Holy City." Although residing in Columbia over one-third of his life, he always considered Charleston the only "town" in South Carolina. Bennett, a transplanted Northerner, a talented artist, musician, and author, whose books gained international recognition, was the true force behind the Charleston Renaissance. It was at Bennett's fireside that the Poetry Society of South Carolina was formed. It was Bennett who encouraged DuBose Heyward, Hervey Allen, and Herbert Ravenel Sass, among many other writers. It was he who taught drawing at the South Carolina Art Association School and who welcomed to Charleston such artists as Alfred Hutty.

The letters of Snowden and Bennett help to reveal the cultural life of South Carolina in the early twentieth-century through the discussion of many facets of the intellectual and social interests of the time. They contain lively anecdotes about well-known, and some not so well-known, historical figures of the Revolution, the Civil War, and the early 1900s. They uncover little-known facts about South Carolina dialect, and they reveal attitudes about literature, music, and art of many different periods and genres. The letters are also important because of their style, that gracious form of addressing friends with love, affection, and kindliness of an earlier era.

The Manuscript Division of the South Caroliniana Library houses the Snowden-Bennett Collection, given to the library by John Bennett in 1949. The correspondence in this volume has been chosen from that collection. In several cases, some sentences of lesser importance have been omitted from the letters selected. Such omissions are indicated by ellipses. Spaced periods used by Bennett in his letters appear as dashes in the edited text.

Since most of the correspondence between the two friends is sent from Charleston and Columbia, the complete letterheads appear in the volume only when they are important to the contents of the letters. Names of persons spelled in various ways have been left as they appear in the originals. A few obvious errata have been corrected, and the punctuation has been standardized.

The notes for each chapter appear at the end of the book. They clarify the identities of or add details concerning many people mentioned, for the ones cited have often been involved in historical or otherwise noteworthy events.

Acknowledgments

My interest in Yates Snowden and John Bennett began in childhood. In Charleston, the Bennett home was at 37 Legare Street, and the home of my great-uncle and great-aunt, William Henry and Ida Imogene S. Shingler, and their children was at 21 Legare Street. *Master Skylark,* written by John Bennett, was a favorite book in my school years. In Columbia, I grew up on the University of South Carolina campus, where my father was a professor. One of my earliest memories is of a figure striding across the Carolina horseshoe, with dark cloak swirling in the wind. Yates Snowden was that figure. My parents were friends of Annie and Yates Snowden, as they were of many other Charlestonians and Columbians mentioned in the Snowden-Bennett letters.

I am particularly indebted to the staff of the South Caroliniana Library at the University of South Carolina for their help in the preparation of this volume. I have been encouraged by the advice and assistance of the director, Dr. Allen Stokes, in undertaking this most pleasant enterprise. To him I wish to express my sincere thanks, as well as to Henry G. Fulmer, whose aid in locating specific materials needed to clarify certain phrases in the correspondence has been invaluable. To the assistant director, Dr. Thomas L. Johnson, and to Herbert J. Hartsook, Laura M. Costello, Eleanor M. Richardson, James R. Hill, Ann B. Troyer—indeed, to all the South Caroliniana Library personnel—I am also deeply grateful.

I owe special thanks to Dr. Mark V. Wetherington, former director of the South Carolina Historical Society in Charleston, and to the staffs of the Huguenot Society of South Carolina, the Charleston Library Society, and the Thomas Cooper Library at the University of South Carolina, who have helped me find additional information.

Besides my family, without whom this book could not have been attempted, others whose keen interest or important knowledge has contributed to its completion are Dr. Carol Drowota, Curator Angela Mack of the Gibbes Museum of Art, Miss Anna Wells Rutledge, Mrs. Philip E. Mosely, Edward Ball, John H. Bennett, Jr., and the late Dr. John A. Hamilton, of Charleston; Dr. Willard H. Davis, Dr. Carol

Myers Scotton, Dr. Michael Montgomery, Miss Peggy Clark, and Preston L. Musgrove, of Columbia; Curator Ellen Miles and Catalog Researcher Ann P. Wagner of the National Portrait Gallery of the Smithsonian Institution, Washington, D.C.; and Prof. Jan Blommaert and Prof. John Everaert of the University of Ghent in Belgium.

Two Scholarly Friends

Chapter 1

The Meeting

THROUGH THEIR letters, two extraordinary men, one born just before and one just after the Civil War, have revealed their lives against the background of early twentieth-century South Carolina. Yates Snowden, a quintessential Southern gentleman and an unreconstructed Rebel, left the Charleston *News and Courier* to become a history professor and an unforgettable figure on the University of South Carolina campus. Snowden fired the love of history in the minds of his students and was in demand as a speaker throughout the state. John Bennett, a stately Northerner and author-artist from Ohio, moved to the South on doctor's orders, made Carolina his home, and became the compelling force behind the Charleston Renaissance. Noted for his poetry and novels, Bennett influenced many writers.

The two scholars met 1 May 1901, in Washington Square, Charleston, South Carolina, at the dedication of the memorial to Henry Timrod.[1] They soon became fast friends.

John Bennett, the son of John Briscoe Henry and Eliza Jane Trimble McClintock Bennett, was born 17 May 1865, in Chillicothe, Ohio. His family was torn by the Civil War—the Bennetts and the McClintocks fighting for the North and the Trimbles for the South. Although William Trimble McClintock, John Bennett's uncle, had a son in the Union Army, he prevented a young Confederate soldier from being hanged on the pretext of being a spy by obtaining the signature of Abraham Lincoln countermanding the order.

As a lad, John Bennett's sympathies were definitely with the Yankee forces in the Civil War. Later, when ill and penniless in the early 1890s, Bennett was befriended by the Appleton family of Salt Sulphur

Springs, West Virginia, who took him in and nursed him back to health. Jack Appleton, whose father had been badly wounded while serving as one of the white officers of the black regiment that made the night attack on Battery Wagner, became one of Bennett's closest friends.

On 11 December 1938 there appeared in *The News and Courier* an article, "Wanted To Draw, Writer by Accident: Bennett's Ambition To Be Illustrator Realized in His Own Stories." The newspaper outlined his career, beginning with his first interest in story-telling.

If the neighborhood children helped a chore boy with his tasks, he would tell them stories—a mixture of Arabian Nights tales and of Irish legends—in the evening. When the lad obtained a better job, John Bennett was designated to read magazine stories to the group. He would add action to what was written, if the story seemed dull. Soon he began to draw pictures and put them with anecdotes and poems on a paper, circulated under the desks at school for two years, until caught. The Ross County weekly, *The Register*, printed parts of the confiscated copy seen by a reporter.

Bennett became interested in the farces presented on the stage in the neighborhood stable loft. One person who performed there for a single time only was George C. Tyler, in later years the New York manager of Caruso and Nazimova, the producer of *Ben Hur* and *The Garden of Allah*, and the man responsible for arranging the sale of the film rights of *Master Skylark*.

When the father of one of the boys had to take a printing press in lieu of a cash payment for a debt, the gang set it up in the stable loft and began to print miscellaneous items, such as jam labels, as well as a paper, *The Little Messenger*. For three years the boys learned the newspaper business—writing stories, type-setting, printing, and selling advertisements and copies of the paper.

When Bennett left school at the age of seventeen to study art, he worked as a cub reporter at *The Register* during the summer to save money to pay his way. In the autumn of 1883 he enrolled in the Art Students' League of Cincinnati, where he remained until the spring, when a flood sent all non-residents out of the city. Back in Chillicothe, Bennett began to work for the new Democratic paper, *The Daily News*. He ran it virtually alone and in opposition to the Republican weekly, also owned by his employer. When he revealed a real estate boom to be fake, Bennett antagonized some local business men and was forced to quit his position. He left town and began to work for the comic weekly magazine, *Light*, until the real estate fiasco died down. He then returned to the *Daily News* to help the paper survive the competition of a new daily in Chillicothe. John improvised a new type cut and was able to produce the first three-color print ever to appear in a newspaper. He also began to use chalk plates. When the opposition paper folded and one of its backers told John that they couldn't win out in the rivalry because they never knew what the *Daily News* was going to do next, Bennett modestly replied, "Neither did we."

Leaving Chillicothe again, he contributed cartoons and verses and articles to several Midwestern magazines and Sunday supplements for a few years, during which he also took any job he could find. He became a painter of scenery for a theatrical troupe, a guitarist in a small itinerant orchestra, an expert taxidermist, and a cartographer with Peabody Museum's field expedition to Indian mounds in Ohio.

In 1891 he became a regular writer for *St. Nicholas* of stories, accompanied by silhouettes, instead of the pen-and-ink drawings he had previously done. It was these stories and illustrations that made up most of Bennett's 1928 book, *The Pigtail of Ah Lee Ben Loo*. Mary Mapes Dodge was the editor of *St. Nicholas* in the 1890s, and it was she who published *Master Skylark* serially in the magazine. When Bennett went to New York to finish the novel, he studied at the Art Students' League half the day and wrote the other half. After first appearing in the magazine, *Master Skylark* was published in book form in 1897 by the Century Company. The success of the book made it possible for Bennett to move to New York to resume his study of drawing. When he was requested to begin a second serial, however, he adopted writing as his profession and began *Barnaby Lee*, a juvenile romance of old New York and Maryland, which was published by the Century Company several years later in 1902. Soon after he started work on the new novel, he suffered gas poisoning in the New York rooming house where he was living and had to leave the city.

In order to recuperate, Bennett came to the South in 1898. In Charleston, he again met Susan Smythe, whom he had first seen at Salt Sulphur Springs when, as a young girl, she was vacationing with her parents in the West Virginia mountains. At that time Bennett had been an impecunious writer, visiting friends at the resort; now he was the successful author of *Master Skylark*, which was to become a classic not only in the English-speaking world, where it even became available in braille, but also through translations in Holland, Germany, France, and Poland.

Susan Dunlap Adger Smythe, the daughter of Augustine Thomas and Louisa Rebecca Hayne McCord Smythe, and John Bennett were married on 2 April 1902. They became the parents of three children: Jane McClintock, John Henry van Sweringen, and Susan Adger. Through his marriage, Bennett became allied with the Smythe, McCord, Adger, Cheves, Dulles, Stoney, and Flinn families of South Carolina and the Wright family of Georgia.

In Charleston in 1902, Bennett finished the novel based on the adventures of Sheriff Gerrit van Sweringen, his own ancestor. *Barnaby*

Lee was in later years filmed by the Edison Company. In 1906 the Century Company published his first adult novel, *The Treasure of Peyre Gaillard,* a South Carolina tale which was reissued by the London *Times* to break the book trust. He had written the story on a dare by Mrs. Samuel G. Stoney. Soon after arriving in Charleston, Bennett began to study the speech of the black people along the South Carolina Coast and in 1908 and 1909 had some of his research on Gullah published in the *South Atlantic Quarterly.* In 1921 *Madame Margot,* a grotesque legend of old Charleston, was also published by the Century Company.

Although Bennett no longer made his living through illustrations, he never lost his interest in art. He taught art classes in Charleston and sent silhouettes to his friends as Christmas presents. In the 1920s, he made designs for the backs of Ambrose E. Gonzales's books.

In 1928 Longmans, Green and Company published Bennett's last juvenile book, *The Pigtail of Ah Lee Ben Loo,* a collection of whimsical tales with his own silhouette illustrations. That year, when he was revising his silhouette tales and verses for publication as the *Pigtail of Ah Lee Ben Loo,* Bertha Gunterman visited Charleston and wrote "The Astrologer's Tower" for the *Horn Book* (volume 4, number 3), issued in August 1928. In her article, she called the Legare Street home of the Bennetts a "place of wizardry," which "is full of surprises and necromancy." She described the top floor of the house, where at one end in a study that overlooked trees and walled gardens toward the harbor, Bennett wrote; at the other end in a carpenter shop that looked out toward the Ashley River, he mended toys or fashioned model sloops and log cabins and kites. She remarked that he had loved to work with his hands since childhood, at one time carving a set of Punch and Judy faces from big potatoes by following George Cruikshanks' designs, and then giving a show with the help of his brother and younger sister. On the same floor of the pre-Revolutionary Charleston home was a library, where young friends and relatives were welcome to wander in to read at leisure.

Bennett's final adult book, *The Doctor to the Dead,* was published by Rinehart in 1946. Throughout the years he contributed both prose and poetry to many magazines, including the *Atlantic* and *Harper's,* and several of his poems were set to music.

A student of South Carolina history and folklore, John Bennett was honorary curator of the Historical and Cultural Collections of the Charleston Museum, a curator of the South Carolina Historical Society, and a teacher of special classes for the South Carolina Art Association. He became an honorary member of the Alpha of South Carolina chapter of Phi Beta Kappa and later received an honorary doctorate from the University of South Carolina. With DuBose Heyward, the author of *Porgy,* and Hervey Allen, the author of *Anthony Adverse,* Bennett founded the Poetry Society of South Carolina, which became the inspiration for the Southern Literary Renaissance. He died 28 December 1956 at the age of ninety-one.

J. Yates Snowden, the son of Dr. William S. and Mary Amarintha Yates Snowden, was born on 8 May 1858 in Charleston. His father, the son of the Reverend Charles B. and Maria Louisa Drake Snowden, died during the War Between the States, while serving as a Confederate Army surgeon. His mother, the daughter of Joseph and Elizabeth Saylor Yates, was educated in Pennsylvania at the primary schools of Philadelphia, at Madame Talvande's on Legare Street in Charleston, and at the Columbia Female Academy at Barhamville, where her roommate was Ann Pamela Cunningham, known for her efforts to preserve Mount Vernon.

Mary Amarintha Snowden was one of the most distinguished women of her time. As vice-president of the Soldiers' Relief Association of Charleston, formed in 1861, Mrs. Snowden became responsible for providing garments for the soldiers in the field and hospital stores for the sick and dying in hospitals, in private homes, and at Second Manassas, on the open field. Left with two small children in 1863, when her husband died of typhoid fever while serving with the Confederate forces, she continued her civic work. For some months at the end of the war, she took care of several hundred Confederate prisoners in Columbia, seeing that they were clothed and fed "with the contributions of the citizens and what she could exhort from Federal authorities."[2] She was president of the Calhoun Monument Association and president of the Ladies Memorial Association, which placed marble headstones in Magnolia Cemetery on the graves of 800 men who fell in defense of Charleston, later erecting a bronze monument in the center of the plot. In 1867 she founded the Confederate Home and School in Charleston for the mothers, widows, and daughters of Southern soldiers. About twenty years after her death in 1898, a marble tablet to her memory was placed on the wall of the State House rotunda in Columbia.[3]

As a child of nearly seven, Snowden witnessed the burning of Columbia. His family had taken refuge in Columbia, hoping to escape Sherman's march to the sea. They, along with a number of blacks from his late father's Lowcountry plantation, were staying at the home of the Reverend Dr. Aaron W. Leland[4] on Gervais Street, the historic house where the Marquis de LaFayette had been entertained on his 1825 visit to Columbia. When General Sherman's Army arrived during the day of 17 February 1865, the residence became the headquarters of a Union Colonel. That night the burning of the city occurred. The memories of those days remained vivid all of the professor's life, for as late as 1930 he wrote to the then retired United States Army General Adelbert Ames as follows:

During the night of the conflagration, the house caught fire nine times, but though the adjoining house (to the west), was burned, it was saved. . . .

A day or two afterward, you came there to see Colonel Stone, you a dashing young Major (or Colonel?), and very handsome, as I seem to remember. You must have been genial, and, possibly, curious as to the character of young "Rebels," for I distinctly remember having a talk with you—possibly on your knee.

I was, like all of us nowadays, "Nearer Heaven when I was a boy"; and I was then imbued with the religious training of my Presbyterian mother. I remember distinctly telling you: "Major (?) Ames, your people have broken two commandments."

With a laugh, you asked me: "*What* commandments?"

And with the impudence of early youth, I replied: "'Thou shalt not steal,' and 'Thou shalt not covet thy neighbors' goods!'"

As partial vindication of those "charges," I might say that, on that dreadful night, the house had been "raided" by "foragers"; many articles appropriated, and one portrait and a handsome wardrobe ruined by bayonet thrusts,—while our cow and all our chickens had disappeared from the back yard.

My mother heard, or heard of, my impudence and rebuked me severely. But, though you may have been amused, you must have been generous and tender-hearted; for the next day you sent, or brought, me some candy! (Where you got candy in Columbia, S.C., in February, 1865, God only knows!) I have never forgotten the taste of it; and I have held Major Adelbert Ames in kindly remembrance for 65 years!

In the same letter, Snowden recounted the following incident:

General Sherman was about to leave Columbia, and thousands of negroes wanted to "follow the Army." My mother (Mrs. Mary A. Snowden), was a woman of force and character. . . . Addressing herself, either to you, or Colonel Stone, she said: "Colonel, I wish you would tell these former servants of Dr. Snowden and mine what it means to 'follow the Army.'" She had crowded thirty or more of our negroes (most of them from the plantation in St. Stephen's Parish), into Mrs. Leland's large drawing-room. Their "leader" was Brutus, my late father's body-servant, and an excellent man. Either you, or Colonel Stone, then told them that, if they followed the Army, they would be made

to "fell trees, make roads, build bridges; in brief, to pioneer, etc., etc."

I think that the word "pioneer" did the business. It
evidently frightened Brutus, for as soon as he heard it, he
interrupted you: "Pahdon me, suh; but wha' dat wud?"
"Pioneer," you repeated. Whereupon Brutus said very
decidedly: "I ent da gwine." Bowing to you, he left the
room, and every one of the 30 negroes (with two, possibly
three exceptions), followed him, instead of Sherman. They
remained more or less pensioners on my mother, until we
returned to Charleston, early in 1866.

Snowden went to school in his native city where he received his
undergraduate education with the class of 1879 at the College of
Charleston, which conferred on him an honorary doctorate in 1910. He
was admitted to the bar in 1882, but left the law profession to enter the
newspaper field, conducting the *Berkeley County Gazette,* a weekly
newspaper in Mount Pleasant. He was for a time an associate editor of
The Budget, a Charleston weekly.

On 25 October 1894, Yates Snowden and Ann Eliza Warley, the
daughter of John Caldwell and Anne Eliza Bailey Warley, were married.
The ceremony took place at the Parish Church of Prince George Winyah
in Georgetown, South Carolina.[5]

Joining the staff of the Charleston *News and Courier,* Snowden
helped cover the story of the earthquake of 1886. He remained with the
newspaper eighteen years before doing post-graduate work in New York
at Columbia University and then becoming a college professor at the
University of South Carolina, where he taught history from 1905 until
his death on 22 February 1933.

In 1901, the year he met Bennett, Yates was still on the staff of *The
News and Courier.* By this time, he had published several historical
articles and had composed one of his best-known poems, "A Carolina
Bourbon." Other poems, written after he had become a history professor, included "Carolina, Hail," "Okrantomottis," and "A Blast Against
Book-Keepers." From early manhood, Snowden was in demand as a
speaker. His depth of thought, as well as his scintillating wit, made an
oration or even a simple conversation an event to be remembered.[6]

Snowden never got the newspaperman out of his system. Throughout the years he wrote articles for and letters to the editors of *The State*
and *The News and Courier.* It was his custom, late at night, to walk from
his home on the University of South Carolina campus to the 1200 block
of Main Street, where he would await the first edition of *The State* as it
came off the press. Other professors or some of his city friends often
kept the vigil with him at the little cafe near the newspaper office.

Yates Snowden had an excellent and extensive library, filled with volumes that he had obtained over the years, which Mrs. Snowden sold to the University of South Carolina after the professor's death. The works pertinent to the history and literature of the state remained in the South Caroliniana Library when the McKissick Library was built, but the other volumes were moved to the new facility, and later to the Thomas Cooper Library, where they may be found today.

Generous in lending books to friends and acquaintances, he occasionally became exasperated with those who neglected to return the treasured works. In *The Story of The State, 1891-1969*, Samuel Latimer told of the professor's inserting an advertisement in the newspaper, which restored to him "a good many valuable volumes." The ad appeared, as follows:

> Yates Snowden
> At Home
> 5 P.M. to 7 P.M. Today
> 803 Sumter Street
> Admission: The Return of One Book Borrowed From Me
> Notice: Positively No Books Lent
> During Hours of the Reception.[7]

There are almost as many anecdotes about Professor Snowden as there are people who knew him. Several have been preserved in the tribute, *In Memoriam: Yates Snowden, 1858-1933*, published by the University of South Carolina in July of 1934. Others have been handed down by word of mouth from friend to friend.

Once, Yates Snowden borrowed another professor's[8] portable typewriter, which, unlike most similar machines, had keys for adding foreign accents. Since Snowden liked to include French phrases in his letters, the other professor assumed that was the reason Yates needed to use the typewriter. Such was not the case, however. Snowden said he simply could not find his. A few days later, he returned the machine, saying that he had found his own under a pile of papers on his desk.

Some time after William Watts Ball[9] resigned as dean of journalism at the University in order to return to Charleston as editor-in-chief of *The News and Courier*, he invited the members of the Kosmos Club to be his guests in the port city. Among those who accepted were Yates Snowden and a prominent colleague on the University faculty.[10] The two stayed in Charleston through Sunday so that they could go to services at the French Protestant (Huguenot) Church to which Snowden belonged, the only church he ever made an effort to attend. At that time, Dr. Snowden helped take up the offering. When he reached his friend, that professor put in a quarter. Snowden remained motionless, with plate extended, until told, "Go on, you old goat." Yates then responded,

"I'm not going anywhere until you put some green money in the plate," and he was as good as his word.

According to a former student, it was Professor Snowden's custom, when writing his examinations on the blackboard, to indicate the special significance of certain questions by placing "D.I.M." before the numbers of those questions. "D.I.M." was Yates Snowden's abbreviation for "Damned Important."[11]

Another student used to tell the story about his class's bringing a jackass into the lecture room on April Fool's Day and leaving it while they hid outside, waiting for Professor Snowden to appear. When Snowden came into the room, he looked calmly at the animal and said, "This is the most intelligent class I have seen this semester."[12]

Great humor, warm friendship, and revealing comments on a wide variety of writers, artists, and historians, including South Carolinians, are found in the correspondence between Yates Snowden and John Bennett. For thirty years the friends exchanged these letters.

Snowden and Bennett sought help from each other on behalf of some struggling young person from time to time. As their friendship grew, they insulted one another with jovial camaraderie. The way they addressed each other in the salutations and the way they signed their letters were relevant to the tone of the letters and to their affairs in the outside world. Both men sought the truth, preferring facts to romantic surmises. Both continued to write verses. They enjoyed exchanging comments on the works of the well-known and the little-known in many genres. Each assisted in collecting material on subjects of interest to the other. Snowden, from time to time, requested help in polishing his own poetic endeavors. Bennett nearly always assisted, although in the midst of his own work. However, he refused when asked to write newspaper tributes to recently deceased persons, for he wished to spend the small amount of time he had free from his daily writing to help living authors and painters.

Bennett and Snowden used many phrases from the works of William Shakespeare. Characters from the novels of Charles Dickens also found their way into the correspondence in appropriate situations.

Snowden, who often expressed strongly his opinions concerning any matter under discussion, was always eager to tout the successes of his friends and to spurn literary works he felt were not absolutely true to history or life. He genuinely admired the poetry and novels of Bennett. Snowden liked Bennett's "The Magnificat of the Hills" so much, both for its central idea and its phrasing, that he often had the poem reprinted in order to distribute it to people he met during the summer months when he went to the North Carolina mountains.

Bennett admired the mental acuteness and the genial companion-ship of the dashing, unorthodox gentleman of the Old South, who was a loyal, ardent South Carolinian. Nevertheless, Bennett liked to needle Snowden about Confederate history, especially in regard to works by South Carolina historians.

Written by hand in pen or pencil on History Department or hotel stationery, plain paper, or scraps, Snowden's letters to Bennett were often dashed off in the early morning hours, when Snowden probably should have been asleep. Nevertheless, his thoughts flowed easily, wittily, and teasingly onto the page.

Bennett's letters were usually typed because of his poor eyesight, but with beautifully printed corrections of the text and additional notes in ink. The phrasing was vivid, clearly expressing ideas and making the reader laugh aloud at one moment and wipe away a tear the next.

These discussions, written in the gracious style of long ago, yet filled with sparkling repartee and frank observations, are found in the following pages.

Chapter 2

1902–1908

Poems of Snowden and Bennett; melodies of blacks; The Treasure of Peyre Gaillard; *Europe; free blacks before the War Between the States; Samuel F. B. Morse exhibit; poetry of George H. Sass; eye trouble.*

THE FIRST letters between Yates Snowden and John Bennett were exchanged some time after their meeting in 1901. In the beginning, the letters were fairly short. The salutations were most formal in 1902 and 1903, with the two addressing each other as Mr. Snowden and Mr. Bennett, but by 1904 they dropped the titles.

From New York and Columbia, Snowden's letters grew longer. Although there were no letters in the collection for 1905, Professor Snowden's first year at the University of South Carolina, he wrote twice to John Bennett in the fall of 1906.

On 1 January 1907, John and Susan Bennett's second child and only son, John, was born. That summer, Professor and Mrs. Snowden traveled to Europe, being assisted in their passage arrangements by Bennett. The Snowdens were accompanied on their tour by Roman Catholic Bishop Henry Pinckney Northrop of the Diocese of Charleston, through whom an audience with Pope Pius X was obtained while they were in Italy.

By 1907 Snowden and Bennett were on a first-name basis and the letters became more jocular in tone. In June of 1908 Bennett mentioned having trouble with his eyes, a condition that continued to plague him throughout his life.

During these years, the Bennetts visited Chillicothe, Ohio, the author's hometown, and Woodburn, the Augustine T. Smythe family place in Pendleton, South Carolina. Bennett published *Barnaby Lee* and the *Treasure of Peyre Gaillard,* worked on the music of blacks, and began research on old Charleston tales.

Bennett discussed art and art history with Snowden, especially in regard to Samuel F. B. Morse and his work in Charleston. Also, the friends critiqued the writings of George Herbert Sass, and mentioned other authors, world-famous and obscure, modern and classical.

THE NEWS AND COURIER
19 Broad Street
Charleston, S.C.

EDITORIAL ROOMS
May 7, 1902

Dear Mr. Bennett:

I thought I had already inflicted a "Bourbon"[1] upon you. It is a fate that few of my friends have escaped. Sam Stoney[2] tells me that your library still lacks the gem and so I send you one.

Yours truly,
Yates Snowden

"Woodburn," Pendleton, S.C.
October [ca. 5 Oct. 1902]

Mr. Yates Snowden
Charleston, S.C.

My dear Mr. Snowden:

I owe you some coals of fire for your "In a (Charleston) Rose-Garden," so I have requested my friends of the Century Company to send to your address a copy of my forth-coming book: "Barnaby Lee." If there is interest in it for you—suppose that it entertain you in spare time—if you ever find any—remember: this is my coal of fire.

Serenely yours,
John Bennett

Charleston, S.C., 6th Octr 1902

Dear Mr. Bennett: [Pendleton, S.C.]

I will read, mark, learn, and, if the pabulum be not too strong, will inwardly digest "Barnaby Lee," just as soon as it comes to hand, and I thank you for it. Next Sunday the wife & I are going to New London Conn. for two weeks & if it only comes in time, it may help to lighten the horrors of mal de mer.

I am delighted to have such coals heaped upon my head. I am used to hot stuff. You seem to forget that I am an amateur Huguenot.

I send you by this mail a copy of the New England Magazine for Dec'r 1898, with an article by Wm. E. Barton D.D.[3] on "Old Plantation Hymns." I hope that you & Mrs. Bennett have not finished collaborating your negro melodies. I don't know that Dr. Barton will help you any; but I did have a newspaper article on *S.C.* negro songs written by a friend of mine which I know would help you, if I could only find it. I am holding those scraps for data for your great South Carolina novel, on which I expect you to begin work next month.

Please remember my wife & self most kindly to Mrs. Bennett and to the Woodburn Smythes,[4] all and singular.

In unwilling haste,
Yours sincerely,
Yates Snowden

Columbia University
in the City of New York
Earl Hall

21st Dec. 1904

Dear Bennett,

T'other day, in one of my *very* few idle moments I dipped into a little book, with a S.C. imprint, entitled, "Natural History of the Negro Race" "*Extracted* from the French" by J. H. Guenebault, and printed in Charleston in 1837 by D. J. Dowling. It is a strange kind of book, in which it is difficult to find where Guenebault begins and where the quotation ends, though there are numerous foot notes mostly from French and German works very many of which are not to be found even in this 350,000 volume library. The scrappy references therein to *Negro Music* I have copied and enclose herewith.

When is the great definitive work on Negro Nightingales coming out? I await its appearance with great interest. Mr. Gilder[5] "lunched" me at "The Players" but I did not boast of being one of your many friends as I thought he might think me puffed with pride. I have shown our book-worm to some of the library chiefs at this University & there was a great "miration" thereat.

I won't tire you with my views of life in New York. The atmosphere (when not freezing) and the studies here on Morningside Heights are delightful; but, the horrible rush and hurry and turmoil down below is frightful. I dislike it even more than I did when I was here for several months in '88.

Gotham is a Hell of a place to *live* in & I long for the sweet tranquility, the unapproachable serenity of lower Church St. The wife & I are comfortably housed & fed at Miss Boykin's[6] at 103 West 48th St. While I am studying my eyes out, she, not being able to get some lucrative job reading to some millionaire blind lady, stays at home and "sits on a sofa and sews a fine seam, and feeds upon strawberries, sugar & cream." Mrs. hommages & the compliments of the season to Madame.

> Yr's sincerely,
> Yates Snowden

I have been looking for y'r article in the Atlantic, but all in vain.

UNIVERSITY OF SOUTH CAROLINA
DEPARTMENT OF HISTORY AND POLITICAL SCIENCE

Columbia, S.C., 15th Oct. 1906

Dear John Bennett:

The enclosed clipping from the N.Y. Ev'g Post may interest you. I scissored it in 1904, and it turned up *yesterday*. Query, Is the Romulus (Africanus) any relation to Uncle Remus?

You are doubtless already familiar with it; but if not, look at that article by Henry B. Dawson[7] on *Slavery in Connecticut*, & you will see a reference to Africans in this country selecting sham kings! I have 60 written "quiz" papers to read tonight & have not time to look through the Year Books for the article. It is since the '80's. When I read it the other night, I thought of you. I think of you pretty often. Strange!

Do you ever come to Columbia, paying your own expenses? If you ever do, can't you turn up your barrel & give South Carolina Collegians one of your fine lectures? Something historical would be preferable, but *anything* from you would be lum tum. I wish we had a fund and that I could write you on this subject other than *in forma pauperis,* but the legislature does not overload us with money as it does Clemson. If you do come, the Flinns[8] will naturally grab you, but can't you spend one night, at least, in my shanty?

My kindest regards to Mrs. Bennett, & a punch in the dept. of the Interior of your enfant terrible!

In haste,
Yours ever,
Yates Snowden

Columbia, S.C., 25th Nov. 1906

Dear Bennett:

I don't know which to thank you more for, your delightful book (which I read as I *walked home in the street,* so absorbing was the interest it exerted), or your wonderful letter, de omnibus rebus et quibusdum aliis, which preceded it, & which was very welcome, barring one paragraph.

Anticipating our friend Toilus Salley,[9] will you kindly answer:

Why, Peyre Gaillard, instead of the French *Pierre,* & by the way the name of the protagonist of the *"Gilyards"* in S.C.? (Peyre, I believe, is English)—O, Man of Morals, tell me why!

And *why* that long lying list of Huguenot writers, "Henri Rodé"; "Jean Carouge"; "Nezerau's *'Philologie* des Francois,'" etc.,(the most I bring of all); "Perderiau's 'Transcript,'" etc.; "Doucinet," "Elie Berchaud," & "Mouzon's Colonial Surveys," etc.!!![10] What do you mean by it? I am glad one of my classes, which has been assigned "themes" on "Indigo Culture in S.C." and on "Early Colonial Highways & 'Dirt Roads' in Carolina," has not yet seen your infernal book. They would worry the life out of me.

Though Dr. Wilson[11] has proved that many of them were well-to-do and educated, they, the original emigrants, left next to nothing in MS! Confound them. That "Liste des François et des Suisses" by St. Julien de Malacare; which the elder Dan'l Ravenel[12] once owned, & a MS. sermon by Pastor Prioleau,[13] and the entry (very pathetic) of his wife's death in the emigré Porcher's[14] Bible (these last two) are all I have ever seen. Nor have we any interesting scraps about them by any contemporary except Lawson's[15] visit to M. "Eugee"[16] and "Galliar"[17] on Santee. Every Snowden in Charleston & Berkeley Counties & in Ga. has Gaillard blood except my sister & myself. I don't know how we escaped, except that my father married outside of the Parish & didn't marry his cousin—against two unwritten laws in St. Stephen's. But, without knowing it, you have brought in one of *my* Huguenot family *LeQueux*. My Grandmother's mother was Lois LeQueux. They have gone to seed long since, though you will find a row of nice slate skeleton & angel-headed tombstones to LeQueux's in St. Stephen's Church yard. When I was born Miss Amelia LeQueux sent me a present. She was a *lady* & I have a book of poems presented to her by "her friend Paul H. Hayne."[18] All the LeQueux's *now* are Tillmanite[19] ash-cats, except my excellent far-away cousin Miss Mary LeQueux, Miss Irving's assistant at the Orphan House.

If you will find out who Lois LeQueux's (Drake's) mother[20] was I will give you my note for $5. Perhaps after all, she may have been a Gaillard!!! But enough of my genealogy. LeQueux does not sound like "little nobility" even; I suppose they were *barbers*.

Dr. Wauchope et ux.[21] are delighted with Peyre G. Dr. W. thinks you a brave man to write a lost treasure story after "Treasure Island" & "The Gold Bug" but he declares that you have more than made good—& so say we all!

I would like to know what *Col. James Cosgrove*[22] thinks of your "Zététique system"!! Look out for an indignant comparison of your & the Col's solution of the problem.

I hold up your good wife, toiling with you in composite work, to my present wife. I bought a type writer six months ago thinking *disipens in loco* or rather on *sofa,* and dictate to my wife. She has written me *one* letter telling me how she loves me, & has not used the type writer since. At my advanced [age] it's hard to learn to think with a machine. I find it hard to *think* anyway.

When you see Maj. Hemphill[23] again tell him all you know about the custom of *"trial child"* on Edisto Island. He wants me to write something for the N. & C. which would prevent that eminently proper family journal passing through the U.S. mails.

I appreciate fully why you can't lecture for us this year; but I sincerely trust that we shall welcome you & your partner early next year. Don't fail to bring her: it would have a fine effect on my frau. With renewed thanks for your kindness and for the book wh' I value exceedingly, I now wish kindest regards to Mrs. B.

Your friend,
Yates Snowden

I have recently had access to some letters of Ralph Izard (son of the Minister to Tuscany & U.S. Senator) to his mother.[24] I send you an extract from one of them wh' I think will interest you.

Presenting the New Year's greetings
and compliments of
John Bennett, Sr.
and
John Bennett, *Junior*
Born, January 1st. 1907
Charleston, S.C.

Dear Yates:

Will not this be some slight explanation of and apology for my delayed reply to your delightful letter of many years ago, which I mean to answer as soon as I recover from the present happy catastrophe!

Sincerely yours,
John Bennett

Charleston, S.C. May 17th, 1907

My dear Yates:

I am very glad you thought of calling on me, and I'm going to do all I can to help Mr. Pott[25] carry out his plans for the summer.

The SS "Effia" is due to arrive here on or about July 1st. She will scarcely be ready to sail on her homeward voyage before the middle or end of the month. Her owners are very nice people and her captain is a fine fellow. It is possible that some arrangement can be made for Mr. Pott to take passage on this ship, and if the time of sailing suits Mr. Pott, I will take the subject up with the Ship's Master as soon as she arrives.

I would suggest that he go as a passenger and it's my purpose to fix it in that way for him.

My little family are in fine trim. The lad sasses his poor old Dad— in the modern fashion, and has already informed his Mother that "Fater is a billy-goat"—& I guess he is right.

With kindest regards to Mrs. Snowden and with "hell taps" to you—

Yours,
John F. Bennett

[*Postcard of Shakespeare's House, Stratford-on-Avon, England*]

24th July, 1907

There is a woman "Spieler" or custodian in the upper room and library to whom you could have talked and listened for eight hours!

Y. S.

I would have given a month's salary to have had you with me for three hours, boating on the Avon, at this house, and rambling round the town. Vive Master Skylark!

Y. S.

[*Handwritten on the back of a copy of* Free Negroes in the South Before 1861; and Slaves Owning Property, *which is printed in blue ink and marked by Snowden* "Confidential !!"]

How much will you charge per *yard*, for what you know about all this, Johannes Carus?

Facts, milord; not from Mermaid stories—funny though they be.

A dear friend of mine, Prof. C. Woodward Hutson,[26] of College Station, *Texas*, writes me that he & his whole family are wild with delight over "Peyre Gaillard," & asks me to write him all I can about John B. "*Who* is John Bennett?" says he.

Over 40 examination papers on my desk, untouched! Capristi; also Carramba!

Adios,
Y. S.

#37 Legaré St., Charleston, S.C., 23rd. [?], 1907

Dear Yates:

I will be glad to drive a screed through my note-books, and send you all that I have relative to free negroes, etc., etc. I send instantly something directly apropos to the subject—Richmond man, Virginian, who owned land out in the "free country" Southern Ohio, Old Virginia Military District—you can see at a glance what it carries: provisions for freeing and for feeing slaves, and a legacy of $1000 to a free negro; also for training, as carpenter, of a negro man.

I shan't send you any mermaid riot business; tho'—as Teddy would spell it—I have collected a bunch of macabre legends here that beat anything I have seen excepting Burton's[27] Arabian Nights—alas! that I have to expurgate.

Have no time for a letter—confound it, Yates! I am owing you a fine reply—and here is Little John, and grippe, upon Mrs. B., Jane B., Johnny B. and myself—just emerging; and the Century Company pushing me continual for some work we have been dickering about for years, a collection of my children's stories illustrated en silhouette. I am going after Paul Konewka's[28] shoes.

I'll write at length; and send what I have at hand; at present conclude with love to you and your good wife; and to Prof. and Mrs. Wauchope, to whom also I owe letters—but, Lo'd, Lo'd! I owe everybody letters—keeping me busy to prevent owing anything else; such is a literary life and the portion of genius—ahem!

Devotedly but busted with haste,
Yours ever,
John Bennett

POST-SCRIPTUM: I enclose the *Notes,* which, having a few moments before dinner, I have copied. Thank you. Do you take interest in such notes, (as I perceive you copy among these), concerning artists settling in Chstn. and advertising to "do portraits, land-and-sea-scapes, battle-scenes, historical pieces, fine china," or "birds and flowers of South Carolina,"—pictures exhibited, engravings planned and drawings made therefor—date, prior, during and closely after the Revolution.

For if you do, I'll be able to give you a few I have taken over from the *Gazettes,* in my note-books. I cannot promise regularity, or instant delivery; but will surely send them, from time to time, as I come upon them in miscellaneous note-work, if you care for them.

Some of them seem to me to be interesting and illuminating.

And, by the way, the author of a recent magazine article of *Morse,*[29] as a portrait-painter, is wrong about Morse's experience in Charleston: Morse came to Charleston BEFORE he was married; failing to get any work was departing disappointed, when a portrait he painted of his uncle, whose guest he had been, attracted attention, and got him so many orders for portraits—some 60 or 70 ordered—that he returned to the North, married on the strength of these Charleston orders, and, the ensuing winter, returned with his new wife, opened his studio here in Charleston, and painted many, many portraits. This was his first considerable success in practice of his profession. I do not know how many Morse portraits are still in existence here; but suggested, to the Art Society, a Morse exhibition, of all that could be collected in Charleston and Carolina—while the Morse telegraphic interest is being worked in the current magazines. The gentlemen with whom I spoke did not even know that Morse had painted portraits here: I had scarcely expected them to. I do not know whether they consider it worth while to act on the suggestion. I should like to see the collection, myself; as Morse was no slouch at portraits, and painted confoundedly well, with a style of his own, distinct and distinguished. Stephenson,[30] of the College, is trying to list and locate such things, in connection with the Museum; and such an exhibit would be in his line directly; I'll flush him with a single barrel.

Can you tell me where I. B. White's—or was it J. B. W.'s[31] portrait of Dr. David Ramsay[32] is? Or who possesses "a profile portrait of Dr. Ramsay, artists unknown"? Lancaster, Pa., Historical Society wants to know.

And so farewell—

Again, thanks for the notes
Yours ever:
Ichabod[33]

Dr. Robt. Wilson D.D., has a delightful Morse portrait—a woman's face: family portrait. Mrs. Smythe has Morse's L. Cheves,[34] a bland and genial draught.

Charleston, S.C., February 13th, 1908

Dear Yates:

God bless you, my child! That is a charming pamphlet you send me; and I am very much obliged. Someday, according to scripture, your bread will come back, buttered, from these dubious waters!

I enclose two rather worthless scraps: the suit of the Randolph[35] negroes in Ohio may interest you.

I am suffering from mental indigestion—too much Voudou, etc.—but am none the less due to submit a paper or two to Messrs. Harper & Bros., this month; so there is no rest for the weary and wicked.

I should like to talk forty years with you—it would be to my much profit, and to your exhaustion. But don't be affrighted; I cannot get away from here!

Please don't forget Tillinghast[36] on Negro Traits in Africa and Here. I'll not remind you that you promised to send it down, at this writing. But if you should seem really to have forgotten to do so, I shall gently hint that the true Bourbon has far too high a sense of personal honour ever to bust a promise, even to a "damn Yankee" like me.

Please present my compliments to Mrs. Snowden—and for yourself again thanks, and real regrets that I did not remain behind to revel in converse with you instead of meandering in futility with females about James Island, the afternoon we spent at Uncle Willy Hinson's![37]

Farewell, honoured Sir! Don't forget Tillinghast—I'll return him—or it as soon as notes are verified.

> Very sincerely, and gratefully, yours,
> John Bennett

Charleston, S.C. [February 22, 1908]

Dear Yates:

Thank you very much for the loan of Tillinghast, which volume arrived safely, several days since, while I was in a pandemonium of plastering a ceiling, papering two rooms, and preparing a lecture for the Federated Clubs of Charleston—unlucky venture! For which I am at present being unmercifully scarified by the gentler sex for being too Boccaccio-like in material concerning the precious legends of Old Charleston—probably an actual error on his part, who thought to address students of entire literature, and, alas! finds that his audience consisted of those to whom only expurgated editions are possible! Ah! had I but taken into heartfelt consideration the injunction of the late Mr. Podsnap,[38] and ventured nothing which might fetch to the cheek of the young person of either sex the blush of outraged shame! But, alack-a-day! the Arabian Nights, Don Quixote—not to mention Fielding, Sterne, Boccaccio, Balzac and Rabelais,[39] have now added to their "ranks and viles" your saddened and chastened servant,

> John Bennett

P.S.: Better not allow anyone to know—just at present—that you receive letters from

> J. B.

Charleston, S.C., April 30th, 1908

Dear Yates:

> Man wants a great deal, here below,
> And wants it right away;
> But—blast his eyes!—for all your work
> He does not want to pay!

The preceding quotation from the poems of a Cheerful Idiot *are* apropos to a demand: viz.: that is to say, namely:

Can you tell me where; and when—for how many years; and by whom, a Southern magazine, styled "Southern Field and Fireside," was published?

Davidson,[40] vide Living Southern Writers, or "Living Writers of the South,"—exactly—N.Y., 1869—says: George Herbert Sass[41] took the prize offered by *Southern Field and Fireside* for the most striking poem on the War. G. H. S. makes no record of this event; the family cannot enlighten us: as I am doing G. H. S. for Kent,[42] I'd like to know.

Does the University Library possess a file of Southern Field & Fireside? If so, is there one in the Library employ whom I can procure to investigate this subject of prize-poem and contest, for me?

Off-hand can you tell me did *The Southern Magazine,* published by Turnbull Bros. in Baltimore, 1870, etc., succeed *The New Eclectic:* I am at fault here; and though a small matter, I should like to be put right-o!

I am recovering slowly from the onslaughts of the insulted populace—Madame Solomon Grundy, et al.[43]—I own I was disconcerted at its acrimoniousness; but much consoled by your cheerful P.C., on which was much GOOD STUFF for WOWNDED SOULS—for which same, heartfelt and ebullient THANKS. Good-by. No more at this writing. Here the CHOIR will please appreciate Y. Snowden's FEELINGS by singing Ye Long Meter Sockdologer:

> Praise Him, from whom all letters flow,
> When writ in kindness here below;
> Praise him, who writes, but owes a host;
> Praise him who answers promptly, most!

The CONGREGATION will now be DISMISSED:

(At this place the congregation may say AMEN; or heave a sigh of relief, and pass out quietly. Don't forget the Poor!)

I shall be greatly obliged for any assistance upon the points questioned.

Very cordially, even affectionately,
Yours:
John Bennett

P.S.: I have enclosed TWO postal-cards. You will see I have not self-addressed them. This is not necessarily for publication, but as a token of good faith. You see how I trust your integrity.

B.

Columbia, 2nd May 1908

Dear John Ichabod Bennett:

I answer the first query of your insane scrawl by a blank page from the Southern Magazine showing that it "evoluted" from the New Eclectic; but *when,* I don't know.

I once owned an odd no. of the New Eclectic containing an article from the Dublin University (?) Magazine on the "Beginnings of the Drama in America" (or some such title) in which the claim was made that the first dramas of any importance in this country (like the best wives: e.g. Mrs. J. B. & Mrs. Y. S.) originated in *Charleston!* One of the plays reviewed, an amazing production, "The Battle of Eutaw Springs" by Ioor,[44] of St. George's Dorchester can be found in Dan Ravenel's collection. I have a batch of "Southern Magazines," not complete or consecutive, & I have jotted in pencil on the other side the nos. containing poems by G. H. S.; some of them doubtless in his published vol; I'm too lazy to look. I will be glad to *lend* them to you, after you have returned Tillinghast. There was one poem of G. H. S. pub'd in the So. Magazine (I forget the title) which I asked Mr. S. to put in his book. It may have been among those thrown out by the pub'r. . . .

Your friend always,
Y Snowden

Charleston, May 4th, 1908

Dear Yates:

Your letter and p.c. of the 2nd received with acclaim! You have qualified for the doxologer! Your information concerning *Field and Fireside* is positively the first received: I still hope to catch a hot trail. None of the poems mentioned—the anonymous one being the only one available—were by G. H. S. I have mss. of all his youthful verses, beginning with ambition in 1862, during the Greenville hegira, and ending with verses written "in the field," when he was with Lieut-Col. Feilden,[45] with Hardee,[46] in N.C., at the closing of the war. I hope yet to identify the prize poem—if persistency may prevail against oblivion. Thanks for the *New Eclectic* clew; that sets me right. Poole[47] is supposed to index the *New Eclectic* and its successor, *The Southern,* but has no mention of "Barton Gray," nor G. H. S. that I can discover—I don't comprehend it.

"Aftermath," "Dying," "Enchanted," and "Disenchanted" were printed in "Heart's Quest": there were a disheartening number of excisions; G. H. S., in his most characteristic letter to you, met the disappointment gamely. "The Crown Unwon" seems to me to speak his heart. Since a poet's best is his criterion, after Timrod, G. H. S. ranks Carolina's best, on a handful of let us believe permanent poems—certainly the "Confederate Epitaph"—I have read the Anthology through to compare: it compares. Equity may have gained; Justice also in a community; poetry and letters lost in making G. H. S. Master of Common Pleas court, Chasn., S.C. He was undoubtedly one of the first promising voices to remove from Southern letters the sharp accusation of being more *poe*sque than poetical. I am obliged to you for the offer of the loan of copies of *The Southern Mag.*, but think I shall hardly need them; I am cramming space as it is; feel like an Archimedean screw.

As to Tillinghast, never fear, Shylock, you shall have back your damned—oh-oh!—butcher-shop—if you need him yourself, at once—if not, as soon as convenient to my usage, awhile longer. *En passant:* I return, herewith, letter of G. H. S., unmarred, but a little shopworn, as received. Credit my honesty. I have not shocked a hopper since last convulsion—but expect to arouse some wrath when volume appears—date as yet problematical—of Charleston's Grotesque Legends—expect thunders of denunciation from Podsnap, Grundy & Co. these be Corinthian tales, not sweet Parthenian fables, sirs. You shall have a copy when printed: get a quiet place out behind the barn, and take an afternoon off. To the rest I say in the words of an esteemed contemporary: To the pure—all things are Impure! I have never quite believed myself as vicious and depraved as reported.

. . . in ten months I have made exactly $26. The panic and hard times literally have the trade gibbering in the corner with fear; and we who live on literary earnings and book-royalty—ye gods and little ichthyans! Let's not talk of this! Let us speak of laughter and spring, of nymphs and love, music and dance—let us indite odes to MIRTH—let us dream that the Golden Age has come again, rejuvenescent, from the moldering corridors of the PAST! . . .

Do you know his [George Herbert Sass's] translations from Simonides of Ceos for the Davis[48] monument in Richmond, dedicatory epigraphs to the Confederate Army and Navy? Yes, of course; what is Confederate you do not know? But this is true: his translations shine superior to all others; there is not one essay comparable to his. There's a great deal which makes true poetry entering into the reasons for this fact, but this is not a lecture nor an essay upon poetics. Only this: those two translations should be quoted and known by every schoolboy through the South, memorized for their sheer nobility and calm beauty. Tell your collection of coming statesmen and geniuses I say so.

With hearty thanks for your aid, and in expectation of specifications, I remain, with compliments and greeting to your charming wife—vive la Charleston! I toast your Wife and Mine!

Very truly and affectionedly your friend,
John Bennett
(Ichabod)

Charleston, June 24th, 1908

My dear Yates:

. . . My eyes have given out almost entirely. . . . I have busted. Hence am re-reading Robert Louis Stevenson's letters, for the strength and support of my miserable spirit, by courtesy of my wife's eyes; have packed up papers, note-books—all the varied paraphernalia and panoply of Hell—and am to do no more work until November; by which time I sincerely trust health and eyes will both be materially improved. If not, please have made one decentish tomb-stun, two by twice in measurement, inscribed: "Here continues, mineralogically considered, Ye Melancholy Jacques. Requiescat! His dim spirit, observe it yonder, perched upon the far stars, doing book-plates through the ages for his friend, Yates Snowden." For which favour, God bless you, Yates! I send also, by this mail, *our* beloved copy of Tillinghast, since, bearing your name upon its face, 'tis more appropriately in your keep. . . .

I must stop this tap-tap-tapping, like Poe's ravings, at your door: my eyes are defunct, and frankly, hurt like

I am off for the Up-country, Pendleton, July 1st, Flat Rock, 10th.

[John Bennett]

Chapter 3

1909–1911

A. S. Salley, Jr., controversy; Revolutionary War research; early South Carolina private libraries.

In May of 1909 an incident involving Alexander S. Salley, Jr., occurred. Salley, the secretary of the Historical Commission of South Carolina, sent John Bennett an insulting postcard, accusing Bennett of making fun of him in a poem signed "A. Z.," which had appeared in *The News and Courier*. Bennett angrily denied the accusation, and Snowden then revealed a choice anecdote about Salley and Fitz Hugh McMaster, the insurance commissioner of South Carolina. Snowden, who had in earlier years been in the old-book business with Salley in Charleston, was now at odds with him. Although he had not spoken to his former partner for months, Snowden acted as an intermediary, and Salley sent Bennett an apology.

Snowden and Bennett exchanged several clippings in the latter part of 1909 and in 1910, but if there were letters for that period, they were not kept by the friends. Snowden's article, "South Carolina Plays and Playwrights," which first appeared in *The Carolinian* in November of 1909, was reprinted in pamphlet form the same year; in the following year a reprint was published of his article, "South Carolina School Books, 1795–1865," from *The Southern School News,* January 1910. On 11 May 1910 *The Columbia Record* noted Professor Snowden's address to the South Carolina Medical College in Charleston, and on 4 December 1910 *The State* printed in full his speech at Georgetown, "The Pathos of Lost Causes." The College of Charleston, his alma mater, conferred on Yates an LL.D. in May of 1910.

The correspondence beginning on 1 January 1911, indicated that Bennett had earlier requested help in locating materials for a book on the Revolutionary War in South Carolina, in which he planned to reveal the state's true Tory side, as well as its true Partisan side, and to show the participants to be, not superhuman heroes, but mortals capable of error.

Snowden began his search for the requested volumes and pamphlets on the Revolution in his study, where his private collection not only filled the many bookshelves, but also the desk, the chairs, and most of the floor. He allowed no one to straighten the room or to help rearrange the papers, books, or magazines. Once while Snowden was absent from Columbia, the cook had tried to clean the room. When he returned and saw his study, Snowden was furious.

One rare gem of the Revolutionary War that Snowden promised Bennett over a long period of time was *The Life of Edward Lacey* by Dr. Maurice Moore. Snowden continued to send Bennett interesting material, but not the biography. Meanwhile, Bennett was looking for pre-Revolutionary material for Snowden. By the end of the year, still not having received *Lacey,* Bennett took Snowden to task, insulting and praising him in the same letter.

Charleston, May 21st, 1909

Dear Yates:

I am just in receipt of the following:

> John Bennett,
> Legare St.,
> Charleston, S.C.:
> I suspect you of writing the "A. Z." poem in yesterday's paper. (News & Courier, Chsn., May 18, '9). Did you do it? If you did I'll roast you so that there will be another guess that the frying does not "smell like Jew."
> A. S. S., Jr.
> Columbia, 5/19, '09.

In gentleness will you tell Salley that one who wishes a question answered must not back it with a threat; and, in the same gentleness, and friendliness, that if upon suspicion he is prepared to attack one who has been—so far as admissible evidence goes—kindly disposed, he may "roast" and be damned to him. Neither threat, nor roast, can alter my present and constant disposition, which, if he does not know it, I recommend him to learn before he commits his pen to any course which might be found to savour of injustice.

With constant esteem, and every good greeting to you, hoping not to impose upon your kindness, I am, as ever,

Very faithfully yours,
John Bennett

[*Enclosed in the above letter was the poem clipped from* The News and Courier *with* "Send this back to me!" *penned in the margin.*]

THE DOOM OF ART

When Whistler wrote his "Gentle Art"
　　So very quid-pro-quo-tal,
He tore them limb from limb apart,
　　The painters "anecdotal."
He scored with satire tempered fine
The Briton's simple joy in line
　　That etched his country's glory,
But never from his mordant tongue
Was hissed "Corrupters of the young!"
　　That's quite another story.

When Jasper did his noble stunt,
　　The artist, it is reckoned,
Was not on hand to share the brunt
　　Of that hot psychic second.
He did not wield his brush 'mid crash
Of cannon by its lightning flash
　　Nor kodac Death's wild valley.
And so we learn his work must go,
Because, of course, he couldn't know,
　　He's doomed by Mr. Salley.

Paint not complacent Mistress Motte
　　Her arrows held (if any),
Because you were not on the spot.
　　What good that there were many?
The Capitol must lose, we fear,
"The Crossing of the Delaware";
　　The ice may be mendacious.
Imaginary scenes, pardie,
Develope [sic] inveracity,
　　And let us be veracious.

Where round the Little Corporal's sleep
　　The heart of France lies sleeping,
Through the Pantheon veterans creep,

Their eyes, too old for weeping,
Light with an afterglow when fall
Their comrades' glances from the wall.
    But—au diable allez!
The word has flashed across the seas:
Mere fancy scenes. Suppress them,please;
    They've heard from Mr. Salley.

They'd like to keep in England's isle
    Some little things of Turner's;
A trifling "Battle of the Nile"—
    But ship them for Avernus.
And oh, where glows in Dresden's shrine
The wonder of the world divine,
    The world delights to honor—
She'll have to go! The truth is rife.
She really wasn't done from life,
    That poor Sistine Madonna!

                    A. Z.[1]

                    Columbia, 25th May 1909

My dear Ichabod:

You have met the enemy, and they are your'n! Salley & I, for months, have *barely spoken* as we passed by. Fitz McMaster,[2] the best friend he ever had in this burg, once almost came to blows with him, when he went with the olive-branch of peace; & three weeks ago when Fitz expressed his views, rather festively, in the Cola. *Record, in re Myths,* Salley *retorted,* as Fitz passed him next day in the State House, by using a most insulting epithet. Fitz naturally threw his great insu. documents to the tesselated floor, "and *went* for him, there and then," and, but for the interference of a mutual friend, Mr. Banks Dove,[3] Salley would have had more than a very white face and a torn coat-tail. I mean no imputation on his *pluck;* for he is as full of *grit,* as he is of damphool.

But more of this when we meet. Let us come to the *res gestae,* as Maj. Smythe would say. I received your sparkling letter; wishing to preserve the original (so that my great-God-children may know that I was honored with the friendship of the eminent novelist J. B.), I had a typewritten copy made, and wrote a letter to Aleck; saying that "my friend Mr. Bennett" did not know of our "strained relations" &c., I put my letter and yours in an envelope and delivered it to Mr. Salley in person, telling him, "Here is a communication which may or may not require a reply; certainly *I* expect none."

Much to my surprise, I rec'd yesterday *a copy* of Salley's letter to you, with no letter; but simply endorsed: "For your information; please return." It's the biggest humble-pie epistle he ever wrote!

It's hard to *fix* any man's *motives*. Probably he was *appalled* by the idea of losing your friendship or good will, for he has been cultivating Whistler's "Gentle Art"[4] more assiduously and successfully than any man I know, since he became Sec'y of the Hist. Comn. *Possibly,* he had the good sense to see that he could not afford, in spite of his omniscience, to antagonize *you!* He recognizes that in a discussion whether Miles Brewton's[5] g.g. mother's middle initial was I. or J.; or whether the B. Jones family landed first at Skull Cr'k, or Toogadoo in Sept. 1712, he would wither you by his erudition!! But when it comes to pure litera-ture, he thinks (in spite of his dainty verses in the Sunday News telling "A Z" to go to Hell), that you would "best" him, and he fears the outcome. His initials, backed by some of his writings, would furnish a fine subject for a companion piece to Coleridge's lines to a *dead* Ass.

And yet he has a wonderful amt. of minute information in certain twin-state subjects (See his excellent Fort Motte speech!); and could fill a very useful role, but for his epigrams and stupendous self-conceit. I have never met his equal. Thomas H. Benton[6]—and J. P. K. Bryan,[7] fade into insignificance before him.

His posing in the N&C as "Mr. Valliant-for-Truth" defending the last bulwark of veracity, or "historicity" (as we Presbyterians call it), *in spite of his "fading eye-sight,"* has many elements of farce or opera-bouffe.

Of course you will reply kindly to his letter, and all will again be "sweetness and light" between Jack and Aleck, but,"all the same," I thought you ought to know the facts. With kindly greetings to Mrs. B.

Yours affectionately,
Y. S.

Hoyt, of the Cola. *Record,* who is a very fair cold-blooded man and very friendly to Salley, told me two weeks ago: "I honestly think Salley is going crazy"!

Salley told Baker (my "colleague") yesterday all about your letter and his reply, and expressed the opinion *that you were not "A. Z."!* Your letter makes "A. Z."'s identity as plain as a pike-staff. The day the poem appeared I told a friend: "John Bennett is the only man in S.C. who *could* write that. I will bet you my next month's salary against a 'Flor de Malaria Segar'"; and he did not take it up!

Charleston, May 30th, 1909

My dear Yates:

Thank you for your very good services; and for your fine letter of May 25th. Would have replied before, but was up to the neck in the criticism and revision of an attempt that is being made by a clever young fellow in Chicago, to dramatize my book, "Skylark," and what with telegrams, scenes, cues, character- lines, and what-not, have been living the strenuous life.

All's well that ends ditto: so, thanks to your kindness, Mr. A. S. and I have avenged our mutual honours, smoothed the wrinkled front of war, and the fair, fond dove of peace is doing a land-office business.

I had not, of course, known of the strained relations existing between yourself and Mr. Salley, or I should not have thus thrust you into the middle of things: yet, according to the Immortal Code, I could not have bettered it, mutual indignation adding increased dignity to our Gullorious Cause.

Frankly I have had a second very excellently tempered letter from Mr. Salley, quite on a par with his excellent communication to the News apropos to Geo. H. Holmes (which latter his communication is fo' laff at)!

Except for his unfortunate poetry, Mr. Salley has distinctly the best of the newspaper discussion, so far as any serious aspect is concerned. The best of all the assaults upon his extreme left wing, his eccentric, emphatic, dogmatic, odylic wing, was the poem by "A. Z."—which verses, maugre your certitude, were not writ by me; nor do I yet know who is responsible for them. They are brilliant, and deserve a place in Charleston's Garden of Anecdotes alongside Miller's[8] "Sans Culottes King," and that other inimitible epigrammatic description of a certain gentleman, as "a biological specimen out of his alcohol." To have done any one of those three were worth a Cycle of Cathay.

A certain—need I be particularly definite?—feeling of sympathy— sprung, pardie! of a certain event a twelvemonth gone—has put me somewhat in accord with Mr. Salley in this controversy—though God prevent I should ever jump to his extremes, or be so dry-as-dust in ways, or lose my own imagination, upon the comfort of which I have so often had to fall back. But, having been myself, in private and in public, controverted unceasingly, and, having been, for many reasons, deprived of the privilege of recoil, and so, like a suppressed pot-kettle, gone my ways, bubbling inwardly and spewing futile gusts of steam, on the main issue I "fights mit Salley," believing that truth is preferable to a lie, however pretty, comfortable, complimentary, or well-established the said lie may be, or in how many damned pitiful school-histories said figments of Satan have been embalmed like chinch-bugs in amber. . . .

All balderdash aside, I admire Alex Salley's pluck and determination and am very grateful to him for circumscribing in Carolina history a little oasis of fact in the luxuriant thickets of fiction. I detest the "dear old legends," most of them are silly, and the major part untrue. I believe with Josh Billings'—who is not much read down here, to be sure, being very much *non grata*—that "It is better to know less than to know so much that ain't so." I purvey fiction; but I do not call it history. Nay, by my halidome! when I write it shall be one of two things confessedly: utterly gratuitous fiction, or some entertaining style of rather cautiously collated facts—or else I'll say at starting off: "Once there was a basic fact; which possessed no interest whatever to the world at large; out of which there grew a strange, a monstrous, grotesque, macabre legend, in which there is a singular interest; it is not, however, to be read by anyone of an impure mind, but only by those of vigorous mind and triumphant, four-square virtue, who can look on mire without themselves plunging into its unhappiness."

As for Mr. Salley's self-conceit, it may be I, myself, have not been innocent on that head—we'll call it a draw: we have got off the field with mutual self-respect, if you will. Certainly we have got off with honest mutual assurance of very kindly disposition one to t'other; so I make a good end.

But, believe me, maugre your suspicions, or Presbyterian convictions, I did not write the verses by "A. Z." and know not who did. You risked losing a segar. I am laboring under—let's see! what did my late correspondent call it?—"fading eye-sight." Mine is not at all fading, only bad; balky, won't stand hitched, and won't work yoked. I lose much time—but, *allons!* . . .

I am trying to do some work, allegedly literary, on my own book, for Macmillan; but go with terrific slow pace, the eyes, aforesaid, permitting few revels. Your letter, however, for the nonce transforms the place to Belgium's capital by night—in consequence of which this sounds like a letter.

Your book-plate rests heavy on my mind; but I have not drawn, and may not draw; so it rests, and rests.

Please to give my compliments most cordially to Mrs. Snowden, and with hearty regard, believe me, ever,

Affectionately yours,
[John Bennett]

1st Jany *1911*
(The first time I have written *that*)
803 Sumter St., Columbia, S.C.

Dear J. B.:

I made the *"first preliminary"* search for Lacy[10] this afternoon; "Nothing doing!"—but, I found the accompanying "Memoirs of William Butler,"[11] which may furnish you with some choice *scraps*. The grammar is faulty at times, and the style is stilted. I wish we could spot where the "Manuscript left by the Hon. A. P. Butler"[12] begins, and where the poetical "T. P. Slider"[13] butts in. Some of Slider's ear marks are perfectly plain. If the matter is worth pursuing, suppose you write to "mi fren" Col. P. Butler Hagood, Barnwell, S.C., asking him what he *and his mother* know of this "MS. left by the Hon. A. P. Butler"!

By the time you *return* this Butler pamphlet, possibly before, I will have found my Lacy pamphlet. I have an idea that I will find Lacy just about the time I get those copious notes on pre-revolutionary S.C. libraries. Have you yet seen the *"Memoirs of Tarleton Brown, A Captain in the Revolutionary Army,* written by himself."[14] It was printed at Barnwell in 1894, long after Brown's death. It's full of *movement* everywhere, but, in the main, deals with fights with Tories in Harden's[15] territory on the Savannah River. He has evidently read Weems[16] & I regret to see a reference to "Cudjo" & "Major Snipes";[17] but though he spells a number of proper names very improperly, the story (only 28 pp.) has an air of truth. My copy was presented me by my dear friend ASS Jr., so if you want to see it, you must furnish bond for its safe return! It has an important reference to "Capt. Salley's Cow-pens"[18]—"the g. great grand father of A. S. Salley Jr."

Remember me cordially to your present wife.

With very happy recollections of a recent charming evening, and the narrow escape of some of my silver-ware, I am,

Always
Your friend
—usque ad nonam (that's Latin)—
Yates Snowden

January 4th, 1911; Charleston, S.C.

Dear Yates: . . .

There are, I find in a hasty glance, some things in these Bailey-Myers ms. I had not picked up elsewhere; wh. I am mighty glad to get. There

are, also, in the Butler memoirs, some facts not elsewhere found—it
would appear from this that there were more than one bloody raid by
Willy Cuningham[19]—all the histories are parlous uncertain and inept,
inadequate and paltry, when it comes right down to the true facts and
exact dates of Loyalist raids and doings. The frank confession of the
peach-brandy episode, in connection with the massacre at Cloud's
Creek, redeems those unfortunate patriots from the charge of being
simply idiots, and restores them honourably to the ranks of men, erring
in judgment of the time to be drunk, but otherwise impeccable and
human—our local historians, apparently—under pressure of modern
transcendental moralities, I suppose—would rather write our heroes
down asses than say, plainly, "they were drunken on good peach
brandy." Everyone seems to gloss over, to avoid, to be afraid to state, the
simple fact, that our ancestors were fond of rum; and that, now and
then—as we, who read our source material, know—it played the deuce
with well-laid plans of mice and men. Now we all know that any
however-well-laid plan, if set in a mare's nest under an intoxicated hen,
will hatch a hurrah—or "hooraw." What's the use of dodging the fact?
There's only illumination in the truth; and I'm always very suspicious
of the motives of the man who is afraid to face or to tell the plain truth
of history—we have had too much of this. Let's be human, and own the
fact that our confoundedly plucky ancestors were neither more nor less
human than ourselves; this done we shall at last perceive and thoroughly
appreciate what nobility, what courage, what admirable persistence,
what genuine, downright heroism in doing, and enduring want, priva-
tion and disease, was theirs. If they were, as our silly historians have
tried to write them down, a race of demigods, what credit is it to them
to do heroic deeds? If they were indeed human like us, look at them, and
see how poor, weak, but somehow glorious, humanity shines in their
heroism! Tut, tut I wax enthusiastic! Enthusiasm is not for historians;
yet no good history was ever writ without enthusiasm. I have seen
"Tarleton Brown," and digested him; one is soon able easily to discard
the sophisticated embroidery which afterthought adds to a plain tale. I
shall extract many extracts from the Butler and the Bailey-Eutaw ms. as
soon as the anguish departs from a tonsilated throat. Say: I have never
had my tonsils excised—not having had the excise tax to pay W.
Porcher[20]—so that I still have tonsilitia; but Mrs. Bennett and Jane, my
daughter, both have had their tonsils excised by the royal gauger—query:
gouger?—since which they both have laryngitis instead of tonsilitis—
inflamation on the fourth story instead of one floor up: where are they
better off?

Truly I will attempt to forward you some of that pre-Revolutionary
library truck as soon as I can get back at the Gazette files: having, as
above-said, laryngitis on the lower floor of my tonsilitis parlours, I

decline adventures in the dust of ages—though Phil always lends me a whisk—query: whisp?—broom with which to ghoul those old bones.

Surely, those who survive these correspondences of mine deserve a place in heroic song! . . .

Farewell—farewell!

> Yours affectionately,
> without any
> haughty furrin' languages, such
> as Latin, which you indulge in
> and surely have the bulge in
> on me—
> Once more—Yrs.,
> J. B.

P.S.: Gratitude genuine. . . .

16th Febr'y 1911

Dear Jack Bennett:

Did I want those gems? Does a duck love water? Do I turn up my nose when the Major offers me Gourdin[21] sherry? Am I a long-eared ass?

I want *everything* you have on libraries & literary life in Cuffeetown Kaffraria before and after the Revolution, and before, endurin, and after *de Wah.*

Which reminds me: scena Edwd McCrady's[22] office: temp. 1898.

> McCrady, loq.—"Yates, here's a queer letter: a prospective Ph.D. at Harvard sends me a long list of questions regarding S.C. history, all of which I can answer. It has taken me years to gain this information which I expect to use in my third volume. I do not like to be discourteous, but I am strongly inclined to give him nothing."
> Snowden, loq.—"General, you are perfectly right; tell the Damyankee to dig it out for himself,"—or words to that effect.

In brief, give me all you can spare, & that you can snatch a few moments to transcribe for me. I know that you are working hard for a living for yourself and the little doves up stairs (*hawks* at meal time if they are healthy), and I appreciate the stuff you have sent me & the valuable time you have devoted to me.

That "Travestie on Virgil" (would that I could *see* a copy!) is possibly among the first specimens of polite literature in S.C.

I had *the title;* from an article in the Gentleman's Magazine giving Robert Wells (the Royal printer)[23] as *author.* I have also a mem. of a note by Wells's daughter Susannah Aikman,[24] saying the "Travestie" was probably by Raymond *Bagley* (evidently the damprinter changed *Rugeley*[25] to Bagley). But your clipping from the Gazette makes the whole matter clear.

John Wells's auction notice in Jan'y 1778 is rich stuff for me, and the sad losses of odd vols by the library & Philosophical Milliner is good reading, as is also the sad story of J. B.'s losses.

Let the good work go on! Is there any record of the size & make-up of the original Langdon Cheves collection at Lang-Syne? The trouble with these notable private collections is that they were generally broken up after death of the owner for division among heirs; e.g.: the Poinsett-Pringle[26] collection near Georgetown (very fine, full set of Tiraboschi![27] (do I spell it right?), etc., etc.)—the big Mitchell King (père)[28] library divided among 11 heirs!! and so on.

Up to this morning (2:30) I have been wrestling with and double damning 140 or more examination papers. This is the first of 11 letters I have answered; so I have no time to continue my first preliminary search for Lacy! but he is sure to turn-up before long, & I shall send him immediately.

I thought I had left no impedimentia at that delightful Smythe home; but they kindly returned my malodorous *pipe* instead of turning it over to Marcia Green.

With 1000 good wishes for "She who must be obeyed,"[29]

Your friend always,
YS

July 23, 1911

Dear Yates:

In or about 1769, Rev. J. J. Zubly,[30] German Reformed Pastor at Savannah, Georgia, translated and printed a funeral discourse on *Peter the Great,* of which entertaining pmpht. he declares that he had sold "at least half a dozen copies." (Original letters of Zubly, to Rev. Ezra Stiles, D.D.,[31] Newport, R.I. in Yale College Library) Date of Letter: April 19, 1769—I don't know that this interests you; or is of any cogency; but if you can find, or possess, a copy of this treatise on "Peter the Great," the CharlesTown Library Society will be very glad to receive it as a donation from its loving friend, Y. Snowden.

N.B.: Darn Moses Kirkland,[32] whose devious path I am trying to unravel! Your absurd Carolina historians (?) have done their best, or worst, to wipe the record of Moses K. from the pages of time—and very near succeeded. I mean to put him back, in all his specious insincerity and picturesque failure. Tell me, Yates, whom did he marry? and where is it recorded?

P.S.: I have other stuff for you, but know you have no wish for it, just now, while rambling about the holiday world—nor have I time at this instant to fish it up and squeeze the colour from the murex—I am in a peck of woe with work promised and undone—and meus damnatus sum—that's Gullah Latin: can you talk it?—to live on wind until said work is accomplished—so farewell, Heaven bless you!

* Sssssssssssst! "Life of Edward Lacy": by Rev. Dr. Moore—Sssssssst!

** Living a bachelor's life here: good-wife and kids in the highlands—a poor apology for happiness, this separative scheme—and uncomfortable!

*** Who was She whom Lord Rawdon[33] so gallantly volunteered to escort across the foaming deep?

**** And She, for indiscreet attention to whom Gen. Robt. Howe's[34] recall from Charles-Town was so successfully urged; etc.?

P.S.: These latter queries are not for the purposes of publication; but for scandal only.

No more—I hear you say, "Thanks be!"

> Yours forever—like unto Ye Army & Ye Navy—
> Ichabod

Nov. 16, 1911

Dear Yates:

I thought I had mailed this. But, since I find it here, am forced to conclude I did not mail it, in July. Well, it is never too late.

> J(cha)B(od).

10th Dec'r 1911, 1:10 A.M.

My dear John Bennett:

Yesterday morning, at 3:20, *I found Moore's Lacey* on one of my tables. It was laid away among unpaid bills, flower catalogues, University catalogues and old letters. Last summer our noble cook, before my return, thought she would "put my room to rights," and piled up four

Pyramids of letters, pamphlets and *olla podrida* (whatever that may mean), on my main table. That's why I have looked in vain all these months among my pamphlets for Lacey, while you have been thinking me half a dozen varieties of liar and ingrate. I put it for safe-keeping *into* my Terry's Hist. of England, to which I referred this morning in my luminous exposé of the early career of Edward III of England. I left the book in my class room, & therefore I cannot mail it herewith. I will mail it to you tomorrow, or Monday.

I have two pp. of mem. to send you; one bearing on references to S.C. Rev. hist. & t'other to "hot" matters in Charleston, scraps from Caroline Gilman's[35] Rose Bud. I handled both of them last week but, tonight, though neither wife nor cook has interfered, I cannot lay my hands on either.

How can I thank you enough for your charming letter & notes, especially from *Ontario.* Mr. Hirsch[36] told me you had made some rich finds there. I loaned Mr. Kennedy (of Kennedy and Kirkland,[37] authors of *"Historic Camden"* who have this *2d vol.* almost ready for the press) your note, *in re* Col. Cary,[38] & I suggested that those Ontario Records might have been rich Tory "finds" for him.

At the meeting of the Historical Comm'n (no quorum) last Wed'y, I asked Alexander the Great Salley Jr. if the Commission had any funds wherewith to buy those 2 vols of Ontario Records, inasmuch as our fellow member Presdt Snyder[39] of Wofford, at the meeting of the Commis'n last year, had very wisely suggested that "it was time we were giving some show to S.C. Loyalists during the Revolution"! Alex'r the Great replied that we had no fund for buying books; indeed we were $160. "to the bad" on one of our accounts.

If you could or *would,* only run up here and spend a week with me in Jan'y, I know you would get some good stuff for your great work, and would give infinite pleasure to my first wife, and

> Your everlasting friend,
> Yates Snowden

December 13th, 1911

Dear Yates:

Vox clamavi de profundis non te Deum laudamus: you're another South Carolina historian: it is not Moore's *"Life of Lacey"* you send me, but *Moore's "Reminiscences of York,"* reprinted from the *"York Enquirer,"* *with a biographical sketch of Dr. Maurice Moore, by Celina Means!*

To be sure, there is material in these *reminiscences* which I welcome; all is the best sea-bass and cavalli that comes to my net. That does not give me the "Life of Edward Lacey," by Dr. Maurice Moore, writ in 1858, as a labor of love, and, like Love's Labours, Lost. *Where can I get Moore's "Life of Lacey"?* I believe you owe it to me to tell me, after thus horribly dashing my primed expectations.

However, I was not, on taking thought, surprised at the outcome: at *1:10 A.M.* you write me—legibly, I admit—that at *3:20,* the preceding morning, you discovered the volume I wanted. I warn you that historical discoveries made at 3:20 A.M. and proclaimed at 1:10 next succeeding A.M., are apt to verge on the milieu devoted hitherto to historical works like "Uncle Tom's Cabin," or J. L. M. Curry's[40] "History of the Confederate Government," slanders and tusheries.

I had not thought it of you; to break a would-be-honest-working-man's heart! For God's sake, tell me where I can find the *"Life of Lacey"?*

I am very glad to have these "York Reminiscences" for perusal: both for local color in my present work, and for future fictional reference: so, thank you, kindly!

This is nothing to the gratitude which shall pour forth upon receipt of the *"Life of Ned Lacey,"* the noble, the pugnacious, the patriotic, and darn-near-forgotten. Try again, among the *olla podrida*—whatever that means—upon your study table. Every now and again I do that, and find something for you; so do you try again, and find something making a sound like Dr. Moore writing a life of Ned Lacey, for me.

You wrong my vocabulary: never, never, never will I call any man "a liar" when I may resort to the superlative, and dub him "a South Carolina historian."

And, by the way, you might suggest to Mr. Kennedy, of our really much-esteemed collaborators firm, Kirkland & Kennedy, that the material you lent him was wrung from remote sources at the cost of bloody sweat and hard work by your friend, Bennett, who is hardly yet handing his finds around at the barbecue, since he must depend on just this new material, and his cursedly hard and difficult grind and search for the success of the book he is now toiling over—the payment for the same being inadequate to comical—something like 50 cents a day for time already spent. Truly, I am not prepared to give this stuff away; *and yet I would be graceful; and not refuse Mr. K. use of Carey data*—though I had the devil of a time getting it, and can only see before me still more devilish times getting the rest of the facts, before I may even begin to put pen to paper towards a finished draught, or even a first rough draught, of my volume. Lord, Yates, 'tis weary work, this trying to tell the truth! But I'll tell you very frankly, I'd much rather lie about a man alive, to-day, than about the dead who can't get back at you until Doom's Morning. It's a coward's job, bearing false witness against a dead enemy; and I hold it to be a dirty coward's job to bear false witness against men dead so long that there is none alive to take their part. But I'll carry a merry face about my labor, swearing only, now and then, in the bosom of my correspondence: *vide* plaintive passages hereabove. Would Mr. K. be kind enough to credit my search with the data concerning Col. Carey? For it has been a long and a hard search: and promises only more before I finish. And before me I see, facing me sternly, an enforced trip to New York—a darned expensive business, to get there what should have been in print, or made accessible to the States concerned, long ago: complete attested statements of our Royalists, as to their losses by forfeiture and war's vicissitudes, and loyal services rendered, military or civil, to King George, in the Revolution—taken by Commission on Loyalist Claims, and filed in the Audit Office, London. These are in MSS. volumes in the New York public library; the Library of Congress has them not; all *South Carolina* claimants are collected in two volumes—*those whose claims were filed in London;* and another volume is devoted to *South Carolina* claimants *whose claims were filed from Nova Scotia,* etc.—there be upwards of fifty great MS. volumes in all, of American Loyalist claimants—and I have yet to see the American historian, not even Sabine[41] or British, for that matter, who has examined them, or digested their meaning. I am going to be one who will attempt it; if I can find the means to get to New York; and money to keep me alive while there—which at present is confoundedly doubtful. It is these records the State of South Carolina wants, and needs; *not* the *Ontario* Records. The *Ontario* Records are only partial, and are out of print; but you may find them by advertising. Owing to my constant urgency in this matter of some showing for the Loyalists, the S.C. Historical & Genealogical society has had a copy made of the Index—list of names—of all the South Carolina claimants for reimbursement, or back-pay, for services rendered the Crown, filed with the British Commissioners on loyalist claims; and we will print that Index in full, I believe, in the January number of the Society's Magazine, carefully edited by Miss Webber.[42] *Vide.* This, I believe, is the first definite opening wedge toward justice for the Royalists that I have run across in Carolina history; it pleases me to have had a stout hand in it: I have heard so much concerning the falsifications and injustices—and seen and deprecated so much—of Yankee historians, that it is a real pleasure to set the bark to somebody else's fox—"to keep the record straight." It is 128 years since the American Revolution; and I've yet to see in print any S.C. effort to be just to the honest gentlemen, and the honest rank and file, of the South Carolina loyalists—as easily separated, by a broad line, from the horse-thieves and Dan McGirths.[43] So I should like no ghosts of honest Royalists, who rose and rode, and fought and fell, bravely, simply, "for Church and King," to stand at my bed-foot, in the gray hours of dawn, and, pointing ghostly fingers at me, hiss in tones of bitter and somewhat mildewed contempt: "Elllll-ssss-on! Eeeelll-ssss-on! Elson-n-n-n!"

(Gracious! what burst of eloquence concerning one's own virtue!)

Now, I hold no brief for the Royalists—I'm a d——d Back Country Scotch-Irish Presbyterian and a Whig—but it's a shameful cause cannot tell the truth concerning its enemy—and I hold this true wherever it applies—if it has ever applied to me, then I'll be hoist with mine own petard!

It cost us $7 odd dollars just to get the Index of names copied of the S.C. Loyalists whose claims merited official attention: of the unlucky thousands who never filed a claim, but submitted, and remained in the State—well, one can only say, "They also ran!"

If I knew that there was material enough to warrant my coming and indulging in the pleasure of a visit in Columbia, I'd accept your invitation. But since the promised *"Life of Lacey"* has turned up to be only *"York Reminiscences,"* what can I hope of the rest? I can't afford, in my penury, to trade knives with Chance, sight unseen. And unless I felt secure of good material, I could not afford myself the genuine pleasure of seeing you and your good wife, and of cussing and discussing, percussing, and da capo, ad infinitas, res publicae, etc. Man, man! the holes in my breeches are shamefu'!

But I'm studying how to get together enough denarii to take me to New York, and feed and lodge me there, long enough to see my way through the Royalist Partisans of the Carolinas, Floridas and Georgia— all of which are concerned in our plain tale of the fighting in Carolina.

N.B.: I've notes, giving the bully prices received at the public sale of books, classics, and standard English volumes, belonging to the fugitive Royal Governor, Martin, of North Carolina,[44] when his library, being left behind in his hasty flight, was seized, confiscated for the public good, and sold at vendue, at Wilmington, N.C.—the Cape Fear settlement was closely allied, in those days, to South Carolina—enough to give these items local application—as in appreciation of literature. I cannot just now lay hand on these; but will send up at first chance. I'll not send you a lemon, either—and you did me—or was it a *pomelo,* neither one nor t'other?

Good-night.
Always heartily yours,
John Bennett

P.S.: My remarks on *Col. Carey, in re Kirkland & Kennedy's "Camden,"* seem, on looking them over, rather selfish—and sound like a man making a bid for recompense. *Fur frummit*—nothing of that sort! *Tell Mr. K. he is welcome*—only just give me credit for supplying it. I look for their new volume with interest, and shall have it for the Library the moment it is out. But, for God's sake, don't let my poverty make me mean, selfish, or petty. With which honest and earnest prayer, let me close this meeting.

Ichabod

Do ye just remember what W. G. Simms[45] did to Sabine?

Chapter 4

1912–1913

University of South Carolina songs; Gullah Jack; *famous artists in nineteenth-century Charleston; death of John Bennett's mother; more research on Revolution; pronunciation of Snowden.*

YATES SNOWDEN, having entered the competition being held for the selection of a University of South Carolina song, received help from John Bennett. Several other professors' entries were mentioned in the friends' letters, including the one by Dr. G. A. Wauchope, which was chosen by the University. Bennett hoped that Snowden could find the two early South Carolina College songs that had been written by his wife's grandmother, Mrs. D. J. McCord, before the War Between the States.

Snowden was intensely interested in the plans of Bennett and the Art Association for an exhibit of paintings by Samuel F. B. Morse, and he suggested possible exhibits of the works of other artists connected with Charleston. In one letter, Snowden showed that the South Carolina pronunciation of his surname was the same as that of the Puritan Snowdens, with the first half *Snow* rhyming with *cow*.

Additional subjects of the letters during this time period include a New York production about 1830 of *Gullah Jack, a Melodrama,* Mrs. A. T. Smythe's daguerreotype of the mother of Francis Lieber, Bennett's Christmas silhouettes, Cole Blease as governor, Snowden's trip to Boston, South Carolinians summering in the North Carolina mountains, Reed Smith and the FolkLore Society, and the health of Mr. and Mrs. Smythe.

When John Bennett's mother died in January of 1913, Yates Snowden sent his condolences. At first, Bennett was unable to reply at length. But in July from Wellesley, where he had been staying several months with his sister, the head of the English department at Dana Hall, Bennett wrote a long letter—the first pages being a tribute to his mother. During his stay in Massachusetts, Bennett worked in the Boston libraries on his American Revolution research. His letters, while he was away from home, were not typed as usual to save his eyes, but were carefully handwritten.

In the fall of 1913 Bennett joined his family at East Flat Rock, North Carolina. He wrote of his future plans and exchanged banter concerning the *Life of Lacey* with Snowden, who once again wrote that he had found it.

New Year's Day; Jan. 1, 1912

Charleston, S.C.[1]

Dear Yates: . . .

Truly, Yates, the best I can do for you and the Psalm is merely to write a few rough stanzas suggested by yours, and let you borrow whatever seems suggestive or by way of improvement, if any there be, and by hacking the two, your version and my redaction, perhaps arrive. . . .

I suggest . . . that, though it may not carry out just your own idea, the *fourth* stanza be made the *third*. . . .

The reason for my transpositions of Gist,[2] etc., is simple: after stating tersely that these men shine in story, and are of deed Time shall extol, the brief fine statement concerning Gist—"how he rode to death, joyous and fearless," comes like someone suddenly blowing a trumpet.

But don't, in God's name, call Hampton[3] such confounded canting trumpery, bastard stuff as a French phrase, a beau sabreur—I beg your pardon, heartily if my anger offend you, Yates! I know that old chestnut borrowing of gallantry and feathers has been worn threadbare at Hampton's spur-heel. Who doesn't know Hampton—or who, not knowing Hampton, will be impressed by calling him a phrase which somehow ever calls up visions of waxed moustachios, high-polished boots, and a young French braggart swaggering through the flowery pages of some flap-doodle tale? Transfer the wellearned title, "peerless," to him; say something significant of Elliott[4]—Hampton's name opens a line like a cannon-bolt, and would make a fitting climax to any military casting of the vision of Carolina's warrior-students.

I suggest nothing for Elliott, not being sure which Elliott you refer to—you must needs pardon the ignorance of a damyankee—at first I thought you meant William Elliott,[5] the Congressman; but he was not a Carolina student, I believe—and, as you know, I have not yet informed myself on these latter-day heroes, save in general way—I can only defend myself in this by saying that of four men I have asked and two women, no one has been able to inform me exactly which Elliott you mean; hence you cannot expect an honest and admiring and honestly fair-minded but damyankee to know. But fill a line with something identifying, or really characteristic of the man, if possible—Gist you have fixed finely, a diamond of concentration; give us something of Elliott not a stock phrase—Hampton can ride a stock phrase and not appear ridiculous—the name carries so much suggestion with it even to the most ignorant. . . . I think, by making a good, strong and vivid impression as the "soldier stanza" must do, we can safely resume with the professorial.

We then at once introduce the universal, not the particular set of men, but a whole panorama of the student-body: "Here came young Love and Life, seeking the High and True Temple of Learning." . . . and the following quatrain of the stanza expresses their sensations, and the varied impress of the men you wish to extol in your verse: Thornwell,[6] Lieber,[7] Preston:[8] I believe my reconstruction of that awkward-to-handle catalogue of Worthies will approve itself to you: I think we can rest on making a picturesque climax of "great Preston's voice!" There was certainly one occasion when Preston's voice thrilled the student-body, if I am not mistaken; when he appealed to the riotous students, "as gentlemen," to follow him to their rooms. Also, I presume you know that the "Preston voice" is famous, even beyond Mason & Dixon's line, for its amazing clarion-clear and carrying quality: I suppose you know the tale. . . .

Then let us have the good touch of lyric and pastoral, classic reference, fitting the place, and presenting a very fair picture to those who have seen the campus—indeed who have loved any quiet campus, at any college. . . . Then suddenly introduce a striking bit of the University's history. . . . All may not know, but easily may guess, the story of the student-volunteers from old Carolina College. . . .

This is all at present writing. I hope there may be in it something of comfort and assistance!

I have sang; you have hearn: nufced—and, with the immortal Samuel peeps, pipes, peps, etc.—"So home!" Farewell—and all that the New Year holds of good to you and yours, I wish ye!

Yours, as ever,
Cordially and affectionately,
Ichabod.

P.S.: Now for the Life of Ned Lacey! Hooraw—yip, yip, yip!

March 31st, 1912

Dear Yates: . . .

Thank you for the several Odes to Carolina: it seems to me that most of your Odesters hopelessly confuse Carolina, the University, with Carolina, the State: it may be that they consider the University a state, of mind; or that they confuse the State with the Universe: which, aforetime, was the habit of Carolinians, who couldn't believe that even the cuckoo Caroliniense ever called anywhere beyond the Border of Carolina: and, lo!, and alas!, I perceive that science at large has named the Carolina cuckoo, *Americanus!* Another outrage of the carpet-bag regime—invading even the chaste domain of Science with reconstruction. But of the several Odes, frankly I think yours the best of these, irrespective of my 'umble aid in that regard. I hope you'll recover Mrs. McCord's,[9] for their historical interest. Who is R. S.,[10] who wrote "Carolina, All Hail!"? . . .

You hold trumps in the "Art Throes"; I had none of them; not having passed with microscopic eye through that period of S.C. data at all. To tell the truth, Yates, I have not yet got into the 19th Century, except some little revel with Gullah Jack, the trick-doctor and insurrectionary. By the way, did you ever come across a copy of "Gullah Jack, a Melodrama," produced in New York, circa 1830? And did it utilize Carolina as its ground, or any of the dramatic incidents or characters of the "rebellion"? It staged "black-face" characters; that much I know— corked Africans; but was it a sort of scare-crow, or a prehistoric Uncle Thomas? I take the privilege of copying your Art Notes; but not of using them, without your permission; believing this to be offered as a privilege by your frank enclosure, and yourself to be, as the French say, "One large generous villain." I will return the notes as soon as I can copy 'em. . . .

J. Bennett

Columbia, 31st Mch. [April 1], 1912

Dear Jack: . . .

No returns as yet to my communication as to Mrs. McCord's songs. Might they have been published in the Columbia newspapers? Does Mrs. Smythe know of no copies extant? I meant you to use any & every line of those "art throes" if they are of any possible use to you; I only asked their return rather than you should throw them away. I am sorry you took the trouble to copy them. Thanks very much for those art Mors*els*.

It's a good thing, a Morse exhibit, if practicable. There is another artist who did some work in Charleston: *Healy*,[11] and I hope Prof. Stephenson and you will "nose out" several of the portraits he painted, when he came to Charleston to idealize Calhoun.[12]

At Highlands three years ago I copied a mem. to that effect from a little book on Healy; but I have mislaid my note. I never *lose* a mem., though some times I mislay it for 10 or more years.

I have a book up stairs that you and Stephenson ought to see: Dr. Jared B. Flagg's[13] "The Life and Letters of Washington Allston"[14] (Bentley, London, 1893). There are a number of letters from *Cogdell*,[15] our only sculptor, who seems to have been Allston's most intimate S.C. friend, and a number of very interesting allusions to Malbone[16] & Fraser,[17] with some letters to the latter. Writing to McMurtrie[18] from Boston, Apl 26, 1819, W. Allston says: "My friend and pupil, Morse is meeting with great success in Charleston. He is engaged to paint the President for the City Hall."

It may be practicable to get up another year a collection of *The Mimics*. Miss Webber at home, & Ben Taylor here can furnish data.

If the Art Ass'n comes out ahead financially in this venture, why not republish the Fraser gallery pamphlet (Charleston (pp. 65) 1858)? In the Charleston Courier for Jan'y 9, Feb'y 11, 13, 14, 16, 17, 18, and M'ch 5, 1857, are a series of articles on "The Fraser Gallery." I think I shall direct Lathan's[19] attention to them.

If you want to see the Fraser Gallery pamphlet, I will send (and *lend*) you my much valued copy, though possibly you are familiar with the copy in the Charleston Library, or elsewhere.

Is there any sketch of Malbone which gives even a tentative list of his S.C. portraits? . . .

> Your friend always,
> Yates Snowden

NB! Send me, if you can spare the time, any note you think would interest me. You never sent me a dry one yet!

May 20, 1912

Dear Yates: . . .

I am sending by same mail MSS—Bailey Myers notes, etc., and two prints, "Will Butler," and what you deceived me into believing (until I saw it) Moore's "Life of Lacey"—alias Life of Moore by Means—which you so kindly put at my disposal—and which I am loth to leave in my house now that I am ordered away for an indefinite stay. Thanks heartily for the loan: when I get back again to work I may ask again for Butler & Moore.

Have you, the University, or any Historical Collection in Columbia use or place for a daguerreotype of the mother of Francis Lieber? Mrs. A. T. Smythe has one for which she has no pressing use, and for which she would like to find a place where it may be desired? I leave town for Flat Rock (East) on Thursday 24th—to remain until Fall—work forbidden except physical.

Jack B.

Columbia, 24th Dec'r 1912

My dear John: [Chillicothe, Ohio]

I don't know that you can imagine how much I appreciate this last and most captivating and artistic of the Christmas creations with which you have honored me; which I would feign regard as evidences of affection, and which I know I have done nothing to deserve.

"By the remnant of mine honor," I will have it framed, if it takes the last cent from my emaciated post-Xmas pocket book, and it shall hang in good company near my two little solitary specimens of high art, a Tisio etching and a Malbone miniature.

By the way, a quick-witted, black-eyed little boy on the banks of the Ocmulgee, and a youngster in Summerville, one of my numerous Godchildren, are probably both reading, and reveling, in the wild career of Gaston Carew[20] at this moment. Before he sent one of the copies, Foxy Godpa thought he would read Master Skylark again; and, like a damn fool, he put aside "quiz" papers (over 100!) and class reports for the month, &c., and read the confounded book *at a sitting!*

When you next see "Mac" Horton or his sweet wife,[21] ask them if I did not ask them *two weeks ago* what was the name of your little girl! Of course I remembered Sockless Jack's name. I wrote to Mr. Isaac Hammond ordering little gifts for seven friends and sent a check for $5, which I asked to be put to your credit; saying that you would call and select something, a fountain pen, or book or some nick-nacks that *would not duplicate what the children already had!* Do so, please!

Christmas P.M. Billy Ball and I start for Godly Boston, to meet the high brows of the American Historical Association. They are coming to Cola. & Charleston next year, you know!

Dr. Mitchell[22] is going too, and though a charming *compagnon de voyage*, we thought he had better take a sea-trip for his health, while *we* go by land.

My present wife is spending Xmas in Hawkinsville, Ga. I had much rather be with her than go to Boston, though I expect to meet some fine fellows there.

With all best wishes for Christmas for you and yours, and a thousand thanks for the picture, which has already given twenty or more people the giggles, I am

Your affectionate friend,
Yates Snowden

NB! This *rondel* is *"woodern"* I know, though the New Orleans Times Dem. paid me $5.00 for it, in 1893; but the lines from De Musset *fit* the little picture to a T; and so I put the three together in the Coll. Maga. "Stoop angels," &c., of course, you recognize as Timrod's; Give it to Mrs. Bennett with my compliments.

The valedictory to poor Gus Pinckney[23] I *know* is not good editorial matter, and you will think it *rhapsodical;* but I loved him, and mean every word of it!

Columbia, S.C., 27th Jan'y 1913

Dear Jack Bennett:

I do not know that *you* can appreciate how much *I* appreciated your sending me that copy of the Chillicothe paper announcing the death of your mother, with its temperate but earnest tribute—I meant to say *admiring*—to her life, lineage and character. I wish that I might have met her, and have told her with what love and admiration we *decent* people of Governor Blease's[24] state regarded one of her brilliant sons. Except for a brief visit to "town," we only know your gifted brother by reputation.

Her age suggests the idea that her passing to the great beyond was grateful to her. To your brother and sisters and to you there is the *wrench,* that only those can feel who have seen the mother grow old gracefully, with "honor, love, obedience, troops of friends." I know what it is from experience, and I am happy to know that my mother died before the mind began to rust, and when the frail body could not permit her much longer to play the earnest energetic part which had marked her long life. I don't know that these shaky sentences convey what I feel; I only want you to understand that I love you, and that I sympathize deeply with you and yours.

Your friend always,
Yates Snowden

NB! I showed the clipping to "Mac" Horton, and I enclose the brief notice from *The State.* "Magazine Writer" is odious; but the clumsy night editor doubtless wrote the head line.

Mass. Hist. Socy. Bldg., Boston
March 11th, 1913

Dear Yates:

Silence means simply that I have been unable to write, not that I have an ungrateful heart. Your extraordinary deeds at Christmas which made my children rejoice—and your further letters to me, far from forgotten are with me constantly with deepest appreciation. Necessity to do great things with slender equipment drives me very desperately. The eventual result of all my labor and study must remain problematic, and I must proceed as a man who is determined on an end but has no promise of any commensurate reward except in the appreciative friendship of a few like yourself: for which always hearty thanks and genuine regard.

And so I must end and get on. Goodby.

Affectionately,
John Bennett

I have asked the Merwin Sales Co., #16 E. 40th St., N.Y. City, to send you their catalogue #504—1913, containing an extraordinary list (a collection) of Charles-town, S.C. *Gazettes* (1783) for sale. *You must see it.*

#12 Brook St., Wellesley, Mass
July, 1913

Dear Yates:

Long ago, and long ago, I planned, and, as you know, never have written a decent and grateful reply to your treasured letter of January 27th, which, for the genuine good it does me, I have read and reread, and have just now read again, with the same sensations that its first perusal gave. Among the kindest letters I have ever read, or had, I keep yours; and shall do so, so long as I keep anything human. After that, my dear fellow, we'll talk it all over at our leisure, or sleep quiet, you and I. And may the good Lord rest you easy, ever, as a very good fellow. I can speak very calmly and happily of my mother: she was full of gentle life, undiminished interest in the real world's work, and of energy more than comparable with her years, and had full possession of a clear, kindly judgment and uncommonly keen, yet gracious intelligence to the last moment, with an odd, quizzical, and good humoured wit of an entirely Scotch kind. Though by a serious fall, years ago, she sustained almost crippling injury, and took what ventures from home she made through the oldfashioned town, in a rolling chair, little stayed her, at home, and none could restrain her ceaseless energy and characteristic determination to be actively engaged every hour, if only in determined rest: if you can understand what determined effort it took, on her part, to leave activity, and repose for half an hour. She was a slight, graceful woman, but at last, by the fall of which I speak, was bent; and was never of robust health, but of enduring fibre, and lived 84 years doing for others the kindly things she seldom permitted others, until she grew old, to take the trouble to do for her. I owe her a great deal: indeed I owe both my parents much more than simple being, though I have not greatly distinguished their real gifts by much accomplishment: and in that lies the honour one is commanded to pay to his parents. I have envied my brother the last several years, knowing that severance must come. And, for two years, last, Mother's health and spirits were uncommonly good, and her companionship charming, and convincing that life is pretty well worth while. As she wrote me, briefly, when I laboured in discouragement and illness: "I have lived eighty years, and have seen much trouble, but the bright days outnumber the dark." She had buried four children, was left suddenly childless; and knew extreme poverty and heavy toil, consequent upon the entire ruin of my father's business: she abandoned a society which sought her, to devote herself to us, and to meet need with her own effort: yet I never knew her unsteadied, nor saw her decline the effort, nor to be in an ill temper with anyone, though high-spirited, nor ever heard her repine. Altogether the despair and admiration of her son, given at times to all these weaknesses. She gave herself unstintedly having nothing else. Her memory is like a summer's day, with fair clouds, sunshine and a fresh breeze, sweet, cool, calm and bright, after drought and storms, and, in despite of them, lovely. So we, each of us, has his own remembrance. Her mind never lost its balance, was keen, and kind and clear to the very last, and heedless of herself: "Is that you, John—my son," she said to me quietly, "you will be worn out with watching." "Oh, no, Mother" said I, "day has come." "Day? Then put up the curtains, and let the light in: I like it. The sun is not shining, John? Put the curtain higher, then: I like to look out." An hour later all she could say was "Come, holy Spirit!" And so, Yates, we said farewell, after forty-eight years. I write these things to you simply because I know you will comprehend, and understand the feeling which has prompted me so to write, and that I need, to you, in such case, neither explain nor apologize for pushing upon your privacy these of my own. Thank you warmly for your letter.

And now, as to my own to-do in the world: I am still here in the Holy City, endeavoring to cover the ground which our too-familiar lack of means makes it hard to cover in the South: I have met, everywhere, a singular and generous courtesy, and much convenience: particularly at the Mass. Historical Society, where, as they are, at present, custodians of many of Harvard's treasures, during alterations and rebuilding at Harvard, I have killed—or thrown at—two birds with one stone. And I am gradually beginning to get, at last, after four years' work, some distinct idea of how little I actually know about my subject—how much there must remain to be done that I cannot touch, and to get rid of that fallacy of attempting "definitive" work. I have found splendid material; and have as much in sight. I am hoping to finish here in the course of a month; and then immediately to New York to see Bancroft's[25] MSS, Rivington[26] and Gaines's [27] files, and the transcripts of Loyalist Claims for Services Rendered and Property Forfeited, in Georgia and the Carolinas, and Floridas: then Wisconsin and the Draper[28] collection: Washington and Peter Force's[29] imprinted hoard, and the transcripts listed by Andrews:[30] DeRenne[31] (I hope) in Georgia; I *ought* to see Wayne's[32] orderly-books, in Philadelphia, I suppose while roaming in these quarters: an acquaintance is reading the Pennsylvania Packet, etc., for me, Massachusetts Post-Boy and Spy, in exchange, and out of natural generosity—and then I've got to get a search warrant, and descend on you and your esteemed friend, fidus achates, Alexander S. Salley, and find what there is that one can find in my field, among the State papers in Columbia. Then, in about twenty years spent in digesting the mass this anaconda will begin slowly to loosen its involved coils, and to writhe (i.e. write). I have lodged in Wellesley all winter and summer to have my sister's society in odd hours during the winter (she has charge of the English Department at Dana Hall, Wellesley), and in summer because it is unmistakably a beautiful spot on the foot-stool, and my way by trolley, to and from Boston-town, lies through charming suburbs, and by pleasant avenues—such as Beacon Street, Brookline Village, and Commonwealth Avenue, and shady Massachusetts Ave. for home-stretch. Of course I have eaten off the arm of my chair all winter, and shall be lucky if I don't have to eat standing on the corner before I get home. On my honor, Yates, search me if I know when I shall see the "dear Southland" (hang the idiot who first invented that maudlin phrase!), again. The foreseen and unforseeable interruptions and un-avoidable delays have set me full three months already behind my longest schedule. So, for goodness sake, anchor the good old State to some stout and immovable post, and prevent Cole Blease from retiring with it into the Dark Ages or Primitive Man Period, before I get back. Between Pillsbury[33] of the American Bar Association and his colored friends, and that un-bury'd Pill, C. Blease, let alone the rude shock of ancient truth which I am recovering, I have been either an armadillo or a porcupine all winter: and when it actually came to the janitor's children, at the Mass. Hist. Socy., walking through the room when I was at work, "to see the gentleman from South Carolina," I thought seriously of having some small hand bills printed "descriptive of same," to hand about as I pass. My only old and cherished Carolina friend, the Duke

Tritta d'Italiancheesi,[34] I did not see while he was here, lecturing on the pleasures of Poisoning, and other ethical subjects; for he was suddenly called back to la bella Spaghetti by the death of some possessive and hitherto-inimical ancestor—and Boston has had to fall back upon the same old clumsy box of candy for its fatalities.

Tell me, what do you know about a "proposed newspaper" "The Ark"—Charleston, S.C., circa 1810–11–12? I was entirely stumped by it. The Mass. Hist. Socy. have a broadside:

"The Philometer:

the Gauge
of
His Majesty's Love towards the
Americans."

composed of four newspaper columns of matter made up in a one-page form under the above head, and with a sort of colophon in the corner stating that "The Ark, a newspaper," is "about to be published by John H. Sargent,[35] at Charleston, S.C." Of course "His majesty" referred to was his French kingship. What can you tell me of Sargent and his Ark? Did he ever float it? If you can inform me, I should be pleased to put the Mass. H. S. wise. As to the historic "high-brows," excepting His Excellency (a most cordial and courteous fellow), Worthington Chauncey Ford,[36] I have not been around the high-brow settlements. Ford was kind enough to take me down to the Club to lunch, which attention, and others, I shall endeavor to reciprocate upon him, or any other accepted Hub historical eminency who ventures to attend the National Association meet in Charleston, next year. (Apropos: Miss M. E. Webber quite in despair regarding same meet: says nothing done nor sign of doing preparatory thereto, scarce even conversation.) My news from Charleston I catch solely by snatches at the "News & Curiosity," in the Public Library from time to time; Mrs. B. and the hive being all at Flat Rock, where I wish I were, to-day.

I have glasses which have relieved my contrary eyes more than I had believed possible, after the incessant misery of seven years misfit, and am, and have been, working like the very old deuce himself to push ahead. But as there is no such thing as hasty thoroughness, I make all my haste slowly. Yet I shall somehow, someday, reach an end to it: as I have, here, to this long-deferred assault upon a good fellow. I do not know in the least where you are, but do not think you can avoid this if I mark it Forward, so farewell—and respect and affectionate compliments to Mrs. Snowden. As for you, my dear fellow—the recollection of last Christmas's doings on your part, and the abiding memory of your many kindnesses, leave me,

> Affectionately yours,
> John Bennett

If you should chance to see George Wauchope, Esq., please recall me to his recollection, with regards.

> South Carolina Club,
> Hendersonville, N.C. 4th Aug. 1913

My dear John: [Wellesley, Mass.]

Let me thank you for your delightful letter, rec'd last Friday while I was sizzling in Columbia, and for that, and 100 other reasons, "as welcome as a daisy in a cow's mouth." I treasure every line of it, but more especially that beautiful tribute to your lovely mother; every line of it ringing as true, and couched in as beautiful language as Cowper's lines to his mother's picture, or Carlyle's, utterly different but wonderfully pathetic tribute to his dead father, the stern brick-mason of Ecclefechan. And I appreciate that friendship which holds me worthy of such confidence.

I have some 10 *long* delayed letters to answer today, and so you must regard this as *section one* of an interminable screed, with which you will be pestered this summer, now that I have your address.

Yesterday, I walked to Hendersonville and ran into about 20 old friends, mainly from Charleston; among them a carriage full of Smythes, Stoneys, Wrights—and best of all a beautiful little boy with sparkling black eyes. Mrs. Smythe *et al* greeted me cordially; I mentioned that I had heard from you recently, and she said, "Why, there is little Jack Bennett on the front seat." We shook hands, and I can see that boy's cherubic smile now!

When you come to Columbia, Annie Snowden says, "Remember, *our* house is to be your home." The Flinns are the most hospitable people in the world and will want you, but you belong to we'uns!

Thank you very much for Sargent's "Philometer" and "Ark" both unknown to me and of *immediate use* for I am scratching off, or revising, a long paper on early labor unions in S.C. & kindred subjects and the extract I send you, on another sheet shows what (unaccredited) use I am going to make of your valuable data. Thank the Lord! I can give *you some* information about *something.* You will find on the other sheet some *scraps* about Sargent. I feel almost as proud as Aleck Salley, for I believe

I am the only man in the world who has those valuable details as to Sargent, & I generously share them with you & the Mass. Hist. Soc'y!!! By the way, Salley & I are on somewhat better terms; we damn Blease together, and fortunately swap jokes; but he never darkens my doors, & I don't think ever will. I have no doubt he will make himself specially agreeable to you.

Here endeth the first lesson.

Yours aff'ly,
Yates Snowden

Your hand-writing does not improve with the years! In giving the title to the "Philometer," *what* is *that word* between "Majesty's" and "towards"? Trade? Trove? In Heaven's name, *what* is it?

#12 Brook St., Wellesley, Mass.
Aug. 12, 1913

My dear Yates:

Many thanks for your generous epistle: 4th Aug. Don't cuss my handwriting: it is the only one I have:

"LOVE" is the "missing word." Do you get it? Your mercantile and usurious mind can think of nothing but *trade* and *trove*. Shame on the degenerate scions of the proud Southland! My handwriting is lovely: curled like young tendrils of grape-vines in Spring. A bas, Philistine!

Thank you much for the excellent information (unique, special, informing), concerning Sargent: I knew even less than nothing of him. I don't associate with Labour Agitations and I.W.W. I shall have a trade with the Mass. Hist. Socy, and am glad to be able, through your generosity on this point, to inform them a bit on Sargent. I enclose a small note, which may be of no value whatever but that belonging to curious fragments: a library in Savannah! Do you suppose "Advocate Farley" was a South Carolinian who merely did business in Georgia? I am pleased that you at least saw my boy. It's near a year since I did. And that is too long. Yet not to be helped. This letter must end as it starts off. I must get back to my dust.

Good-by—but always my most hearty compliments to your charming wife—

Affectionately—but much pushed
by futile labours—
Yours,
John Bennett

———————

State of South Carolina
Executive Department,
Columbia.

U. B. Hammet
Chief State Constable

6th Oct. 1913

My dear John:

That was a noble response to the folklore booklet! Where did you get
$3., *for a society not yet formed?* Smith was much pleased; showed me your
note. I am afraid to try your New York address, so I address this to
Legaré St. I want to know when to expect you & I have a *MS.* to show
you that may furnish some *kudos;* something no one else has tackled; &
it is at your service, though it cost me $16, some years agone!! But you
shan't see it , or even know of the subject *unless you stay at my house* in
Columbia. Yerry, budder?

You won't believe it; but, I also have *Lacy, at last,* loaned me by a
grandson of Prof'r. Rivers;[37] but he may ask its return any day.

Answer me immediately! Herein fail not in penalty of my everlasting hatred.

Yours aff'ly,
Y. S.

———————

"Many Pines" E. Flat Rock, N.C.
Oct. 9th, 1913

Dear Yates:

Yours of the 6th to hand. The $3.00 can be satisfactorily explained:
there was really no need to write on the State Constable's letter-head to
extort a confession. I would never explain upon coercion, even if I am
only a ——— Yankee. But laying aside the terrors of the Executive office
and the Chief Constable, and making a long story short: I had totted up
my accounts, and found, beyond possibility of a doubt, that, some time
before January 1st, I shall be in a literally bankrupted state, dead stone
broke. I concluded therefore to have one free-handed fling before I hit
bottom, to do one thing to which my natural bent attracted me, though
it should be the last: three simoleons of the realm, though a large sum,
would little extenuate and no wise postpone the approaching crisis:
while joining the Folk-Lore Society was a considerable and pleasant

indulgence, a loosening of the tight Scotch reign of economy (Aberdeen variety), to which my adored profession drives me. Look upon it as a sort of pseudo-scholarly spree; but as naught in any way criminal; and, if you wish me to return to South Carolina, avoid the State Constable's paper in future.

As to when I am coming to Columbia, my dear fellow, I cannot possibly say. My personal plans are totally upset. It has become unavoidably necessary for me to go direct to Charleston from here, with my family, and to make plans there for the ensuing months. I must go to the hospital myself for a very minor trick of surgery before I take to the road again: and shall undertake that joy as soon as I get my family settled. In present conditions, Maj. Smythe being much crippled by his last winter's fall, and Mrs. Smythe suffering to a crippling degree from rheumatism, it is impracticable—in truth it is impossible, for Sue—Mrs. Bennett—to leave her father and mother. The fact that I am not to be in my own house, thus, further, muddies the branch: I am uncertain just how we shall be settled; except that we shall dwell at #31, while I have my study at #37 Legaré, if, not being blown away, it has not mouldered into ruins during the past year's vacancy. Further maneuvers will depend on the wealth or penury declared by my publishers, in January, as to royalties —a rich word which covers a multitude of extremes. I do not know, and cannot guess, what we may expect, until that dread messenger, the January statement, arrives. Hence, being broke, and my garments, the purple and the fine linen, being depleted by a year's campaign, I cannot say when I shall be on the field again: I fancy not until after the first of January. I have thus advised my attractive sister-in-law Nancy Wright[38]— apropos to a proposed bit of work at DeRenne's Georgian library at Wormsloe. I have entered into this over-particularized and tedious explanation of shackled movements not because you deserve such punishment, but in consideration of your most cordial and continuous invitation to be your guest in Columbia. None but uncontrollable conditions prevent the early acceptance of your invitation. I shall be glad to be your guest, if, when I can, the time is convenient to that good wife of yours—and providing that you have not changed your mind, from which such reckless cordiality springs. I shall be only too pleased. Why tempt me with rare bait, and tantalize me with nameless, Sixteen-dollar MSS? As to the alleged "Lacy," do you really expect me to believe that? Tush! Tush! That fabulous "grand-son of Prof'r Rivers" will, I am sure, have "asked its return" by the time I reach the place: or some other more original, more ingenious method of disposing of the myth will have occurred to you. There *is* a "Lacy" in Wisconsin, not fabulous, mythical, ghostly and unreal—concrete, tangible, visible: Thwaites[39] vouches for it. It has become merely legendary in So. Ca. But hold to the Sixteen-dollar MSS. I shall earn the sight of that by complying, wholeheartedly, with the conditions prescribed. Would I could say when. But, lo! I am become a creature subject to circumstances—I, once a free Bohemian! Tempus-etc-in illis. Yet, to let you know my wishes are free, I enclose two more small—one quite interesting—Colonial library notes: and to say, as I have said before, that I have others—buried under a mountain of So. Ca. memoranda—which are yours when I uncover them in the process of my present work. New York was gorgeous, with material to my end—but otherwise as sordid, unresting and inimical to my rural disposition as ever: I was glad to be out of it: I out-ed on the 30th ulti., landing here the 1st inst. I find the San José scale has got a heavy start in the orchards while I have been away; so I have my hands full; and shall have until we leave, on the 16th, according to present plan. Thus you are preserved from more, at this writing, from me: a cause for joy, as you may now for some time still assume a bold front, on the Constable's letter-head, as one who *has* a copy of "Lacy." I shall yet expose your duplicity in that regard. With my compliments to that good-looking—and as good as she is good-looking—wife of yours—and sincere thanks to you for your intrepid South Carolina invitation—which, believe me, I shall accept, when I may, with pleasure, and look forward to with much anticipation as a red-letter time. I am, my dear Yates,

Affectionately yours,
John Bennett

P.S.: Meantime, when in Charleston, in God's name, look me up, and at least pass the time of day: my central station, #31 Legaré, apparently for an indefinite season: playground, the Charleston Library and I. Hammond's.

Columbia, S.C., Oct. 13, 1913

Dear Jack: [E. Flat Rock, N.C.]

Your insolent letter has been received, and "contents noted." I have not tried the experiment; but, I heard at College, and I have been told since, that if a man tells the same lie, 100 days in a year, he not only persuades *himself,* but he persuades *other people* that he is telling *the truth. Ergo,* for God's sake, stop telling me that you are a Damyankee.

Far away from the Western Reserve; in Chillicothe (glorious, for that fact!) you first saw the light; and killed sleep thereabout by your horrific infantile yells. I have not looked into the "Barnaby Lee" for points and authorities as to JB; but, as a matter of fact, I have a horrible suspicion that *I* am one 64th Yankee! The Chas. Library Soc'y has a copy of Cotton Mather, with the name of the owner *Jedediah Snowden* on the title page, and the New Eng. Hist. & Geneal. Register has several references to *"Snaughdon"* & "Snoughdon"; showing that the infernal Puritans pronounced my name, just as I do.

Cow = Co*u*

Snow = Sno*u*

I shall not die happy until I am persuaded that "Joshua Snowden Walter," who I *know* could write his name in 1764, for I have seen it, was not kin of those nasty yankees. But, nonsense aside—

Come to see us, and bring your favorite wife, just as soon as you can! If the shanty were not so small, we would say bring those lovely children; but, I shall have to ask you to put them *pro-tem.* in some of the orphanages. The Enston Home is reserved for older and choicer spirits— like you and *me.* I expect to land there yet: my family (Snowden) has lived and paid taxes in S.C. since 1743, and, so far as I know, none has been an occupant of the jail or alms-house; I have a *right* to go, with wifey, to the Enston Home. Q.E.D.!!! The Am'n Hist. Ass'n meets in Charleston (2 days) and Columbia (1 day) just after Xmas. That's the time I want to be known and recognized as the friend of John Bennett!!! Do you catch on? I shall be as proud as a monkey with three tails—if I can stalk through Columbia and introduce *you* as my friend. You are apparently going to loaf in the "holy city" for an indefinite time. I hope the Major & Mrs. S. will so improve, that you & your dear wife can come to us *early!* But, if you really want to see *Lacy,* say so; & I will send him to you by registered post. That "$16. MS," means the letters, published and *unpublished,* of Mrs. *Eliza Wilkinson*[40] (See Trent[41] "Southern Writers"; & Wauchope's S.C. Literature for estimates of Eliza's unique position as an early American letter writer).

If you so wish, I will send the $16. MS. to you in Charleston.

I will or *shall* explain to you later, what part *I expected* to play in the new edition of Eliza Wilkinson. As soon as you have killed the San José scale, write me what you & your wife wish me to do.

I am so sleepy: I can scarcely scrawl. My love to your wife.

Yours always,
Y. S.

———————

E. Flat Rock, N.C., Oct. 15th. 1913

Dear Yates:

We are "putting the big pot into the little one" here, to-day: as we move down en caravan, with a dozen trunks and dozens of bags, tomorrow, and are shipping the horses and other impedimenta this afternoon. Hence this disrespectful card, for which apologies profound. Your Chinese perpendicular letter rec'd. I *do: DO:* want to see the "Lacy"—and the $16 MSS—I sure do! It will be a great favor. Do not send them, however, until I advise you I am safely settled—don't let's run any risks with our pearls and jewelry. I can get through the Lacy nimbly & return at once. Will advise you as soon as we are settled in Charleston, and next time I meet the Pope will get you a special dispensation. Will advise you later as to our movements: and shall expect to chirp under your wing, as a bona fide Southerner, sir, during the incursion after Xmas of the historians.

Affectionately yours,
John Bennett

Chapter 5

1914–1915

Henry Timrod's Katie; *more on Revolution in South Carolina; Huguenot novels; Lacey* at last; *Susannah Wells Aikman's* Journal; *survival of anti-Tory prejudice; Annie Snowden's illness;* The Countess Pourtales.

IN 1914, besides a short note, there is only one letter in the collection. It is Yates Snowden's New Year's Eve epistle from Hawkinsville, Georgia, concerning the past summer, Christmas gifts, a song by John Bennett, and Snowden's lack of musical ability.

Early in 1915 Bennett thanked Snowden for the Christmas present of a beautiful copy of Henry Timrod's *Katie.* In the same letter he referred to his illness the previous summer that prevented his helping while Major Smythe lay dying.

A monograph by Yates Snowden, *Notes on Labor Organizations in South Carolina,* was published by the University that year. When Snowden, for a proposed speech at Clemson, requested any material Bennett might have on George Washington's connection with South Carolina, the novelist, in reply, teased the professor about South Carolina historians.

In April Snowden finally found and sent Dr. Maurice Moore's *Life of Lacey* that he had promised Bennett years earlier. The rare pamphlet, which was lent to Snowden by the grandson of Professor W. J. Rivers, delighted Bennett. In May Snowden lent Bennett his copy of Louisa Susannah Wells Aikman's *Journal.* Bennett, after looking over some old manuscripts from the Laurens house and checking into the Scotch

Church's affairs, sent to Snowden notes on South Carolina Royalists and Partisans.

The friends exchanged stories of anti-Tory prejudice remaining in the twentieth century. They also discussed the works of several South Carolina authors, including Annie Raymond Stillman, Mary Elizabeth Moragné, and William Gilmore Simms.

In July of 1915 Annie Snowden underwent an operation. In December Snowden sent Bennett a newly published pamphlet, *The Countess Pourtales,* with an introduction, "A Study in Scarlet," by Snowden, but signed with the alias "Felix Old Boy." The booklet was a reprint of Julian A. Selby's *A Checkered Life,* first published in Columbia in 1878 at the presses of *The Daily Phoenix,* and reputed to be by "One Who knows."

Hawkinsville, Jaw Jaw
31st Dec'r 1914

Dear John:

I don't know what you think of me—not acknowledging your beautiful song (*both* editions!); not seeing you last summer, though I was not ten miles away; &c., &c., &c. . . .

I brought the 2d ed'n of your song here with me, & have had my lovely niece Pauline[1] (She is as pretty as a picture!) *play* the accompaniment for me three times. It sounds well, but unfortunately Pauline cannot sing any more than a cow, and I cannot read music, and my whole vocal repertoire consists of Moody & Sankey,[2] "Come along Moses" and "Sleeping, I dreamed, Love"! And so I will not *know* how lovely your song is (I mean the music) until I go back to Columbia.

I would have liked to have gone to *town* this Xmas, but my first wife longed to see her two sisters who married two cousins of mine and live in this God-forsaken Jaw Jaw cotton town—"twelve miles from a lemon." My love to you and yours!

Yours affectionately,
Yates Snowden

"Winter" adorns my mantelpiece in Cola., by the side of the Xmas Turkey & Turk that came to me three years ago. I am afraid "Katie" was coals to Newcastle. I mailed it to you from Augusta (en route to this place) just to let you see that I had not forgotten you. It is *not* Timrod's best, by a long shot; but, that edition is rarish.

That cut of a Colonial note of 1723, I put in "Katie," may interest you. Judge Smith[3] & Langdon Cheves[4] have "translated" the signatures for me. The original is in the possession of a Columbia school boy! I had the cut made.

We will be back in Columbia, by Sunday P.M.

#37 Legaré St., Charleston, S.C., Jan. 13, '15

Dear Yates: . . .

I have long since forgiven you, sherr ammy, for not complicating my situation at Flat Rock by a visit, last summer: I was truly in no condition for receiving visitors, or for enjoying even the sight of a good friend— if you know what I mean, I will remark that I was enjoying a thorough-paced physical grouch; and physical disability was ably seconded by a species of mental fury, a rebellion against futile desires.

Joking aside, I was in miserable condition; I was pinned flat on my back and unable to stir down-stairs to support, by my presence, or to assist, on the days that the Major lay dying, and on the day that he died. My wife had to carry it all, alone—and in part to look after me, into the bargain. Truly, women are wonders, and a glory. . . .

Let's blame all that we have longed to do, yet failed to accomplish to the bright fullness of the dream, upon the times, which are about as much out of joint as usual. Which makes me think—an unprofitable exercise—have we diagnosed the situation rightly? Are we really broke; or is it only that our affairs are also out of joint? Query.

February 9th, 1915: Same address as above:

Dear Yates:

In looking over some old MSS found in the Laurens'[5] house, just demolished to make way for the bonsoir railway line, the above valuable bit of Carolina source-material was discovered. I send it to you simply as evidence of good faith. This proves effectually that faith without works is a dollar watch. Post-card asking about the weather received this morning: had a horrible fit of compunction immediately. In reply will state it is a very foggy morning with me: sunshine glorious outside, however. Vive la (firm name here)!

Thank you, withouten hyperbole, for "Katie," and its joyous old English woodcuts by Harrison Weir and Birket Foster, del., Sculp. by Bolton, Green, Palmer and Wimperis: "it may be through some foreign grace and unfamiliar charm of face; it may be that across the foam which bore her from her childhood's home, *by these strange spells,* my Katie brought, along with English creeds and thought—*some English sunshine, warmth, and air!*"—so writes H. Timrod, and so write I. I rise to stir my dying fire into renewed activity, and see if I can find in "Katie" apt quotation for this chillblain morning? Yes, here it is: "It scarce would seem amiss to say: Katie, my home lies far away, beyond the pathless waste of brine, in a young land of palm and pine. There by the TROPIC HEATS, the soul is touched as if with living COAL, and glows with such a FIRE as NONE can feel beneath a NORTHERN SUN—*Such is the land in which I live.*" I wot well the peach-trees are pinkling in the wastes, and that breath-of-spring is tinkling its soundless golden bells along the reviving bough; yet "these houses, free to every breeze that blows from warm Floridian seas"—again aptly to quote our poet, with his eye in phrenzy rolling—retain, within their happy wall, an unmistakable touch of Fall—"Ay, let them jeer and laugh who will"—I'm going to mend that draughty sill! It's cold. "Thus much, at least, a manly youth may hold— and yet not blush—as truth." You notice Timrod said "Thus much," not "this much." Buck up, man! that was some grammarian!

I'm fit for little beside nonsense, this morning; I am restless as a cat in a snow-storm: I don't know whether it is my worthless sight, or mere reluctance to grapple with the grind; perhaps the latter. I refer you to M. Mantalini.[6]

(You see, luckless wight, you are in for it!)

I am in my own house, or my original wife's, whose guest I am; and have been hoping to get forward with Magnum Opus. Another sort of magnum would come handy this morning; I'm down-spirited over the fearful difficulty of ascertaining the truth about you South Carolinians. And, lo! Miss Webber—a fine young woman that, and able: nicht wahr?—tells me that some Englishman, who has not the fear of God in his heart, is preparing to print a dozen volumes upon one of my chosen topics: "The South Carolina Royalists." He writes to ask her to aid him in information concerning the genealogical remains of John and Peter Blewer, of "Ninety-Six." I hope he will delay printing until he gets that information. Such information anent those two is like Boarding-house butter:

CHOICE	"Serving maid enters from pantry; speaks
ANECDOTE:	aside to Mistress: 'Missus B., you know
No. 1	the butter?—well, it AIN'T!'"

. . . .

Sorry you lost your courage, fearing conviction; you should have the courage of your convictions: should have sent me your able article in The State. Now, thanks to your well-meant modesty, and to the unfulfilled promises of Mrs. Ray Horton, and to the fact that I could not read newspapers, last summer, because I had forgot to dot my eyes—I have failed, to this time, to recover that precious screed, which I want for my scrap-book of commentary upon the rapid downward career of a bright and promising young man—you to furnish the clipping—I the down-ward-career. So, if you come upon it, please forward! Oh, by the way: What did you ever do to that really nice young fellow, Sidney Cohen?[7] Rabbi Marcuson advises me that the said S. Cohen came back to Charleston with the opinion, somewhere imbibed, of repute on my part, not warranted by the evidence submitted. That's a nice boy, Cohen; have made his acquaintance through young Albert Simons,[8] the archi-tect, another nice boy; spent an evening with me a short time ago; and are coming to tea, Saturday evening, 13th, if the 13 doesn't interfere: young Sam Stoney[9] coming, also: making three very nice young chaps fallen under the baleful influence of a bankrupt genius.

I have just read through—kiver to kiver—your Bulletin on "Labor Organizations in S.C.," and with great interest. . . . I have never, anywhere, come across anything further concerning John Noah Sargent's ARK. Query: was there Ararat in it? If Union Labor, could there have been?

I am not prepared to comment upon your last, the closing, para-graphs. My contempt for all so-called aristocracies has ever increased with years; my admiration for the man of brains and power who rises into well-earned position and esteem was always great: I had hoped to be one of them myself; instead of which I live in Legaré Street—reductio ad absurdum. I cannot consider this subject seriously. I must leave that to Charlestonians; I am only an outsider, as you know. To contemplate how greatly the old-time Charleston mechanic of brains and grip succeeded, and to see how greatly I have failed, is humiliating. Why, man, that song of mine—which you once so impudently relabelled and printed in the News & Courier; d'ye recollect?—was written twenty years or more ago!

You forgot to state what the translation was of that remarkable signature on the Colonial note enclosed in "Katie." I shall have to get out my oyster-knife, open Mr. Langdon Cheves, and secure the information. Thank you. By the way, what do you know, or do you know anything regarding the residence in Charleston, S.C., of Hugh Williamson,[10] (Hist. of N.C., etc.): about 1777-8? He was in N.C.—Wilmington, I think, in 1780, and volunteered to go into Camden town after Gates's[11] debacle, to attend the American prisoners-of war, since the American surgeons of the army, like the Three Jolly Welshmen, had "all run away" with the militia. Did you ever run across a trail of him? What do you know of that story (Worse and worse, eh?) that Maj. André was in Charles Town during the Siege of 1780? The tradition persists, and I have a small house in the Bay pointed out to me as one in which he lodged, and in which he was seen and recognized. I am going to take a picture of the house, just for tradition's sake.

You would have enjoyed the "petrified head" found in the Laurens' house: 'twas a flint boulder from a rockery, used by old Mrs. Aymar[12] to keep her piazza door open on windy days, when she resided there, some years ago; and was so identified by her, spoiling all the sport for Pickwickians who love to see that BILSTILSTUMPSISMARK! Unfortunately I happened upon Mrs. Aymar, who now lives up at Half-Moon Battery.

Thanks for the clipping from the Springfield Republican, regarding Negro Melodies, with the expostulation of Dieffenbach, Beadle and Stevens; I still hope to work out something on the music theme, some day, by and by, if I don't break my fool heart beforehand in vain endeavors to accomplish the impossible—viz., namely, and to wit: to write the truth of history. Man! I long to be back at real fiction—but I am hooked up hard with the present effort for Macmillan, who will probably not want it when they get it. And, likewise, I long to be doing the Charleston Legends, of recent notoriety. What a mess a man can make without the slightest intention to offend! Ai, me! And I shall probably spend the remainder of my life sedulously burying myself beneath gathered material for an undigested and unfinished magnum futilis! I was happy to be able to use a little of it, last week, in supplying some notes for a brief screed, for Miss Webber and the Hist. & Genea. Mag., on the 2nd Continental South Carolina Regt. of Foot, having recovered the names of some 200 non-coms. and rank and file of Motte's[13] Own, in 1777, when they were part of the garrison of Charles Town. I will return one of your compliments by sending you the same when it appears.

I am supposed to be writing an historical romance of S.C. in the Revolution. I find it the devil's own task to carry on fiction and historical research and construction at one time—one so contradicts the other in mental method—imagination being fatal in history; and the method of history deadly to imagination.

As to your chat on "S.C. as a Back Ground for Fiction," I wish I could get forward with my own prospect of it: it is as good a canvas as ever was stretched, take it as you will. I sometimes wish the State were a little less of a background, however, and a little more foreground of sorts. But it will be, when the long row is hoed at last.

I do not know when I shall be able to get to Columbia, or Wisconsin, or Washington, or Philadelphia (may not have to go to Philadelphia); and, the last time I saw DeRenne, he was so drunk that I have hesitated since to return to Georgia for the much I have great need to see there in DeR's wonderful library at Wormsloe. I have a wonderful bit of stuff on

Sumter:[14] and, if his life did not go out in a sort of spiritual collapse, I should like to write a life. If I can once get to Wisconsin, to verify and complete some sketchy spots, I mean to do something entirely new upon the Game Cock—and filled with thrills as any moving-picture melodrama. Dreams, dreams, dreams—the work so long; the life so brief!

Farewell! and believe me, I greatly miss you, year after year, since you have gone from this place: which has none too many good companions—and a fearful vacancy in your place.

Accept this letter as an apologia pro vita, etc., or as an aggravated assault-and-battery; but remember it goes with the hearty love of

John Bennett

Heartiest compliments to Mrs. Snowden, always.

Columbia, 14th Feb. '15

Dear Jack:

Bless your heart! You don't know what a "giggling joy" your letter was to me, in spite of its occasional pessimistic strain! Why don't you get a bottle of Simmons's Liver Regulator?

I have 60+ examination papers before me, *still unread,* and I cannot answer you now; wish I could. I *don't* know anything of the S.C. side of Hugh Williamson; Wm.son of the Council of Safety I barely recall. I don't know anything of the Blewers of 96.

I don't *know* anything of Major André being in "town." I believe it is one of Johnson's[15] Traditions, which has a basis of truth. If you could summon the spirit of Mrs. Dr. John B. Adger[16] (a lovely old lady; I wish you had known her!) you could find out something about it. I think it was her ancestor that spotted him. I gave away my Johnson's Traditions (I was *a* ass to do so!) and can't refresh my memory.

What *I* would have you do is to write a romance on S.C. Huguenots! Some brilliant pp. in Peyre G. show what you *could* do with such a theme. God knows it would require a deal of imagination & mendacity (judging by some latter day specimens), but you have both! Miss Stillman's[17] fine Sundayschool book "How They Kept the Faith" (which does not *mention* the S.C. Huguenots) & a measly little novelette by a Miss Moragné[18] of Abbeville are all we have on the subject except Simms's hastily written "The Lily and the Totem." So get busy, as soon as you have finished your Revolutionary lucubrations!

Apropos of Royalists: Did you ever read Col. Chas. C. Chesney's authentic *Memoirs* of "A Carolina Loyalist in the Revolutionary War" (pp. 323–40) in his military biography? It particularly attracted me because of the references to Lord Edward FitzGerald. I will lend you my copy, if you will give me one of your photographs! What say you?

But, I *must* get to work. God bless us all! including young Jack Bennett (who, I am told, is a beautiful boy), and his mother too.

Yours affectionately,
Y. S.

We never drove Sidney Cohen away. The rascal *left us*, and not for a handful of silver, either.

S.O.S. CALL!

I am to blow myself off at Clemson Coll. on Birthington's Washday, 22d Feb'y. Have you any *choice bit* of G. W.'s scant connection with South Carolina—which you have found, after years of research, & which you intended to use in your forthcoming *m.o.*—which you would mind *giving me* to work off as my original research at Clemson? I know all about George Mercer's nasty picture of the Holy City, wh' he wrote to G. W. in 1757, and I "know about" G. W. as a mule-raiser (Miss Webber told me!) and I know about a certain letter as to "Royal Gift" (a Spanish jack-ass) wh' G. W. wrote to his cousin Wm. Washin' in Charleston, which (pray God!) Miss Webber will never see, but at which I can barely *hint* to my mixed audience at Clemson. To conclude: if you have any choice South-Carolina Washingtoniana to *give away*, for Lord's sake, spit it out!

I don't yet know *what* was that rich Laurens house "find"!

SOS SOS SOS SOS SOS SOS SOS SOS SOS SOS SOS

Wednesday, Febr'y. 17th, 1915

Dear Yates:

Yrs. Recd. I haven't one —— thing anent G. Wash. and So. Ca. If I had I would have sent it, as the King said about the Black Pig with the Blue Tail. It would have been thine without a qualm. It's a pity. And me living in the house of the traditional Izard! I do not know Mercer's truthful comments on the New Jerusalem. Since you call them either n-asty or h-asty—I can't be certain which it is, for in your h-asty penmanship the *n* and *h* closely resemble each other—mean to look them up. A little malevolence now and then is relished by the most charitable of men: of which I am It. I won't say that you true-born South Carolinians have a fashion of gilding the lily; but I strongly suspect your historians of icing a hoecake and passing it on as angel's-food, now and then. . . .

Wm. Wmsn, of Council of Safety no connection, so far as ascertained, of Hugh, signatory to Constitution, and historiographer of N.C.; discredited fiercely by portions of said N.C. not praised by Hugh. . . .

I don't know the "measly little novelette" by Miss M, of Abbeville; and am afraid of the measles. . . . I haven't yet attained the "Lily and the Totem." There are, any way, only three things worth mention in Simms' novels: his touches of scenery; his heroic, break-a-trace patriotism, otherwise hold-a-brief partisanship, and his vulgar rogues, who are uncommonly well-done every one—not his titular Villains—but his Nym, Pistol and Bartolph fellows.

. . . Revolutionary lucubrations: good words; but I am writing an historical Romance, not a lucubration. The research comes on so slowly that the title of lucubration is hyperbole—about the light and progress of the agile glow worrum along a chilly wall. . . . Went through Chesney's Memoir twa year sin, thank you. Am pleased to hear that you have it, in case my copious extracts prove—whenever I get to them again—not to have been sufficient unto the day. Did it in Boston; with much else. . . .

Sorry I have no Washingtoniana: but I have absolutely nothing on that line. Farewell. . . .

Yours in haste,
Jack

2d. April '15

My dear John:

I enclose that clipping from *The State, in re* Rose Garden, which you desired (or pretended so much to desire) to see. . . .

I am sending you, under official cover, *Lacy.* You have jibed, & snarled & doubted my temporary possession of that *rara avis* so long, that I think it well to shut your mouth on *one* subject.

The durned pamphlet *does not belong to me,* but to the good-natured, good-for-nothing grandson of Prof'r Rivers, who was my student for two years, and who "loaned" me 10 or 15 of his grandfather's rare pamphlets. He has gone to the plough, probably, for six months, & has not yet called for his pamphlets; I would gladly give $7.00 for them.

I doubt if there is much in it new to you; but, send it back to me in two or three weeks, *s'il vous plaît.*

I see, in Peter Force, that the Rev. *Paul Turquand*,[19] several times, opened that Constitutional Convention!!! of 1775–6, with prayer. That shows that Mrs. Jack Bennett's ancestor was true blue at the beginning of the fracas. I hope he *stayed good;* especially because of his *connexion* with my frau's people, the *Warleys.*

Tout à vous,
Y. Snowden

Clarum et venerabile nomen (That's Latin!)

Sunday P.M. [Apr. 4, 1915]

Dear Bennett:

Here is Dr. Maurice Moore—at last. Te Deum Laudamus!

Yours ever,
Y. S.

I know, though a Presbyterian, that "I have left undone those things I ought to have done, and have done those things I ought not to have done"; but, don't cherish those things against me, but continue to send me library slips; and I *may* leave my silver mara spoon to your enfant terrible!

April 6th, 1915

Dear Yates:

I have telephoned for the police to open the mysterious package you forward. I know you state that it contains Revolutionary material: viz., namely, i.e.: one copy Moore's "Life of Lacey"; but I hesitate to accept that statement, and feel some trepidation about opening the ominous envelope.

Many hours later:

We are all still alive, and IT *IS* THE LIFE OF LACEY! Mirabile dictu! Well, well, well! wonders will never cease!

Thanks, honoured sir, many, many thanks! I will extract what seems to me desirable, or necessary to the great cause, and will return said pamphlet to you about the 19th current, in a golden casket, marvellously chased, and set with radiant diamond designs, interspersed with rubies, jacinths, emerauds, and many other precious rocks, of which I would make the list longer but that this type-writer ribbon is wearing out and conservation is a hobby of the times. There is just this about the "Life of Lacey": while I may find little in it new or valuable, it is not permitted one to write history without having examined every possible source of the facts; and Lacey contains material not to be neglected in the study of Sumter and Williams.[20] It also contains facts concerning affrays considered unimportant by previous historians, and therefore really important.

Still later: IT STILL REMAINS, UNALTERED: "The Life of Lacey."

Well, well, well!

Your insinuations that I would ask for a newspaper clipping which I do not want are beneath your usual standard. Don't stoop to such badinage; hitch your persiflage to a star, and you will get a higher perspective, perhaps; but I promise you a darned windy ride. Thanks very honestly and boney fidey for the clipping—I desired it very much, to keep the record straight. I am, moreover, obliged to you for extravagance of diction employed, as well as extravagant hopes entertained— not too extravagant, perhaps, after all; for, at last report from the Bond Shop, over 60,000 copies of the song had been sold in spite of preoccupation of mind occasioned by the war and the Jesse-Jack[21] combaw in Havana. This has enabled me to pay for two years' school for my boy, Jack, and half a year for my two girls, without asking their mother, God bless her, to foot those bills out of her estates, with which she has been always too generous and too ready to drag me out of the hole in which a firm trust in Heaven and a hope of earning a livelihood by literature have put me. . . .

Having gone to hear Hugh McGillivray[22] on Balladry, I have been humming, for some time, the old ballad of "Lord Lovell," to the old tune my mother used when I was a small dumpling-headed child with the expression of a boiled pudding. I hear Jack picking it up, and even Susy, the youngest, came up stairs, yesterday, carolling irregularly, but enthusiastically: "Wey is you goin', Lord Luddell, SAYS SHE!" The children are to be vaccinated to-day; I think my wife suspects this outbreak of balladry.

I am trying to get for McGillivray several ballads which, as a boy, I often and often heard sung by the hill-fiddlers, on the public square, on stock-sale days, market-days and during the country fairs: "St. Clair's Defeat," "Perry's Victory," "Wayne at Fallen Timber." The airs to which they were sung are, I fear, as dead as the fiddlers.

PAUL TURQUAND, and the contumacious TACITUS GAILLARD,[23] fled from the State in 1780, fearing lest they be elected to dance a pas de deux—or suthin that sort—in a lang tow; they went by way of Red Stone Fort, down the Ohio and Mississippi to New Orleans; there Tacitus passed away to the Islands of the Blessed. It is certain he passed away; all South Carolinians *pass away;* nobody ever dies down here but negroes. Just which way he went I have no satisfactory authority for statement. Paul remained in the Missippi (I will supply the missing letters at the foot of this page) Valley, until all uncertainty—and the war in its entirety—was ended, before he returned to Carolina.

Mrs. Smythe remembers a MS. diary he kept during his stay in the Valley, and during his overland trip, through the Indian country, returning to Carolina, which was in existence when she was a girl; but which has now disappeared utterly, she knows not where, nor when. She has a volume of his sermons, and I think this volume contains one of the prayers or sermons preached to order on occasion, for the Provincial Congress.

I think the reason Paul and Tacitus fled beyond the confines of the Colonies was that they arrogated to themselves, perhaps, greater distinction as rebels than I think was attached to either. They did not pause in North Carolina, I have fancied, from the reason that Tacitus was always, as I understand, attached to the Church—be his forebears what they might; while Paul was a turn-coat Huguenot who had taken English orders, and could scarcely have been immensely admired by our good Presbyterian brethren around Charlotte. I have heard him bitterly and scornfully referred to by family connections as a turn-coat, even at this late day.

In spite of his excellent connection with members of Mrs. Snowden's ancestry, I have never heard of his doing anything very dashing or distinguished, and his surviving sermons, like those of the revered Thomas Smyth, D.D.,[24] are futile reading and dry. He was, no doubt, an estimable character. I regret that none of Dr. Smyth's war-time sermons got themselves into his collected works; they would have added amusing interest to that publication. He knew just about as much of the questions involved as he did about the Declaration of Independence, Mecklenburg brand, on which he pronounced at length and in error, of course—being a Presbyterian.

But my remarks seem to be growing passing pessimistic and carping. 'Twere better I cease: hence these ceasings:

> Tout, tout, tout, tout!
> This is a French horn, as you see:
> also affectionately,
> Jack Bennett

Ever my compliments to your good wife.

John Bennett

P.S.: I suppose you saw me keeping the submarine record straight. I have to print something, now and then, to keep from acquiring the impression that I am dead.

N.B.: The missing letters: ISS

1st May 1915

My dear John:

For, I was delighted to note, during that charming Sunday P.M. chat, that *the Melancholy Jacques* was a thing of the past! You are a poor actor in a lachrymose *role* anyway; it was always a misfit; cut it out!!

I expressed you this P.M. Susannah's Journal, &c., &c.; I have no idea that there is much in it for you; but, some of the *scraps* may help you. The *really* distinguished Wm. Charles Wells'[25] report of his last visit to the city, and his scathing denunciation of everything and *everybody* there, except one branch of the Harlestons,[26] is significant. The appendix will probably interest you more than Susannah's belated journal; e.g., that short sketch of Robert Wells and the *"Travestie on Vergil,"* in verse, attributed to him. In the note of correction Susannah (or Mr. Aikman) attributes the "travestie" to Roland Bagley, Ala.; it means of course *Roland Rugeley.* I just missed *by a mail,* buying a copy of that rare bird from Cadby of Albany, N.Y., for 3.00. *Now,* if I want a copy, Wilberforce Eames[27] of the N.Y. Public Library (which got ahead of me) says I must send him $10. for a photostat. I want it *bad;* but I can't afford $10.00, in these awful times; for these blanked Columbia tradesmen, *force* me to "fritter away my money paying my debts"! The Rev. Henry Alex'r White, D.D.,[28] who had my copy of the *Journal,* asks me to impress upon you that Susannah's intimation that most of the Scotch Presbyterians were *loyalists,* is incorrect. *He says* that the claims of the S.C. loyalists on the British Gov't contain the names of only *two* Scotch Presbyterian families; and that some few families like the *Brisbanes*[29] (See S.C. Hist. Socy Mags!) were arf & arf. Harry's pamphlet proving that the Circular Ch. congregation was *Presbyterian,* and that David Ramsay prevaricated; will soon be in print; the revised proofs have been read. The gentle Harry had better not go to Charleston after that lucubration is published. "Holly" Mitchell[30] will shoot him! If you *wont* come to Columbia and walk up Main St. and through the campus *with me;* & visit the Kosmos Club, and address the students in chapel, *introduced by me;* all my prestige as being John Bennett's intimate friend; & all my chance allusions to what "Jack Bennett" wrote, and said to *me;* and my occasional exhibition of "Jack's wit" in "his last letter," which I always have in my inside pocket, will go up in smoke! *If you wont come,* at least send me a photograph; but when taken, kindly remove those enormous gig-lamps you wore the other evening. Let me have your eyes "in wild 'phrensy' rolling." It's only 2:30 A.M., which stops me from more prosing! My love to your lovely wife, and those charming children!

Yours affectionately,
Y. S.

There is not *anyone,* outside of your wife's & your family connexions, who awaits your novel with more interest and intense expectancy than

Y. S.

May 5th, '1[5]

Dear Yates:

Louisa Susannah reached me, O.K., by express; followed, later, by your characteristic impertinence of May 1st, for both which heartiest thanks from jocular John, who, according to your account, is substituting here for the Melancholy Jacques. Jacques, I must confess, shuns good company. Would I had more of it here in Charleston. It is my own fault, no doubt. I could bring some exonerating evidence; but haven't time.

I deny, however, the lachrymose. I may be dour; not lachrymose. I have to use those unfortunate ducts over time during hay-fever season. A truly melancholy Jacques is merciful to his ducts. You have read the character wrong. Get out your Wully Shakespoke and study again that delightful character-sketch. Was never lachrymose; never! He only frivolled with lachrymae. Nor was dour; which, being mostly Scotch, I take the liberty of being from time to time: any change is then so delightful and so welcomed by my family. Do you not remember the story of the small boy, found by his mother beating his thumb with a hammer and crying wofully. "Why do you do that when it pains you so?" she demanded. "It feels so good when I stop!"

Show this to any friends.

I have not had time, yet, to dip into Susannah; but have been peeping like an Elder; and see considerable that interests me; more than you imagine: you know not the devious system of my lucubration.

I love diatribes against Charleston. They help me get all such thoughts out of my system; and then, indirectly, move me much more to love the town, hearing it scandalized by others, non-resident; just as one will abuse his own kindred, but will permit none other to vilify. There are two natures struggling in me when it comes to Charleston, affection and dislike; what I break with one hand I am ever moved to repair with the other.

Gee! Man! You don't mean to tell me you had a chance to get Rowland Rugeley's Travestie! I had the opportunity of straightening Evans[31] out on Rugeley and Wells, while I was in New York, a year or two ago: he didn't seem much obliged. I am sorry you missed the Travestie, genuinely sorry. I wonder if there is another anywhere in the wide world, loose, that can be got for South Carolina? I wonder if the Rugeleys in Texas—if there be any left—chance to have a copy. Doubt it awf'ly: Whigs trimmed the Rugeleys too clean when they chased 'em off the earth.

My esteem is great for the Rev. Henry Alexander White, D.D. But, with all regard, I will be impressed by such evidence as I accumulate on the diverting question of the Toryism of the Scotch church, rather than by anything less certain. I have been through the claimants—Loyalist Commissioners' Reports—complete. I have no opinion in the matter: I only wait on the evidence. I shrewdly suspect that any church of which Sandy Cheves was a member in good standing, and in whose graveyard his bones rest, had a leaning toward—well, one side or the other!

As to the Circular Church and whether it was Presbyterian or Congregational, Mugwump or Bull-Moose Baptist, far be it from me to meddle with church polity or dogmatic theology. I look forward with interest, whetted to a keen edge, to the promised pamphlet—and shall be delighted to offer my house as a refuge to the author when in the danger zone. The number of those good people, members of the Scotch and Circular congregations, who make use of our good secretary, Miss Webber, and of the material of the S. C. H. & A. S., for their own ends, being neither members of the society, nor paying Miss W. her due fees for services rendered, is peculiarly astonishing. Does this prove that their forebears were Whigs or Tories, Congregationalists or Presbyterians?

Do you expect me to come to Columbia, EVER, if you threaten an address to students in chapel? Don't you realize the fact that I have gone permanently out of the address business? If you chatter so ill-advisedly about me and my flub-dub I'll go North and West by way of Florence and Augusta, and dodge Columbia: don't you realize that I am bashful? Or unsuccessful. Success hardens many a shy man's face.

Alas! I had expected to see "Master Skylark"—known to the elite as "Master Mudlark"—in moving-pictures; but the Essanay people cannot find a boy to play the lead, and decline to dish up Hamlet ungarnished by Ham.

About the photographs, with or without goggles, they charge for them down here unless one is on the track-team. Would send one if had one.

In the glorious romance at present stewing over the blaze of need, there is nothing doing just at these present instants. I find that it is a great mistake to engage with anyone to write a book according to *any* specifications: for the specifications instantly become impossible: imagination will not follow specifications; if it does it is darned sure proof that it is hatchet and saw botchery, not literature of even primary sort as mine is. Thank you for the persevering interest and encouragement you lend—to me, as to every aspiring or despairing genius: you are one noble fellow: which is not altogether a jest.

And I am, with thanks for Susannah and her portion of the Apocrypha, regards to Mrs. Snowden, and souvenirs to all mourning friends,

As You Like It:
John-Jacques:

May 6th, 1915

Dear Yates:

I send by parcels post, to-day, Journal of Louisa Susannah Wells Aikman, late of Charlestown, Jamaica, and the World, with many thanks for a most appreciated loan.

I got more out of it than you would suppose. In fact I practically copied out 10,000 words, extracts, and put in a slip cover for myself, so that I retain the meat of the volume, ready for real digestion at leisure.

I found what she said most interesting from the light it sheds on a bundle of other material I have in hand.

There is no doubt about it, our friends, the Loyalists, had a d—— rough deal in the Carolinas and Georgia. They also had an equally d—— rough deal in the rest of the Colonies. Wm. Chas. W. faintly shadows forth the happy life of the loyalist, in his notes on his visit to Charlestown in 1783—and but suggests the iniquity of procedures against such as had any money which might with advantage be laid hold upon by our noble ancestors. Our noble ancestors were not a bit more noble than we ourselves and those we have around us; some of them weren't as noble, but have been sedulously glossed and gilded in a way that is sickening to a man who likes the truth in history.

A study of the difficulties experienced in removing from the Province, by such loyal folk as refused the Association and the oath of abjuration, would make a stunning thesis in history, and be as full of picturesque material as Esquemeling's[32] History of the Buccaneers—or near it. They sure were skinned on every pretext and at every turn.

And, once more, as to the patriotism of the Scotch Church—ho hum! The bats in the belfry were Hanoverian bats. By this statement I do not mean to go on record as saying that the Scotch Church has bats in its belfry—except theologically—ho hum! the bats are petrifactions.

As to the attitude of you thin-skinned, or erring, South Carolinians, on the Tory ancestor business, it is enough to make a harness-maker's wooden horse laugh. Why, I asked Mr. Jack Ball if he could give me some information—not in the Ball book[33]—about his Tory relatives, and the boy blushed to the roots of his hair: Anno Domini, 1912. And the Rev. Mr. Williams[34] told me, recently, that, among other parish work, ten years ago, on the border of North Carolina, he endeavored to organize a boys' brass band; he selected a particularly good cornet-player for his leader, and was surprised to find stubborn and bitter opposition, with no apparent cause; which finally came down to admission, upon . . . [my] question, that "Well, you know, Mr. Williams, that boy's . . . were just Tories during the old Revolution!"

Ho hum! Why, even the children down here still say, when . . . [play]ing tag, "Americans!" for a moment's truce, instead of the . . . honored pass: "King's X."

Hullo! Paper's out: I get off here: much love, much . . .

Ever affectionately yrs.,
Jack

Columbia, 10th May '15

Just 10 lines, my melancholy Jacques, to tell you how much I appreciate your letters and Royalist data. . . .

In addition to the *Ball* & *Williams anti-Tory prejudice* survival, *I* can give you a fine specimen. In my II History (one term, American) classes, four or five years ago; talking to a *frosh class Edgefield* student, about a former Edgefield student, whom he knew, I said: "That's *a fine* fellow, about the best old Edgefield can produce; we are going to *hear from him* before many years!"

"No, Sir*ee*, Professor; you don't know him! *He's* descended from Tories in the Revolution!"

I don't like to crush a butterfly, and I respect your injunction, and I rather like the wild-eyed H'y Alex'r Wh.— otherwise, I would horrify the Historian-Divine with your shocking exposures *in re* Hewatt and his hot-Scotch flock. God bless your wife (ink's out) and your ugly self, and your lovely children!

Yours aff'ly,
Y. S.

I enclose "Dum Vivimus Vigilemus,"[35] with my *fool* introduction. You will recognize the prodigy of learning W. W. Ball!

June 7th, 1915

Dear Yates: . . .

I had no postal-card; hence was compelled to wait until the price of paper fell, and until my wife bought stamps; hence this inexplicable delay in replying to yours of 27th May.

Also, am just back from adventures in the wilds of Washington, D.C., where I interviewed and was interviewn by a noculist: hence gig-lamps adorning this noble visage.

N.B.: While in Washington a distinguished amateur—namely Mrs. Edith Pratt Dickins[36]—shot at me with a camera, minus gig-lamps. If said shot has reasonable results will forward one choice shoot to your address. Perhaps if you wish to avoid infection it were well to remove early.

I did not attempt to see any librarian or historian while in Washington, though this was deuced impolite to the generous and friendly Jameson.[37] I was busied with ocular scrutiny, and in haste to get home to enjoy briefly the society of my wife and children before they remove to Flat Rock, on or about June 18th current. I saw only an old friend, in the Agricultural Department, who has been studying Pan's pipes among the Incas of Peru, etc., and wishes me to furnish a brief screed upon the African application of the "quills" to music, as found still lingering remotely in S.C., on which I have some data—if I can ever lay hand on the stuff. He was tickled to death over the simple superposition of tetrachords which I found in two instances—but as you don't know what a tetrachord is without a musical dictionary, I will discontinue this. . . .

A print of St. Philip's Church, 1753, was sent here to be sold for $5.00 for the benefit of the Belgian Relief Fund, by Mrs. Adger Smyth,[38] patroness. From Gent's Maga.; is to be had of Metcalfe-Morton, #1, Duke St., Brighton, Eng., opp. G.P.O., for 1s. 6d. A good many things are done in the name of sweet charity.

But, speaking of antiques, the Book Committee of the Charleston Library Society owes, and most cheerfully and heartily pays you a vote of thanks for your interest in our behalf, anent the two City Directories, 1790 and 18-something-very-early, neither of which we had. It was truly generous of you to wrest the same from Alex Salley, to divert them from yourself and University, and send to us. The map in 1790, from survey of 1789, is excellent; I have already affirmed two uncertains by it, and am going to copy it for my own use. So, personally, and officially, many and most appreciative thanks. . . .

> Farewell! Farewell! I must get back to
> a romance in which I have no interest
> whatever, and which is half pilfering
> and half piffle:

> To Sir Fretful Plagiary I haste to make it known:
> What's good in this book I borrowed; the pitiful truck
> is my own.
> Again farewell!
> Yrs. pessimistically
> as usual:
> J. B.

Regards to Alexander Salley:
if you are at present speaking.

11th July '15

My dear Jack:

That visit to Charleston, *barring*

I. My poor sister's sickness,

II. My failure to go to Sullivan's Island, and see the Porchers (Walter's female "department")—and to see my dear old friend Bp. Northrop,

III. My failure to see *you,* and talk you to insensibility *in your own shanty;*

IV. The damned mosquitoes in Walter's house *the first* night I tried to sleep there; but, "for goodness' sake don't say I told you"!

—was one of unalloyed pleasure, with three notable mint juleps (Sam Stoney Sr. should have been a bar-tender!) and "innocent merriment"!!

Next to seeing my sister and Dr. Vedder,[39] & our friend Miss Webber, the main object of my visit was to see *you!* I saw you and *heard* you (You always make yourself heard; sometimes *too much!*), but *only in a crowd,* but not as R. B. puts it:

> When hand grasps at hand, eye lights eye in good
> friendship, and great hearts expand and grow one in the
> sense of this world's life.

I thought I would find time in the four days to break into 37 Legree St. and spoil your morning's work; but, it was impossible.

And all of this prelude only *proves* that you *must come to Columbia,* & vegetate three or four days—a month, if you will, with we uns!!!! Q.E.D.

I returned to this frightfully progressive, New South, burg; tired and dirty; but, very happy, for I had dined with *old* Teddy Guerard, with Walter, & my old college-mate John Pyatt; and a beautiful ox-eyed Damyankee R.I. girl Miss Bogert (a niece of Mrs. G's); but, I had a cruel setback when I reached this house. My first, present, and only wife, informed me ten minutes after my arrival, that she had been to see (and had been seen) by the ablest mid-Carolina surgeon, Dr. *Guerry* (brother of the Episcopal *soul* physician!)[40] and that he advised an operation on the throat, for a little growth there (presumably, *a small tumor*), and that she had made up her mind to "face the music," "like a little man"! I kissed her (an old trick of mine, for two decades!) and heartily concurred in her decision. I "carried" her (Charlestonese) to the Cola. Hospital yesterday, and went to see her today; and she is in excellent spirits, and I hope to see her at 12, noon, tomorrow, after the operation. The doctors tell me there is *no* element of danger, & that the operation is slight; but neither of us has ever been to a hospital before, except to visit sick friends!

The Moore's Creek "story," from Ashe,[41] which I enclose, is, I am afraid, "ancient history" to *you;* I pray God you never heard of the heroic young bride-groom *McLeod*[42] before. I should be awfully proud to find the story in *your magnum opus,* & to hear that *I* gave you the "pointer."

Yours affectionately,
Y. Snowden

P.S. Monday, 12th

The operation was successfully performed this morning, and a "pesky" little growth about as big as a pigeon's egg was removed. She is in some pain; I have been at the hospital for over four hours; but I am greatly relieved, as it *might have* developed into goitre!

I send you a "grind" on Sidney Fisher's[43] book, a work with which you are doubtless familiar, and I am not! There are some rhetorical flourishes about Tories which may be new even to a Philistine like yourself. Send it back to me!

Y. S.

No. 1.
24th July '15

Jacobus Carus:

After eight days in the hospital, she is home again! Looking and *talking* well, altho' Dr. DuBose[44] comes every third day to dress the little wound on that really lovely neck. I rec'd the surgeon's bill yesterday, and I judge from its *three* figures that it must have been a *terrible* operation; so terrible that I doubt if we shall get away from this Earthly Paradise (or shed) this summer! I read your more than kind letter to her. Receive sir, the assurances of my most distinguished consideration! When may we expect you *here*? If not; why not?

Y. S.

No. 2
24th July [1915]

Jacobus Carissimus!

I neglected to mention in my post card No. 1 that—Stewart, Britisher,[45] the alleged *"last of the house of Monteith,"* is buried in that young forest the Westminster Presb. Ch. graveyard on Archdale St. (Is *it* the heir of that *"false Monteith"* who betrayed Wm. Wallace!!![46]) You have not the money to explore that graveyard; but, you can go and see that really charming Miss Clara Bruns at Dr. Vedder's Church St., and she *will tell* you a very interesting family tradition as to her ancestor Stewart.

I send this for what it is worth. It *may* give you a fine "pointer" for your pestiferous work.

Yours ever,
Y.S.

Where's that *photo*? Is *it*, or are *you*, a failure?

July 28th, 1915

Dear Yates:

Nos. 1 and 2 recd: contents noted with mingled emotions. "Stewart, last of the House of Monteith" is fine; had not come across this worthy.

Thanks for same, and three cheers—I don't care a bawbee though he betrayed Bruce, Wallace, Malcolm and a', ancestrally: but I explore no more churchyards in dear old Charleston: my lamented friend and coadjutor, Doctor Ryngo, got me into pickle, as it is, with his graveyard adventurings. Must try to be a gentleman and see Miss Bruns; had a delightful note from her once, long ago, apropos of my FIRST lecture in Charleston. . . .

. . . How heartily glad I am to hear that Mrs. Snowden is home again from the hospital. Hospital hospitality is all right—I know—but Home is Best. Please, again, and constantly, give her my compliments and best wishes for quick recovery from every indisposition.

As to expecting me in Columbia—there is no end to "Great Expectations." Why not? The author is dead. I recommend you to consider that men have, for many years, remarked over hopes long postponed and still indefinite, that it might be, perhaps, that they were coming: so was Carissimus!

Excuse decent correspondence for a week or so; I am in the agony of beating the opening chapters of a GREAT ROMANCE into shape—rough first draught—I assure you it corresponds with nothing.

As to the photograph: you will drive me to drink water if you do not give me peace! Have I any photograph of you, that you should presume to Hector me? The picture taken in Washington City was executed by that talented amateur, Mrs. Edith P. Dickins, formerly Chief Officer of the late Admiral F. W. Dickins, U.S.N. I have not yet so much as heard the explosion of a copy in my morning mail, let alone seeing the horrid plot. Mrs. D. sent a copy to Mrs. Bennett, at Flat Rock; which my good wife says she did not altogether care for; but, sir, I assure you, on my word of honour—spelled with a "u" to increase its weight—I have neither seen nor heard further of it. I must, therefore, refer you to Mrs. Bennett for any information supplementary to the preceding damnable design—for, since our late marriage all my affairs are in her keeping; as you should, indeed, know, being yourself, also, entirely married. I have kept a close watch upon all local mail; but have to this time discovered absolutely nothing suspicious since the explosion at the White House. I regret that as much as you or anyone.

N.B.: I am going into photographic bankruptcy. Aha!

Ichabod, Carus et Co.
per J. Bennett
B.R.

9th Decr. '15

My dear John: . . .

I am sending you, under other cover, a pamphlet entitled *The Countess Pourtales;* pray God, Mrs. Bennett does not look at it.

"Felix Old Boy" is a friend of yours; the rest is an imprint of a pamphlet by the late Julian A. Selby[47] of Columbia, sometime publisher of the Cola. *Phoenix.*

Keep your mouth shut, & drop me a line sometime, as to the crazy introduction by Felix O.B.

In haste & *sleepy.*

Yours affectionately,
Y. S.

Chapter 6

1916

Shakespearian festivities; Art Association classes; Master Skylark *as drama; Charleston legends; Gullah research; early Charleston suffragette movement; Flora MacDonald; Bennett's recorded songs.*

IN THE letters of 1916 John Bennett commented on the Gullah language, of which he had made an extensive study. He also noted why the two friends corresponded.

In January Yates Snowden explained the reason for the republication of Julian Selby's work the past December. Snowden was a participant in the April festivities of 1916 that marked the three hundredth anniversary of William Shakespeare's death. During this year, he also helped found the Columbia Art Association.

When Bennett was again urged to work on his Carolina Tory romance, including Flora MacDonald and the Scots in North Carolina, he informed Snowden that he had no inclination to proceed with his Revolutionary War novel because of the World War I carnage in Europe. Bennett taught classes for the Carolina Art Association and began work on legends of old Charleston, making a list of tales to write and seeking a new style that would create an atmosphere sometimes found in artists' paintings.

Explaining to Snowden why the dramatic version of his *Master Skylark* was not suited to silent film production, Bennett assured him that it would be performed on stage at Wellesley and Boston during the Shakespeare tercentenary. The play was also being considered for performance at Stratford-on-Avon.

When Bennett sent samples of two quartets fashioned from his earlier poetic works to Snowden, the professor had the Carolina Glee Club perform "Today" and "A Hundred Years from Now." Several of Bennett's songs were recorded for Victor-Victrola and the Emerson Phonograph Company.

Also discussed in 1916 was an old unpublished poem, "The Devil Among the Baptists," concerning a suffragette meeting held in the First Baptist Church of Charleston in the nineteenth century, in which Snowden's grandmother, Elizabeth Saylor Yates, played a role. And Bennett promised to read from a prefatory chapter of his Charleston tales to the Kosmos Club in Columbia in the spring of 1917, if he could make headway with his manuscript during the family trip to Ohio.

Columbia, 2d Jany. 1916

Vir clarissime,

That's Latin (I copied it from a letter of John Locke), and it means: *most illustrious Jack Bennett.* Before I shut this Locke book (anno. MDCCXXII), perhaps I had better wind up this letter on the first page, by startling you with *Tui amantissimum*—that's Latin too, and means: Yates Snowden loves you like the Devil.

I am sorry you sent that stuff to Mrs. Smythe, or showed it to that dear lady you fooled into marrying you, in a Charleston Rose Garden. I had nothing to do with the republication of old Julian Selby's "grind," though I had a copy of the original pamphlet in my collection. James Holmes,[1] a *fine* fellow, who has had unmerciful disaster follow fast, &c., and young Selby thought they could make some Xmas money by republishing the stuff. Jim complained that it would not make a big enough pamphlet for their price, *one dollar;* & I said I would write an *introduction: hence* the more or less damphool "Study in Scarlet" & the "foreword" from Dr. Warren, to give it an ethical, highly moral touch! As a matter of fact I have *bought* two copies, and stranger still, *paid* for them.

Of those ancient scandals, at which you *meanly hint,* I know nothing. *I am* no scandal monger. I fear I will have to come to see you before I can hear them. Of course, I *ought* to hear them, tho' I am not "professing" sociology or ethics—still: "I am a man & nothing concerning humanity is foreign to me"; "*Homo sum*"; &c., as you recognize, my Lord!

Scott's Random *Recollections* is a crazy book, which I would send you, had not some rascal friend borrowed my copy. It's very "scrappy" and has several statements as to the loose morals in *Saxe Gotha,* which they stupidly changed to the Damyankee "Lexington" County.

The dramatization of "Master Skylark" pleases me more than you imagine. Thank you for the little brochure which I loaned to Mrs. Ball (one of the 2 or 3 women in this burg who know anything about the drama!), and tonight I see the notice in the N.Y. Times (Satd'y Magazine Section) of a "Five act dramatization of John Bennett's novel of the same name." Are they the same? I shall get my copy from Mrs. Ball tomorrow. . . .

Come & see me *someday;* & see that last silhouette, with several others of yours on the walls of my dining room. Lord! *If I could laugh* as does *your* fool in cap & bells!!! "Come back again my olden heart!"

I hope Jane is herself again! Give her my love & to Jack Jr. and you & yours.

Yours aff'ly,
Y. S.

I too have heard that Marie Boozer (Pourtales) was "beheaded, by order of the Mikado"! But; who *knows?*

5th Mch. 1916

My dear John:

I won't delay any longer! I have postponed writing you and thanking you for your much prized gift until I could write a decent letter. Your letter & the play came in the midst of exams—one of the two periods of *horror* every year—but, I put aside the exam. papers, which were then one week late, & read the charming dramatization from cover to cover. *Why,* especially in this Shakespeare revival period, has not *Master Skylark* appeared in the "movies"? I can't understand it. You are an artist, why don't you prepare the scenario yourself. . . .

Now, I am sending you a string of extracts & quotations *a part* of the "remarks" (not "oration" or "address") before the Huguenots, or "Juggernauts" as Ker Boyce[2] called them. I had a few "separates" printed & have corrected some of the numerous errors. I saw *one* proof, but several of my corrections were overlooked.

Don't read it, unless time hangs *very* heavy on your hands, but roast it at your leisure & let me know the result. That speech of Alfred Huger[3] is *ringing;* & old Sam DuBose's[4] "Saby" letter is *good; me judice.*

When *are* you coming hither? The newly formed "*Columbia Art*

Association" would rather hear a *speech* from *you* than from any other So. Carolinian. *Won't* you, *can't* you come?

Yours affect'ly,
Yates Snowden

Pretty Polly Snowden, who fell in love with you, kissed me last night for your sake.

Foolish Question, No. 1472.

20th Apl. '16

My dear John:

I have no right to pester you again—for the 419th time—but, I want some information immediately and you are better qualified to advise than anyone in the Carolinas, and Jaw Jaw too.

I am to be Sir Walter Raleigh in the Shakespearian *page*ant here next Tuesday.

(1) *Would it be proper for me to smoke a long stemmed Powhatan pipe, in the presence of the Court, at the theatre, or in the pageant proper on the College campus?*

(2) I have some genuine brass armor (back & front) brought to my mother from Mexico in '48. *Would it be proper for me to wear that either at the theatre at night, or on the campus in the morning?*

God love us all!

Yours affectionately,
Yates Snowden

NB! Horror of Horrors! Her Majesty *"the Virgin Queen"* (Mrs. John Sloan[5]) has *been married twice,* & wicked rumor says is on the lookout for No. 3!

George Armstrong Warhoop is to be the Earl of Lindsay; & is to appear in *kilties* as a braw Scott! *That* alone will be worth the price of admission: to see Wauchope's legs!

April 24th, 1916

Dear Yates: . . .

If contribution to Carolina's store of folk-stuff be collateral acknowledgment, I mean to acknowledge just as soon as I can cast into magazine, literary shape, the infamous Legends of Old Charleston aforetime so objurgated. I am, at present writing, deep in the endeavor to get those queer tales into shape for printing, transformed into something rich and strange. This once successfully done—which will call for every ounce of wit I may possess; perhaps more—I mean to turn the original notes for the whole lot, legends and folk-stories, over to the Journal of Am. Folk-Lore, if it will take them: so that the general may, I hope, enjoy the one, and the student, the other. Does this meet with your approval?

With able assistance from Mrs. Bennett, I have managed, also, to get most of my Voudou material roughly grouped. It may be I can grind something out of this for the glory and amusement of this ancient, quaint State. Does this meet approval?

Heaven knows I am as slow as Martial's barber, who shaved so slowly that the beard had begun again to grow upon the one side before he well had begun to shave upon the other; yet I hope to get something done, some day, some how—to merit the surprising confidence revealed, by error, in your varied correspondence.

But this is not making Sal's baby a night-shirt!

In response to your F.Q., #1472, would say have telegraphed information desired, date above, and refer to same for opinion. Hope 'twas satisfactory to Sir W. R., more glory to his bones! Whose cloak had you? I wonder if you enjoyed the amusing series of Elizabethan caricatures used a few months ago in *Punch* to advertise Chairman tobacco? Jolly things, full of spirit and comedy, and without one touch of gray age to mar their festive humor. My mother-in-law and I had much mutual solace in them. They were as superior to and as far from the dirty realms of Mutt and Jeff as God has given men limit to rise; to Whom be thanks and praise for these and some other mercies I could name. I trust the Columbia Art Association may be one of them: Heaven knows we need both art and association against the barbarism in its name in this antique and glorious uncommonwealth! Your free invitation to address said Columbia Art Association, so touchingly worded, per your missive of March 5th, hitherto unanswered . . . is tempting; but, truly, Yates, I have need to get a bunch of main-line work finished and marketed before I think of the pleasures of any side lines, or of rambling down the daisied lanes and primrose paths of dalliance such as, from time to time, you open so seductively to my longing eyes: viz., namely, to come to see you, etc., etc.

I somehow missed account of the organization of the said Columbia Art Association: can you afford some particles informant. I have a sort of morganatic alliance with the Carolina Art Ass., in Charleston, by holding a student membership card in it, and criticising the drawings of a men's life class two evenings per week, and a union sketch class, girls and men, Saturday afternoons. Sidney Cohen and Albert Simons were the prime organizers of the Class. Can you inform me whether or not there was ever before this a men's life class in S.C. I am persuaded this may be the first. Do you know? I should like to make that record, if no more, for the sake of decent drawing and an actual knowledge of what good drawing is, in this proud sovereign (three shilling six) State. Few show talent; and fewer persist; but a few can draw, and draw well, or will if they will stand the gruelling essential to mastery of an art. Some of the girls are more than clever; if life gave them chance they could attain to excellence; but I fear much it will not; means lack, generally, and, alas! Art, though divine, is no G.R.Q. profession. Young Paul Bissell is ready for cartooning, if any newspaper here had soul and sense to use him. Miss Marguerite Miller,[6] W. C. Miller's daughter, is doing capital work at the Pennsylvania Academy; lacked Antique, but yet made the Life Class in three months, I believe. I ever regret that Miss Alice Smith[7] never studied, either at the North, or elsewhere; had she done so, achieving breadth and much which observation lends, she had been distinguished, far more than thus locally notable. She has personality and more than common talent, and has achieved much; but Art cannot spread its wings for flight in a cage built 2x4. . . .

As to your raging, apropos of the fair personage you so vilely style "a Columbia str——p-t," the less you have to say on that subject, the better; that you were willing to lend your talent to scandal in hopes of "making the d—— thing sell," is shocking. That is the sin you impute to the lady herself. Need one say more to show you your position? I have pleaded with you for definition of several horrible epithets hurled at the unfortunate female's lovely head by "the garrulous Selby" or his coadjutors; and am come to the conclusion you don't know what they mean. Now, categorically, answer me: is an ASYMPTOTE any kin to a LEMNISCATE? And, granting identity, which your utter mathematical ignorance well might do, IS there anything ignominious in having tacnodal acnodes at infinity? I could tell you things about these ASYMP-TOTES which would horrify you; but you would not understand them.

And why, having slandered the lovely Pourtales, do you now throw out insinuations concerning the great Elizabeth, in your last hasty scandal? You can't blame *that* on Jas. Holmes.

Eh, mon! would we had a chance to perceive Johnny Armstrong Wauchope in kilts! Man! but that wad be an inspirin' sicht tae see the Lindsay plaid a-swirlin' roond her hurdies! Worth a' lying north o' Tweed to clap ane's twa een on! Ho iero, tae the noble Yerl o' Lindsay! Ye'll no be singing "Leezie" when he cooms linkin' doun the campus?

You ask why "Skylark" has not appeared in the movies? The Essanay people had it in hand over a year ago. They thought they had a lad who could do the part; but something failed to connect, somewhere. The difficulty is that without the music out of the boy's mouth the thing falls a little flat; and there is, I fear, hardly enough gun-play in the denouement. If the hero would attempt to escape in an automobile, and ditch it about twenty mile sousouwest from Coventry in a natural bed of daffodils, something might yet be done. As it is, the Wellesley Seniors will put on the drama by Burrill[8] for their play, this year; and the Teachers' Association of Boston town will also give it, in connection with their tercentenary performance at the Arena. They say they expect an audience of 5000—they might have 5000 spectators. There is a remote chance that the Benson players at Stratford-on-Avon may give the play during their regular summer run at the Memorial Theater, in August. Would not that be the summit! I should like to see the Wellesley Senior play; it would be a pleasant gratification.

The College gave a very charming Tercentenary performance, and accomplished clever wonders on a horrible minimum of means. Harris[9] gave us a pleasant talk on Will, in the evening. I must suppose he appreciates Will's infinite magic; but he says S. can never be to him what Carlyle was at twenty years, Meredith at thirty, Henry James at forty, and GEORGE GISSING to-day. I fear that Harris has gone down some side alley of appreciation, and misses the wide wind that blows and roars over the main road. GEORGE GISSING? Gods!

You ask me to roast your Huguenot peanut, but send me no nut; hence these paucities concerning.

There is so much bloody horror across the sea I have not heart to go on with a sword-romance, such as the Revolutionary War promised, in the tale of "Margaret Cameron," late in hand—killing men for amusement even on paper, in the face of such actualities, is more than I can stand. I should be more callous; yet I am not. This delightful "One, two, and the third through your heart!" is all well enough when death and murder are remote and incredible things; but daily diet on it nauseates. I have laid the merry yarn aside until Time in its infinite mercy shall a trifle have outed the damned spot I find upon the world's red hands each day. Hence the *Legends*, referred to in my opening chorus. Being utterly fantastic, and nothing real, one roams at will among them; the only disagreeable thing being the memory of my experience. All jesting aside, that same most unexpected experience came close to ending imaginative days for me. One thing I would have you remember is the fact that these legends are *not* funny: they may be singular and grotesque; and they may be amusing from their fantastic unreality; but nobody but a fool would think them "funny." And as to appealing to the audience which so welcomed your volume of the unfortunate Contessa, those who discover that in them discover their own hearts. They make a sort of an Arabian Nights series, though unconnected by any such artifice serially. I believe them to be better things than Tom Janvier's[10] Mexico City set—but I do not yet know that I can cast them rightly or word them so as to convey to others the impression I have myself.

You seem always to be the most generous hearer I have, and simulate an interest often so well as to persuade me to think it genuine; so here is a list of Legends and Folk-Tales, which, soon or late, I hope to contribute to Carolina's share in American fantasy:

I	The Physician to the Dead
II	The Gray Man: or the Gift of Strength
III	The Black Constable
IV	Madame Margot
V	When the Dead Sang in Their Graves
VI	The Avaricious Woman and the Dish of Silver
VII	Slipskin Lady
VIII	The Army of the Dead
IX	The Death of the Wandering Jew
X	The Little Harlot and the Broken-mouthed Pitcher
XI	The Wings of Rest
XII	The Measure of Grief
XIII	The Mermaid and the Apothecary
XIV	The Drink of the Dead
XV	The Waters of Perpetual Desire
XVI	The World was Turned Over
XVII	The Devil's Mercy
XVIII	Come Back Mother: (The Mother Who Came Back)

Good-by, long-suffering, erudite and distinguished friend: please present my humble greetings to the noble Earl of Lindsay and Lady Lindsay, whom we always recall with affectionate remembrance, though it has certainly been long between drinks; and now good Scotch is against civic polity and law!

Good-by, thou malevolent and scandalous commentator!

Good-by, you abominable, generous, reckless and beloved representative of this down-at-the-heel commonwealth.

And so, God save the State, and forgive her many virtues, and our own personal iniquities, in one general amnesty and omnibus oblivion.

One sensible remark in closing: give my compliments and respectful regards to your wife—

and believe me, in spite of all
to the contrary foregoing,
Most affectionately yours:
John Bennett

N.B.: And when next you are fortunate enough to see Pretty Polly S., tell her one of the acute regrets of my life is that I am too old to be greeted for my own sake, and too young to be greeted for yours; I'll send no more greetings to you: I care not to be gloated over by any happy patriarch. I am growing old; but bless her, she's sweet and charming!

> To: Sir Walter Ralegh,
>   c/o Yates Snowden, Esq.,
>   #803 Sumter St.,
>   Columbia, So. Ca.

Haste: on the Queen's business!

18th Sept. 1916

My dear Jack:

Let me again implore you not to doubt my love and loyalty because I don't write to you. I had a wild hope that I would see you this summer, but it came to naught. I spent a few weeks in Brevard, and the nearest I was to you was *one day* I spent in a dentist's chair in Hendersonville, for which I had to pay 21 simoleons, *cash!* After *that* I gave up all idea of hiring an automobile and visiting you *et ux* at Flat Rock.

I read a book in Brevard, with which I am afraid you are entirely familiar, for you know too much. It's name: "Our Southern Highlanders," by Horace Kephart.[11] On p. 203 you will find this paragraph:

> A "cooter" is a box tortoise and the name is turned into a verb with an ease characteristic of the mountaineers.

Now; smart Aleck; it strikes me that twelve years syne, you held that "cooter" was *African*. Whoever heard of an African, or of African lingo among the Great Smokies, the Blacks and the Balsams, where Kephart says he heard the word used both as noun and verb? Verb sap.

My best regards to you, your wife, your children and to Mrs. Smythe.

Yours aff'ly,
Yates Snowden

To: John Bennett,

Gentleman, scholar, and judge of good whiskey.

Many Pines, East Flat Rock, N.C.
September 23d, 1916

Dear Yates:

It is such a boon to get a letter from you, old man, that if you but realized its depth and reality you would multiply your good works. I have no reproaches to unload; who am I, indeed, that I should reproach anyone; I am in the same boat. I have had your valuable historical minute on "The Planters of St. John," before me, all summer, with honest intention, cross my heart! to write you in reference to it; and have not done so.

You are right to perpetuate nobility, gentleness, honor, straight-seeing and truth-speaking. The Yankees—call me one if you want—have sought for the flaws in the South, from habit, long engendered in bitterness of economic difference and political rivalry; the Southerner, on the contrary, has, for the most part, especially the ladies, God bless them and improve their judicial minds, which is about the only thing about them needs much improvement—inclined too often to throw Frangonard's atmosphere over the past, and to depict only the golden sunlight—to record the idyllic, and to forget the sordid tragedy that so often underlies the surface, be that as idyllic as Frangonard. Truth sees both, and perceives the past and present one in common humanity, the good good, the vile vile, and the mediocre a majority.

I had read the paper, in the Transactions of the Juggernaut Society, with pleasure and interest; but am better pleased, always, to have the autographed excerpt pamphlet from your hand for my shelf of memorabilia. Thanks, noble Snowden, thanks!

As to your tragic tale of adventures in the mountains of North Carolina, it would appear that you have reversed Scripture, and that in your mouth speech has become golden. But this is cheap wit; if it be wit at all; which I doubt; unless it be what the Connor family scathingly label, "Sunday wit." Why? •

"Our Southern Highlanders," H. Kephart; read, marked and remaining still undigested by me. Its remarks on "Cooter" too old for excitement regarding them.

* * * * *

N.B.: All this my hard earned knowledge—sent only as a sign of good faith, not for gift or publication.

* * * * *

Cooter: a box tortoise.

Cooter-backed: with a hump or ridge in the center; the crown of a well-made road being the cooter-back.

To cooter: to shape as a cooter's back, in a rising ridge or mound.

To cooter-back: to crown a road so that it will drain on both sides, and not shed one way only as does the side-hill road—also, to cooter-back a stone wall with a ridged coping-stone.

These are common usages of the mountains, found everywhere understood of the people: noted, 1908, by yours truly, on first visit to the highlands of North Carolina.

Cooter, or KUTAh, as more generally pronounced "down South," is an African word, in the languages and dialects on the Upper Congo, and otherwheres; but for our derivation probably the Congo tribes, the Bolobo tribe in particular, will suffice: its African form is preceded by that peculiar sound so often heard in African tongues, where *m* and *n* precede a second consonantal sound as initiala as in *nsheigo mbouve*, a small monkey—NCUDU, the box-tortoise, Bolobo dialect (I think); about whom are told many just such folk-tales as Harris collected concerning B'Rabbit. The initial n-sound has long disappeared in America; but Low Country Carolina preserves the remainder of the word in a purer form than does the mountaineer, pronouncing it, as you know, CUDU or *Kuta*; which is more correct in literation than *cooter;* you never called the word COOT-*ER* in your life, nor COOT, but KUTah; it is only in writing the mistake has ever been made, in Low Country Carolina, of erroneously spelling the last syllable ER. The Low Country Carolinian pronounces all words ending in ER just as KUTAH is spelled, with an obscure, non-trilled sound, not R in its vehemence. So much for the pronunciation and corruptions of it in print and outland speech. If you want to find further to the African source of the word, see Verner's[12] book on Central Africa, a book by a South Carolinian.

Our words, pinder—pinda and goober—gooba, likewise African, both in the original form begin with the murmured, nasal sounds MPINDA [and] NGUBA—in the Congo and coast tribe dialects: both these, also noted by South Carolinians, like Verner, missionaries in Africa.

As to the use of the word by Carolina and Tennessee mountaineers in any sense, derivative, or directly applied to the box-tortoise; it is in no wise more singular than that they call their big yellow apples Yellow John apples; why the devil should they talk French more than African? They borrowed both readily, long ago, both by migrant and contiguous usage: our language is far from a heritage, it is an accomplishment.

Shucks! next thing you know you will be talking about "our glorious Anglo-Saxon civilization and blood, preserved purer in the South and the Southern Highlands than anywhere else in America," as I have heard other misinformed or uninformed Carolinians and Southern scholars generally—particularly orators and editorial-writers—do. When the mass is Scotch, Scotch-Irish, Irish, German and Welsh, with your pet strain strong in streaks, Huguenot French, not to include Ref. St. Dom.

Why, my beloved wife returned us to the U.S. Census inquisitor as of English blood; when all that is English about her is her name, Smythe, which was, perhaps, Yorkshire English in James's reign, and never since; and all the rest since then, Scotch, Irish and French; while, as for me, I have hardly one drop of English blood flowing in my veins, if that: Scotch, Scotch-Irish, Huguenot French, Welsh and Holland Dutch.

What can you tell me of the word *side-godlin'* or *side-gadeling*, meaning a greater or less degree of obliquity in a line off the straight; a wandering off the direct line or way? Has it anything to do with the ancient *gadelyng* a wanderer out of the straight path?

I am trying—have been trying, all summer, with little success—to shape my Grotesque Legends and Contes Droles, etc.—to create an atmosphere somewhere between Frangonard's romance, Gustave Doré's mystery and an old German Dance of Death, with a little touch of Botticelli's wistful pallor—I want to contribute one bit of real literature, if I can, to local record; but it is hard to create real literature; it is confoundedly like essaying to play the bass part of one of Wagner's most excessively Teutonic operas upon a piccolo. I hope, however, to do something.

We leave here, October 2nd, for Charleston; and in November, if nought interferes, go to Ohio to visit my people until mid- January, the first visit in years together. We are all very reasonably well; my eyes as eccentric as ever; my children as wonderful, my wife as good—and that is not a jest, about my wife—and I must admit that the children are children, just. My compliments and respects, ever, to Mrs. Snowden; remembrance to any friend met; and to you, undying love:

Aff.,
John Bennett

25th Sept. '16

My dear John:

In a grand and awful initiation into a college society, which I shall never forget, I, the trembling neophyte, was compelled to say:

> "Confiteor frumentum.
> Confiteor me asinum consummatum esse."

My complete obfuscation at your hands, *in re "Cooter,"* convinces me that I have not changed much intellectually in thirty-nine years. I'll never try to be "smart" with you again. You always make me *smart!* Hereafter I will be smarter. I never did know or care much about *words* anyhow. Old Hobbes[13] was eternally right; "Words are the counters of wise men, and the money of fools." Why the editors of Murray,[14] since the death of the old man, did not send for you I cannot divine; you could finish the rest of the alphabet in as many weeks as they will take years. But before they "catch on" to your omniscience, will you play logomachy with me just once more, and answer a question put to me by a friend in Washington several months ago?

In one of Tolstoi's minor novels he refers to a small, tough, little horse in common use in the Caucasus as a *mash tak.*

Will you, oh learned lollypop, oh pessimistic megalomaniac, will you kindly inform me of the etymological connection of the South Russian equine with the wiry little animal on the S.C. seaboard, known as the *"mash taky"* (marsh tackey)?

Your letter was so delicious that I dropped in at Chamberlayne's[15] (one of the two or three *scholars* on our campus), and read him the whole *roast,* omitting your kindly and affectionate opening paragraphs.

"Ah, that is the author of 'Master Skylark,'" said C. "Why cannot you get him to visit Columbia and read a paper for the Kosmos Club?" I told him *that* had been my darling wish for three or four years, but that you were as obstinate as five government mules, &c., &c.

Chamberlayne did not know anything about "side-godlin," or "side-gadeling," & referred me to Harry Davis,[16] whom I will consult tomorrow.

Of course I knew nothing about the word, but I find the following in my edition of Skeat,[17] (Ed'n 1882):

"Gad (2) to ramble idly. (*Scand.*) 'Where have you been gadding?' Romeo IV, 2.16. . . . The original sense was to drive about—Icel. *godda* to goad. . . . I see no connection with Middle English gadeling an associate, for which see Gather."

"Gather. . . . A shorter form appears in the A. S. gaed, society, fellowship, company: whence also the A. S. *gaed-el-ing* an associate, comrade."

I send you that stuff for what it is worth. So far as I can see it is worth nothing. . . .

Thank the Good Lord you married in the Holy City, otherwise I would have been your far-away admirer, but not

Your affectionate friend,
Y.S.

"Many Pines," East Flat Rock, No. Ca.
September 28th, 1916

Dear Yates: . . .

Yours of the 25th, showing a happy revival of spirits . . . received gladly, joyously, tumultuously. I would be less humiliated if my correspondents used less Latin; but that's a minor matter. You were always smarter than ever I dared be. Your quotation from Old Hobbes has ruined me: "words are the money of fools!" Alas! They're all *I* have!

If the editors of Murray had sent for me, they would at least have avoided one of the most ridiculous, inaccurate and asinine of etymologies; the one they give for "Cooter." How could they imagine that with the derivation they allege, any Carolina gentleman could have used the word in common parlance? A closet etymology and most idiotic.

But you ask another game of logomachy: I used to play it with the late Rev. Josiah Strong's[18] father, who took it sore to heart if he were beaten; but, having part of a rabbit's eye grafted to his own, and seeing narrowly, played badly.

I am exceedingly interested in what you say of MASH TAK as the name of a small tough horse of the Caucasus. Laying aside the billingsgate you heap upon my head, I have sought for some explanation of the term "marsh tacky"—pro. ma'sh takky—for fifteen years without success. I wish you would be a scholar, now, and let me have the exact reference, volume, edition and page, as employed in this sense by Tolstoi; there's a good fellow! The only reply I can make is, can you explain why in their original nature, before Good Housekeeping and the Ladies Home Journal stole the idea from Charleston, JOGGLING BOARDS were found in two places only on earth: South Carolina low country (and its

immediate derivatives) and RUSSIA (observed in the vicinity of
Petrograd, then commonly styled *St. Petersburg,* years ago, by observant
travellers). This I was told, some years ago, by a number of old South
Carolinians—their exact authority I cannot cite. George Holmes[19] has
always cited some connection between the *ma'sh takky* and some Greek
word, TAKAS, of which I have no knowledge, knowing no Greek at all;
but which he says, if I quote him correctly, means *fleet-footed,* or *light-
footed,* or some such. Search *me!* Let me have more, definite citation of
Tolstoi, to add to my hard-pursued clues.

Thank you for the notes on GAD and Gadding: I had not rooted in
Skeat: same noted; indebtedness herewith acknowledged. What the
notes are worth one only learns later; never decry; all is possible in a
language as impossibly contrived as English.

Apropos of mountain idiomatics: we all know HOLP; but I heard
one of our men say, the other day, that one of our horses in fooling
around the paddock, had BRAST the fence; sweet savour of ancientry!

Have you ever heard the "ballad-song," "In the Pines, in the Pines,
Where the Sun Never Shines!" or "Polly, Pretty Polly"? I rambled a little
this summer, gathering fragments.

As to coming to Columbia to read a paper before the Kosmos Club.
If I had anything to read I would be glad to come. True. I will tell you
what I will do: if I can get the introduction: *Prefatory Chapter, Critical
Commentary Chapter, and Fantasy Introductory* to my *Grotesque Legends
of Old Charleston,* into shape, this winter, I will read it for you towards
Spring, if you still are in this mind, and the subject appeals to you. If I
could also get the legends into literary shape I should add several to the
preceding matter: otherwise I could but briefly scan rough notes.
Perhaps Kosmos is pure-minded, or arrived safely at the age of reason,
which takes no offense where none is meant, nor reads double meaning
where none exists; or are we delicate, and prurient, lewd and fine? Faith,
on my word, there's nothing in these offerings to bring a blush to the
cheek of the young; and never was but to the foul. Or have you any
habitual card-writers beside yourself in Kosmos, old *Vino Veritas, Pro
Bono Mexico, or Justitia?* Avoid card-writers! They be pestilent dogs; and
far worse, being females! Do not betray me! I got little or nothing done,
this summer toward the above, beyond collocating notes: I may not get
forward much until January, as we are to visit in Ohio from mid-
November to early January. What else may happen to prevent progress
Providence alone knows: typhoid fever and measles in the family
prevented great things last winter: verily the fining-pot is for silver, the
furnace is for gold.

One thing out of the hurly remains clear: I never did you for ten
simoleons on a book-plate, how much otherwise I have grieved you!

I have been looking round for reasons other than marital for not hating The City of My Discontent: I match your close, finding one in the privilege of signing myself,

Affectionately,
Jack B.

You are a good soul, never to comment "caustically" on my misspelling of Fragonard or didn't you know how? my Huguenot hero! Hey?

Charleston, October 17th, 1916

Dear Yates:

that is to say Fidus Achyates:

I have just received from the maker samples of quartets for Male and Mixed Voices, manufactured from airs and harmonies to songs of mine with which you are acquaint. Knowing no one in all my acquaintance who has a more male or more mixed voice than yourself, I enclose you specimens of this mysterious process. I hope to hear you sing them when next we meet. I said "sing."

with more affection than ever,
yours:
John Bennett

I have not dared venture into Gittman's, being possessed of 0000000000000000000 $

even more affectionately than

above,
J. B.

Is there a College Glee Club which I might work some of these quartets off upon? Gratis, to be sure.

Columbia, 20th Oct. 1916

"Hail to thee Blithe spirit,
Bird thou *always* wert"!

How can I thank you sufficiently, Jacobus Carus, for your many kindnesses? One day it is a brilliant letter which I "carry around" and read to my friends—I have read *two* such to Chamberlayne, who is unquestionably the ablest man in our faculty —and two or three days later come such delightful morceaux (that's French!) as those beautiful songs. I immediately consulted my old student (and a lazy one, too) Hodges, the leading man in the Glee Club, who has a ravishing basso-profundo, and who called at this shanty yesterday evening to say that the gleemen would be delighted to have copies of "Today," with which he (Hodges) was very familiar. Strange to say, he was not familiar with "A Hundred Years," &c., but said he would practice it today. *Mille graces,* Milord! . . .

In re Marsh Tacky; I will send you Tighe's[20] letter regarding "Mash Tak," as soon as it turns up. He *may* give in it *the title* of Tolstoi's book which prompted the inquiry.

In re your promised visit and "paper": The Kosmians will welcome you *magno clamore* (that's Latin!) next Spring whatever Saturday night you fix upon, and I will hold you to your promise if it kills me!

I send you, for your eyes alone, a very *rough* proof which I had a printer on The N&C make for me years ago, of "The Devil among the Baptists." It would, obviously, give offense to some very excellent people (e.g.: Dr. Brodie's[21] relatives), if it ever *got out.* This is one of three "roughs" I had the printer "set up" & "pull" for me. It never has been published even for private circulation and "Betsy Yates's"[22] grandson never wishes to see it published!! There *was* such a row in the 1st Baptist Ch. (on Church St.), and I believe it led, eventually, to the establishment of the Citadel Square Baptist Ch. It was the first *suffragette* victory in S.C., methinks. My uncle J. D. Yates had a fight with the author, the late Col. S. Y. Tupper, because of the references to his mother. Read, mark & inwardly digest it and read *some selections* to your blessed wife, and then put it in your strong box—or tear it up. Have you seen the handsome "boost" for *Flora MacDonald College?* Get a copy from George Moffett,[23] and get busy & *finish* your Moore's Creek—Flora McDonald—S.C. Tory tale.

Yours, to the last drop,
Y. S.

> "As for Fitz Heron, he is so very selfish,
> he always wants his letters answered"
> D'Israeli: *Sybil.*

Did you ever see the chapter on "Negro Spirituals" in Col. T. W. Higginson's[24] "Army Life in a Black Regiment"? I have the book (1st Ed'n).

Charleston, October 23rd, 1916

My dearest FitzHeron:

otherwise fil-du-po'jeau—that's French:

Yrs. this day sustained. Briefly in response:

I do not disdain Col. Higginson's Life in an Ebonized Army; but saw Hig's grind on Sperrituals in Atlantic Mthly., a long time before the book was published: you forget I am awfully old, and read well while you were still struggling with your horn-book of AB. I have notes from said Higginson's chapters on Sperrituals; search the scriptures and me if I can find 'em; but safe in one of my unindexed scrapbooks: I'm hoping my son will index them for me when he comes of age; yet hope even more that he will have more sense than to mix himself up with my madness.

Great and appreciative but very secret thanks for the surreptitious broadside sent: a certain safe person will be amused, this evening, at close of day, by this dithyramb. It is intensely interesting to know when the Devil did get amongst the Baptists: I knew he was there—or had suspected it ever since Jones left Citadel Square to die quite as much of heart-break as of anything else: one can't fight the Devil and one's congregation, too. I love these wisps of ancient history; thanks, thanks, thanks!

Thank you for reminding me to get Flora McDonald redivivus from George Moffett; had meant to do so, and forgot; had noted the alteration of the college-title a year ago. No hope of getting at the Scotch in N.C. for a century or so. My eyes are so cursed bad that I lag like cold tar. The murdering on the other side the water made joyous fictional slaughter impossible; and now I am endeavoring to find the style in which to cast a queer collection. Must have a perfect illusion, and preserve it throughout, without winking to friends on one side; air of absolute sincerity essential to all incredible tales; must translate from Gullah and common Charlestonese into such choice English as will carry the dream exactly, yet convey some sensation of strangeness comparable to dialect—must flood with color that the foreign reader may perceive the scene set—and somehow feel the atmosphere, too; by what peacock phrases one should replace those of the jackdaw it is a difficult problem to affirm; yet dare not use such language that the style should drown the story.

I will do my worst to have something for Kosmos; but am yet limping painfully along through introductory: good introductory, too; will persevere through love of you.

Thank you for Glee Club: you say "copies" of "To-Day." Owing to public demand am unable to send "copies," being plural; am forced, regretfully, to send "copy," singular—but send *in both cases,* which may make a grammatical amendment. To your address, not having further Glee Club details; for delivery, through your ever ready hand, to Mr. Hodges, he of the ravishing bass. Will be happy to think that the Glee Club can use either or both songs, or find for themselves pleasure in trying them out. Will you please convey that sentiment with the songs?

Elsie Baker[25]—I believe it is Elsie—has done "To-Day" for the Victor-Victrola; record will be out October 28th, I am told by Dick Voigt. The Emerson Phonograph Co. have records at 10 and 25 cts. if one thinks more too much to pay for the pleasure ensuing.

Tried a more recent lyric on Mrs. Bond,[26] short time since; but failed to stir her muse; she wouldn't wish any, thanks! I suppose she had duckeys in the pond already sufficient for the company.

You use so much French, Latin and other foreign languages that I am unable to write further at this time; so farewell, fervently and ever fondly—I assure you that in the words of the mountain song-ballad, "Your name is writ upon my heart in shining letters of gold," never to be erased therefrom "Ontil the hills of the mountains grows old!"

Farewell to the Nth power!
[John Bennett] . . .

P.S.: Dinna forget "mash-tak."
NO MOE
I forgot to be brief.
Very latest forget:

Also forgot to say that Sam Stoney went to the hospital to-day, to have a splintered bit of his dislocated shoulder— off the head of the humerus, but hardly amusing—removed by Cathcart.[27] Ford machine in September did it.

Columbia, 3.20 o'clock A.M., Lordsday
[Between 23 Oct. & 17 Nov. 1916]

Cara Mio:

I am not going to church this morning. As you know, I am a devoted Huguenot, my grandmother's mother being named *Le Queux,* and I cannot wander after strange Gods, and I cannot afford to go 132 miles to church to hear Pasteur Veuve Cliquot[28]—*ergo,* I shall have a service of song in my bath-tub at 12 o'clock meridian, while my dear wife is listening to my suffragist friend Kirkman Finlay.[29]

I don't know whether it is worth so much of your valuable time, but I send you to read, *& send back to me,* this wholesale denunciation of the Charleston bar by John Lide Wilson[30] (Governor; Code of Honor man, & versifier of a part of the Golden Ass of Apuleius), a very sportive & attractive gent. It is, obviously, not for publication; but, it may give you a "pointer" or two. Hodges says the Glee Club is to sing both of your songs. God bless you, and me too.

Y. S.

I dubbed this stuff "A Pasquinade of the Thirties"; is that correct?

November 17th, 1916

Dear Yates:

Dash your furrin tongues! I have no confidence in them. How can I tell but that under a fair-seeming exterior your ambiguous and caressing phrases may carry an irony a yard long, piercing as a stiletto!

But I am bold. I conceal my fears beneath a placid envelope, and return to you herewith your lewd, lascivious and classic verses, of which I admit, with a frankness characteristic of my nature, I have just made a copy. God keep my character if my descendants discover it among my remains! I lay the blame at your door for all that I may suffer from these indiscretions in future: 'twasn't I, dear grandchildren, but that notorious old roué, Snowden! I hear the future say, "Thank God!"

What a night you must have been making of it, drafting, to amuse a friend and fellow-sufferer of a dull world's banalities, these caustic and escharotic lines at three-twenty o'clock, a.m., of a Sunday morning!

I recently met, casually, our mutual friend, Graeser,[31] of the Citadel; who, inclining his head, with what seemed to me to be a certain gentle weariness, upon his hand, told me that he had been indiscreet enough, and so far favored of Fortune, to spend an evening, until it was well-worn away, with you, W. W. B., and others, I think, in the recent past, in Columbia. He admitted the company to be gifted, and the dialogue ambrosial indeed; but, slowly and feelingly rubbing his depressed forehead, he suggested that the company was, perhaps, a bit too young and gay for him; that you had read him verse ("The Devil among the Baptists," and other things), and that he was not used to it. I told him that this might be a warning to him, and a lesson as to the bright face of unrighteousness and the murky retrospect thereof: *hic fabula.*

Also, recently—a little less recently, to be very exact—let us keep the record straight—those woeful words, so woefully misused to justify the angry recriminations of the hopelessly ignorant—recently, I repeat, I met, also casually, upon a corner, Rev. Barnet Elzas,[32] Ph.D., Heb. 1, and ii to O—who confided in me with some acrimony, no doubt justified—I leave this to history—that he could not get a letter out of you with a cotton-screw. Having fully objurgated you, we had some divertissemong, *in re* Baptists, *vide supra Graeseri*, wherein he informed me that once upon a time, when you and he and the world were young, you jointly printed a work of fabulous delicacy, ycleped the "Toilet Paper Edition of the Poets of South Carolina," privately published—that is an Irish bull—at the galley-press of the *Courier*; n.d.; in clear, readable type, most unreadable verse, on a paper appropriate to contents. You are worse than I am willing to admit to my wife; to whom, cautiously, I read, expurgating, brief extracts from Snowdenian gems. I try to keep her uncontaminate, despairing of myself: for the sake of friendship I endure much.

"Pasquinade" is all right; but "Faux Pasquinade" has merit. I do not know Wilson's *versif. trans. Apuleius*. Why do you not issue "Poets of Carolina, from Rowland Rugeley down to date," including Miller's "Sans Culottes King"? Not for their wantonness, which was much, but for their wit, its quantity uncertain.

I am very much gratified to hear that the Glee Club is to use both my songs; I should like them to know this—make it graceful, good fellow!

I am wrestling desperately with the conglomerate of years, which requires every critical faculty I possess, to separate the trash from the otherwise, in making something worth a body's while of the immortal Grotesques. We leave for Ohio, Nov. 24th; I take work with me, whether to work or not the times must tell. And so, dear lad, farewell, farewell.

God bless us both. We need it.

J. B.

Chapter 7

1917

Work on legends; Master Skylark *on stage; World War I; art and Lewis R. Mignot; unveiling in State House of marble tablet to Snowden's mother; Gullah stories by Ambrose Gonzales.*

IN OHIO for the Christmas holidays, John Bennett had found no time to work on his book in progress, because he had to tutor his children in mathematics. In January 1917 he lamented that he had not written a line, and since Susan Bennett planned to accompany John's sister to Jamaica that month, he expected to get little done while in charge of the children full time. Before returning to Charleston, he sent Yates Snowden old papers that he had rescued from a cousin in the Ohio countryside.

In May, Bon Air, Miss Annie Bonham's school in Columbia, presented the dramatic version of *Master Skylark*. Snowden persuaded Bennett to attend and speak, since he was already coming to Columbia that week for the Kosmos Club. "The Elizabethan Genius of Goodfellowship: Will Shakespeare" was Bennett's chosen topic for the drama night, and "A Literary Experiment," the opening chapter of his Charleston legends, was the paper he read at Kosmos. In June, Snowden wrote that he had bought an old landscape, which he needed Bennett to help him identify. Snowden thought it might be a painting by Louis R. Mignot.

By November, with America's participation in World War I well under way, Bennett again had to postpone work on his new book, this time because of his involvement with the Red Cross and the War Recreation Service.

For work during and after the War Between the States, a marble tablet to Mary Amarintha Snowden, Yates's mother, was unveiled in the rotunda of the South Carolina state capitol in November of 1917. An editorial on the memorial, written by W. W. Ball, was commented on by John Bennett, who assured Snowden that true loyalty and devotion, such as his mother's, were to be honored, no matter which side of the cause was espoused.

It was during 1917 that Snowden, becoming exasperated with acquaintances' not returning books they had borrowed from him, began writing verses about the problem. In December, Snowden sent the Bennetts copies of his poem, which John had helped revise: "A Blast Against Book-Keepers."

In his last letter of 1917 Snowden wrote about Ambrose Gonzales' stories in Lowcountry Gullah. Snowden told Bennett that Gonzales was being urged to publish in book form his new stories, along with some that had already appeared in *The News and Courier* or *The State*.

#76 West Second St., Chillicothe, Ohio
January 4th, 1917

Dear Yates:

Yours received, cargo of poetry and good will noted with pleasure, and hereby acknowledged, with corresponding greetings and good wishes for you and yours for the New Year!

I am sending by mail by this same post a roll of old papers, hardly knowing what they are, or whether they are worth the postage required to forward. I am aware that you have probably seen all the "Madisonian" contains, and may have no possible use for these broken numbers. All this and more I acknowledge.

But, dear heart of my heart—translate it into Latin if you don't like the crude English—I found a cousin of mine, at an old country-house near this town, burning old papers, letters and books; and, after a furious scolding from myself, and a kindly reproof from my better half, she emerged from a closet, bearing these. "Does anyone in the world value such stuff as this?" she demanded, as vindictively as one very fond of me (deluded affection!) could. "Yea," said I, for the sake of example, "with great and enthusiastic care and interest." "Take 'em, then," says she, with tragic air, but comic inflection, "or I'll start the fire with them in the morning!"

Hence this unwarranted descent upon your innocence and occupation.

I had no time—my wife and I are frantically packing clothing,

Christmas plunder, etc., etc., leaving for Charleston, Monday morning, Jan. 8th—to look into or to glance over these papers to see if they are worth your while at all. I only trust you to know at a glance whether they are worth more than throwing into the waste-basket. You will probably get as much per pound for them, war-prices-and-high-cost-of-living, in S. Carolina, as we can here in the fat and satisfied Middle West, a Jeshurun, if ever was. Peruse, if you care to, or cast away, as you choose, I shall remain yours unalteredly ever.

Apropos of the "Grotesque Legends of Old Charleston," I brought the introduction thereto with me to Ohio, expecting to do considerable work upon it while here; but the tutor we had engaged to tute our brilliant offspring, failed us, and I have been busy coaching two young ideas in mathematics—Heaven save the mark!—I who was an unutterable duffer in mathematics all my days, and have not even looked at an algebra for thirty-five years! Have not done a line—nay, beloved, not a darned phrase—upon said "Legends"; and, unless the ensuing immediate months at home show better result of intent and hope, there will be no foray into the Holy City by me as a horrible example of would-be literature for the delectation of you and your friends.

Whether those months now impending will give off a better sound than the past is problematic. Mrs. Bennett is going to Jamaica, the latter part of January, with my sister, who has been ordered there by her physician, to cure an exhausted system, worn with teaching in Massachusetts air; and will be with her there a month. During which time I shall be father, mother, housekeeper, etc., to the best of my ability, and author on the side, when moments avail. Therefore the problematic is uncertain, and things that are not clear must remain stupendously vague, awaiting upon the descending sword Damoclean suspended o'er me.

"All rot, all rot!" I hear you say, in the old accustomed way. Putrid if you will, my dear boy, but Fate!

And so no more at this time, from

> yours enthusiastically;
> but reluctant victim of
> circumstance:
> Ichabod

Hope to see you, sometime, somewhere!

With compliments to the best wife a scamp like you was ever blessed by Heaven with, and regards to her and yourself from the best wife a rogue like me was ever honoured by Heaven with, once more I remain, buffeted by Fate, and swimming hard against a sea of multiplication and division of monomials,

> devotedly, despite asininity
> of expression herein,
> John Bennett

Columbia, S.C., 9th May, 1917

Jacobus Carissimus:

Miss Annie Bonham's[1] school will present "Master Skylark," with all the honors on the 18th inst. (School Edition of course). She has been trying to fix upon some scholar who could briefly introduce the play, by a few graceful remarks as to Shakespeare, & Stratford-on-Avon; Queen Bess, &c. *temp.* Master Skylark; but all in vain. I suggested that tho' you were modesty personified, you *might*, be induced, to be present and say a few words at the initial presentation in S.C. of your beautiful work. I told her that you had sacredly promised to visit Cola. this spring & give a lecture before the Kosmos Club, which, by a happy coincidence, meets on May 19th, and I told her that I would implore you to make *her* and the Kosmians happy on the 18th & 19th!

Now, old socks, won't you put the esteemed Miss Annie Bonham

—Some women use their tongues: she looked a lecture;
Each eye a sermon, and her brow a homily—

and myself, your loving friend, under eternal obligation by coming?

Come and stay with me, "blithe spirit"; the room is very small, but the welcome will be hearty. *Telephone me if you will come,* and follow by a letter telling what you will talk about. I will make arrangements for the Mayor[2] to welcome you, with a brass band, and I will see that the triumphal arches are erected in time.

Always yours aff'ly,
Y. S.

NB! I was 59 years old at 9 o'clock yesterday morning, the 8th of May, a *great* day for South Carolina! John B. Adger[3] born about the same time! No signs of senile decay have set in; but the *financial* breakdown is complete. Lexington cow (aet. 20) 30 cts. per lb! Good Lord deliver us.

#37 Legare St., Charleston, S.C.
May 12th, 1917

Dear Yates:

Whatsoever you call me, you're twice it. No more curses now; but to the business:

Yrs. recd., 9th May; contents noted; telegram in reply, evening May 11th, date of reception of same appeal.

Glad to grant Miss Annie Bonham's invitation. Subject will be "The Elizabethan Genius of Good-fellowship: Will Shakespeare."

Am not a scholar, nor a dignitary; but a drudging ass of letters. Think you simply unloaded this eminence upon me. Rejoiced to save your life!

Address should and will be short: slight reference to Stratford; casual mention of good Queen Bess; brief reference to Shakespeare's career, contained in all academic literature texts; more stress upon my own feeling regarding Will as a good fellow among a charmed ring of good fellows: two-three words modestly adverting to the play—the play's the thing!—and then no more of me but charitable oblivion's dear embrace upon the bosom of supporting "friends," perhaps yourself in role of S. friend. Notice very short; but will do what I can not to be tedious and banal for a few moments.

As to Kosmos, I cannot say at this hasty writing that I can give them anything on the 19th. Let me have two days to look into this. Will then let you know what I can give. If it won't do, say so, and I shall be far happier.

I have only one thing in view just now: a piece of more or less graphic descriptive, introductory to my collection of Grotesque Legends and Contes Droles of Old Charleston. If I can get this into shape for reading, which I am not certain that I can do, I shall let you know by Monday night or Tuesday morning. If it won't do, shoot your liquid fire, flammenwerfer, and I'll duck!

Shall esteem it a proud distinction—as well as a pleasure, to be guest of Mrs. Y. S. and her irresponsible consort during my stay in Columbia, S.C.

Your reference to arches confirms previous opinion that you have long been in close and intimate correspondence with the Arch F. As to age, how did you get ahead of me? Must have lived faster.

I have a birthday, myself, this week; betray me not; I will not tell you how young I am; 'twould affect my impressiveness upon occasion. Financial breakdown popular dance. Know original steps. Private lessons to promising pupils. Must be graceful. Heaven preserve much vegetable, and your charming wife: the Deil will take care of

you and ME.
[John Bennett]

————

Monday Night [14 May 1917]

Dear Jack:

I am overjoyed to hear that you are coming. This evening, without hint or suggestion from me, Billy Ball informed me that you were to be invited to attend a little stag dinner at his shanty where you will meet 10 noble gents, including myself, Friday P.M.—after which you will adjourn to Miss Annie Bonham's and blow off that fine spiel, of which you have kindly sent me a forecast; it's fine!! It will be a short-coat-tail party at Ball's & you are not expected to wear your swallow-tail at Miss Bonham's.

You *cannot*, you *dare not* crawfish out of that *Kosmos* paper. Read *anything you want:* preferably the story of Charleston's early wonder-love & scandal, such as you have outlined.

Let me know on what train you expect to arrive here. If the little cuddy-hole, in which I am going to house you, were only a little bit bigger, I would insist upon your bringing Mrs. Bennett with you. I wish she were here.

In unwilling haste,
Yours aff'ly,
Yates Snowden

————

May 15th, 1917

Dear Yates:

I am busy as—oh, well, something busy. But I looked over some stuff, yesterday evening, between leaps. If you think it will be acceptable to Kosmos, I shall be glad to read before that august body an opening chapter of the book I have in preparation on Grotesque Legends of Old Charleston.

This chapter I must entitle "A Literary Experiment," as it is written for a peculiar purpose, and peculiarly contrived to fit that purpose.

That purpose is to prepare the mind of the average reader for the queer tales which are to follow it, which are bizarre, amusing, tragic, and not without a certain strange beauty of their own, and are, without exception, tinged with Oriental fantasy to greater or less degree.

It is a sense of this fantasy, this Oriental character of the legends and *contes droles* contained in the proposed volume, I wish greatly to stress:

I wish also to make emphatic the presence of beauty and tragedy, as well as grotesquerie.

To do so, and to bring to the mind of the reader from outside some actual sense of the scene of their birth and being, Old Charleston's back streets and kennels, is the purpose of this chapter.

Whether it is a success or not is not yet proved. The opinions of Kosmos will help to prove whether it is or is not; if Kosmos is willing to sit through it, and act as "dog" on which the thing is tried.

I have tried—and am still sedulously trying—in this chapter, to produce so strong an impression on the reader's mind, of the beauty, the Eastern character, the exotic strangeness, of all that lies around us in neglect, that until the end of the book, story by story, the effect will be as if a stage had been set for the production of scenes out of a strange drama of life, entertaining, and uncanny, and filled with a color all their own.

If this will do I shall be glad to read before Kosmos. If it will not, I have nothing else to offer.

I shall leave Charleston, Friday morning, reaching Columbia at 12:45 p.m. I shall be very glad to hear the band playing on the plaza as the train rolls in—but play me no more melancholy songs, for I am sick of woe—stir up my blood with jovial harmony, and enlivening strains of martial, or deputy-martial, music!

I have had, this morning, a very pleasant note from Miss Bonham, more than courteous, and expecting greater than your humble servant. She must put up with yr. hum. servt. and his best endeavors, which are cheerfully at her disposal.

She tells me, a great relief to my mind—that you are to preface the play with some judicious explanatory commentary; relieving me of all need to allude to that joint product of E. W. Burrill and yrs. truly, which spares many a mutual blush, original product and proxy.

Further than this, dear Y, nothing at this time.

I do not know how trains run, coming by Columbia to town; but must return with decent promptness to this burgh; for I have need of it, and it has need of me; as I am trying to do "my bit" as publicity for the Red Cross; and God knows there's little time to lose if we're to be on the job!

So no more, dear lad; but my compliments to Mrs. Snowden, and ever the deepest description of honorable and youthful affection for yourself—

Yrs.,
John Bennett

1:30 A.M. (*Not* "just from Ball's")
May 22d. '17

Dear Jack:

Let me thank you from the bottom of my heart for your visit. You charmed everybody. Like Cascarets; children cry for you; old maids love you; everybody wants you. You resemble Cascarets in another obvious particular; you work while other people sleep. Selah!

Mrs. Ball tells me that the women are pestering that extraordinary female Miss Bonham for a *repetition* of Master Skylark. She has had the decency to return my copy of the drama, but without a word of acknowledgment. She shall *never* again borrow *that,* or any other book from me! Never in a thousand years.

I cannot imagine one of our archaic Charleston gentlewomen acting as she did. Why without *me* she would not have had the play in time, and she might not have had *you,* the *deus ex machina,* Johnny on the spot!

Chamberlayne regretfully told my wife, and later "kicked" while talking to me that he had not seen something of you; that he did not know you were here until Saturday, &c., &c. I wanted you all for ourselves on Friday. I *did think* of asking him to dinner on Saturday; but if I had, he would not have seen you for over half an hour.

There are 100 things I wanted to show you, or talk about. I did not see anything of you myself; confound the luck!

My kindest regards to your wife. Annie has been asleep for 2 hours.

Yours affectionately,
Y. S.

When you see my friend Miss Annie Sloan, Miss Alice Smith, Miss Willis,⁴ or any other Art Association officials, beg, borrow or steal for me some C.A.A. pamphlets, reports, or "literature," for me to add to my pamphlets, so as to make an art volume. I have not enough to bind.

Residence of Ichabod: Charleston, S.C.
May 24th, 1917

Dear Yates:

Bottom of your heart recd. Many thanks. There is no bottom to mine. Or, if there is, heart has crawled down its own interior, and disappeared from mortal ken in intolerable dejection, following brief period of joy while with you and all those noble, unconfined souls I met and dallied among, in Columbia, what time we were there.

There is deep, abysmal crape upon the *arbor vitae* of my intellect for inspiration that was, and is no more.

Would blow out cavity where alleged brains are for a quarter, cash.

Visit in Columbia seems a fairy tale frequented of stately queens, dainty damsels, lovely elves, and various gnomes and sorcerers requisite to keeping the game going at good gait—among these both guests and hosts upon occasions.

But, on my soul (preserve me from rude betrayal!) among these happy stars I do not count Miss B—n——m one; although under immediate press of excitement she permitted one speech or two of graceful import to escape through that stern crust. She stood between me and the stage too often and too persistently for me to be enthusiastic over her attitude: since then methinks the lady's dead! I'm glad you got your copy of the drama back again! "Extraordinary female," says you? Well! I'll no deny yer obsairve. If she *is* dead, R.I.P.!

But heaven lengthen the days and nights of all those goodly gentlemen whose guests we were! They took the leaden heels off several hours! And that deserves exordium and bays.

And as for you, with all your many and evident faults—such as allowing me to be an hour late to Mrs. Snowden's excellent dinner, for which you shall die unshriven!—I love you still; and shall be glad at next chance to sit until 2:30 at collogue, while treasures literal and pictorial, new and old, and gems of wit, appear and disappear, from unknown sources and abodes.

What a pleasure it is even for a little while to forget "M. Mantalini" and his like, and for a little gap feel sure that life is *not* just a demnition grind! If you don't get it, ask W. Ball: he is full of the true Dickens vaccine—that life-long and remitting fever of fondness for C. D.

As to Mr. Chamberlayne: this furnishes another reason for my return to Columbia at some future date. I am complimented he should care to meet this ragged remnant of repute. I shall tell you frankly, I am pleased to meet all and sundry that you wish that I should meet and know in Columbia: and count it acquisition—both University and beyond. Kosmos is a capital circle: commend me to each and every, heartily: they stood it stoutly, and indeed are men. Heaven be good to them all! And t'other place lenient.

You know well that, often as we might meet, there would always be another story to tell, and another yarn to spin, out-doing the famous 1001 Nights. Only 100 more things you had to show me! Tush! man: innumerabilia. Go to, thou great Caliph!

Mrs. Bennett was greatly pleased at your remembrance—I don't know where she is—I haven't seen her for two days—she's purchasing thousands and thousands of yards of myriad materials for Red Cross work—and bids fair to out-do her revered grandmother, Mrs. Louisa Cheves McCord.

The children and I get on somehow.

I will commandeer what I can in the C.A.A. line, and forward. Many, many thanks for the two express parcels, which arrived by post, entirely safe, at your expense. And for their contents I am yours, indeed.

But that damned suggestion rests heavily on my heart—with memories of old obnoxiousness filling my recollection—that Charleston will not welcome what I write. And so no more; but my heartiest regards to Mrs. Snowden, ever; my compliments to Mrs. T. S.; some jovial message to all good hearts; and to you always, as ever: much affection:

Yours truly,
Jack Bennett

Many thanks for the clippings. I shall file them with infrequent similar much-treasured memorabilia.

I hear something making a noise like a good wife down-stairs: so dinner must be ready; and I must run, having Columbian delinquency ever before me!

J. B.

"Mum's the word"!!!
Grave-yard!!
Sub rosa!! et al.

June 5th, 1917

My dear John:

That I am a long-eared ass is a proposition you will not dare deny, after you have read a few lines more of this extraordinary epistle!

I have bought an oil painting called, I believe, "Twilight in the Tropics" (for I have never yet seen its backside), which I am afraid to bring home, until I have paid one or two pressing debts. It has an ugly rent in the side of the canvas which must be repaired—that is if the picture is worth the expense. What I want to do is to send you the picture to get your estimate of it; *who was the probable painter?* (it *may* have some telltale painter's "mark" or name); *is it worth restoring* & a new frame? the probable cost of such restoration and the name of the man to do it? &c., &c., &c.

I think it beautiful, of course, or I would not have paid $15.00 for it!! *but*, as you know, I *don't know* anything about painting. It's worth either $1.50 or $150.00; of that I am certain. It belonged to the *DePass* family (I never heard of any virtuoso DePass!) *is said* to have come from Georgetown or Beaufort originally, and is evidently old. I have a *lingering* hope that it is the work of Mignot,[5] altho' I am afraid he did not begin to paint tropical scenes until long after he left Charleston. Be my good friend still; look carefully at the picture; give me your honest opinion of it, & I will write you what to do with it. My only fear is that you will soon start for Flat Rock; write me *when* you expect to leave, & if you can undertake this task for me before you go to the delectable mountains.

You probably know of Lewis R. Mignot; he was a native of Charleston; & I have a *grave suspicion* that he was the *mulatto* or octoroon son of that "Mignot, R, confectioner, 170 King St." (See Morris Goldsmith's Directory of Charleston, 1831.) I have never heard of or seen any of Mignot's work in Charleston except two landscapes, formerly owned by the late Dr. Chazal,[6] & now, presumably, in the possession of his son Philip, or his daughter Mrs. Williams of N.Y. Neither of them, *me judice*, is of startling merit, or give promise of Mignot's after fame in London, where there was once a special exhibition of his paintings, & where he died *circa* 1871. Like Zogbaum,[7] Charleston was nothing to Mignot. If *he was* a mulatto, the explanation is more than simple. I have copied on another page nearly all I know of Mignot from Benjamin's[8] book "Art in America."

Write me if only a post-card, saying that if I have anything old to send you, that it must come before June—as you expect to go about that time to Flat Rock—or some such non-comittal, cabalistic epistle.

Yours remorsefully & affectionately,
Yates Snowden

N.B.! Your very interesting clipping from the Gazette, *in re* John Drayton[9] & the literary Negro Caesar, was *very* interesting. I read it to the Kosmians Saturday night. For this, all thanks!

Miss Bonham objects to a reproduction of "Master Skylark," with her cast, until later in the season!

N.B. 2d. Where's that photograph of your ugly phiz for my rogues' gallery? Of course I would prefer a portrait of the artist by himself—a little more elaborate & antique than that you pasted on the title page of Lutkenhaus's "Master Skylark."

Charleston, November 2nd, 1917

Dear Yates: . . .

Unable to do you favor asked: I know not, and, being in S.C., can find no one who does know *color of Thackery's eyes:* Rev. Robt. Wilson says *gray-blue:* will not take oath. Others, who saw T. when children, either noticed not, or have forgotten. Literature on shelf. The *Charleston book* indefinitely postponed by work for local Red Cross and War Recreation Service, for which was in Washington, ten days ago, where met Reed Smith, and lost him all too soon; alas! Also Ch. Benet, Esq.[10]

Yours until Death and after, if you go my way.

J. B.

I am on the Federal Grand Jury which holds in Columbia on and after Tuesday, 6th Nov. I need the rest. Will be hung up at the Jefferson, and will see you if I can and Judge Smith permits. I cannot yet make out whether I am 1 part genius 3 d. fool, or reverse.

25th Nov. [1917]

Jacobus Carus: . . .

I don't know why I sent you the newspaper clippings *in re* M. A. S. and the tablet, except with the idea that you might turn it over to Mrs. Smythe. I do *want you* to read the little *editorial* by Ball and when you have leisure & inclination I want to know whether, as an alleged Damyankee, you regard Ball's statement as "a most enchanting paradox." Can that tablet to a woman of the old regime ever so faintly be metamorphosed into an incentive to the women of today; one hating *"the flag,"* the other glorifying it? Honor bright.

And here endeth the 101st lesson.

Yours aff'ly,
Y. Snowden

I approve the banns in the Stoney-Simons prospective alliance; two fellows well met!

November 27th, 1917

Dearest and most
        Effervescent of Geniuses,
                and Most Valued of Friends:
Yates the Golden:

Yrs. Recd. Regret no time to commit persiflage epistolary. Hurry call R. C. publicity 'smorning, etc.—damnable haste, etc. . . .

You sent me the newspaper clippings, dear fellow for the reason that you think I know your feelings in this matter. I trust I do. I read the estimate of W. Ball: I see no paradox: only a slant vision does, dear fellow.

("Dear fellow" is not an odious epithet, terrible as it sounds).

Those who are true to their cause are exemplars always; causes change, and flags are substituted one for another; truth, loyalty, unswerving faith are things ever to be expressed in the present tense: while standards follow the dead brave past to the dust. What odds which flag she loved or hated? To the one she loved she was true until death. It is this abstract attitude, not the concrete, specific flag of the starry cross may be commended to the women of to-day: it makes no difference that their flag, through the vicissitudes of war and time, is the flag your Mother hated. We all shall be truer to what is fine in the past if we will but be true to what is brave in the present; and far better represent the nobility of the old by being, if we can, a shred of it, to-day.

Sermon is over: there is no paradox: creeds and confessions of faith go down into the irrecoverable dust with dead religions; but righteousness remains:

"Though I perish, Truth is so!"

Good-by, God bless you! And send us peace and honor and victory!

Yours,
[John Bennett] . . .

22d Dec'r, 1917

My dear John: . . .

Chamberlayne's death is a heavy blow to the College and the State and, though we were not very intimate, I feel a keen personal loss. He had in some matters as fine a critical judgment as yours and his patriotism was as ardent. That cold-blooded economic interpretation of history (See Seligman![11]) though often correct *falls down* absolutely when we contemplate a character like Chamberlayne's. The trail of the money devil is *not* over all! —And he warmly admired you; I don't think you had a more enthusiastic listener in your Kosmos paper.—By the way, Bernard's impressions of the Holy City did not impress you as they did me. I send you three copies of the "Blast"; give one to Mrs. Sam Stoney and one to Mrs. Smythe, if you think it would amuse her.

With all best wishes for you and yours in which my favorite wife would join were she not asleep, I am

Yours affectionately,
Yates Snowden

NB! Already, as a result of the enclosed fool local by Koon, a State reporter, the Blast is having good results; *two books,* one of them very rare, have already been returned to me! And "still there's more to follow"!

———————————

24th Dec'r, 1917

My dear John:

I swear it is a shame to interrupt your quiet but unobtrusive works of philanthropy by my perpetual appeals for information; but, this time I have a reason as well as an excuse.

Ambrose Gonzales,[12] one of the most generous of men and one of the finest fellows I ever knew, is slowly sinking of a wasting disease; but, his brain is as active and sprightly as ever. As you will see by the enclosed clipping he is a master, *facile princeps,* in *low-country* Gullah. I have got up a list of over 150 men and women who have begged him to publish his negro stories in book form and have subscribed each for from one to 10 copies. The old man just now is strongly inclined to collect his old stories, as pub'd years ago in the N&C. & The State, and to write some new ones. He has rec'd a long letter from Brabham, an admirer, who says his wife was a linguist, and that *she said* that the dialect of our S.C. Coast darkies is a mixture of African, English, French and Spanish. The old man sees the absurdity of any *French* influence and doubts if there is any Spanish. I tell him the machinations of the Spaniards at St. Augustine were traced in the Stono (?) insurrection and in the Yemassee (?) and other Colonial wars and that there *may be* a trace of Spanish influence upon the talk of our Coast negroes, tho' I doubt it.

I told him that *you* were the best authority in the world in this matter and that if he could only have a short talk with you, he could get at the facts. I did not tell him I was going to write you this letter.

Now, to the point: Can you settle for me *this question of possible Spanish influence* upon S.C. Gullah?

I don't want you to give away any of your "thunder," upon which you have been working for years; but, if it is perfectly fair, would you mind answering that one question: *Did the Spaniard have any appreciable influence upon S.C. "Gullah"?*

Just dash off a few lines to me, if you can do so, in justice to yourself, and that precious boy Jack Jr.—who, if I mistake not, will be ten years old one week from tomorrow—only 49 years younger than

Your affectionate friend,
Yates Snowden

Chapter 8

1918

Gullah origins and usage; World War I; translations by J. A. Symonds and G. H. Sass; Gonzales's Laguerre.

DURING 1918 the Gonzales stories and Gullah remained subjects of the friends' letters. The other main topic of the year was, of course, World War I. While Bennett was working for the Red Cross, Snowden became a board member of the Fatherless Children of France, a Columbia committee organized by the Alliance Française.

John Bennett wrote of the origins of Carolina Gullah, its tonality and enunciation, and the influence of various cultures on its development. He considered, in relation to these aspects, sources of information from the 1705 English translation of the Dutch work of William Bosman, *A New and Accurate Description of the Coast of Guinea,* to the 1903 work by Samuel Phillips Verner, *Pioneering in Central Africa;* and he commented on remarks by La Rochefoucauld, Colonel Asbury Coward, and Professor Charles Woodward Hutson. Bennett noted the impact on the patois by the immigrant British peasant and London cockney bond-servants and laborers, as well as the effect on Gullah by other nationalities. He also listed some of the words surviving from the African language still in use during the first two decades of the twentieth century.

Snowden wrote Bennett about seeing Sam and Loula Stoney on the streetcar when they came up to Columbia from Charleston to spend Sunday with their son who was stationed at Camp Jackson. Snowden further noted that young Lieutenant Sam Stoney, Jr. had purchased from

Gittman a small book of English verse to carry with him to France. Bennett told of Albert Simons's seeking poetry volumes from a North Carolina bookstore while he was stationed at Camp Greene. Other topics mentioned in 1918 were Lord Bolingbroke on the wisdom of mirth and a comparison of the poetry of John Addington Symonds and George Herbert Sass.

In December Bennett recorded some of the family occurrences of the past summer, while the war was still raging in Europe, including his fashioning bows and arrows and a hay-filled sack effigy of the Kaiser, which the children used for target practice. For Christmas Snowden gave the Bennetts a book of poems, *Wine, Women, and Song,* and Bennett sent the Snowdens a silhouette.

Jan. 18th, 1918

Dear Yates:

Have tried three times to get an answer written to you anent questions asked concerning *Gullah:* interrupted every time. Answers to such queries should be explicit: ought to have common-sense in 'em, also. *Mr. Gonzales is welcome to all information I can give, and more.* I would give something to have the privilege of a long talk with him on the patois of which he is certainly past-master perfect. If his collected sketches are printed put me down for half a dozen copies (6), I MUST have that many, sure. Am writing; this is just to reassure you of yrs.

Affectionately,
John Bennett

January 23d, 1918

Dear Yates:

A few words to keep the record straight. My long delay in reply is discourtesy of circumstance, not of choice: it is none of my liking, I assure you. I should long ago have answered your original query of December 24th, but that I have been up against adamantine diversion: first Austin Smythe's[1] illness with pneumonia—which, though, heaven be praised, a light case, was critical in his instance: second, his mother's immediate desperate illness from grippe, followed by a most serious attack of dilatation of the heart—from which she is, happily, now making excellent recovery: and third—an anticlimax, perhaps, but none the less hindering to free correspondence even with a well-beloved friend—namely, yersel', juist—my three children took advantage of the bitterest weather, no water in the house, fuel short, gas low, and their mother greatly occupied with the cares of the other house—to have, one following the other, measles! They are all, at last, out of quarantine, and back at school.

To add a touch of humor: I have a wife in public life in addition to efficient family service on the side.

Yet, if the matter has been broached to him at all, I must ask you to make sufficient apology for me to Mr. Gonzales, high dean of our local dialecticians and past-master of the Gullah patois of the Carolina coast country.

Would I could write Gullah as he writes it; would I knew it as he knows it; would I had the opportunity to talk the whole subject over with him at length and leisure for my own instruction and immense profit! But as that cannot be, speed the publication of his collected works, with all the expert comment from his knowledge you and he and his other familiars judge proper to append or prefix thereto: and don't forget my order.

As to the several queries you make, perhaps they are best answered in general commentary; so I take that way with it.

Recollect, please, that I am not speaking as an authority, but as a student. It is dangerous to dogmatize in etymology; and perilous to be cock-sure. But, as far as researches go to inform, these are my conclusions up to this time:

In the first place the Gullah negro is an African from the Liberian group of tribes: formerly powerful and numerous, they have been crowded and over-run; their remnant remains about thirty miles inward from Monrovia. From this coast many negroes were brought to the West Indies and the Carolinas at an early date; the earliest were tempered by servitude in the islands, Bermuda, the Bahamas, Jamaica, San Domingo, etc., before arrival in Carolina; later the untempered Africans were brought direct from the West Coast to Charleston.

At the time of the arrival of these negroes in the American provinces a considerable proportion of the population was composed of white bondsmen, indentured mechanics and "redemptioners" the laborers of the colony, among whom the newly-arrived negroes learned their English. Their vocabularies were small and very markedly dialectical, in the majority of instances a dialect which had been handed down from father to son for several generations, preserving closely the peculiarities of earlier times, in many cases Elizabethan and Jacobean.

The African, plastic as he is by nature, quickly lost their own languages and acquired imperfectly the dialects of British peasantry among whom they worked, and by whom they very generally were directed. The main reason was, perhaps, that, at the height of the trade, owing to the danger of conspiracy, large groups of negroes upon great plantations and in any considerable establishment, were generally made up, by preference, of negroes of different tribes, speaking languages and dialects unknown to one another; they were mostly young; youth was preferred for many reasons, one being that youth soon forgets, retains no bitter or lasting memories, and acquires a new language with greater ease. The new negroes were parcelled out among the early bond-servants, and, later, among the trained servants, preventing their congregation in a body, hastening their familiarity with their new duties, and more quickly learning the language of their monitors and wardens. This plan was operative from very early days in obliterating the many African dialects and tongues native to the negro slaves.

Among the many African tribes brought to this country, the presence of very many Gullah negroes is apparent from the earliest times. On some plantations, before the days of experienced precaution, it is highly probable they formed a majority of the hands. As early as 1730 a plan had been hatched against Charleston by these negroes. Some years later St. Paul's Parish saw the outbreak called the Gullah War. In the Gullah Jack rebellion of 1822 there was actually a Gullah society which met in conspiracy in the parishes about Charleston once a month; and one large and evidently influential group of the most active insurrectos was the "Gullah Company" headed by Gullah Jack. I am told that within the memory of persons living—or living a very few years since many Gullah negroes were still plainly distinguished upon Cooper, especially at the former Washington plantation.

The dialect of the West Coast from which came these Gullah negroes was early commented upon as peculiarly harsh, quacking, flat in intonation, quick, clipped and peculiar even in Africa: Bosman,[2] the Dutch sailor, describes its peculiar tonality and called its speakers the Quaquas, because they gabbled like ducks.

The clinging together of these Gullah tribesmen as indicated above, and their apparent resolute and persistent character evidently assisted in impressing their dialectical peculiarities on weaker and more plastic natures brought in contact with them, and fixed the tonality of the negro dialect of the Carolina low country. I do not say that this is so; we cannot establish the fact; but it is a surmise of much probability, based simply upon what we know has happened elsewhere.

For the above reason of prevalence and domination as a peculiar dialect with singular and marked tonality the characteristic patois of the districts where these negroes most abounded came to be universally referred to as the Gullah dialect.

The tonality and mode of enunciation remained, perhaps, African; the vocabulary became peasant dialects of Great Britain, with fewer and fewer survivals of African phrases and words, until in 1853, the Southern Planter found that with exception of a few old people born in Africa and brought away in advanced youth the negroes seemed entirely in the dark regarding their native tongue.

The body of their dialectical vocabulary remained archaistic English, unlettered dialects of the 17th and 18th centuries, of which there are many instances surviving. Thus the untempered African direct from the Guinea coast lost his African dialect and acquired that of the British peasantry.

But there were very many tempered Africans, bought at second-hand, accustomed to servitude, from the West Indies, whose speech was tinged by French, Spanish and Portuguese, some slight admixtures of which remained in their vocabularies for a time, and, perhaps, have left traces behind them, indistinct enough, it is true. After the attempted negro insurrection of 1760, in Jamaica, many negroes were sold to the continental American provinces out of that island, deported by order of court, and disposed of by their masters. The Spanish influence was still strong upon many of these West Indian negroes. Likewise many of the negroes in the West Indies from which large purchases were made in the provinces had already been transported out of French and Spanish islands, the Spanish islands and out of Martinique in particular.

The Jamaican negro dialect is still said to be English spoken with a Spanish accent; yet to be very closely akin to the rice-field Gullah spoken with a curious Cockney twang.

That there was undoubtedly French influence exerted among the Huguenot colonists upon the speech of their negro servants is no doubt true, especially in the Santee settlement. The extent of this remoter influence is entirely conjectural. Before the American Revolution Parson Peter Levrier of the endowed French church lamented the decline, decay and dissolution of the church owing to the disuse of the French language. It would tend, therefore, to decline among the servants of French-speaking settlers of the Huguenot faith. Whatever surviving French influence there may be perceptible upon the Gullah dialect is therefore, perhaps, more attributable to the greater and later influence of the San Domingan refugees, of whom there were many found sanctuary in sea-coast Carolina, who brought negroes with them. Rochefoucauld says that in 1796 Charleston was full of Frenchmen from San Domingo, many of whom earned a livelihood by letting their negroes whom they had brought with them in their flight. He speaks of the French planters of that day as a class considerable and distinctly defined. The trades of the city itself were filled by them, and the handicrafts by their trained servants; music, letters and the arts were greatly in their hands. For some years a French theatre flourished, and there were one or more French newspapers essayed, while to cater to French subscription and trade there were numerous contributions in French printed in the English papers, and many French advertisements. The letting of trained and accomplished servants and tempered laborers must have produced an effect beyond the city limits. That this was so is shown by the evidence at the time of the Gullah Jack rebellion in 1822, at which time there appear to have been many negroes throughout the country who were known as "Frenchmen negroes"; there was, among the insurrectos, a group who spoke no language but French among themselves, and were known as the "French band"; there were witnesses examined who spoke nothing but French; and interpreters for such were maintained in the courts until circa 1829, subsequent to which I have no record as to this usage. It is quite certain that the speech of many negroes on Cooper river was markedly French in accent; and Col. Asbury Coward[3] told me that the negroes upon Silk Hope plantation in particular, up to a short time before the States' War, where a body of servants and field-hands had been maintained unchanged for many years, spoke a dialect so markedly French that negroes from neighboring plantations across the stream frequently found it difficult to understand the speech of the Silk Hope men; he had understood this to have been the case upon several other plantations, in St. John's in particular where the French accent was distinctly traceable in a peculiar throwing-forward of the stress to the closing syllable of a word in quite the Gallic way, as in sta-shun, a-gent, plan-ta-shun, tukrey buz-zahd, trel-liche for trellis, and cor-niche for cornice, and the like.

There is enough surviving evidence of French influence as to believe it to have in some degree affected the rice-field dialect; it can, perhaps, safely be said that both Spanish and Portuguese had a remote influence upon it difficult at this time to dogmatize on. It can also be said, with every necessary evidence to support the statement, that the greater portion of what is picturesque in phraseology and diction in the dialect was gathered from illiterate English, Irish, Scotch, Scotch-Irish, and London cockney bond-servants and laborers who lent the first negroes their dialect to be passed on from one generation to another unchanged as all folk-dialects pass. It was and is a lingo inadequately heard, incorrectly spoken, crushed, abbreviated and corrupt, with the intonation and lazy articulation of the African negro lending its most distinguishing note.

Many of the phrases characteristic of Gullah are to be found also in the dialect of the Jamaican negroes and in Sierra Leone.

There are to be found in the Carolina gullah a few words of dubious Moorish or Arabic; but I do not think either Moorish or Arabic had any effect upon the dialect; or that the coast-trade Minorcan Greek from the

Turnbull[4] settlements at New Smyrna had more than a problematical contact with it, the one or two possibly Greek words found are far more like to be school-boy Greek as commonly used by English school-boys.

Of words surviving from the African, from any African language, the list is brief, perhaps fifty words or phrases within the vernacular, a few of these in common use, the rest but cabinet specimens, still in actual use where primitive conditions maintain, but affecting the dialect not at all.

Buckra, nyam, cona, swanga, du-du, goober, pinder, cooter, okra, geechy, cymbi, bakalingo (obsolescent), guffer, penepne, da, da-da: these are, perhaps, most commonly met; and to these Mr. Gonzales can, no doubt, add others.

To sum up: the body of the Gullah vocabulary is archaic peasant English mixed with Scotch and Scotch-Irish pronunciations and uses; in some localities its accent is apparently influenced by French; and there may be some much more remote influence of Spanish and of Portuguese difficult to define; its peculiar intonation would appear to be African, and its articulation negro in its negligence.

I do not know whether this will answer your questions satisfactorily or not. I hope it may. I could, of course, string this brief essay out into an article with example and citation; but scarcely fancied that was what you want, so have been as brief, but as explicit as I might off-hand. You may, perhaps, gather from the preceding gabble what you want truly to know; but if there be anything further desired write, in particulars, and I will be particular if you choose.

Further than this I shall not delay to write; but shall mail this at once to you.

With my compliments to Mrs. Snowden, always, and my respectful regards to Mr. Ambrose Gonzales, to some meeting with whom I look forward with great interest if these disjointed times permit—and with bung jower and other language of affectionate intent devoted to you, I beg forever still to remain

[John Bennett]

1st Febr'y 1918

Dear John:

If you have not destroyed them all, rake up half a dozen letters of mine to you in the last ten or more years! Read the first eight or ten lines of every other letter and you will find profuse and profound thanks for many kindnesses, and solemn pledges never to pester you so again.

Well, your invaluable letter *in re* Gullah, was rec'd; was read with infinite delight & great profit by old Ambrose, who still has it and who will write you himself. I won't write any thanks this time: just *ditto* to what I have so often written you.

I had two copies of the bulk of your "essay" made, one of them I loaned to Reed Smith. I enclose his letter to me which explains itself. What he says about me and Gullah is all fol-da-rol. I am no expert, & have never attempted a line of it in my life; but it interests me, *mainly because* it concerns *South Carolina negroes!* And I am infinitely wise in one particular: *I know how little I do know!!!* Altho' born on the S.C. coast, I doubt if Sams⁵ knows any more about Gullah than I do. *Still*, Smith's letter is interesting.

The other copy I have sent to my dear old friend Prof. Chas. Woodward Hutson of New Orleans. He was born & bred in Prince William's Parish, or thereabout, and is something of a linguist and if his mind has not recently weakened with his 78 or more years, I know he will write me something good. I have asked him to criticise your "essay" freely; especially your claim (new & very plausible to me!) that our rice field negroes speak a much transmogrified 17th-18th century, bondservant, cockney English.

One word more: Can you identify the negro word *poon-tang;* or poon-tank? *Don't ask any woman* about this!

Yours aff'ly,
Y. S.

6th Feb. '18

Dear John:

I did not write to thank you for your most kind response to my S.O.S. Gullah call. Old Ambrose was delighted and has referred to your contentions and admired your brilliancy and scholarship time & time again, and talks about getting an automobile and going down, with me, to see you in the merry spring time, if you have not the decency, meanwhile, to come up here. I am far behind in my College work, as usual, & can't write more tonight in the thank line.

I had a copy of your screed made and sent it to my dear old friend, Chas. Woodward Hutson, who tried to teach me *Anno* 1895, and asked him to send me his criticisms.

Judging by the roast you gave me and the ass you proved me in Sept. 1916, when I sent you what Kephart wrote about *cooter* in "Our Southern Highlanders," you know all about that toothsome bird: *but,* I am struck by Prof. Hutson's Spanish *cota* surmise, and by "swan-guh," and *Indian* influence in negro lingo. With all best wishes for that wife of yours,

I am yours aff'ly,
Y. S.

Prof. Hutson was reared in "old Beaufort," the Combahee country.

Charleston, February 10th, 1918

Prof. Yates Snowden,
      Earl of Sumter Street,
         Columbia, South Carolina.

Dear Yates:

    etc., etc., etc.,

First let us dispose of the Hon. Reed Smith: Have been collecting Gullah, and prying into its structure these twenty years, summer and winter, snubbed by everyone but yourself and two-three other noble souls, yet gradually getting to somewhere. Should like nothing better than to produce a really adequate article on the subject, in conjunction with others, like Mr. Gonzales, who were born to Gullah. But what's the use of stuff like mine. Mr. Gonzales amuses a tired world and causes infinite delight. There be few of us who care for theses on the Gothic conjunctive, for instance; hence why analyze, probe, surmise or dig out the roots of this most remote of all negro dialects, bar the Louisiana creole patois as spoken among the blacks yonder? Nobody would read the thing but just ourselves. And war has left no time for doing things just for the love of it. We might do for Gullah all we can, but never what Page has done for Virginia, Harris for Upper Georgia or Cable for New Orleans; for nobody can read Gullah in the great outside world. Jones[6] fell flat. It is kind to say that Harris and Uncle Remus gathered the popularity, depriving Jones of that fame which might have been his; but it mightn't! Who reads Jones? Or comprehends him out of the Holy Land? Not one. I sent a copy of his valuable Myths to a student of English dialects, who thanked me for my interesting gift, and couldn't read it. Not Jove himself could do for Gullah what Page did for Virginian and Harris for Upper Georgian. This is sad, but true. I sent some gentle Gullah once to Richard Watson Gilder, hoping acceptance of the Century. He sent it back expressing much interest in my subject, but suggesting courteously, by advice of his readers, that I learn to write negro dialect, and then try again. Gullah is only for the Chosen People. I wrote an article on Gullah and its relation to archaic British peasant dialects, and after difficulty got it printed in the South Atlantic Quarterly, at Durham, N.C. And within six months the thing was dead of financial meningitis—the Quarterly was dead!

I have the citations, the examples of usage, the differentiations in many instances; and sources. I have, also, African vocabularies to substantiate origins; and wish to God I had more.

But how to get on with this War and write about Gullah passes my small ability!

Where, too is our audience? Nowhere, nor anywheres else, beyond the Charmed Circle.

Tempt me no more! My compliments and regards always to so hopeful a spirit as Prof. Smith possesses.

I enclose his letter: it pleased me.

Second: let us speak of that kindly scholar and gentleman, Prof. Hutson. A man who was reared in the Combahee country should be authority on Gullah for that district. *You*, however, should not accuse me of saying that rice-field Gullah is transmogrified *cockney* English; for I certainly never said it. British dialects from country shires far more affected the negro's speech than London cockney, of which there are but a few—tolerably distinctive—traces, in Charleston and vicinity, such as vax candles for wax, Ventvorth street, for Wentworth, wolley, for volley, wine for vine, etc. Prof. Hutson's very kind comment upon my hasty epistle I am very glad to get; and thank you. In speaking of British peasant dialects I include the Scotch—Lowland Scotch—and the own cousin to it, Scotch-Irish of Ulster—which McCrady with some cranial perversity persists on calling Irish in his history. McCrady was singularly ignorant of things outside of South Carolina; and inevitably fell into errors, of which this was one most notable. Of Highland Scotch, or Gaelic, I know too little to discover a trace in Gullah. There were many Highlanders in Georgia, and many upon Peedee, below Fayetteville, N.C.—and much trouble they made Francis Marion.[7] They used Gaelic bibles until the '50's; but I can find no traces of their dialectical English, which has peculiar marks of its own, unless we conclude that the usage of "carry," meaning "escort," is due to the Highland usage in English, and not to the Lowland Scotch of which the country was full—more in the Piedmont, however, than in the tide-water—you remember the "Irish" from Ulster were not welcomed nor wanted in the coast-country, but were urged to pass on to the frontier to open up the back country, to increase the trade moving through Charlestown, and push back the Cherokees. The preachers, however, who had most influence on the negroes were not the Presbyterian Scotch preachers, but the early Baptist and Methodist preachers and lay exhorters, who, compared to the Presbyterian ministry, were singularly uncultured, and were constantly in trouble for meeting with the more ignorant negroes: some were English, some Welsh, some Scotch—Lowlanders—and some Scotch-Irish Ulstermen forsaking the sterner Presbytery for the more genial air of Methodist futurity, a more generous speculation—"Titty" and "Titta" for sister, and "Daddy" are Scots.

The vocabulary of the gullah speaking negro is full as large as the vocabulary of the lower peasantry of Great Britain; larger than the estimates put upon the actual vocabulary of the peasantry by some students—which is certainly too small, the actual number of objects handled and familiar to the lowest rural life being far larger than the conjectured vocabulary of these stingy students.

As to my conjectures relative to words of African origin, few are so conjectured without tolerably certain identification in African vocabularies. I think Prof. Hutson quite mistaken in regard to "oona," which occurs upon the West Coast, broadly distributed, as *ona:* I have felt that the identity was quite certain.

As to "Swanga" far be it from me to dogmatise. I don't know. Swank is common British slang to-day. I have found half-a-dozen examples current of swank and swanking in the most colloquial English. And what Prof. Hutson says would carry it further back to an origin beyond all Africa. I have found but one African citation—not a vocabulary of language; and I believe, off-hand, used in Sierra Leone, which proves what? That there were a good many negroes in Sierra Leone from the British West Indies, and numbers from the Carolinas, who had been carried to Nova Scotia after the American Revolution, and thence to Sierra Leone. It is no surprise, therefore to find in Sierra L. a great many parallel usages to the rice-field Gullah; and such is the case. I thank Prof. Hutson for more data on "swanga" than I had previously possessed.

Prof. Hutson is again entirely wrong with regard to "Cooter"; he is almost as wrong as the Oxford Dictionary, but more decent, indeed; I am happy to state. The Oxford is a singular case of closet etymology. In such a place without excuse. The word "cooter," which is as we all know not pronounced "cooter" at all, but, if we use the Oxford's system, is Kut.; or as the Century dictionary would, perhaps, indicate it, Kutu—the first *u* as in full, the second as in put—or, say, like the final Teutonic *e* in Steibe—is broadly speaking, Bantu the great family tongue of the Triangle of Central Africa, as spoken in the Baluba tribe, among the Balunda, at Ndombe on the upper Congo. A group of words here are illuminating to the etymologist: nkusu is the parrot; nguvu, the hippopotamus; ngubu, the ground-nut; ngumbu, the okra-pod (or gumbo); ncudu, the terrapin. Vide S. P. Verner's "Pioneering in the Heart of Africa." (It's there: I haven't the page-number at hand.) As to the Oxford's closet etymology, which, on my soul seems water-closet etymology, they coolly evolve, without an example or citation to follow their track, the name of the terrapin from an intransitive verb, coot, and a participial, cooting-time, of mating-season's most intimate period—as follows:

COOT, v.: obs. intr, of tortoises. 1667, H. Stubbe, in Phil. Trans. II, 500; Dampier, Voyage II, index, s.v.; 1750, G. Hughes, Barbadoes, 309— "in cooting-time."

If they had but gone a little further they might, perhaps, have found a side-light on this use in Philip Henry Gosse's "A Naturalist's Sojourn in Jamaica," 1851, London; p. 319: "This knotting together (of yellow Boas, in the intimate mating-season) is called by the negroes 'cooting,' perhaps from the Spanish *coito*."

Had they followed the word to Africa as they should have done, and as they have done in so many instances, as in "buckra," the Baluba Bantu would have given them their source without such a bungle as this.

I know of no Indian influences perceptible in Gullah, beyond the suggestion of Gen. Alexander,[8] that the word "culla-culla," used round Georgetown to mean wild-duck, is Indian. As Prof. Hutson says the influence of the Indians upon the slave population appears singularly small—and I know too little of Indian tongues to note anything at all.

As to your own interrogatory, in re the dark word *poontang,* I do not converse with ladies on this topic, and—seldom with gentlemen. I would ask you, with real interest as to the word's usage where you found it current? In Carolina? I have not yet. But in the Alabama black belt it is vernacular for *to cohabit.* I should truly like information on this word— as to extent of its common usage geographically: what can you tell me?

Also what do you, or what does Mr. Gonzales, know of a dance called the "gitchin"?—neither turkey-dance nor coonshine.

I have a letter from Mr. Gonzales, of February 2d, which I purpose to answer within a very few days, direct; so will here enclose but my cordial respect, if you will be so good as to deliver.

And, as for you, you waster of time, that golden thing, you're ever welcome, as you should by this time, very well know, to almost anything I've got—including the golden time referred to.

I have not done some publicity which is due for the morning press; but, for once, it may go to, as Will Shakespeare so gently says—

My compliments always to the ladies of your household—remember me to W. W. B. and such others as you deem proper and worthy—and now no more, from

Your humble servant of etymologies,
[John Bennett]

P.S. I forgot to say that J. Leighton Wilson[9] cites "swanga" in the native language spoken near Gaboon with the meaning of gay or elegant. And that swanga-nyabga is found in Jamaica with the sense of pride or superciliousness, self-consequence. These are practically the meanings Prof. Hutson finds for swank running back to Dan Chaucer. I'll leave it to the better scholar. As I said in my former letter, it is dangerous to dogmatise in etymology. I am not a partisan of my own position: I am hunting the facts; I thank any man who can prove my etymology in error and settle the fact.

P.S. No. 2: Etymologies are all very well, and much interest me; always have, always will. But let's have A. Gonzales, his book. We are all dull as ditch-water; but he will give us more than a laugh. What are his plans for the book—when, that is?

P.S. No. 3: Until this war's over my time is all done for: I have stolen an hour for this.

N.B.: There's no immediate chance of my coming to Co. I would that there were, and that we could congregate and sweetly wrangle.

How would a Gullah evening, program to be arranged, do for Kosmos, next season? Huh?

Goodby! Goodby!

———————

24th July '18

Dear John: . . .

I met Sam & Miss Lou on the street cars Sunday & learned your address. They had come up to spend the day with little Sam.

Today I saw at Gittman's a *small* copy (onion skin paper) of the book of Cambridge Verse (Quiller-Couch's), price $4. & I asked who is buying *this* book in *this* town? And Gittman, that abysm of reckless youth, answered, "an officer at the camp, Lieut. Stoney." So, the rascal is going to carry some choice poetry with him across the briny!

I don't like the sinking of that *transport* leviathan *the Justicia!* My God! Suppose she had been struck going over!!! All sadness in this shanty: poor Willie Warley has had another stroke, and is, practically, dying in the Baker Sanitorium in Charleston, & my wife & her sister are anxiously awaiting news that must come soon!

Yours aff'ly,
Y. Snowden

"Many Pines," E. Flat Rock, N.C.
August 20th, 1918

Dear Yates:

Yours of July 24th received. I am ashamed not to have replied before. I can only say that weariness of wits occasioned by much war, and some personal complications, are the only things which prevented immediate reply. . . .

I have very little of the French spirit in me. And nothing, or little of the English; but am intolerably Scotch in mood; and where I get my pleasure in a jest, search me, dear lad—not from the Scots fork—my Uncle William[10] never saw a joke from youth to eighty-four years—and my grandfather never was known, though genial, to jest. It may be Welsh for all I know: for my father loved to laugh—but did na Rab Burns like jests and lauchter?—and my faither worshipped Rab, and knew him end til end! As near as I get to real vers de société is in my verses "In a (Charleston) Rose Garden!" Carolyn Wells insists that those verses are vers de société. But I told her they were too damned serious to me to bear that title. "Oh, well," said she, "If that's your narsty fancy, keep your nasty verses!" and didn't print 'em in her book.

I was much amused by your discovery of young Sam Stoney's purchase of the Oxford Book of Verse. The boy is a delightful reader, of taste and discernment, and has carried his verses to the transport, and across. Miss Harriet Stoney's man, Albert Simons, Dr. Grange's son, is another charming—but far shyer fellow—with a happy love of loveliness, either prose or verse, and when at Camp Greene, fairly set the style in verse for the literary metropolis of western North Carolina by insisting on the book-shop there producing various volumes of immortal beauty they never had heard of before. I understand they since have had a run on them—whether among Charlotte's intellectual ring or among men in camp I know not.

I have been trying to rest up here; not to much purpose; the yeast-cake seems stale; I don't rise. Mrs. Bennett, I am pleased to say, declares that she is beginning to pick up. We shall be here but three weeks longer, at the outside; then we go to Charleston to complete my girl's outfit for school at Dana Hall, Wellesley, Mass., where my sister has had charge of the English department for near twenty years—and where I hope a change of climate will strengthen my girl, physically, as well as mentally. We go on to Boston with her in mid-September.

I have watched for news in the Charleston papers of poor Willie W.; but have seen nothing as yet. I am sorry for everyone who has a grief.

Mrs. Bennett joins me in sincere regard to all of you; and from me please accept for yourself a full measure of affection from . . .

[John Bennett] . . .

———————

21st Dec. '18

Dear John:

I send you, with all best wishes for you & yours, a copy of Symonds's[11] "Wine, Women & Song." It's a favorite of mine, and it's barely possible that I have sent you the same before. For that reason I have not written your name on the flyleaf; for, Heaven knows, *one copy* of a book of this kind is enough for an old man like you.

So, if you already have a copy, send this along to some poor chump for Christmas. That's what I, and possibly you, did with some superfluous berry-spoons, when I was married once upon a time.

I think I have already called your attention to the beautiful dedication of this book to Symonds's dead wife. I discovered—me and my wife—that *every word* of the beautiful tribute was *faked* from the dedication by J. S. Mill[12] to *his wife,* about 1850, of his celebrated "Essay on *Liberty.*" Mill's tribute is all the more wonderful from the fact that his wife had a more or less shady record before she married him.

"One more word, and I am done," as the pulpiteers so often falsely say—Look at stanza three on p. 73:

> "In the public-house to die
> Is my resolution"; &c., &c.

That is perhaps the best verse in "The Confession of Golias"; the celebrated

> "Mihi est propositum
> In taberna more."

Now, compare Symonds with *Sass.* (I quote from memory)

> Let me in a tavern
> Hear my final knell 'O,
> Wine, from cool, green cavern
> Floating to me mellow;
> While, in tones sonorous,

> Shout the angel chorus;
> "God be kind and merciful
> To such a merry fellow."

Mr. Sass beats Symonds all hollow!!! I don't care to pester him, but the next time you see Herbert R. Sass[13] ask him for the rest (?) of his father's translation.

I don't know where I got that single stanza, I don't *think* it was ever in print; perhaps he did not write any more. Somehow you can't associate G. H. S. with students' drinking songs. I doubt if he was ever tight in his life.

So glad both of Sam's boys are safe & sound.

> Yours affectionately,
> Yates Snowden

Old Ambrose G. published or, rather, printed, an excerpt (?) from his forth-coming vol. of Gullah: "Laguerre" (Sidney Legaré), to be used by Mrs. Barton Wallace & Teddy Guerard when "entertaining" in France. I send you one of them. *Entre nous* the old man is evidently getting weaker and has not yet written that learned *introduction*, though I have urged him time & time to do it. Should he die (absit omen!!) *you* are the only man who could write it.

Charleston, December 27th, 1918

Dear Yates:

I should mightily like to sit down, this morning, and write a letter in praise of fellowship, and of folly, which dissembles the truth which abides beneath the goodly cloak of careless laughter, diverting the minds of the ignorant from the deep below, and bedazzling their blind eyes with the dancing of the glimmer on top!

How often, when soldiers meet, the greeting "God d—— you, you old son of a longshoreman's shame!" truly means "God bless you, old man!" And "Where the h—— have you been, destroying the happiness of everything with your d—— benighted soul?" meaning "I'd hug you like a girl if we were not men; for my heart is fair overflowing with pleasure, lad, to lay these eyes upon your face again!"

We're all more or less fools, in that we seldom say what we mean most, but pass it off in a jest. Just the same, I am game, this morning, to say to you very frankly, that if it were not for just such messages as I get from you and one or two other choice souls, I think that life would lose its finest light—brighter even than the steady glow of duty. A few words from a friend will pull the dead cow out of the mud where everything else fails.

I have read and pleased myself with your Bolingbroke, beyond expression: "That in comedy the best actor plays the part of the droll, while some scrub rogue is made the hero or the fine gentleman. So in this farce of life, wise men pass their time in mirth, while fools only are serious."

Often I fear that I am failing in sense, sinking into the Fools' Slough, growing serious as an ass; but, praise be to God, there still remains, a golden thread in the tattered rags, a grin!

I remember how, when I used to box, years ago, the boxer's grin got set on our faces like a Japanese mask, taking wallop after wallop unalteredly, though at the latter end of thirty minutes rather drawn and hard.

That's about the way of it yet, at the end of Life's busy Thirty Minutes with the mitts.

Yet, when a man feels that somewhere on earth there is another lang-lugged beastie—somewhat like himsel'—who appreciates his side-stepping, he takes his wallop better.

I enclose you some evidence of sane folly from my summer: you may not know that I have been bowyer and arrow-maker and head-devil to the children who gather at Mrs. A. T. Smythe's place every summer, and have kept them playing at "Robin Hood" as if I still were young. This year they shot the soul out of The Kaiser, often putting a three-foot arrow clean through the hay-stuffed crocus-sack: I built the Kaiser, whose photograph I send you with Jane, Jack and Susan Bennett, and Jenks Robertson's boy.

I sent you also, previously, a silhouette, as proof that my soul is still not wholly corrupted with age, but climbs the fence and fools about the green fields still, once in a while, though Time keeps crying after, "Hurry, hurry!" and work waits. My wife, who has French, says this design possesses *espieglerie!* What the Hun she means I leave to you: it's Greek to me. I have little use for those barbarous tongues: English, South Carolinian (Charleston variety), and Gullah are all the languages I speak intelligently—or understand when spoken carefully.

Which brings us to "Laguerre," that gem of merriment from the revered Dean, A. E. Gonzales, Esq. Already I have admired and chuckled softly, read on and burst into the joyous cackle which defies convention, and makes my good wife sit up and say "What's that you've got there? Some nonsense from Yates Snowden?" I have not heard her laugh heartily for a long time as she did over Edisto's critique of "Dick T'ree Time," and the "Sons and Daughters of I Will Arise." Don't let A. E. G.

Esq., remit his labor until the volume's done, complete, replete. I do not know its like anywhere. It will be rare Caroliniana of the future, far better than is Georgia Scenes. Urge him to do the introduction: he's Sir Hubert Stanley in commentary on his text; knows Gullah complete; have it done. I thank you for the compliment implied in your suggestion as to this intro. if Mr. G. *will not* round out his own inimitable volume. But A. E. G. Esq., Dean of Low Country letters dialectical, alone should complete that volume of glorious Gullah and laughter—which we have followed, in odd numbers, in The State—on which I congratulate The State. (I had not known that Mrs. Wallace and Guerard really were aiming at France, further than Guerard's eager desire to go across in any sane capacity: he has worked too hard here already.)

Now, "Wine, Women and Song": I confess, as to my holy father behind the curtain, I never saw the volume before; so never had it: so we join, not part, these light things and I, though, at my age, man, it is a scandal. (I confess the berry-spoons; and add thereto several sets of pearl-handled carvers, ditto three superfluous gravy-ladles, which, re-engraved, did new duty well and won acknowledgments sincere and ignorant of our guile.) But, for God's sake, Yates, don't search out the many sources of happy phrase in my writings, and identify the writers of them, as you do Symonds's beautiful dedication, stolen—as you have told me—from Mill. But you err strangely, my lad, in thinking that Mill's wife's uncertain record aught might militate with Mill or any man who really loves a woman: I believe that love forgives greater things than shady records: there is something so generous in it by nature, and the noble pity a fine man feels for fine woman broken is so near in spirit to the truly divine that it becomes, in love, a thing superior to the flaw— however hard it may be to comprehend the workings of the soul. The pity of it is so great, if she be truly fine—and, sure, pity is akin to love— no more of this; I am no amative essayist: I have done some verses, may be, in a generous and difficult youth, concerning the instinct which is so mixed of grape-juice and gall—and is, I say, rebelliously, full of beauty and of glory, however much it fail perfection.

I have also just writ the last—or latest, certainly—verses to a "students' song" of my own, which at intervals through years comes out through the warp, and makes a comical spot in the sober pattern of my correct and moderate existence. . . .

Don't publish this[14] abroad among the unsanctified: one reason being it is not copyright yet; but will be; and, perhaps, is to be be-print with music for the use of the elect. Mrs. B. has written down the air for me, by her violin: I am looking for a harmonist, now. The thing will sing; that I know: but will anybody enjoy singing it in these dry days and moral? These are no verses for Walter Eichelberger[15] to find in man's possession.

I am interested in the Sass version, and will ask Herbert concerning the text. I have not seen him since receiving your letter. Symonds is not the only translator Sass beat hollow. His translation of the epigraph—on Jefferson Davis's monument in Richmond—of the Greater Simonides on those who fell repelling the Persian invasion, is the best in English—I should not be surprised—were it possible to commeasure languages disparate in nature—if his were the best translation in any tongue; but do not know any languages myself, so have no base for comparisons. But, certainly, his translations from Simonides, on the Davis monument first made actual epigraphs, I think, are beautiful transmutations; and by any comparison with English translations—at least so far as I have found these lines translated: as by Sterling, John Herman Merivale, Burges, Lord Charles Neaves, Edwin Arnold, and John Edwards—Sass's rendering gains in dignity and exquisite fitness of phrase.

As to associating G. H. S. with students' drinking songs, I knew him pleasantly, but too little to associate or dissociate him as to bibbing: the theatre seemed his indulgence, a star first-nighter, cribbed, cabined and confined in the provinces.

But then, here's *my* song: *I* have not been *so often* drunk, nor immoral, nor commonly goat-like and hircine—does it truly need be? I'll bet you, even, there's many a good drinking-song penned by folk not given to next-day headaches; many an amorosity writ by hermits: just as it is said that the best description of the Grand Canyon of the Colorado was done by a man who was all his life never west of the Mississippi. But, to be sure, a Judge in Equity looks odd as saturnalian poet, especially when quite purblind by night when revels mostly do rev.

But good and bad things all have end: so does this: here:

Give my respects and best wishes to Mr. Gonzales when next you meet him; and my regards to W. Ball Esq.—and to any true and enquiring friend of the proper sort. Forget at your peril my compliments and cordial regard to Mrs. Snowden, and to her sister, if still with you; and, with the New Year's best greeting and regards to yourself, believe me, briefly—though in letters voluminous—

Honestly and affectionately yours:
J. Bennett

Chapter 9

1919–1920

Work on Madame Margot; *Smythe nicknames; scarlet fever at Christmas; Hampton anecdote; Sams and Gonzales's Gullah glossary; D. J. McCord house; Confederate ladies; J. F. J. Caldwell's poem; literary figures; formation of South Carolina Poetry Society.*

In August of 1919 John Bennett thanked Yates Snowden for his humorous poem, "Okrantomattis," and acknowledged a clipping that Snowden had sent about an English Thomas Smyth family with odd first names, commenting on the Charleston Smythes' penchant for nicknames. Bennett, then in East Flat Rock, North Carolina, at "Many Pines," the Smythe-Bennett summer mountain home, also included an explanation for his long silence: he had been deeply absorbed in, but had been making little progress with, his Charleston legend, *Madame Margot*, although it was now two-thirds completed.

Other 1919 topics were the Stoneys' attendance at the World War I victory parades in New York and Washington; Bennett's early poem, "A Rose Garden"; Snowden's tribute to Walter Peyre Porcher; the University of South Carolina Bulletin on Robert Mills; Robert Browning's lines from "Rabbi Ben Ezra" on growing old; the necessity for thoroughness of preparation and intensity of work in writing a story; young Susan Bennett's illness with scarlet fever at Christmas time; the compilation in progress of a Gullah glossary by Ambrose Gonzales and Stanhope Sams; and an anecdote about one of the Wade Hamptons.

In April of 1920 Snowden taunted Bennett about an Edisto Island story told by Croft Williams and a comment by Ambrose Gonzales in regard to Gullah. In Bennett's reply, he responded to Snowden's remarks and mentioned being fined for driving twenty-five miles an hour up Meeting Street.

During the summer, the death of Susan Bennett's kinswoman in England was the occasion for Snowden's asking Bennett to write a tribute for the newspaper as if "coming from an old Columbian." However, Bennett refused, as he would all such requests in the years to come, to praise the departed.

The friends discussed the Poetry Society of South Carolina; Reed Smith's wedding; and the continued popularity of *Barnaby Lee,* as well as *Master Skylark.* Critiques of or references to a number of authors were contained in the 1920 letters, ranging from the famous, such as Christopher Morley, Stephen Vincent Benét, Arthur Clough, William Gilmore Simms, James Thomson, Don Marquis, DuBose Heyward, and Hervey Allen, to the lesser-known, such as R. W. Memminger, James FitzJames Caldwell, and Beatrice Ravenel.

"Many Pines," East Flat Rock, N.C.
August something, I don't
just know which: 1919

Most Cherished of Carolinians, Hail!

Since my discharge from the service I have been here at Flat Rock—now three weeks—endeavoring to recover from shell-shock, and at the same time to complete the legend of "Madame Margot," who sold her soul to the Devil—to whom you refer so irreligiously—that her daughter might be white. She succeeded in her aim; I succeed in neither. Instead of recovering from shell-shock and mental depression I find myself worse, and wake every morning frightened to death in apprehension of everything that may go wrong—a totally idiotic state, I know; but one that seems hard to cure. In the endeavor of the legend (which is two-thirds done, and is said, by some who know my past work, to be, perhaps, so far as it goes, some of the best work I have done—in some things better than the past)—I make little progress, if any, and have done nothing since arriving here—a rotten state of affairs when a man depends for his income—at best a pitiable, almost negligible dream—upon the completed output of his pen. Eh—what? As the English are said to say. Therefore I may reply that while upon the "mountain top," I am not "tiptop"—rather tipped-over, emptied, futile as a dumped can. I have sought vainly for the "great unutterable thought" to which you refer, with your addendum foul as to the internal apparatus of compassion—I have read 1st John, Ecclesiastes, Psalms (some of 'em), 9th and 10th Romans, slathers of Proverbs, carefully avoiding entangling alliance with doctrinal points, and refusing each theological crux, Romola, Kreutzer Sonata, Anna Karenina, Judgment House, Bleak House, Col. House—and find myself worse and worse with each, and less provided with great thoughts, utterable or otherwise. Nor can (Apropos of Great Unutterable Thoughts, etc.) I answer the *Transcript's* "Gizzey Gamme"—nor do I hold myself responsible in the slightest degree for the vagaries nomenclatural of the Smyth family, past, present, or future—a family which dubs a charming old lady "Totty," when her lovely name is Charlotte; which calls a boy Cheves—which is ill enough to strangers—"Chimpy"; Austin, "Ocky"; David McCord, "Cordite"; Louisa McC. Stoney, "Gary Evans"; Loula Stoney, "The Old Woman"; Aunt Sarah Ann, "Taddy"[1]—may shoulder the responsibility of "Gizzey Gamme," and explain it, if it can. I refuse to be held responsible for the eccentric performances of those dead and dusty this many a moon, I reckon—as those defunct Smyths of Gloucestershire; moreover, I believe these, our, Smyths, Smiths, Smythes, or What You Will, came out of Yorkshire into Ireland—which still further lightens my responsibility for any eccentricity. We had a full table the day *Okrantomottis*[2]—classic Greek, that!—reached us; and your verses were read aloud, lifting a cloud with their genial rays—and I'll be hangit, if, every day since, inspired thereby, Mrs. Smythe has not had okra soup for dinner! Its "Panacea," however, has not yet "revivified my powers," imaginary trouble still lowers behind the plenty unimaginary of the same—and "troubles," real and false, such as you refer to, beset me round day long—your "revivifying sedative," what paradox! refuses its aid in this case: am I too far gone, or is it that I am not a true-born Charlestonian, and, being entirely decamouflaged, demirouflaged, depersiflaged, forever must remain beyond its genial aid—only a damned Yankee? Tell me soon, please, how many plates of *Okrantomottis* are requisite to cure *natal Yankitis*—and how many potsful will mend a mind diseased, and greatly relieve your most melancholic

Jacques

Being which I should have my soup served "As You Like It." The madame is all be-swollen with pleased vanity at your signature; her "egregious admirer"—noble and ingenious.

"Many Pines," East Flat Rock, No. Ca.
Sept. 16th, 1919

Dear Yates: . . .

Wish I had time for persiflage; but we are packing ready for our return to Charleston, via Dodge, Highway & Bye-Way, Tuesday next, to reach the classic but mildewed city by the sea on the following day—

We have just shipped our eldest, Jane, to her school in Mass. by automobile, with Miss May Parker and Miss Sue Alston, via Washington, where she will view the great peerade on the 17th—and perhaps see Lieut. Augustine Stoney, Loula's boy, in all his glory with the 5th Artillery of the famous First. Sam and Loula are already in Washington, having been also in New York, glorifying in the parade there. I hope the excitement of the parade will stimulate my daughter sufficiently to make grade in her Latin exam., she having been conditioned in that deceased thing last year owing to insufficient ground-work at Ashley Hall—breathe it not abroad, however.

Paper is out—so is your admiring and confectionary follower:

J. Bennett

Please remember me to His Honour W. W. Ball and give my great respect to your wonderfully sweet wife, whom none knows but to admire.

#37 Legaré St., Charleston, S.C.
December Steenth or sich; Anno Dom: MCMXIX
[22 Dec. 1919]

Blessed Youth:

Yours of September 25th, cursing me, and refusing further to be my Romeike[3]—who asked you to be? anyway?—and yours of November 8th, subsequent thereto, apparently reconsidering and romeikeing again, received, several years ago, and forgotten hurriedly, as one does obnoxious perfumes during the Paradise of the year, somewhere between jessamine and June. I further acknowledge—to keep the record straight— as South Carolina newspapers always say when bolstering up some historical falsehood with asseveration, in a flamboyant style with which you are familiar—receipt of a really touching and well-deserved tribute to Walter Porcher, which I had read and recognized as yours, unmistakably, in the Courier of Nov. 4, '19, and an exceedingly interesting monograph on that forgotten man, Robert Mills—being a bulletin of the South Carolina University, No. 77, by Chas. C. Wilson[4]—why do I not receive ALL such bulletins? Or is a stipend connected with it? Say, and I will borrow from my wife such pay as may be necessary to have them delivered regularly at my study-door—further, received, among the ruck of above, two perfect copies of that wonderful poem, gem of gems, song of songs, much better by far than Solomon's, and far less fussed up by theologians—namely "In a Rose Garden," by Me, clipped from the New York Times Book Review, of April 2, 1910, apparently by you, and from the Springfield Republican, of Sept. 22, 1919, ditto: which would go to show, what I once believed, that the only successful rival to "Home, Sweet Home" is a castle in Spain—in the passionate affection of men's minds. It is only when men have given over the hunt for the mirage, and abandoned all dreams of the castle in Spain, that they really long with unspeakable yearning for the door-step of Home, Sweet Home! But it puts hooks in their hearts then!

Now, how to acknowledge your courtesies, catalogued above, how to tell you what a wonderful fellow you are, and what persistence is yours, thus to pursue a silent correspondent into every hidie-hole in oblivion until this holy season rolls around, and even the grouch mellows, and returns to the charge, thus, and thus, and thus!

Dismiss the futile effort, and let's get on with the rodent-killing. You're a good fellow. That brief phrase is crammed with hearty feeling, appreciation and what-not. I do not deserve your constancy: I never did; but, my dear, did I ever pretend to? . . .

You ask me why I do not send to the compiler of "From the Golden Books" other verses of mine than the perennially blooming Rose Garden? There was a time when I did that, and when I sought that bubble reputation at the cannon's mouth. But I think I should reap little benefit for myself from requests to print further verses that seem naturally to have died, and to have been permitted to die by the general, and kept only by the few. Folk will not have variety; it is the old familiar line they want. And, truly, I am pleased enough to have furnished a few old familiar lines to bloom like monthly roses in the Query Column. "Write another beautiful poem," you say, as if the writing of poems was carpentry or snug-joining. Don't you know, dear fellow that the writing of beautiful poems that convince of their sincerity and their passion is a matter for youth and not for limping eld? Songs are not often written on the icy side of fifty, and most of those then written earn early and appropriate forgetfulness for themselves—for they're dead as the devil. Browning's lines have been an inspiration to me for several years; a blessed older sister of mine sent me the quotation—I think out of her own experience of their light—at a time of intense depression: "Grow old along with me," she began with, and so through to the end of the passage. Knowing how hard it is to her to perceive age stalking at her side, and already to feel his rugged gripe upon her ardent spirit, the power of the lines came home with force to me. I had met them, years ago, reading Browning with my other sister—the better half of me, head of the English department at Dana Hall school. I'd like to believe it true in my own case, that "The best of life is yet to be." I admit my courage shakes, and fears assail me in the cold gray dawn in a manner sickening. I must pass over much; some things I cannot comment on. I am now working at the queer legend of "Madame Margot," the San Domingan milliner who sold her soul to the Devil that her daughter might be white.

I have been at it over a year—was too stale to do a fit line all summer—
have been back at it since October—but had to work up to it by means
of writing verse of several sorts—on old beginnings and metres, things
twenty years old and over. Several of these I finished, and spurred by
your suggestion, have been trying them upon the better class of editors—
for I will not print with the worse class—but the better are worse for me;
they will have none of it. But the training put my hand in trim. I may
have said all this before. And I am now putting speech into the mouth
of the Devil himself, whom I have just introduced: a fine, original Devil,
resembling Marc Antokolski's[5] Satan—though I may have spelled the
Bolshevik sculptor wrong—Judge Smith, John Marshall and Old
Moreland[6]—there's a star gathering equal to the recent cataclysmic line-
up in the heavens. I had hoped, long ago, to have had this tale done, and
done to suit myself, and, perhaps, there being charity abroad, to have
had opportunity to read it before that gathering of critics, the Kosmos
Club of Kolumbia; but it could not was; not till; so I work on, sometimes
with hope and inspiration, oftener with fear and prayer—for I do pray,
and fervently, although a hopeless heretic and an outcast with dogs and
sorcerers.

Truly, Yates, I should like to leave behind me a book of strange tales
of Old Charleston, of a quality to live a generation or two after me, if
only to justify my pretensions to ability—of which I have made very few,
God knows—and to prove my right to exist. I just can't talk about this
much; the matter lies too deep at heart; I'd write my fingers to the bone
to do it; but God Almighty only knows if I shall have the chance
uninterruptedly to toil until the thing is done.

I have now been in the South for twenty years; and have almost
nothing to show for it. But this is one of the things I cannot talk about;
so we won't. But as to writing beautiful poems at request, dear lad, do
you remember what the lady in the morning lesson said to the angel who
suggested that she bear more children: "Sir," she said, in a modest tone
of rebuke, "It isn't done, at my age!" Those may not be exactly her
words; and as I think it over, I do not believe they are; but they were
somewhat to that effect.

I want, completing "Madame Margot," to write next either "Doctor
Robin Russell, who Borrowed a Man's Soul, and died of it because the
other fellow's time was up," or "Doctor Ryngo, Physician to the Dead,
who fell in love with a beautiful woman a hundred years in her grave,"
and went to the devil from thwarted regard of the impossible. Sound
interesting, eh? Seems so to me.

I have also been trying some brief sketches, dialect, humorous,
illustrated by myself en silhouette: I have sent you the reverse of one as
token of undying affection. You may fancy it: *no editor does.* . . .

Facility is not mine. The lovely things that I have done from time to time which so excite your envy and admiration—and upon the multiplied earnings of which one might, perhaps, if economical, discomfortedly starve, are all the results of sweating toil. I was three years and over writing that Rose Garden song you like—and got $4.00 for it—from the Chap-Book, Stone & Kimball pubs., Chicago. No more of this. I only wanted to add new wonder in your mind as to why my good wife married me. Search me! I do not know; and never shall, I guess.

It often causes me to lie awake at night wondering. Do you lie awake at night wondering why an angel married you?

The price of one of my books has riz to $1.75; another has gone out of print: the gain on one seems to me to be quite offset by the entire loss of the other. This is chaos. We must get the Reds deported, rid the country of the Bolsheviki; we must sell more—of my—books!

What about the enclosed sensational anecdote, concerning death at a wedding from D. Federal shells, in Charleston? The reply annexed cannot possibly refer to the occasion of the query; not even a Roman Priest, be he never so transcendental, would "proceed with the ceremony" of marriage when the bride was shot to pieces. Tell me what is there in this tale of de Rochelle and Anna Pickens. I can find nobody seems to know; Johnson's Defense[7] is mum, as I discover. Return stuff, please.

How about the "new verse"? Amy Lowell and the rest? Use it any? They used to print it prose form and call it "etchings." Now they break line and call it verse. What do you know about it? Approve?

Tried "The Abbot of Derry" on a dozen editors; all said times too dry for drinking songs; Life ventured behind its hand to whisper that the sentiment was good but too ricochet for prohibition days. I have a deuced good air to it. Do you suppose tipplers would dare sing it sotto voce, behind closed and bolted cellar-doors? If so, I'll print.

We are having a comical Christmas, the gude wife and I. Our youngest is hard and fast abed with scarlet fever—a very light case, uncomplicated, and thus far, in no way alarming—but stringent quarantine just as necessary for protection of others. We have been locked in behind a fine yellow label three weeks: shall be in quarantine until mid-January.

(Second volume Gibbon's Rome:)

. . . Jane is home for the holidays from . . . school in Massachusetts—you have no such schools down here: see, I hurl it in your teeth! She and Jack are staying at Miss Sarah Annie's, next door—we talk with them across fifteen feet of "safety first," that we may not frighten and stampede the neighbors—you'd fancy us lepers by the way many turn and dodge on sight, though we be stenchified, disinfect and fumigated to the Nth power of purification. The remainder of the family will join in hilarious orgies at Loula Stoney's, Christmas Day; but we, alas! shall sit by the dull fire and suck our thumbs, the Missus and I—unless I shall previously discover a bottle of Madeira somewhere in the empty locker, on which she and I may warm up some temporary joviality for the appearance of things upon this Feast of Christmas-keeping folk. The way we smell is awfully carbolic. Smell close; you'll note formaldehyde upon this letter.

Guess you'll wish quarantine were not so close which gave opportunity for such a confounded, long-winded screed as this turns out to be! Sorry, Yates! But I have not seen anyone to talk to rough for so long that my feelings were not to be restrained. Although a Yankee I find no joy in rough talk to my wife. By the way, wasn't it the older Wade H——n, whose wife finally refused to come down from her room to eat at table with him because his methods with her were brutal? And, when he started for the stair, saying "I'll fetch her down!" was confronted by his daughter, with a chair, and a promise, to which she was equal, of knocking him down if he tried it, and, staring at her one moment, laughed, in his pleasant way, and said appreciatively "Humph! Chip of the old block!" Tell me the truth of this tale, won't you? Or is it only slander? I get so puzzled what to believe in studying South Carolina history—that is why I fear to print what I know—and the whole falls still-born.

We drove down by your house in the Autumn; but it was closed fast; no one seemed at home; and you, we found, were giving lectures to the prisoners. I said, fervently, "Thank God!" and left a card for you with a specious, pleasant and well-mannered youth, who promised to deliver it as soon as we were out of town. We hurried on. The children got many pictures round the Campus, of the old College buildings, and of Col. McCord's house—he was another genial, disputatious old-time noble! Eh, what?

But this is too much.

You've said it!

Blessed man, if ever you read it through; and see in it what I've been trying to say: I send deep affection to all who are yours, with my wife's regards to you and Mrs. S., and honest wishes for a Happy Christmas and a prosperous New Year. May good fortune of every sort attend your days, and ever cheer your stout heart!

Merry Christmas!

—also Chris'mus giff', boss!
I remain always—apologetically,
but truly—
Yours,
Ichabod

Truly, man, forgive this infernal memoir!

Nothing you have ever done, not even passing on poems for me to decide on, deserves such treatment.

Please give that gallant editor, W. Ball, my regard and speak my courteous compliments to Mr. A. Gonzales when you see him. Will printing never lower so that we may see his book?

John Bennett

Sam Stoney's automobile shot him in the wrist the other day, and laid him up with a back-fire. Avoid cranks.

23d Dec. '19

My dear John:

A thousand thanks for Rev. Brown of Edisto. I would have carried it to show Ambrose Gonzales, but he is weakening every day, methinks, and just now is staying out at his (?) country-place, preparing for a visit from the Ambassador to Peru. He has not touched his Gullah stories and dialect studies for over six months, tho' up to that time he worked on them every day, & sometimes had Stanhope Sams at his house until 1 A.M. working on his 2000 (?) word Gullah glossary; I fear now, it never will be finished, tho' he says he is going to work again "after Willie goes." The charming little silhouette card with its thrilling inscriptions, came this morning. The airy-fairy, "come-with-a-song," graceful mov't of that youth reminds me of myself some 48 years ago. You should have known me in my golden (or brazen) prime before I married.

If ever you have a chance to "call-up," from the great beyond, my old friends Charlie O'Connor, Palmer Lockwood, Hartwell Ayer,[8] or dear old Walter Porcher (who, strange to say, had a great fancy and admiration for *you!*)—ask *them!* You could scarcely imagine what a jocund, jovial, jocose, genial Jeems I was before marriage, old age and prohibition soured me!! . . .

You said nothing about the chillun. Blessings on them and their mother too from me & mine.

In the usual haste and with the same d——ned pen,

Yours affectionately,
Yates Snowden

Columbia, *5th April 1920*

Cara Mia,

I have not heard you *roasted* for many years. Until today I would have believed you, if I trusted to common report, an Admirable Crichton[9] in learning; a St. Francis of Assisi in moral character; a Bysshe Shelley in "honey dew" and "milk of Paradise" consumption. *But* my friend Father Croft Wms. stopped me this A.M. Quoth he: "Have you seen that bodacious (so he called it) act of John Bennett? *Stole* my Edisto earthquake story, word for word!!! Capristi. Sacre bleu. Mille tonnerres," &c., &c., &c.

A few minutes later A. E. G. *loquitur:* "Those silhouettes of Mr. Bennett's are remarkable! He has caught the *exact* pose of the Coast nigger, &c., &c., &c.; *but* his dialect is defective in several instances. I expect Old Brabham is right, *I am the only* now, Tighe possibly excepted, who *knows* Gullah!" The dear old fellow is a little vain methinks. I only remarked: "All the more important then, Ambrose, that you knuckle down, & finish, & *publish* your Gullah stories and 2000 word Gullah Glossary!"

I like to tell my friends agreeable things like this.

Here endeth the 15th lesson!

Yours very much,
Yates Snowden . . .

April 9th, 1920

Dearest Beloved and Detestable Yates:

A murrain fall on your friendly reports! If your opinions of me were at fault, God knows I have never painted to have them. Revise them at leisure, and, as I said to your fidus achates, Alex Salley, be damned to you! Name your lethal weepon, and appint the fatal place!

As for the perjured Father Croft—that earnest agent of futile reform in this State of perdition's inheritance—he told me I might use his bloody story, two years ago at Flat Rock: if he denies this I bite my thumb—observe, I bite my thumb!

Two obeisances as we approach the Dean of Dialect for the District of South Carolina, Low Country. Please, sir; I was not trying to write good Gullah, but something the damned fools would print. Let it be known of all men, Gullah is a precious and esoteric thing for home consumption, unknown to philologists afar, and anathema and contemnation to those who sit in the seats of the scornful magazine editor. Why strive in vain with wild beasts at Ephesus? I must get my stuff printed, or how in hades get money? In humility and respect I offer this apology for trifling with so sacred a subject, such a sanctum sanctorum, as REAL GULLAH.

N.B.: Not to label the Editor of The Southern Review as a damned fool. Far from which, he seems to be a very pleasant and appreciative gentleman.

I'm not ass enough to think I can write Gullah as the Master can.

God's sake, clear me of imputations!

And repeatedly urge Mr. Gonzales to complete volume and glossary. Who is to print it, the State Printing Company, or God?

Sounds irreverent; but isn't: I've tried near every common or garden publisher: they won't have Gullah. Mine's rotten, however; I admit; I don't claim to excel; I have only a few parlor tricks. . . .

We have . . . no expert magistrates . . . unless Theodore Jervey[10] is one; and he fined me ten dollars—TEN DOLLARS—for running 25 mi. per hour, up Meeting Street road—if that is expert magistracy, God save the mark!

I have appealed to heaven a number of times in this letter; after your vile assault upon the troubled peace of a man engaged upon the most difficult labor of his fool career, I have need to call upon some superior thing! Should I express frankly and fearlessly my opinion of one of my calibre attempting to earn a livelihood or earn a just repute by literature, the message would go smouldering through the mails, and burst in flames when it was opened to Columbia's oxygen.

So, farewell, thou deeply troubling spirit!
If you meet any other kindred spirits
—of any sort—remember me as
Yours Intentionally,
Sir Fretful Plagiary[11]

Sabbath Morn.
4th July 1920
Sheol, S.C.

Dear Jack:

I saw the notice of the death of Mrs. Feilden in the N&C; cut it out & then promptly lost it. I told Ball it was "good stuff" for a neat little semi-editorial, or better perhaps a "local"; but he could not find the notice, or did not look for it; and there the matter rests. If *I* had the clipping I don't know enough about the lady perhaps to write it myself.

There *now!* Sit down, sweetness, and write a semi ed or local or "*communication,*" as *coming from an old Columbian;* give the main facts referring incidentally to Col. McCord's house at the corner of Pendleton and . . . [Bull] streets; say that the late Mrs. (Col.) Thos. Taylor,[12] or Miss Isabel Martin[13] *would have remembered* her; say that "the girls of the Sixties" (a very *live* organization of sprightly old ladies here) *may have* some members *now* who remember her, e.g., Mrs. S. Rhett Roman; Mrs. Berwick Legaré, Mrs. Cornelia Davidson, Mrs. Clark Waring (?) and others, & wind up with "a stick" about Col. Feilden! I will copy in my own beautiful chirography, and I will insert some little details that you (old stoopid Yankee!) could not possibly know, and so everybody, including Ball & Fitz McMaster and *especially Mrs. Smythe* will be fooled & will think it is a home product. Try to come down to my level in style & content, oh effendi!

Or, if you are still roasting in Legaré St., write this stuff and carry it 'round the corner to Mrs. Beatrice Ravenel[14] who is an editorial writer for The State. She will thank you for a splendid filler for her colyum, and you will save a 2¢ stamp.

Either send it to me or Mrs. Beatrice R. I don't care which, so long as you write it. I am confident *it would please* Mrs. Smythe even at this late day. My regards to your gude wife.

I kiss your hand (if washed),
&c., &c., &c.,
Yates Snowden

9th July 1920

Dear Jack:

You don't deserve any of my charming letters, so I will not write you one.

You have not answered my last proposal; it may be a fool idea; it may be too belated. If so, why don't you say so? Not a word from you! But—I can't help sending you this clipping from Christopher Morley's (*he can* write!) column in the N.Y. Ev'g Post; a poem of S. V. *Benet,* "Song in a Summer Garden"!*

It no more compares with "In a Rose Garden" than Hercules to Snowden; Hyperion to a satyr; wine unto water; Lee unto Grant, &c., &c., &c.

"Shall I compare Lee to his successful antagonist? As well compare the pyramid which raises its majestic proportions in the Valley of the

Nile to a pigmy perched on Mt. Atlas!" Old Jubal Early, pyramid, & pigmy! Rather mixed metaphor!

&c., &c., &c.

Yours, as you show yourself!
Y. Snowden

* NB! I have read some most excellent stuff by this Stephen V. Benet, who is, I believe, highly regarded by the intelligentsia; but this does not suit my mediaeval, or Mid-Victorian, fancy any more than "Troy Town's Afire."

"Many Pines," East Flat Rock, N.C.
July 15th, 1920

Dear Yates:

All right, lynching-party—where's your stake and kerosene: I don't deny I'm unforgivable.

I had not the clipping, either, and after search, could not find it, the current newspapers being used to kindle fires with. I knew no more than you about the lady; neither did my wife, whose kinswoman she was; we were here at Flat Rock, and Mrs. Smythe in Charleston, due to come later, but engaged in packing Mrs. Austin Smythe for the trip.

There was a time when I should have enjoyed writing a "semi-editorial" about a lady of whom I knew nothing; but it has passed; about thirty years ago, I think.

All Mrs. Bennett could tell me certainly about her British aunt was that Mrs. F. had become so completely Anglicized as to be no longer able to understand United States currency or news; and that she never wanted to return to the dear old States. If that would be good material for your semi-editorial from the standpoint of a Columbian, get to it yersel' and write: I'll not.

By the way you reel off the blessed old ladies' entitlements—which, in your hasty, but beautiful Italian hand, I found it difficult to decipher—I don't see why you didn't just interview yersel', insert some of those little details of golden Confederate glory—save the mark!—which insure the authenticity and home production of Southern articles—and let it go; 'twould be quite as authentic as most Southern history and biography, and more interesting, being the handiwork of genius, not of a purchased hack.

I have done, tried to do, and am ready to do a deal to please that revered lady, Mistress S.; but, Yates, take my word for it, I am too damnably out of spirits (non-alcoholic), to write. I am trying to get something of my own done, and making hard going of it these past two years, and that buoyance of soul which formerly made me envied of the men and beloved of the ladies, has been, some time, as dead as your own nullification—of which I do not speak lightly, but hurry to lay another rock on its bier—Volsted Act.

I am taking little interest in things; but hope, by the end of summer, to find some. I am thinking of putting in three weeks in Ohio with my people: perhaps among stoopid Yankees I may regain my soul, lost in South Carolina.

I shall leave my wife and daughters here; the boy at Rob Perrin and John Moore's Camp, Transylvania, near Brevard, making up math. and Latin, which he flunked at Porter's.

I should have told you I could not write the lady's remembrance, long ago. But I didn't. As it is you, I apologize, asking pardon: to anyone else neither. She is dead, and in peace, one trusts; and so far to be envied truly; it is a fine thing to be in peace, I think—for I am not, certainmong, as your Huguenot ancestry used to say.

As to S. Vincent Benet's "Sung in a Summer Garden," all that you say as to its inferiority to "In a Rose Garden," I admit. As to Christopher Morley's ability—he can write. By God, I wish I could again! I am too mouldy and too old, pardie! Time hath dropped his monkey-wrench in my machinery.

I know nothing of Stephen Vincent Benet's stuff—Father, I confess with shame! But I am not of the intelligentsia, which I take it is the latest formula for cognoscenti? I belong forever'n'ever to the Ignorami. I can't help thinking that your quotation from Jubal Early is rather asinine— piffle and tush! R. E. L. was, without doubt, the finest thing we've done on this continent, he, and the earlier and simpler nobleman, G. W.— both Virginians, prythee! But it's the poorest way on our green earth to praise a man by simply down-crying his antagonist. I used to say, with a boy's honest fervor, "Thank God Grant won!" I am not sure I say so now. The old enthusiasm wanes, and here are Cox and Harding, and Lodge and Tom Watson[15] and Hon. Richard S. Whaley[16] and William Turner Logan[17] and Rumty Rattles, The Crisis and Burghardt DuBois, and Eugene Debs, campaigning for President in jail, and the sorry affairs of our Allies, and our present pusillanimity on the face of the earth, and my old firm belief in the American common people, and foreign opinion of us, part-deserved—and, worst of all, my own lost happy opinion of mysel'—just that—and all gone to ballyhack together!

God bless you, and preserve your indomitable soul, world without end, amen! If you but belonged to the one True Church I should be sending you a dollar to put up a candle at some kindly shrine for me: I need illumination of some sort.

It's far too late to do what you suggest regarding Mrs. Feilden. No, it's not; but I can't do it—not while thus wrestling with blue devils as I am—and the roads soup, and the rain raining Shakespearially!

Lead me to your stake; libate with kerosene; apply the torch! Farewell, dull world, farewell!

Yours per best Scotch blues
or something sair depressant
to the soul of man:
Jack Bennett

Burn this—and me.

---

803 Sumter Street, Columbia, S.C.
Saturday Night, June the 24th I believe
[July 24, 1920]

My dear old crazy John:

That was the sourest epistle I ever rec'd from you, and it has worried me. Get out of that "grouch"; it ill becomes you, and is not fair to that devoted wife of yours or to those little ones—not so "little" now, by the way. And it is not fair to those people among whom your lot has been cast; narrow, provincial and all that; but very many of them love, and thousands of them admire you.

Go to some neighboring "cave"; get some of "the fiery bright dew of the mountains, yellowed by peat-reek and mellowed by age"! Get on your first drunk; *anything;* but get over that grouch!!!

As to your literary output. I read, t'other day, of some fool Englishman accounting for Arthur Clough's[18] "mental laziness" by the fact that from the age of 4 to 10, *he had lived in Charleston,* and his mind had been permanently enervated by the sub-tropical climate. In your present insane condition I believe you are durn fool enough to apply that idiotic idea to yourself.

Simms ground out very much stuff (too much) in that enervating climate, which is the same latitude as Jerusalem, where several big men worked, and which Signor Gener y Macias, sometime vice-consul for Spain, told me very much resembled the climate of Charleston.

If you wish to encourage and insure permanent melancholia, let me know, and I'll send you my grandmother's copy of Zimmerman on Solitude, and better still, the poetical works of *James Thomson* which includes his "City of Dreadful Night." That Reverend Republican politician R. W. Memminger[19] (father of the judge), who was crazy too, wrote "The Diary of a Recluse," while living in the delectable mountains, at Flat Rock I believe. Get *that;* it will put you in a whirl of excitement.

Have you read *Madam Constantia,* by "Jefferson Carter"? The agt. of Longmans, Green & Co., the publishers was here last year, & I asked him *who* "Jefferson Carter," evidently a pseudonym, was? He said if I wrote to the publishers, he had no doubt they would tell me. The gentleman lied; I wrote to L. G. & Co. two weeks ago, telling them how much I liked the book and why; how glad I was that S.C. was the scene &c., &c., & asked who *he* was? Nary answer!

I told them in my letter that *you* were the only person in S.C. who could have written it; but that I was sure you were not the author—one reason being the utterly impossible pen picture of Francis Marion—of which *you* could not have been guilty! Tell me, when you next write, what *you* think of the book.

Here I *must* stop; I've owed my poor sister a letter for over a week.

Yours affectionately,
Yates Snowden

NB! I am not an ardent admirer of Dixie Whaley; but, Good Lord! he is far superior to that slick renegade Turner Logan! Why does not *Austin Smythe* run?

Your explanation as to the English lady, & why you cannot and will not send the stuff for an obit, perfectly satisfactory! R.I.P.

I put that Jubal Early Grant-Lee comparison in my letter to rile that Yankee spirit (which you imagine possesses you). You bit!

Chillicothe, Ohio: Aug. 15, 1920

Dear Yates:

Peccavi! Also Apologia pro Vitae Sua: I am here, where I was foaled, faithfully endeavoring to cure the grouch by bringing to a successful end work which thro' these years of casualty, has remained hanging like the proverbial millstone, around my neck. Not absolutely certain I can do so. But on my word, Doctor, I'm taking the medicine you prescribed—although it trespasses boldly on the Harrison Law against narcotics and nepenthes—since one may no longer—at least he may not here!—drown

Sorrer in the Floin Bole! Thanks for the prescription, Doc! N.C. previous to Aug. 26 when rates are raised; or I'll be stranded!

Yrs.:
Pertinax Surly[20]

My compliments ever to Mrs. S.

J. Bennett

Columbia, [2 Dec. 1920]

My dear old John:

I have not pestered you for some time, and I hope you are duly grateful; but, here goes!

Read these lines "At Eighty-Three," by my old friend Major J. F. J. Caldwell;[21] and *if, as I think,* several stanzas have real merit, simple as they are, write me a line if only a postal card, to that effect!

If *I* were to write him, he would argue to himself very properly, thusly:

(1) "Snowden is no critic."

(2) "If Snowden were a critic, he lets his friendship blind him as to the merit or demerits of my verses. It's only a *succes d'estime!*"

But, if I were to enclose him a few lines of favorable criticism from the eminent John Bennett of Chillicothe-Charleston, arf and arf, it would tickle the dear old fellow all over. If, as is probable, your critic's eye sees nothing in the old man's verses above the deadly commonplace, then don't write me a durn thing.

Reed Smith was delighted with your beautiful letter. Whether it was mock modesty or not, he said he did not "know how to answer such a letter"! The truth is (when he brought me your letter) he was so busy loving and preparing for that "dreadful leap in the dark" that he did not have a mind for anything else.

When I marched up to the bride & groom, at their crowded reception, as soon as he saw me he turned to his bride of an hour, and said presumptiously: "Kiss that man!"

And she done it very gracefully!

I saw a momentary gleam of defiance in her eye; it was the first *order* he had given her; but she had just promised to "love, honor & *obey*"! The

Presbyterians still retain that mediaeval promise. My blessed wife also made that same promise, but—

(See the advantage of 62 years and gray hair!! You will be old some day yourself. Cheer up!)

Twice I have been asked of late at the Kosmos Club: "Can't you get John Bennett up here again?"

1000 good wishes for you and yourn.

Yours aff'ly,
Y's Snowden

Sabbath Eve.
[Dec. 12, 1920]

Dear John:

Having rec'd no answer to my inquiry as to the merit of J. FitzJames Caldwell's verses, I must conclude that you find *no merit* in any of them—just what I feared. Now, effendi! don't think that I swallow *all* your opinions without a gulp, but as to the literary merit of poetry, I think that you—like the Pope and Aleck Salley—are infallible.

James FitzJames has not quaffed the divine ichor; he has not fed on "honey dew" or "the milk of Paradise"; his inspiration must have been the "tussick" of Newberry's back woods.

Turn over this page & you will find a rough copy of a letter sent by me this day to the Century Company.

Love to all.
Thine,
Y. S.

Glad to see poems by DuBose Heyward[22] & Mrs. Beatrice Ravenel listed in Stanley Braithwaite's[23] anthology. Why have *you* written no poems, lazy bones?

Charleston, December 14th, 1920

Dear Yates:

You're certainly one of the best chaps going, and I must get a printed form of apology for not replying to your letters.

Yours of December 2 and 12 before me, with the Episcopal prayer book, opened at "We have left undone the things that we ought to have done, and there is no health in us."

The lines by Maj. Caldwell made me think of a quotation which very well expresses what I want to say first:

> "Kind hearts are more than coronets,
> And simple faith than Norman blood."

There is a frank, manly simplicity about Maj. Caldwell's verses that disarms adverse criticism; it is simple, unacademic poesy, sincere in its inspiration, pleasantly excellent, and full of a courageous, generous solicitude not for himself, but for others, which is refreshing to see in a day of morbid introspection and radicalism such as we find too often everywhere. It opens like a saddening verse, but closes like a hymn—a sort of brave meditation. It is a little long for its impulse; but eighty-three years may very well be excused the grind of condensations, and commended for its clarity and simple faith—to which I referred above.

Dear Yates, there is something in "an old man's verses"—as you style Maj. Caldwell's—that makes them fine, however far from classic fire. The heart that sings at eighty-three is brave; and though it be a hymn, the simple piety of the Major's day is not to be despised of us of none—and is not, but much wondered at in a crazy world, and envied in its grave confidence.

I am glad Reed Smith was pleased with my epistle; I was immensely pleased with his essay on "Great Prose Passages." I have been trying to write some such myself; and had thought I had done so—at least to the limit of my gift; but I am unable to persuade an editor—nay, not so much as one among the throng—that there is any merit in my stuff. It is the grotesque legends of Charleston—they don't give a damn for 'em; and perhaps—as writ by yours truly—they are right. I am allowing the MS. to lie resting from its travelling until after the Christmas jam subsides, lest I lose my papers in the mails, and mess my MS. beyond ironing fresh again; but, after Christmas, off it goes again to try a few more of the Jove-like brains that control the current magazines. Meanwhile, since they do not seem to fancy these grotesqueries—or those they've been offered—I am considering a picaresque novel, a romance of adventure in the West Indies—say Jamaica—and Charleston, circa, 1810 Anno Dni. God knows what!

Your account of amorous adventures among the innocent salutatorian brides of Columbia, and reflections upon the marriage ceremony which provided your happy distinction for favors far beyond your merit, breed some envy in the hearts of youth, I admit: if, at sixty-two, I shall come at such, 'tis something to be lived for still! My hair, my dear fellow, is gray as yours, though I admit not so hyperion in its coil. As to the former obedience of wives, why drag in archaeology? And Presbyterian paleoliths, more kept in the breach than in the observance?

Had I something to read at Kosmos, I'd be delighted to be again the guest of that royal group; but truly, I have nothing whatever that will serve—and seem not likely to.

As to your sensational epistle of SABBATH EVE: I know not where you received your information that "Master Skylark" is *"out of print."* It is incorrect, extremely. "The Treasure of Peyre Gaillard" is out of print: I have his plates in my garage, neatly boxed: some day a South Carolina-printed edition, with glossary of facts and notes. But, far from being out of print, "Skylark" is in I know not what edition—the last I noted was the fourteenth, and like Johnny Walker, still going strong. In fact "Skylark" sells steadily and well; sold more copies this year than in any (save two especially opportune) years since the book was published; and the dramatized form sells in its small, special way, a few copies every year. So I am sorry your informant was himself so ill-informed as to prevent copious sales of this classic tale. Harry Kirk, at "Hammond's," *Broad Street, Charleston,* can always get copies for you—perhaps supply them immediately himself—if you cannot obtain service in your little town. Kirk has the book always in stock, except when the clamor has just bought him out clean; then he restocks. The only disadvantage that I know—it may, perhaps, be worth while to mention—is that, owing to the stringency in the book-making business and to the shortage in paper supply, particularly in plate-paper, almost all the charming illustrations by Reginald Birch[24] are having for the present to be omitted from "Master Skylark," and the kiddies have to be content—as I should not be, and am not at all—with but four or five pictures—and, instead of the pleasant green binding with red and white Tudor roses thereon, we are reduced by the printing-and-binding stringency to a buff back with single brown-ink stamped design, that I like exceeding little. And the retail price has jumped from 1.25 & 1.50 to 1.90 and $2.00!

Both "Skylark" and my second book, "Barnaby Lee," continue to sell steadily, I am happy to say: why not take a try at the second story, sometimes? They say it's not so bad—my brother, and Rev. Dr. Robt Wilson like it much better than "Skylark." That's as one chooses and is pleased. I send you enclosed a squib from Don Marquis's column in the New York Sun of Nov. 29th—to give you one lad's opinion—a pleasant note. Please return the clipping to me, Yates; I wish to preserve it in the Golden Book of newspaper clippings alongside of "In a Charleston Rose-Garden." At any rate please return it after you have read it four or five times and can repeat it from memory accurately enough to quote often.

Your appreciation of the book, however, will do the Century Co. good. I trust it falls into the hands of my friend, James Abbott, a good fellow.

Like you I was happy to see the poems by DuBose Heyward and Mrs. Ravenel in Braithwaite. It is not laziness, old top, which keeps me from writing poetry. I have no inspiration to do so. Poetry is for youth; and for age the oft-repeated line, "It might have been, but ain't!" Hence—

Have you seen that we have a Poetry Society in South Carolina—and that *I* am its *Vice President*—DuBose Heyward its Secretary, Miss Josephine Pinckney[25]—a charming girl—its Treasurer, or its treasure, too—and Frank R. Frost[26] its President—and that we are to fetch Harriet Monroe, Vachel Lindsay and other such *rarae aves* and pater nosters down this-a-way to read and lecture to the tradition of culture in this State? Go to—go to!

Life and I have not found so simple a solution as Maj. Caldwell's in a serene and childlike faith. I write no poetry: I have before referred you to Scripture for sufficing reasons why. The South is a fair land; but it has been my ruin.

How is that for Greek tragedy, my beloved? Fill the cup that cheers—to-morrow I shall be in these same clothes which I have occupied these half-a-dozen years—And as the gardener comes around to the Garden Gate to lock it, here at the corner of the way all I turn down will be an empty pocket.

Not that I care a darn about an empty pocket: in my mind empty pockets are synonymous with happy days and brave companionships. But, bless us, I have accomplished nothing of good things I dreamed to do, and the reasons why are inscribed in lady-like-and-violet writing-fluid and a fine Italian organ-grinder-and-a-monkey hand upon Rabbi Ben Ezra's[27] Day-Book or Journal.

If I seem depressed in aught, I'll tell the reason: I had my yard filled, a few weeks ago, to get it above tide-water, and I'm hanged if they didn't fill it with earth from a grave-yard—there are teeth and bones and coffin-nails and pewter rosettes all over everywhere, and naturally I am moved to brood upon mortality. No more just now—save a myriad good wishes and pleasant remembrances to your good wife and her sister—and for you, though you do little to deserve it, the very sincere affection—entirely hopeless of reward—of

Your friend,
John Bennett

Don't forget my clipping: I must have something exhilarating now that we are all so out of spirits.

Remember me to Smith and Wauchope and Holmes and Ball and Salley when next you meet them, one, or all.

My daughter, Jane, near 18, will be home, Friday a.m. from Bosting for the Christmas holidays.

We have a young fellow named Hervey Allen,[28] down here, at Porter's—who can write POETRY verily.

Chapter 10

1921

Acclaim for Master Skylark *and* The Treasure of Peyre Gaillard; *picture of Louisa Cheves McCord for a University publication; Snowden's commencement address on William H. Trescot, James D. B. DeBow, John McCrady, and Paul H. Hayne; publication of* Madame Margot *and its reception.*

IN JANUARY of 1921 the two friends wrote about a painting by John Beaufain Irving and also discussed a wood-cut portrait of Mrs. Louisa Susannah Cheves McCord to be used in a University of South Carolina Press publication.

In April Yates Snowden sent an admirer of John Bennett's *The Treasure of Peyre Gaillard* to Charleston to meet the author. On 17 May, Snowden gave the 1921 Commencement Address at the College of Charleston, "Four Names To Conjure By," on the accomplishments of several earlier graduates of the institution: the diplomat William Henry Trescot, the editor and statistician James Dunwoody Brownson DeBow, the scientist John McCrady, and the poet Paul Hamilton Hayne. Many other prominent South Carolinians were mentioned in the speech, which was published in full in the Sunday *News and Courier*, 22 May 1921.

At the end of the month Snowden sought to elicit help from Bennett for a proposed memorial to Paul Hamilton Hayne. In June, before the Bennetts left for Massachusetts to attend their daughter Jane's graduation from Dana Hall, Bennett assured Snowden that the Poetry Society of South Carolina had already proposed a scholarship at Converse College in Spartanburg in Hayne's memory, but that since such a tribute had not brought an immediate response, perhaps a different kind of memorial might be considered in the coming season.

When Bennett's grotesque legend of old Charleston, *Madame Margot*, was published in November, Snowden informed his friend of an article about to appear in *The State* praising its style but condemning its subject matter. Subsequently, Snowden received a delightfully imaginative letter from Bennett, who pretended to be in exile in Switzerland.

By December Bennett's new book had received much praise. That month Yates went to Greenwood to see the famous French commander, Marshal Ferdinand Foch, who visited South Carolina on his American tour after World War I.

Charleston, January 8th, 1921

Dear Yates:

My feeling of impatience and dull indignation with the perfunctory and ill-informed memorials printed in the News & Courier, is, perhaps, not equal to your native frenzy; but is very genuine. But I cannot embark on any career, however brief, of rescuing the already forgotten from undeserved oblivion and neglect—blame it on your proud and haughty State, or this Notable Community, as you may prefer, not upon the stranger within her gates, who finds it difficult to keep his own head above water without extending a helping hand to the departed worthy. The dead past must indeed bury its own. The living ask hope and friendly encouragement: this, like an ass of seeming conceit with his own quality, I endeavor to give to sundry young: I can no more. . . .

Pictures drawn on sunny days, perennially sunny—and like John Keats's Grecian loveliness, unchanging—silent but serene, and filled with the old charm of England's rural counties—which, God knows, one trusts, may still survive the wreck of fabrics and the overturn of times—though walk among its comfortable lanes and bright-grassed fields one may never—but in dreams. Such dreams gave me my first successful book: do you see the New York Sun: Don Marquis and I, by accident, gave quite the biography of my book, a few weeks since, in his popular column, the DIAL: did you know that Brandl, the great German English scholar, called my tale "Ein Meisterwerk," and said of it, in the Vol. XL, of the "Shakespeare Jahrbuch," "Aber die Absicht is gut, and die Abbildungen auch"?—in the most important Shakespeare journal on earth? No? Well, now you know. Farewell, and ever, thanks and affectionate regard,

from
Jack Bennett

My sincere compliments to Mrs. S. and her charming sister: regards to Ball, and Holmes, and Wauchope—ay, and A. Salley—should it chance.

Your visitation was as the outburst of cold water—or fine wine—in a desert place.

Columbia, Sabbath Eve, 9th Jan'y 1921

My dear Johannes: . . .

By the way, have you & Mrs. J. B. seen the historical pt'g by J. B. Irving[1] (Sir Thomas More going to execution), which some very generous friend at the North has *given* to Dan Ravenel? When next strolling through the beautiful Boulevard Saint Michel, drop in at the corner and look at it.

Tout à vous,
Y. S.

Sunday Night 23d Jan'y [1921]
In a hurry!

Dear Johnny:

I know your artistic eye will be hurt by accompanying cut; you can tear it up if you will; but you will see it again! Miss Fraser tells me she is reading the proofs of her "story" of Mrs. McCord very carefully; and well she may, for the product of Green's[2] "University Press" is generally pretty poor.

Green has had a cut made of the McCord bust in Mrs. Smythe's beautiful pamphlet. It was made *here* and I hope it is good. Last week I stumbled upon a cut of Mrs. McCord on p. 250 of Vol. II of Duyckincks' Cyclopaedia of Am'n Literature, and as we only had a picture of the *bust*, I carried my big book 'round to the engraver and asked if he could not reproduce the portrait wood-cut. He said "yes" & that though a small vignette (?) he thought he could make a good picture. He changed his mind however and *enlarged* it so as to suit the page of the "Bulletin."

I am going to have printed *under* this picture: *"Enlarged from a wood-cut portrait in Vol. II of Duyckincks' Cyclopaedia of Amn Literature."* Send me a postal card saying *if that explanatory note is correctly worded!*

I am not familiar with the lingo of you artists. Would "vignette" be better than "wood-cut portrait"?

Write "only that and nothing more"!

Yours aff'ly,
Y. S.

Jan. 25, 1921

Dear Yates:

Yrs. rec'd.

"Enlarged from a wood-cut portrait," etc. *is correct.*

A: From a photographer's, or portrait-draughtsman's stand-point, this wood-cut portrait is *vignetted:* that is, it *fades away into the background.*

B: From a particularly correct and technical book-making stand-point, this wood-cut portrait is not a vignette, in that it is not the head or tail-piece to chapter or title-page.

C: Loosely and familiarly speaking, almost any portrait—particularly head or bust, is a vignette, no matter by what process—photo., wood-cut, copper or steel engraving it is produced.

Note A: In such sense vignette means only the *style of picture,* which is evident: *wood-cut portrait* tells the method of its production, thus explaining its peculiar character: *Wood-cut portrait* it is: and pretty good, being instantly recognized by Louisa Stoney without the signature. Mrs. Smythe quite satisfied and much interested: says "Use by all means."

All much interested in approaching publication:

Immense regard:
Pro Bono Publico.
[John Bennett]

1st Ap'l 1921

Dear John:

This will introduce to you Dr. S. W. Woodhouse[3] of Philadelphia.

I will let him speak for himself. If he interests *me,* who know so little, how much will he charm *you,* one of the cognoscenti, the Aleck Salleys of Charleston!

It is but fair to say that Dr. Woodhouse is laboring under one remarkable obsession; he really believes and stoutly asseverates that that nine days' wonder, "The Treasure of Peyre Gaillard," is a wonderful and beautiful book! I mentioned your name to him yesterday afternoon, and he instantly broke in: "You don't mean the author of that beautiful 'Treasure of Peyre Gaillard'?" "Yes," said I; and then, he told me a long story of buying the book in France, & of its infinite charm, &c., &c., &c., &c., and how he gages a man's, or woman's, taste and intelligence by asking him whether he has "read 'Peyre Gaillard,'" &c., &c., &c.

Now this pardonable weakness of the Doctor may appeal to *you*, and so, I rest.

> Your friend,
> Yates Snowden

———————————

June 8th, 1921

Dear Yates:

Your letter, dated May 31st, in an envelope stamped June 2d—enclosing your capital address on Trescot,[4] Hayne, DeBow[5] and McCrady[6]—reached me a few days ago. Your idea that I did not read your speech is erroneous: your statement that I stayed at home is correct: my sins are ever before me! You did not miss me: and I did miss you. My early wife says she discovered you gazing tragically at my mansion in an attitude of one about to throw a bomb, while I was absent, toiling like the devil for a thank-ye—as usual—I admit, to avoid argument—that I was always an ass.

I agree entirely with your indignant thrust at Charleston's forgetfulness of Hayne. Doubtless he loved Charleston: but Charleston? I cannot grow enthusiastic over Charleston's remembrance of those whom a city might well remember but forgets. I care little for *vers libre*—prefer Tom Hood's "Song of a Shirt" to Sandburg's: but, though I would like heartily to agree with your generous estimate of Hayne's too-prolific and level verse, I cannot. Yet if Timrod deserves a bronze bust—and I am not at all sure that he does—though a wisp of his work is very genuine —if he deserves a bronze bust, Hayne deserves remembrance in some more substantial form than a friendly and admiring tribute—even by yourself—in the Sunday News. It was proposed, last winter, through agency of the Poetry Society, to establish a Hayne scholarship for Charleston students—at Converse: but the reaction does not appear to have been at all vigorous—or the response immediate. Whether this will again be broached, next season I know not: I shall keep it in mind. The Converse Alumnae had this matter in hand, whether a tablet to Hayne, or a shaft could be erected is problematical—after my full experience during the war I should not join gaily in a "drive." But, somehow, there may be something done in Hayne's memory. But, God save you, Yates, I find not one in ten knows a line or a poem's title even, that he wrote. So will it, doubtless, be with the rest.

I would have writ you a nobler letter—and worse, being longer—but Mrs. Bennett and I are leaving in fifteen minutes, for Massachusetts, to attend the graduation of our daughter, Jane —and you may be grateful.

I shall remember Hayne next season—to what end I know not at all. We are all so damnably engrossed with forwarding our own position in the world. I hope to have one of my grotesque legends of Old Charleston issued, this autumn: "Madame Margot"—the little San Domingan milliner who sold her soul to the devil that her daughter might be white. I do not dream that the public will care for it. I hope only that a few may—and wonder if, indeed, the work is worth it?

Affectionately—and always unsatisfactorily yours—
John Bennett

From the sign of THE WANDERER
Somewhere Abroad:

Schweizerhof Lucerne
Hauser Freres   November 20, 1921
Prop.   *IN EXILE:*

Dear Yates:

Thanks for your warning. I fled at once to escape the anticipated outbreak of acute sociological sensitiveness, and am already comfortably settled here, in an obscure hostelry. The winter has already set in; there was a heavy fall of snow, last night, and all the mountain-crests are dazzling white with new snow. The wood-fire, however, snaps and sparkles merrily, and my only care is that I do not speak Swiss well and cannot in any of the stores find a Swiss phrase-book such as may readily be found in other languages: a damn queer oversight. I had just time to pack my heavy underwear, so I shall be quite comfortable, I think, until the Spring. And by that time I trust your hair-trigger emotionalism may have abated, the fury of an outraged populace have been soothed, and, in some light disguise, it may be safe for me to sneak home again! Home, home! None but the exile knows the true love of home! I was saying that to a very pleasant fellow, named Payne, J. H. Payne,[7] whom I met upon the train on his way to Algeria, a few days since: he was very much moved; looked suspicious, and said he hoped I did not mean to write upon the subject, as he himself had, the night before, dashed off a few lines on it, that he was *just waiting to borrow an envelope and stamp* to send to some American publisher. He incidentally showed me the verses; and though, as you know, I don't care a damn for poetry, they were not without a certain popular touch, which, if set to an old, familiar tune, such as school-children sing to "Our Father in Heaven," might achieve some brief success. He seemed so anxious about it, and so suspicious of me, that I said no more about home, did not ask further why he was going to Africa—of all places—and he was good enough to omit asking me why I travelled so hastily abroad, which, of course, he could easily surmise through my having snatched up only my last summer's broken straw-hat as I dashed from the premises where your timely warning reached me. God bless you, dear old fellow; I am deeply in your debt. If you will but stop by, from time to time, and assist my family (may I hint grocer's bills?), while I am secluded here, I shall be yours for life. Adios! Adios! I hear that Tom della T——re is in Zermatt. If this is so, I must fly again! How unfortunate; but I must not spoil his journey; he would be put in a devilish close place if he met *me* here, thus under a cloud.

I had seen the review of which you speak; and told the writer to print it, in the STATE, or anywhere; while it toasts one side and roasts the other it is both discriminating and appreciative, keenly so, and *well* worth while.

I am not greatly troubled. A lady, caught buying four copies at Hammond's, yesterday, remarked "It *is* beautiful; *but* IT IS NOT CHARLESTON!" Perspicacity, thy name is woman! It is perfectly true, it is not Charleston; but a wonderland, I think. As to what Mr. JOE B——ll[8] may say, I do not very much care; I hope it may be as sensible as emphatic.

The book is done, and, good or ill, is launched upon the sea. If it can win approval and repute as an adventure in English, I care very little any more for the adverse opinion of those whose over-delicate prejudices are offended or shocked by the "immoral beauty" of the tale.

But it is very funny to those who know the truth of many things. Pardon me, revered and honored paladin; no more—I hint no more!

But with my ears strained to the ground I listen with considerable interest to hear the echo from the book's impression upon the first reviewers; after whom the public. It is but a little, little book, squeezed out to one hundred and ten fair pages, a little square of type on each; it were very easily altogether lost among the 10,000 volumes a year the country prints.

I wonder very much.

And am figuring upon a second to the series—did you note the series?—which may be either "The Death of the Wandering Jew," or "The Doctor to the Dead," preferably, perhaps, the latter, as more likely to produce a social shock.

But, Yates, the winds may blow their bellies flat if they will but find that I have written singular English singularly well, and lent true loveliness, wistful beauty and tragic charm to a drab and sordid story, made an atmosphere original, not like aught that anyone anywhere has produced before, and created the unreal.

But while I am away, in God's name do not permit my innocent and unfortunate family to fall into obloquy undeserved or actual want, but see that they have food.

And when the storm is gone, and I once more may creep back cautiously, very cautiously, along the midnight streets to the old, familiar door—dear friend of magnanimous soul and noblest heart, I'll somewhere, somehow, borrow money to repay you this that you have done for me and mine.

Adieu, and yet again adieu, gesundheit and ausgeschpiel! Give my present post-office address to W. Ball, as I have asked him to send me some papers in which he has printed *Beatrice's Tribute to Dante*.

No more, no more! I am overcome; I also think I smell something cooking, kraut or sausage, or other trifle; and I must away, away!

Since I cannot by any means, anywhere, come at a Swiss phrase-book, I shall have to address this letter to you in English, which I trust these infernal foreigners may read sufficiently well to forward this to you without delay.

If Payne's song should be printed, please send me a copy; I think there is something in it: I shall send you in repayment some verses of mine, being short of money.

> Gratefully yours, dear Yates,
> and again assuming the old,
> familiar disguise,
> Yours once more:
> *Ichabod*

11th Dec. 1921

Dear Johannes: . . .

I had seen Digby's nice little notice & I shall look in the Satdy Evg Post tomorrow for more. Surprising that the N.Y. Times Supplement of yesterday had *nothing!* I steal *The Transcript* from Ball's desk whenever I get there first; I went to G'wood to see *Foch*,[9] & so perhaps missed Wedy's issue which *may* have had a notice; nothing in Thursday's. . . .

Gittman has sold out all of his first batch of *Margots*; his 2d batch about 25, I judge, is now on sale. *Ca ira; ca ira!*

My congratulations to your blessed wife and sweet Dantesque daughter, on having *such* a husband & father!

[Y. S.]

14th Dec'r 1921

Dear John:

I cut out W. W. B's notice to send you (boost for Montrose Moses's Children's Drama book); went to The State office; found that Billiam Ball had already sent you one! This P.M. I cut out Warhoop's fine screed from *The Record;* dropped it in at *L'Etat;* found that B. Ball had mailed you one. The creature really thinks that *he* is the head of the Columbia Bennett Booster Bureau! So, I send you a duplicate of Wauchope's anyhow. No answer from *Kittredge* yet! Gittman has only 7 left this P.M. of 50 copies he has had on sale. Muller ordered another small batch Tuesday P.M. The work goes bravely on! A friendly nature fakir (*not* Ambrose Gonzales!) complains that you make *tulips & oleanders* bloom in the Unholy City simultaneously! How dat? My love to your wife.

Yours ever,
Y. S.

Wauchope is a *Presbyterian* elder, or deacon, and yet he approves unreservedly of Margot! Whoop-e-e!!

Not a line in last Sunday's *Transcript!* or in the Springfield Rep'n of same date; or in the Times Satd'y Review. What's the matter?

D. Jno. Sam Stoney has asked me to go to Back River Xmas. I can't & don't care to *shoot* off anything but my mouth! *But, are you going?* Answer, if only by post card!

26th Dec. '21

Dear Jack:

'Rah for Lawrence Mason! That notice of Margot, in Literary Review of Dec. 24, caps the climax. The State Co. has only one copy left, & had to wire for their last shipment. Gittman has had heavy sales, for a Columbia market—over 100 certainly.

Ball thinks of republishing Mason. Thanks for your beautiful card & that telling inscription. *My* voice "charming"!!! And dear old *Walter's* too!!!! "Angels & ministers of Grace defend us!"

My love to your entire family. My family has gone to Main St., to spend the last of my Xmas money at the movies.

Yours affectionately,
Yates Snowden

Let me know *when* the 2d "printing" of Margot is announced!

Chapter 11

1922

Sunday State *"Writers and Books" page;* Madame Margot *reviews; Jane Bennett's engagement; a War Between the States love story; Rowland Rugeley's burlesque translation of* Dido and Aeneas; *early South Carolina writings; the MacDowell Colony and work with DuBose Heyward and Hervey Allen; Salt Sulphur Springs memories; Heyward and Allen's* Carolina Chansons; Gonzales's *Black Border.*

IN THE month of June Yates Snowden complimented John Bennett on the "Writers and Books" page that he had begun for the Sunday *State* newspaper. Under the pen name "Alexander Findlay McClintock," Bennett was including some poems that Snowden did not like, because they were written in free verse. He sent Bennett a new Confederate bibliography, and he referred to Jane Bennett, John and Susan's older daughter, as the "Dantesque" maiden. He had heard that the lovely girl was to marry a "damyankee."

Snowden informed Bennett of the enjoyment Bishop Kirkman Finlay's father-in-law, J. Otey Reed, had derived from *Madame Margot* during his illness. The little volume continued to win praise across the country. Bennett, however, refused to allow a writer in New York, who was preparing a movie scenario of *Margot,* to proceed when the young man proposed dodging the issue of miscegenation and changing the outcome of the story.

Bennett, who was spending the summer in East Flat Rock, North Carolina, apologized for not having answered Snowden's December 1921 communications and replied to Snowden's taunting notation about the oleanders and tulips mentioned in *Madame Margot.* He recalled the first time he saw Snowden, and he admitted that his daughter, whose debut had taken place in December, was going to marry—in about a year and a half—a Yankee from Indiana, Forrest Hampton Wells.

Bennett explained that he did not collect Confederate history, having learned, after collecting Revolutionary War history for six years, that he still needed about six more years of collecting if he were to have enough neglected facts to proceed with an accurate novel. Bennett then recounted a curious story about the engagement ring of Julie McCord, Mrs. A. T. Smythe's half-sister, and Henry Feilden, a British officer who joined the Southern cause during the War Between the States.

Bennett mused over the possibility of obtaining a copy of Rowland Rugeley's burlesque translation of *Dido and Aeneas,* which the friends had discussed years earlier.

Snowden attended the 123rd anniversary dinner of the St. John's Hunting Club. He pondered the sale of his two lots on the outskirts of Hendersonville, North Carolina, which the Board of Water Commissioners wanted to buy. Snowden promised to spend the day with the Bennetts if he came to the mountains on business, but he concluded the sale of the lots through Fitz Hugh McMaster and did not travel to North Carolina.

Snowden related an anecdote told him by Ambrose Gonzales about an old schoolmaster of Charleston. The friends discussed "Omnium Gatherum," "Omnium Botherum," and other early South Carolina writings, as Bennett looked for material for his weekly page in *The State.* Snowden offered to send a two-volume set of Francis Kinloch's letters, so that Bennett could write something about them before A. S. Salley, who had recently obtained a set, did so. Snowden was again at odds with Salley for a recent slur against Bennett.

In the late summer Bennett went to the MacDowell Colony in New Hampshire to work with DuBose Heyward and Hervey Allen for a few weeks. In September the Bennetts entered their son Jack in Exeter Academy.

In December Snowden told Bennett of a paper on Arthur Hugh Clough, which he would like to give in Charleston if feasible. Delighted, Bennett arranged for Snowden's appearance before the Poetry Society of South Carolina in 1923.

Snowden's purchase of a new edition of *Master Skylark* resulted in a discussion of the merits of the art work in the volume. Remembering the days at Salt Sulphur Springs, West Virginia, when he was writing the book, Bennett mentioned the young hopefuls assembled at the resort and their success as authors in later years.

Bennett praised *Carolina Chansons,* the recently released book of poems by DuBose Heyward and Hervey Allen, and informed Snowden of the review of Ambrose Gonzales's *Black Border* that he had written for the New York *Post.*

Columbia, 14th June '22

My dear John:

Bp. Finlay's father-in-law,[1] who has been critically ill at a hospital, has had "Margot" read to him *twice!* The Pontifex returned me my copy this P.M.

Per-contra. A distinguished editor to whom I sent a copy of "Margot" last week, wrote me: "Why does John Bennett write such stuff?" &c., &c., only a little worse! I had written reproaching him for not having written a review of the book. *De gustibus.*

I send you a very dainty piece of book work, a tentative Confederate bibliog. of Walker, Evans & Cogswell publications. They sent me a few copies. I don't know that you particularly affect C.S.A. publications; but I know that you like fine type & paper, & I trow that you like me. I have many proofs thereof. It is not complete; nothing but Charleston *is;* but pp. 9–30 have some fairly good work in them.

And so that lovely Dantesque girl, who kissed me at her father's command, is to marry a Damyankee! If he is a good fellow I don't object, *if he only lived in Charleston.* We need all of that type at home.

You are getting out (Mac Horton adjuvante) a first class page in the Sunday State! Can that pace be kept up? That's the rub. I don't admire all of Angus McGlockity Fergus *McKlintock's*[2] vers libre, tho'—I don't admire any *vers libre.* When is the 2d of the Margot series to appear? My love to your wife & respectful greetings to your mother-in-law.

Your Early Victorian friend,
Yates Snowden

N.B. I was 64 on May 8 ult. Wait till *you* get to 64! "You don't know how nice it is," as the foxes (who had their tails cut off) said.

"Many Pines," East Flat Rock, No. Ca.
June 23rd, 1922

Dear Yates:

One guess that you made in your epistle of June 14th which is correct: you trow that I like you. It's true; I always have, and always will, even when we are the dustiest of dust, should there be liking left.

Passing rapidly to less personal matters, to relieve your bashful confusion after above frank declaration—

I discover on examination of my check-list of errors and omissions episcopal, that I do not owe you as many letters as I had been doing ashes penitential for; having discharged yours of August 4th last, and of all dates previous thereto, by apologia pro culpa—thus leaving me in your debt for only FOUR real letters, of Dec. 11th, '21; Decr. 14th do.; Decr. 26th dodo.; and your recent welcome indication of godlike forgiveness, dated 14th June, '22. And that's too many, God knows, for a man to owe anyone, let alone a friend of—let's see, it's just about a quarter-of-a-century standing, now, isn't it? Wasn't it just about that time ago you printed certain verses of mine under audacious and impertinent heading—all your own, so far as the bearing o't was concerned—in the Snoozing Courier? You were pointed out to me as the guilt-reddened culprit, by my present wife—who was then (well, she still is!) the effulgent star of my existence—at the dedication of the monument to Henry Timrod, in City Hall Park, Charleston? From that moment I conceived the idea it were safer, considering the power of the press, to be a friend of yours, than otherwise; and through the long years I have sedulously endeavored to play that part. Some genuine emotion has been involved, which latterly has been, perhaps, satisfactorily discharged through one "Dantesque daughter"—whose services in this capacity, alas! it now appears will not be permanently available for such transmission.

"I never had a dear gazelle," etc.

He *is* a damyankee; that's the fact; and a very fine young fellow—one of a group of fine young fellows we had the good fortune to know with peculiar intimacy all winter, through our habit of trying to keep up a tradition of hospitality. The Dantesque daughter and her Miltonian mother have just returned to Flat Rock direct from Philadelphia and Newport, R.I., where they have been, saying good-by to said group of young fellows in general, and to Ensign Forrest Wells,[3] in particular, ordered to the Asiatic, for duty, in the demonstration of readiness and force at present making in oriental waters, as a sort of prescribed "N.B." to furrin nations, particularly them of saffron complexion—that, although our naval teeth are pulled, we have our eye-teeth left. The young folk fancied each other, I think, on sight; and time appears but to have confirmed their opinion; as it has very happily confirmed ours of the young man. He is a Lochinvar—that is, come out of the West—Middle West—Indiana, to be notorious about it—next door to my own. How he got his most confoundedly Confederate, yet Christian, name, "Forrest Hampton," he does not well explain, for his people, praise be! had nothing to do with the Knights of the Golden Circle or other Copperhead conspiracy of the '60's. His father is the man who took the bit in his teeth and introduced American agricultural machinery successfully to England and to the Canadian wheat-lands of the Northwest. The boy has the same drive and determination, has old-fashioned loyalty, old-fashioned principles, old-fashioned ideals, and makes them drive most successfully in a new-fangled world; by his successful handling of a rotten, old, out-of-date craft he has just won preferment to chief engineer of the Truxton, #229, on which he goes out to the East. The only objection one could make is to the wandering, dislocative life of the navy; but I have one pet niece already happily living that life—Mrs. Billy Popham, now in Japan; and the courage of the young seems, as always, equal to anything, and their willingness to meet whatever fate awaits them is as phenomenal as it was ever in the story of Greece, or of that great Mother of Sailors, England: So, Father Terence, your blessing! And they're to be married, please, Father, when the young man gets his Junior Lieutenant's commission—so I'll have my girl for a year-and-a-half more at home; and for that brief companionship I am grateful. And then, my dear Yates, farewell to vicarious expressions of emotional affection per Dantesque daughter!

Bishop Finlay's father-in-law is a gentleman and a scholar and an excellent judge of literature: I hope he recovers his health; that hope is without jest. As you do not nominate your "distinguished editorial friend" to whom you sent a copy of "Margot," and received postscript condemnation thereof, I refrain from opinion. Yet he is not alone. The reviewer of the Detroit Free Press states it as his opinion that "the author of Madame Margot was *delirious in spots.*" And the Philadelphia Record quotes choice passages under heading of "Miasma from Madame Margot." I can only say it sells like a masterpiece; and we shall probably clear the edition; and that the cordial appreciation of my friends at home in Carolina is reinforced by the quite positive declaration of Dr. Chas. Graham Dunlap[4] (a well-known critical scholar of Shakespearean editions and the like), that the book is a masterly piece of English. I had hoped, for many a day, at some time to win just such a statement from him, and am quite happy in doing so. Yet there's another much-esteemed, though younger and more radical, friend of mine, in the English department, Ohio State University—himself a writer of high-quality English—who says "You are all too academic down there!" Meantime—the book not yet written, indeed, scarce begun—Harry B. Kirk, of Hammond's, has already ordered 100 copies of *the second of the series* of "Grotesque Legends of Old Charleston," of which "Margot" was first. That's on faith, sure! I understand that several English departments in advanced schools to northward are using the "Madame" for reading and theme-work in advanced classes, and have had sent to me for my entertainment, a group of senior themes from one institution which pleased me very much by appreciative ability. So we go. The next one of the legends is to be—if it is ever—the legend of "The Doctor to the Dead," whose practice lay in Charleston's graveyards, and who, unhappily for himself, fell desperately in love with a lady dead for a century—and the odd results of this outre infatuation. I am using my work for *The State* to endeavor to get a hold upon this legend; as the power to write seems sometimes to depart beyond control. I had thought to do a genuine romance from the life of my own father, as an orphaned Virginia boy upon the frontier, in the '30's and '40's of the last century; but something—may be the war, may be just time—has somehow withered the vein, and I found the story growing stark and stern as I began it; and do not wish, certainly not yet, to write it that way; so was compelled to lay it aside. Yet it has great elements of romance in it—in something akin to "Vandemark's Folly"—and I should like to tell it, some day, some how—gad, how many things, some day, some how, we should like to do! Eh?

But *you've* got your book-room! And for that hooray! And, during the winter, *I* managed to rebuild for my boy the model sailing-boat I built for myself, forty-three years ago. So we get something done. We have sailed it on The Pond, and the small boat *sails!* And someday I'll take a chance at Columbia to see your books again, arrayed in orderly glory, shelf by shelf!

As to keeping up the pace in the Sunday *State,* I can, I guess, if the rest will, and am glad to do what I can to push the endeavor along. I have never been able, since you left us, to get a Charleston paper *to even attempt* (don't mind split infin.) such a thing as a "Books and Writers" page—not so much as a column to letters, but Edson's "Whimsey Board," which is as unequal as it is surprisingly facile. I am sorry you do not like this young Scottish rhymester—or, faith! is he a *rhymester?*—Alexander Fergus Aeneas MacGillicuddy of that ilk. I'd like you to cover his identity, since you are aware of it, and just let him write in one form what he no longer has heart to try to put in another—and which, perhaps, is better in this. It is genuine, what there is of MacGillicuddy, and will be found not without meaning, whatever its form. May be, a little later, he may abandon *vers libre* for an older, more accustomed mode, more to your liking—I'll ask him as to this when we meet. But, please, Father Terence, not too much publicity as to Sandy MacGillicuddy's personality: there is, as you know, opportunity concealed in a pseudonym. Early Victorians were fond of 'em, too.

The Boston "Transcript," so far as I and my clipping-bureau were able to discover, contained but the brief mention of "Margot," as received for review; and never . . . ; Braithwaite didn't take it kindly that a cullud lady should be willing to serve the Devil that her daughter might be white.

In one of your December letters (for which I was profoundly grateful—I was horribly tired, and Drs. Simons and Wilson held an autopsy over my remains, shortly after, and told me I must travel and rest, at which I smiled and did neither: they put me through the Third Degree and the Presbyterian Shorter Catechism, and there wasn't a thing the matter with me but acute society diversion owing to one Dantesque daughter's debut. Travel and rest! Where, and on what? Name of Glory!)—

But, to resume that abandoned topic: in one of your Dec'r letters you report that various nature fakirs in Columbia complained that I make tulips and oleanders bloom simultaneously in Charleston. I do NOT. I suppose they refer to p. 14, where in describing Margot's garden it is stated that the shade of the great magnolias "fell heavily on the sleepy oleanders and over the rows of tulips down below, that lifted up their golden cups and filled the air with odor." Sure, the tulips were in bloom; it was tulip-time. But who said the oleanders were in bloom? Not I. Aren't they oleanders except when in bloom? Both magnolias and oleanders bloomed when their time came; but even in a book not in tulip-time; and who said they did? Not I. If this folly be repeated, tell them to go *to*—in the Shakespearean sense. But, no, it was "a friendly nature fakir": assure them that I know, though but an immigrant on sacred soil, that oleanders do *not* bloom in tulip-time, tulip-time, tulip-time—they do not bloom in tulip-time, though it's not so far from London!

As to the French mistakes, we have had as ridiculous a time about them, as about the scriptural quotations: for the asses in the Century office would insist on correcting quotations from the Vulgate by the text of the King James version. (I say "asses," and won't retract.)

I had a tentative proposal to do "Margot" in Swedish, as you may have seen by *The State;* and a scenario was started, by a brilliant young gentleman, in New York; but when he proposed to dodge the question of the color-line and alleged miscegenation, and the Afro-American situation altogether, by making "Madame Margot" Japanese or Chinese or Malay, and turn the grotesque, fantastic, tragedy into cheap melodrama by having "Gabrielle" marry the only son of a noble South Carolina family, her mother's betrayer being an intimate old friend of the family—I deliberately turned off the gas, and told our young phenomenon to run along. If the heart and intellect must be taken out of the tale to make it a movie, 'twill never be a movie!

Let me see; what else is it I have to say?

Oh, yes. You remember old *Rowland Rugeley,* author of the *"burlesque translation from the Story of Dido and Aeneas, just published by R. Wells,"* etc.—"fragments of the Fourth Book," 1774; *S.C. & American General Gazette.* Did you tell me that you had seen this unique bit of Caroliniana? Or did you say you had bid once for it and missed it? Do you know how many copies are in existence, and who owns them? I'd be greatly obliged if you would let me hear from you on this subject. I'd like mightily to get my hands on a copy. Do you know at what prices the surviving copies have been held? Whose authoritative list of early Americana had "*R. Rugeley*" listed as a nondeplume? I met him once—the authoritative list—in New York, and warned him he was in error; but never heard further from him regarding any correction. The whole thing weighs on my mind, and I must purge me.

I have not particularly affected Confederate publications, chiefly because I cannot afford to affect publications of any rarity whatever, save such as are presented to me by generosity. It is like my not specializing in Confederate History: I have neither time nor means to afford to attempt the exploration of even one corner of so wide a subject. Six years almost, devoted to Revolutionary War history, led me through miles of fancy to the ridge of the mountain of knowledge, from which I viewed suddenly a wide valley of utterly neglected facts. I put down my pilgrim's staff and bag and scrip, and abandoned the pursuit; for the unexplored valley before me exceeded in breadth the land that I had traversed; and the story of that country could not be told without adequate knowledge of both. Since that I have essayed to probe no history; but, ever, the facts, the glimpses of forgotten men and things, fascinate me. I think you knew that. And so knew that so choicely-printed and interesting a bit of the almost-lost interior history of the Confederate War as the Walker, Evans & Cogswell brochure would be an irresistible bait to my fish. *I do not like the paper back, imitation of morocco;* but the interior is as lovely a bit of book-making as I have seen for many a day, type, paper, and format. I had read the original draft in *The State*, January, a year-and-a-half ago, and kept it; but replace that unsatisfying form by this appropriately printed and unique bit of history: I could wish that you owned every item mentioned, a complete collection. I have seen some of them; but not many. Thank you heartily for the remembrance.

I have just received another, far different remembrance, with a most romantic story, which I know you will find interesting: When young Henry Feilden threw up his commission in the British army and joined the South, when he met and became engaged to Julie McCord, having no ring to give her, and nowhere to get one, she gave him a little plain gold ring which had been given her, as their token of engagement. In Florida, early in '65, before the end, on military business, he heard of the opening of the tomb of an Indian princess near by, and took a hand, actually, in excavation; during which the ring, given him by his fiancee, slipped from his hand, and search failed to recover it. With regret and chagrin he was compelled to pass on. In 1867, after he had married and returned to England, the ring was returned to him by the children of the family at whose house he had stopped at the time of its loss. They had recovered it from the sand of the princess's grave. He had kept it close by him all his life. His wife died two years ago; he followed in a twelvemonth. Before he died, having had some correspondence with me, he prepared, to be sent to me as a personal remembrance, this little gold ring, which I now have, and shall keep, as you may guess, for some fit and devoted purpose in the end of my possession. I thought you'd like the story of that ring and staunch old Henry Feilden.

I note: p. 28–9, "War-Time Publications," ref. to S.C. Tract Society's wide circulation of the tract of "that eminent educator and theologian, J. H. Thornwell." Was he the vapid critter who wrote that dear, sweet, birds-in-their-little-nests-agree alleged history of the Confederate Government? making cherubs, seraphs and archangels out of the most human of honest, earnest men? He deserves a monument for his literary efforts therein next to Parson Weems! If I could believe that his point of view and statement was accurate I should the more deeply rejoice over the failure of your ancestors: for had such a government as he describes established itself upon earth there would have been no longer any need of Heaven, and all my anticipatory practice upon the harp—per vicarious guitar—would have been futile.

And tell me why, Father Terence, it was considered essential, at this day, knowing what little we do, for our friends, the vets., to take their little hatchets and nail poor old Abe Lincoln to the cross as *personally responsible* for the arguments of '60: God's sake, why not let the old man sleep under the sod with Anne Rutledge—though that sounds a bit free— the row began before he was born.

And why, dear Father Terence, the *"Second Tallest Monument in the World"* to Jefferson Davis? Granted fitting that a memorial should be piled to an honest, earnest, brave and tragic figure, such as in truth Mr. Davis was, why the *"second highest monument in the world"?* Unless, perchance, dear Father, it is a bitter-ender cry of "Scissors! Scissors!" to the Yankees—them goths and vandals, etc., etc.—Isn't that fine memorial in Richmond fit to keep his memory? I grant you a mountain carved greatly in memory of the armies of the South is nobly dreamed and, freely, well-deserved. But dear Father—and Father with an Irish accent— why the *"second highest in the world"* to Mr. Davis?

Having got these monkey-wrenches out of my machinery I run freer.

I have sent some comparisons to "Barton Grey's" translated epigraphs from Simonides, for printing in The State. What do Smith and Wauchope think of them in comparison with my citations? I think Sass leads far in dignity and beauty.

Dear Yates: All these things could, perhaps, have been more briefly and beautifully said. Had I waited on the assured mental grip essential to brevity, I might not have written. You would, perhaps, then have been preserved from the gale which I have blown herein. But I should not have shown even by intention my regard, and gratefulness to you.

Hence these much speaking.

My compliments always to one of the best wives in the world—yours—and to what friends of mine you meet; you know them; and to yourself, always, unchanging, the deep regard of

Yrs.,
John Bennett . . .

The Miltonian Mistress B. and the Dantesque daughter send their affectionate regards to you and yours. Mrs. B. fell down stairs, yesterday, trying to escape the yoke; but fortunately failed.

J. B.

12th July '22

[Dear John] . . .

Your charming, voluminous letter was rec'd; read 2 or 3 times, with frequent cachinnations, & then put into my 98¢ negro-parson, pasteboard valise when I set off for Monck's Corner to attend the 123d dinner (anniversary) of the St. John's Hunting Club. I stayed at Henry Dwight's[5] (wild Isaac Porcher[6] was away!) & next day went to Charleston. When I opened my 98¢ valise, *your letter* was *missing*, & still is. H. Dwight is an exceedingly careful cuss & I am hoping that I left y'r letter *chez lui;* if so, I know he will return it, as it was in your handsome blue envelope, addressed in your wonderfully fine chirography to me.

The *Margotiana* were of very great interest, as was also your half-baked scheme to perpetuate your father's perigrinations & perambulations in the Middle-West. An excellent theme! Push it along!

Now, as to Rowland Rugeley. The Travesty on Virgil (*ca* 1773 or 4) was offered for sale ($3. I think) by Cadby of Albany. I immediately borrowed 3 simoleons & dispatched them to Cadby. He replied by saying that I missed it by *one mail,* & that it had been sold to the N.Y. Public Library. (Bad cess to it!!)

My colleague Baker went to N.Y. a few summers ago, &, at my request, visited the Public Library, called for the "Travesty" & copied some salacious or suggestive stanzas for me. I reproduced a verse or so in my anonymous introduction to the Boozer-Pourtales pamphlet, which I was fool enough to send to you, & *you were mean enough* to show to Mrs. Smythe!! The *only* mean trick you ever served me. That dear lady, I fear, thinks *my mind runs* on that kind of "literature." It doesn't; you know *it doesn't!*

Night before last "long distance" rung from Hendersonville. Mr. C. E. Brooks, Chairman of the Board of Water Commissioners, "wanted" me. He said the new town reservoir is to be built on "the crown of the hill" just on the outskirts of H'ville. It so happens that I own 2 jewels in that crown! I phoned him to make me an offer in writing. Today he offers me, by mail, the paltry sum of $300. for each lot! I shall write him that his offer is unsatisfactory & that I shall come to H'd'ville within a week to investigate the real value of my property.

Query! Will the jury of condemnation assess those lots higher than have the comm'rs? East Flat Rock is not 1000 miles from H'd'sonville; my Lebby cousins live at Flat Rock; so does John Bennett. In short if I "close the deal" with those land-pirates in a short time, I shall run over and spend a day with the Lebbys & Bennetts.

"Joyful, joyful will the meeting be"—to me at least. I have several things to tell you & your wife *et al;* & I want to see that *ring,* &c., &c., &c., &c.

Yours affectionately,
Yates Snowden

I shall bring Ludwig Lewisohn's[7] amazing article on "South Carolina, A Lingering Fragrance," with me. It will amuse & perhaps enrage Mrs. Smythe & Mrs. J. B. & my sweet Dantesque friend, if she is with you.

———————

31st July '22
Sheol, S.C.

Dear John:

I am going to write on decent paper in ink to Mrs. Smythe thanking her for her very kind invitation (for which I know I have to thank you & Mrs. B. mainly)—and I shall write *you,* in pencil as suits the Bohemian ash-cat that you are!

How dare you expose the *poverty* of Y. S. in *borrowing* "three simoleons"? Yates Snowden L.L.D., Professor of History, husband of Annie Warley; cousin of the Snowden who owned "Snowden's Speckled Cock" which made the 2d highest record known in S.C. cocking annals (13 straight fights), &c., &c., &c.—Ah, as Petronius or some ancient wise guy said, "The greatest sorrow, or affliction, of *poverty,* is *that it makes one ridiculous,*" or words to that effect.

The best paragraph in that delightful causerie on Sunday is in the lower half of the 1st column, "Now it is Petronius": the "That was what it was I found"; &c., &c.

Before I moved my great library into new quarters, I had a copy of the "Satyricon." A cheap, N.Y. ed'n, pub'd by Lamar Blanchard (?) an American free-lover. Bain[8] had loaned it to me, & when he died I wouldn't return it to his boy son, & of course Mrs. B. & his girl daughter would not know what it meant. (That was before the advanced-woman, "he-woman" days *we* live in; now when every girl of 12, who goes to the public schools, *knows more than her mother* or grandmother knew *when she was married* & after.) The dirty little book must be upstairs in a lot of other rubbish.

I *hope* all this change is for the best; but, poor old Victorian cave-man that I am, I can't see it.

Now, to business. I sent you (*lent* you) by registered mail this morning "Omnium Gatherum," "Omnium Botherum," "George Tale-Tell,"[9] and J. Lide Wilson's "Cupid & Psyche."

"Gatherum" & "Botherum" with the aid of the notes I send herewith from Simms's articles in the XIX Century, will furnish you *meat* for at least ½ column in *your* Omnium Gatherum.

"George Taletell" is not worth what the binding cost me, but *some* ass *must* preserve such lumber! Why not *me—or I?*

I send it mainly for identification. *Was it* old Bee, the Oxford or Camb. graduate of whom Crofts et *al.*[10] made so much fun in "Botherum"?

I don't know old Bee's initials; he was an old intellectual *sponge* who came back to Charleston & taught school & published "Gatherum." (I am a little intellectual *sponge* myself, & feel for him, & envy you & H. A. & DuB. H. *et al.* who feed on "honey dew," & drink "the milk of Paradise"!)

If you use Bee, *you must* tell the story old Ambrose told me his aunt *"the late venerable & accomplished Miss Elliott"*[11] told him: Old Bee[12] was so obsessed with *every* thing *English* that he sent to perfidious Albion for *birches* to thrash the seats of *honor* of his Charleston pupils!! Old ass to think that *anything* could hurt more than a S.C. *hickory* switch!

"Can such things be—without our special wonder?"

In re Wilson's *Cupid & Psyche,* Smelfungus[13] had a mind to address a line to "Writers & Books" something in this vein:

> To the Editors of the Weekly Farrago:
>   Sirs:
>   If it were possible to conceive that John Bennett would write on *obscene* literature for a *Sunday* paper I would take him to be the author of the article on the Golden Ass of Apuleius. How *could* that writer *omit* John Lyde Wilson's scholarly &c., &c., &c.—No it cannot be J. Bennett for he

thinks he knows as much about S.C. literature, as Aleck
Salley knows about S.C. history, &c.,&c.,&c.

Smelfungus

But I have concluded I would spare you this time. Still, you might
write a paragraph about John Lide Wilson, & you might add that the
public anxiously awaits the completion of the "Life" of that brilliant S.
Carolinian, author of the Code of Honor; author of *The Rules of Betting;*
author of a work on "Artillery Tactics"; translator of Apuleius; Gov'r
of S.C., &c., &c., which has been in course of preparation for some years
by *his grand-nephew Dr. C. W. Kollock!!!*[14]

Entre nous, Kollock *has* been working off & on on J. L. W., ever since
Mrs. St. J. Ravenel's[15] contemptuous *slur* on the versatile old booze artist
and sport in "Charleston, the Place & the People."

But, here I *must stop,* after thanking you dear people for that
delightful invitation to take a peep at the Flat Rockracy. Altho' I am a
sick man, *entre nous* (I have not told my wife even!) I did want to come
immediately to the delectable mountains, for I am burning up here. But,
Fitz McMaster *en route* to Asheville, looked into the question of my lots.
I have wired my acceptance of $600. for the two. They are not such land-
sharks after all!

Always yours affectionately,
Y. Snowden

"Many Pines," East Flat Rock, North Carolina
Aug. 2, '22

Dear Yates:

This is no letter, God bless you and preserve you, and give you swift,
sure riddance of all your present disability! but only an acknowledgment
of the safe receipt of your LOAN of Four (4), more or less worthless, and
correspondingly precious, volumes of ancient South Carolina ribaldry
and wit; to wit:

> The Omnium Gatherum
> Omnium Botherum
> Recreations of George Taletell
> John Lyde Wilson's Cupid and Psyche

Ash-cat as I am, these abominable clinkers from the furnace of dead
wit shall be cared for sedulously, perused with estimating eye, trans-

formed into A ARTICLE, as chance may prove, of great worth—or none—as soon as I can catch my vein for transformation. Why the postal authorities should have sent your plainly-directed letter to FLAT ROCK, and not immediately hither, passes human wit; but, since they did, I shall not be able to turn these pasty gems into a diadem this week. I'll dream upon 'em like the guest upon the cake; then write my *causerie*—I do envy you your consummate command of all these foreign languages!

You must know, though, at once, that Mrs. Smythe entertains for you a very genuine regard and affection, and no agency of ours is ever necessary to secure from her a cordial invitation to you to be a guest at "Many Pines." We should all be mighty happy to have you here if you come to the mountains this summer. We are sorry you are not presently coming.

I, too, am but a Victorian cave-man; but clad in a disguising ass's skin, I caper among the modern meads as if accustomed to 'em, emitting many a hoarse, vicarious bray.

There is richness in the stuff you so generously send; and I pray the gods to put me in good fooling for it! Once more, as so often in the past, I am indebted to Y. Snowden for the encouragement a doubter needs, and so painfully limps on without. I think your letters and personal friendliness come close to being the real golden spot in South Carolina's personalities for me. Let me thank you heartily, now, to make sure it is done.

As to your sarcastic flings at my morality—look out, or I may calmly borrow your own well-worn and patched cloak and cover, that pseudonymous "Smelfungus," and write my article over it, which would shift most acrid blame to you! Be good, fair maid, or you may be unhappy in default. But pray, let me admit, it's little truly that I know of South Carolina literature—I deal in the trenchant, casual scrap; and only give it a different look by basting it on the bias. If you do not know what that means, ask one of the world's perfect wives—I need not name her—but with you, God bless her, and preserve her charming all her days! I had not known that C. W. K. had a literary bee.

We are glad you dealt to your satisfaction with the H'ville reservoir; but we are genuinely sorry we shall not, at this time, see you here. Welcome is always yours; always a bed, and always a portion of lentils. Come if and whenever, you may.

Affectionately yours,
John Bennett

N.B.: Thanks to your scholarly resumé: "Poems on Places"—the STATE gave its benighted clientele a real and informing number, on July

30th. What! Yes. Do more of similar diversities, and push the page along.

11th Aug. '22

My dear John:

Thanks for your delightful epistle. I don't know that you can make more than a half column out of that "raft" of Charleston *light* literature I sent you. I doubt if it is worth more than that, tho' *you can* find mare's nests sometimes where ordinary people can find nothing. The cause of this intrusion is to say that I have a copy of Kinloch's Letters, published anonymously in Boston in 1819. You will recall *Francis Kinloch* M. C.[16] shortly after the Rev. from the Georgetown District. These letters "from Geneva & France" addressed to his daughter "A Lady in Virginia" are full of turgid learning with a batch of local S.C. & Virginia allusions, some of them very interesting, & some very foolish. *E.g.* He was a rabid Federalist and denounces Jefferson for the useless & extravagant purchase of Louisiana!!! *Now; if you have time* & *the slightest inclination* to review & comment on some of Kinloch's lucubrations & extravaganzas, I will mail you these 2 rare volumes. The Charleston Library had the book, but *did not know the name of the author,* until I told them some months ago—or that is my recollection. Salley is gloating over the recent ownership of this book & I have no doubt will write about it some day, & I should be delighted if you forestalled him!! I did not *feel so,* until yesterday when I saw the proof of a communication of his anent a *Dr. Killpatrick*[17] who practiced inoculation in Charles Town, before Lining[18] I imagine. In this he refers to John Bennett as "a dabbler" in *S.C.* literature & history. You will see his letter in the next (Sunday's) *State.* The cheek & impudence of Aleck has not decreased, tho' marriage has improved him in several ways.

What do you say? Shall I send Kinloch?

If he interests you, & you care to elaborate a little, Mrs. Henry Cheves can get from Mrs. Langdon Cheves all you want to know about Kinloch. They are descended from him, per old Henry A. Middleton.[19]

I recognize that you can't fill up your *"Books & Writers"* exclusively with *Charleston* stuff. It's a red flag to these up-country Bulls! But, Kinloch will shift the scene largely to Georgetown & Va. I got Mac Horton to hold my wonderful "Bibliopegy (only one "g," please!) in S.C.," until Sunday week, so we can bring out that silhouette of Wm. Henry Timrod.[20] That will be 2 columns *more* of *Charleston stuff!*

Those Hendersonville landsharks have not *yet* sent me my money!

Yours, till the trumpet
shall sound,
Y. Snowden . . .

East Flat Rock, N.C., Aug. 27th, 1922

Dear Yates:

I have found no time to do a paper on those Gatherum-Botherum-Taletell-Cupid-and-Fish volumes: have been bedevilled to distraction as usual. I am off to the MacDowell Colony, Peterboro, N.H., Tuesday, per engagement to meet there Hervey Allen and DuBose Heyward, for some mutual mess; join Mrs. Bennett and Jack at Exeter, Sept. 17; enter Jack at Academy; and so home, via N.Y. and Phila., last week in Sept. Meantime books in safe hands and care. Unless I shall discover myself to know more about men and times—when I can sit down to take thought upon 'em—I may, through sheer terror of Alex Salley's white-hot scornful pen, just send 'em back, at last, that you may do your own devoirs upon them. Your "Biblio*peggy*" with silhouette was a very good grind: where on the green earth did you get the silhouette? Why not something on ancient libraries—private gents'—in S.C.? You studied that topic once. When I get back to Charleston in Oct., I may—MAY— have chance to get down once more to somewhat regular work. Last winter's social whirl was something beyond words, or works. I pray, and trust! Don't send the Kinloch to me now—may be, God bless you never. I know nothing about him or his times; and could comment only blindly. Do it yoursel' who are admirably prepared and gifted for it beyond any man in S.C.—the God's truth, that! You suggest information to be got from Langdon Cheves, Esq. You cannot get information from said L. C. Esq., with a jack-screw or cotton-press! Nobody can.

I am tired to death of thinking thoughts. I mean to resolve myself into a jelly-fish brainless, thoughtless and blessed. I ran in an anecdote of McCord, Simms et al., for direct purpose of varying the Charleston tone of my stuff to middle country. I shall try for more of this, if the Books and Writers develops any sort of defined policy—I have written at random—having no advices as to plan or intent of THE STATE's erudite and gifted directors—nor of where we all are directing our energies. I shan't be able to do a p.c. for said Books & Writers until I return from the Northward, in Oct. It will not, I fancy, expire.

Lord, Yates, if I just didn't have to think—I get so darned tired of thoughts—I wish often I were a noble manual laborer. Then I might amass a competence. I shall never do so in a profession—nay, not even in most honest professions of love for Y. S.

Until I return from one inclemency to another, permit me to remain, with real affection for one whom L. Lewisohn accounts the last and noblest of Romans—

> Yours devotedly and just at
> present chaotically:
> John Bennett

I know almost as little about S.C. literature and history, as Alexander Salley does of good manners—I admit this without a quaver.

———————

(Hilaire Belloc in the *London Mercury*.)

"When I am dead, I hope it may be said,
'His sins were scarlet, but his books were read.'"

There's a good motto for Melancholy Jaques!

Dec. 8, '22

Dear Jack Bennett:

I have spared you any epistolary infliction for a long time—but, here goes!

Your fine little tribute to Reed Smith, *et alia,* in Sunday's State shows that you are not dead yet, tho' I feared from your silence that you were moribund. By the way, Reed was very much pleased, and I suppose will write you.

I have bought the *deluxe* "Skylark" and it's *a beauty,* tho' I don't particularly like the Queen's picture on p. 217; but the others (notably Ben Jonson on p. 245) are exquisite. You know what a supreme artist I am, & will be affected accordingly. . . .

And now I make another proposition, but, if you love me, *in strict confidence.* I have written an appreciation, or "grind," about Arthur Hugh Clough, which I worked off upon the *Kosmos* Club last week. Ball & Sams and one other man, a Ph.D. from afar, spoke well of it, tho' I rather think Ball looked through *friendly* spectacles. I want to impose it upon some *small* gathering in Charleston, as it has some Charleston stuff in it. If the Poetry Club is disappointed by the non-appearance of the main guy at some meeting during the next two months, I shall be glad to distract them for an hour. Perhaps some less hypercritical organization would be better? Think it over, & don't think I will feel sore if you can find no vent for my lucubration. About 10% of it would interest you I think.

Old Ambrose is busy on the *2d edition* of Black Border, tho' all the 1st edition has not yet been sold. He showed me some of the proofs this P.M. and *tried to talk*. It's pitiful, and wonderful too.

En route to Rudolph Singley's this summer, I passed through *Many Pines* and saw your little chateau. I thought of you and yours; but all had gone and many of the flowers were withering or dead.

My affectionate greetings to your wife and that sweet Dantesque damsel!

> Yours affectionately,
> Yates Snowden

NB! After Xmas I *may* run down to "town," & will drop in and get my "Gatherum-Botherum," &c., if you have not "hocked" them or left them on the mountain tops.

———————

December 13th, 1922

Dear Yates:

Thanks for the motto. I guess they're scarlet, all right; but it's a great life, if one can get the commas right.

But what sins do you refer to, old timer? What have I done compared to Amy Lowell? . . .

DE LUXE "Skylark": Don't like the Queen's picture, p. 217 myself; delight in Ben Jonson and Will, p. 245, as you do—those two dead hearts go deep in my affections; though they, very like, don't know, and do not care; the boy singing in the inn-yard, p. 65, is very good, pleasant in temper, and truly charming, a good historical bit, too; though in nothing better than Reginald Birch's previous, guiding drawing of the same, in the former editions of the book; the frontispiece, also, is excellent in its way; the end-papers delight me: to me they represent, not the Lord Admiral's players, blowing down the hill to Stratford-town, but a little group of old friends who were gathered together in uncommon friendship, years ago, at the old Salt Sulphur Springs, of West Virginia (where, incidentally, and when, I met my wife), the while I was working on this story, and who all went out together from that ancient, gray hostelry, leagued together as "Cheerful Idiots," to seek our fortunes—namely, E. J. Appleton, of Cincinnati, author of "The Fighting Failure" and "The Quiet Courage"; J. R. Taylor, of Ohio State University English Department, author of a slim volume of distinguished poems, "The Overture," Houghton Mifflin, 1903; Henry H. Bennett,[21] who wrote a song you unreconstructed rebels can hardly appreciate to its fine, courageous full of never-altered loyalty to one bit of cloth, perhaps, "The Flag Goes By— Hats Off!" and lastly, Melancholy Jaques. Pitz[22] has done very well—and we *must* have color, these days, for holiday editions in quarto—and Birch will color not, no more. I first noted Pitz for attention in Century Magazine, last summer, with pen-and-ink of new, refreshing quality among vicious degeneracy's scrapings. Nothing, however, could better Birch's original pen-and-ink illustrations as in the first edition of the book; and none can ever quite take their place in my affection; but the new volume is charming, and a very happy thing, as you may guess, for me—after twenty-six years. . . .

NEXT PROPOSITION ("strict confidence"): Fudge! Fellow! The Poetry Society of South Carolina will be delighted to have one of the most popular men in all Carolina, and one of the most brilliant—though he never seems to recognize that fact—address it *at a January meeting,* somewhere—as closely as convenient—to the 15th. I have not a calendar by me to fix that date by its diurnal label. Will a Friday, or a Saturday, night best suit you? Dodge the St. Cecilia, Jan. 18th, which, being always Thursday, affixes the best available dates for us, *Friday, 12th*, or *Saturday, 13th, January, '23.* Now, I was not clear, from your letter, what your terms are, Yates. Nothing stated. You simply say, in jocular passage, you will be glad to distract us for an hour. I shall speak frankly on this matter. We usually arrange to supply two or three speaking dates to all our visitors from the North. This splits our costs; we put them up while here. But beyond our imported strangers—who, at times, more by being strange than by being able, divert us—we are unable to offer fabulous sums; in fact, the best we are able to do for our odd meetings, on which we attempt to offer no foreign and distant celebrity or notoriety, is to offer you your railroad fare to and from Columbia, namely, the sum of an insufficient $10.00, and put you up while here, if you are not determined upon being the guest of friends beyond our management. DuBose Heyward, Hervey Allen and I, representing the Programme Committee—and well voicing the sense of the Society, as I know—are delighted to have such an opportunity to complete our evening bill for January with your talk on Arthur Hugh Clough, if you can find it feasable to take these terms. Clough's boyhood residence here, his brother's grave in St. Michael's (his suspended state of judgment in so many vitalities, yet his sound soul—these latter interesting the cognoscenti more than the general)—will give such an address an instant local bearing and a cause, which your further ability will make absolutely valid, or more. If you are able and willing to come on these terms, let me know, and we will at once arrange for our preliminary notices and advertising—and be hugely happy so well to come off in our search for a really adequate inspirational offer to our members for that month— that is, yourself and Arthur. We await your reply.

Kirk tells me—ditto Legerton—that "Black Border" is the best-selling book of the season; perhaps to share position now with DuBose Heyward and Hervey Allen's book of verses, "Carolina Chansons," which you must see—and doubtless already have seen—a slim book whose publication marks a date in local history, I am persuaded, so fresh and so authentic is the sound—a new voice. The book had its inception at our fireside, and I am proud of the fact, and heartily approve the volume, though barred awkwardly from public testimony by its affectionate dedication to me by its authors—a pair of very good, and really gifted, lads.

I reviewed "Black Border" for H. S. Canby, Literary Review, "Post," N.Y., printed Sunday last; you must have seen this. Horton kindly writes me to say that Mr. A. Gonzales likes the review. I had great hopes that it might please him in quality; for it was to press the interests of his book, and to please him personally I undertook the review; he being pleased I have succeeded so far; and hope the rest.

If you see him, present my personal felicitations and regards; we all owe him much, I think, for his spirit and quality in life and letters.

As to "Omnium"—I have gone so far and so fast, for me, since they came to hand, and have been so drawn from letters here of late, that I never have formulated a good cry about those odd ends of antiquity, though there is a good rattle to them, and an article, informing and amusant. Could you talk them over—and tell me something about them—I know little there, of their dates in Carolina—it may be instant fancy might stir into a gentle, genial flame of journalism—for THE STATE. Whatever—we'll everyone be glad to see you whenever—and every time—you come to Charleston—I am assured of this by Wife and Family—including Dantesque Damsel.

With compliments and regard to Mrs. Snowden,

Affectionately yours,
Jack Bennett

16th Dec. 1922

My dear John:

No Sir*ree!* Nary a cent! I ask *you* to *have me* "*askt*" to spiel before the poets and poetasters, and you offer to pay my way. I never, for an instant, expected and I would not accept a stiver (whatever *that* is!), or a fiver either. I shall come down on Saturday morning train, Jan'y 13th prox., leaving quizzes for classes in II History, shall blow myself off on Saturday P.M. before, I hope, a small audience; shall attend the Juggernaut Church (as Ker Boyce called it!) in the morning, dropping my annual $5 or $10, when the collection is "lifted," and shall return to this delectable burg Sunday P.M. Deo volente.

Don't "play it up big" in the papers; the smaller the audience the more pleased I shall be. Honest!

I am so glad to hear that old Ambrose's Black Border is selling so well. I told him of it, & he was mightily pleased. Everybody here including A. E. G. has the sense to see that your review is easily the finest, and the old man was delighted. It comes in very nicely; for, as might be expected, his other book *on N. G. Gonzales* does not present a popular appeal, and only sells by fits & starts. I am expecting a sympathetic review of B. B. by my old friend C. Woodward Hutson in the New Orleans Times-Picayune, and can't account for the delay. I have bought two copies so far of "Chansons" (one, for C. W. H.); much of it, but not all, appeals very strongly to me, and I was glad when Gittman told me 'safternoon that he had sold out, and was going to order a fresh supply.

Such fine notices of the deluxe Skylark! That was a fine send off with a big illustration in the Literary Digest's new publication! God bless us, everyone.

Yours affectionately,
Yates Snowden . . .

As pay't in full for my great effort you might send me a copy of the Society's Annual! Gittman asked me, t'other day, where it could be bought. I told him from DuB. Heyward, or "Hammond's."

Chapter 12

1923

Last English licenser of books; Billy Sunday's reference to Col. Alfred Rhett; Arthur Hugh Clough and Charleston; William Rose Benét and Henry Seidel Canby and "The Abbot of Derry"; Apothecaries' Hall; *Hervey Allen's reaction to a Snowden article; Orient and Jane's wedding.*

IN JANUARY Yates Snowden suggested that John Bennett write an article on the licensing of books in England, since the last of the licensers was for a short period the chief justice of South Carolina. In March Snowden sent a clipping of part of Billy Sunday's sermon in Columbia on Saturday, 3 March 1923, which referred to Colonel Alfred Rhett.

John Bennett, in his March letter, explained how William Rose Benet and Henry Seidel Canby had not been able to interpret the overhead added to "The Abbot of Derry," which was to appear in the *Literary Review.* When Bennett's *Apothecaries' Hall,* a monograph about the second oldest drugstore in America, was published in April by the Charleston Museum, he sent Snowden a copy. Bennett, who was an honorary curator for the museum, was disappointed that the notes which made the brochure of historical value had been edited out.

In June, when Yates Snowden's badinage in a letter about John Bennett to *The State* was misinterpreted by Hervey Allen, Bennett hastened to warn the editor of the paper not to use Allen's explosive communication in his defense. In July, in the midst of preparing the Poetry Society's Yearbook, Bennett sent news about the bride-to-be and the family's appreciation of the Snowdens' gracious gift. Bennett included a fine tribute to young Hervey Allen.

In August Bennett thanked the Snowdens for visiting the ailing Sam Stoney in East Flat Rock. In Snowden's answer, he included a compliment from Annie Snowden about young Jack Bennett and a request that John bring him a small bottle of rice liquor from Cathay. Near the end of the month, Bennett sent Snowden a goodbye letter, describing his and Jack's latest musical performance and giving news about Mabel Webber.

Bennett's epistle from the Orient at the end of October was really a series of three carefully handprinted picture postal cards, depicting a temple of Pootoo, the Bingoo Pagoda, and the Peak Tramway Hong Kong. An amazing amount of information was squeezed into the small space. He recounted their travels in Japan, their visits to Shanghai and Hong Kong, his inability to find the liquor requested by Snowden, and life aboard ship on the way to Manila, as well as the latest changes in the plans for Jane's wedding, which had just been rescheduled from 5 November to 1 November. After Christmas in Japan the Bennetts were to return home in February by way of San Francisco. They had heard about DuBose Heyward's marriage, but had received very little other news from home.

Bennett's final communication about the Far East was written on stationery from Kobe, Japan. He was unable to carry out his friend's wish for rice liquor from Cathay, probably the Chinese samshu, for he had found only the Japanese sake and a Chinese liquor made from the nipa palm, both unpalatable in his estimation. Deciding on a substitute gift, he gave the Snowdens a small ivory carving of an oriental god of merriment and happiness.

Columbia, 2 A.M., *1st January 1923!*

Dear John:

I intended to bring down this little trifle (Areopagitica) with me; but, as you know, I was disappointed at the last moment.

I am organizing a *Husbands' Protective Association.* I have no reason for believing that you are suffering under the *Matriarchate;* but, *if you are,* let me know, & I will enroll you among the charter members.

There's a good "grind" suggested by Mr. Milton's speech "For the Liberty of Unlearn'd Printing." Do you recall that *the last* "licenser" of books in England was one Edmond Bohun, sometime (and a very short time!) Chief Justice of South Carolina, & that he was sent to Charleston largely because the Commons, in a rage, abolished the office, & he was jobless?

If you want all the facts I can bring them to you next month; tho' this sort of *grind* suits the Aleck Salleys & Yates Snowdens best for *they* have not "the vision and the faculty divine"—with which *you* are overcharged!

Yours affectionately,
Y. S.

Everybody is admiring my framed Ben Jonson & Skylark!

All the "Chansons" sold out, & Gittman & The State have both ordered more! I have bought three copies.

6th Mch. '23

Dear Jack:

I am pushed for time & have no business to be writing you; but, it's time you were getting another disagreeable verbal dose from me; so, here goes!

Your reference to "pasquinades" in the old town, long ago, suggests that *it's possible,* you never saw the enclosed by John Lide Wilson, which made Lang. Cheves *ripping* mad when I showed it to him years ago because of its reference to Minister Plenip. Henry Middleton!

I gave a copy to Dr. Kollock. *Nag* him to finish the "life" of his uncle J. L. Wilson! John Lide *was* a rare old bird!

I once had the fool thing printed; but foolishly loaned the last printed copy I had to a miserable creature, *who lost it; so* the enclosed is all I have! *Ergo: please return it to me.* If you have no stamps let me know, and I'll send you 2¢.

I also enclose an extract from Billy Sunday's[1] sermon last Saturday. You will recognize the amazing reference to Col. Alfred Rhett![2] Lord knows his record was bad enough; *but,* Mrs. Smythe & Mrs. J. B. will tell you that his services in stopping the negro pandemonium on Citadel Square (they thought "the Judgment Day has come"!) were *invaluable* & highly appreciated.

I told Ball how nicely the poets and poetasters treated me; & he commented: "Yes, the Charleston people are very polite." Ass!

Danny Reed[3] was *delighted* with *you*, Mrs. J. B., indeed with everything he saw and ate & drank (specially the *gin!*) in Charleston.

Your lovely daughter was very sweet to me after my long lucubration. Sorry I did not have a minute to stop at your shanty; but I am coming down this month to talk to Mrs. Arthur Jones's club,[4] & hope to see you.

Yours aff'ly,
Y. S.

March 15th, 1923

Dear Yates:

When I wake at four a.m., and sleep refuses more, the world gets all sicklied o'er by the pale cast of thought, and nothing seems worth doing. This early rising business, formerly much commended, is, excuse the language, all your eye! I had not meant to write you for a very long time; but your recent intrusion of the 6th has quite upset my honest intention and thus betrayed me to these whoredoms.

Once, long ago, you lent me John Lide Wilson's "pasquinade," of which I made unto myself a golden transcript, and—upon my word and honour—returned to you the original printed copy. Thus I feel removed from your excoriation. As I still have that transcript I can at little cost be virtuous; so return herewith your Italian pages, and many thanks: I borrowed a stamp from the Missus, who had a pigeon-hole full.

The extract from Billy Sunday's astounding sermon, containing his reference to Col. Alfred Rhett, remains a nine days' wonder. Does his pretext of evangelization preserve him from rebuke; or is there no friend to Rhett and his family remaining to protest? Not that I feel the slightest sympathy with the departed Rhett: least said soonest mended; of him I have never heard an admirable thing save his lack of all physical fear; wolves also exempt from that as from sensitive decency: oh, yes: de mortuis nil, and be hanged to him!

Tell Ball for me that you gave a great company of old friends, and a growing company of new, an evening of genuine pleasure; and to me an explanation of a lack, which has puzzled me, in Clough, and puzzles me no more: a man who could spend the years of his childhood in a town such as old Charleston was, and retain no more impress than he did of unusual circumstance, was of a nature to receive no deep or lasting impression ever from the world and humanity, and was more concerned with his own debate than with a brother's death: not a line to spare to remembrance and affection. And not to remember Charleston, the sunshine and the ships—nor the wind and the rain of boyhood blowing across his face: whose fault it was, his or his mother's, the end is deplorable: take him away, and add this to his fortifications! I guess he deserves to perish. Snap judgment? Well, the truth is so!

D. Reed had no drink at my house; assuredly not gin; I have but the emptied bottles of old perilous delight. We enjoyed D. Reed immensely, and expect to enjoy him more.

My daughter *is* very sweet; I take no credit for that; but every time I draw a draught of cool water from that well I see the white sand in the bucket: I shall miss her; but that is life: as ancient a saw—dear Lord, give her happiness! I shall miss her horribly.

I am sending you by mail, insured at $100, the volumes you sent me, last summer, concerning which I do not know enough to write sagely or wittily. That is a period in which I have done no informing research whatever; knowing none of the men, and having a mind as blank as a baby's of circumstances and events. You do; and your humor is ample to encircle the theme with light, with badinage and irony. When my foot is on its heath, and when good sleep lends a gusto, I may divert; but if I sleep I am haunted by days of poverty; why that should be I cannot tell; and the moody Scotch creeps over me, souring merriment, half of the time awake. Moody Scotch is not Haig & Haig; it's a' pituitaries. I'm trying to dig myself from under God's own avalanche of unended labors; like digging in the sand; as fast as I reach the table, down comes another dump, and anither, and anither, and all the smother of the glens comes smoking up my craw. Dear fellow, there's a round hundred charming things somewhere I meant to do—the few I've somehow managed to get done good folk have seemed to like—and my whole fool heart is hungry to do one or two more—and life's damnably interrupting—this is just comment, not information, dear Newcastle, you have coal-houses of your own.

I've just sent some stuff to Horton: does it get to anywhere? What is your impression of the value of their page? Is the manual labor warranted by the number it diverts? If not, I've got a hundred things I could put the time upon.

Did I ever send you a copy of one of the very best of my songs, a mildly ribald bacchanalian song that once was intended to fill a place in a glorious historical romance: then the historical went out of fashion— and I forgot the rest; and have just inserted the point of it between Wm. Rose Benét's ribs, so that, feeling its peculiar piquancy, he will print it in the Lit. Review? Lest you should escape I enclose a fair copy. . . .

To amuse myself I just set an overhead to it: "Lines, from a lyttel Booke of Balettys and Dyties enscribed to Richard Nix, Bishoppe, by his admyring, faithful Friend, John Skelton, Rector of Diss:"

And I'm blessed if Benet and Canby did not write down, in accepting the thing, to ask, seriously, was the thing mine, or Skelton's—and could they not alter the overhead to make sure their readers would not be led astray in the matter, and attribute to-day's merriment to yesterday's liquor, as it were? What do you think of that? But the song's on the enclosed sheet. And all that is left is departure, and affectionate greeting, and genuine compliments to Mrs. Snowden upon that paper, which I read most interestedly in The STATE, on our Revolutionary Monuments. And no more at this time, from

Quite petulantly, but most genuinely,
Yours:
John Bennett

N.B.: My best to Mr. Gonzales, and to W. Ball, if you see them.

April 19, 1923

Dear Yates:

I am sending you, by this mail, a Charleston Museum monograph on Schwettmann's[5] Apothecary Shop, which I began for Billy Schwettmann's amusement and my own, years ago, and finally, on securing the exhibit for the Museum, as a permanent memorial to Billy, I turned over to Miss Bragg,[6] with the notes which made the story historical material: these were entirely omitted—as you will see: the meat was in the notes, much of it; but here is what is left for collectors of my brilliant product.

Yrs. entirely:
John Bennett

Gaffney, S.C., 13th July '23

My dear John:

I did not "get to 'town'" until the day after you left—much to my regret, & to your good fortune.

I saw your delightful letter to Mac Horton *in re* Hervey Allen & his prospective blast against innocent me. It did not reflect highly on Allen's keen intelligence (that utter incapacity to see the true inwardness of my screed!) but it proved the force & warmth of his affection for you, his guide, counsellor & friend. And, after all, *that's* what counts in this "glad, mad, bad world." . . .

I am not staying at Gaffney permanently. I am only here for two days on somebody else's business—truly a labor of love. Tell that sweet child not to let the celestials confine & torture her little trilbys, in the approved Chinese bride fashion. I tremble when I think of her hobbling along in Legare St. in the years to come, & tumbling down at every crossing because she cannot stand or walk on her "pins." Dante's Beatrice had normal *feet* I believe.

My pious regards to the gude wife, & my blessings on you both.

Yours aff'ly,
Yates Snowden

"Many Pines," East Flat Rock, No. Ca.
July 16th, 1923

Dear Yates: . . .

You certainly made a young girl happy, a few weeks ago, Yates; her happiness is hardly less ours. She has been in Chillicothe, my old home, having a very good week's visit with my brother and sister, in the old house, and among my own old friends—such as remain (and they seem many)—or their sons and daughters, who have entertained her generally. Just now she is in that difficult place, the home of her fiance's parents and sister, meeting them, alone, for the first time; and quite uncertain as to whether they are pleased with her at sight, or otherwise. We expect her back here, Wednesday, from her trying experience. I sympathized with her—and (*somewhat less,* to be sure) with them, *knowing her;* but it was to be done, if it could be; and she has the world to meet, almost as much alone, in but a few short months: one might as well begin, be the temperature of the water what it will. I'll give her your solicitude when she arrives; her feet are shapely but sufficient; no pent-up Utica will restrain 'em, celestial or other. And as to "The Abbot," I am yours immensely; H. Allen's fury added to the fun; he was so crest-fallen when I pushed a pin, pff-ff-ff! into his little red balloon. Allen comes of a scrapping line for the last two hundred years—and came home (to a vanished *home*), *rough* and raw to the soul, from the army, and murder, and horror sustained most courageously, hated most wholly, with great personal suffering, passionate and physical, from great wounds and visible death of many a friend. His first thought is to fight, then think it over, and discover a singular, almost disconcerting gentleness, hidden under the noise: I have seen him with my daughter, Susan, and person-ally attending sick and terribly sunburned and unmanageable boys—a gentleness large and gracious as a woman's. But, gad! he has a rough tongue! And much, as yet but half-shaped, ability—at times an unmanageable, disconcerting temper, yet with it, great charm. We wonder much what Fate will do with him and his most genuine love of wonder and great beauty, splashed as they are in a rotten world of wrong-headed criticism such as surrounds us all, to-day—and from which we seem so very slowly turning. Allen is just now at Peterborough, MacDowell Colony, where he is occupying the newly-opened John Alexander studio, a beautiful stone replica of a little Italian chapel. Allen is the first to occupy it—which is a graceful thing; for his grandfather was the man who first saw genius in John Alexander, and took him, practically from the street into his own home, and started him on the road to distinction, years ago: and Mrs. Alexander remembered it.

Heyward has built him a little oak shack of some real structural charm, under two big pines beside a guggling brooklet, near Hendersonville—but safely beyond the vulgar impingement of that name—and is hard at his poetry, aimed at a book.

And I: oh, well; I'm going to China. That's enough—meantime I'm in chaos and old night combined, putting a Year Book into shape. Soon as shaped, I come to Columbia to lay my dummy before The State Co., and get their terms for printing; they are to put it forth for us, if our limited funds suffice. I hope they will. I hope I'll find you in Columbia when I come down. I hope this may be in the fortnight—but God knows what my poet friends will be doing to delay it! A plenty, no doubt. I am certainly glad I am no real poet, but only an occasional scribbler of bacchanalian and erotic canticles, and an atoning moral hymn or two! But I must at that Year Book, counting words and pages, portioning out poetry and alleged prose—God save and bless and keep you and your wife and kinsfolk ever!

> Gratefully as well as carpingly
> and critically, yours,
> J. Bennett

"Many Pines," East Flat Rock, North Carolina
Sunday, Aug. 12, 1923

Dear Yates:

I am hoping to get to Columbia with the MSS. and baggage of the YEAR BOOK of THE POETRY SOCIETY OF SOUTH CAROLINA, this week. . . .

I am bound but to two things, to arrange as nearly as possible some terms for issue of the Year Book; and to get back to Flat Rock immediately on completion of that business. We are to leave here on August 26th; the time grows short, and the days terribly few with us. It may be a great adventure to youth to go to the ends of earth at summons of romance, and hope, and the bright promises life sets out for all who are young, as are my girl and her boy. But to me this is fantastic, bizarre beyond belief: that I should go to China, to Manila, and should leave my eldest daughter there—to see her again—some day, God grant, all well, and home again awhile—but God knows when! But we're embarked upon this cast; and a finer young fellow I have not recently known. Their chance for what of happiness the world gives is as good as all I see, better far than some, and truly more positive than many that I know. No pious philosophy, however, from me. God be with her and keep her ever! I'll see you when I come. . . .

> Yrs.,
> John Bennett

"Many Pines," East Flat Rock
August 22nd, 1923

Dear Yates:

Your visit, yesterday, did Sam Stoney worlds of good; gave him something to think about beside himself and his sorely discomforted body, and brightened him immensely. It was good to have you with us, if for only a few hours. And your talk of publications and plans projected his mind forward to definite futures and to action, rather than to dejected conjectures on health—such as, quite naturally—have worried him. He is better, and will be, if he can cheer up his mind; and that most sincerely we all will hope he can do; and that the winter will see him much better than he has been for many months. . . .

My compliments to Mrs. Snowden, always; and to you; God bless you, old man!

[John Bennett]

Hendersonville, N.C., 23d Aug. '23

Dear John: . . .

Annie, on our return, intimated something as to Sam's melancholic condition derived from "Miss Lou"; and your letter next day persuaded me that Sam *was* depressed. *I had not noticed it.* I have written to Henry Dwight asking him, if he possibly can, to *express* to Sam that Santee Jockey Club MS book. *That* will give the old fellow something to think about.

When Sister Clare (?) (in the world "Stoney") visited Cola, in the 80's, she asked Capt. W. E. Stoney what were the characteristics of the S.C. Stoneys? He answered: "Near-sighted; *drink-loving; horse-loving; woman-loving,*" or words to that effect. Sister Clare (?) said: "Then *we must be kinsfolk,*" or words to that effect.

Tell Sam for me that I have written to Miss Sue Jervey, & will inform him when she replies, & *what,* & tell him, further, that I heard from Annie (Eutawville) Snowden today. I hear from my Annie Snowden every five minutes.

My wife sat with your reckless chauffeuring son, & with dear Jane on our return Monday. Both of us were mightily pleased. Annie says she has not talked (or rather listened) to so delightfully ingenuous, accomplished, charming young fellow in many years; and I tell her she should have met *me* 15 years earlier!! . . .

I had not seen Mrs. Smythe for several years, & I had somehow got the idea that she was showing signs of age. She intimated that she could not see so clearly, but I saw no change. All the old charm and esprit.

My love & best wishes & "bons voyages" to all you blessed people!

Yours aff'ly,
Yates Snowden

NB! Bring me from Cathay a "phial" of that powerful *rice* liquor that makes a man beat his grand-mother. I want to feel frivolous, *once* again!

———————

Hastily, Aug. 24, 1923
"Many Pines," E. Flat Rock, No.Ca.

Dear Yates:

Jane says you asked mailing-points: would glory in a letter!

Mailing points at which those who so desire may reach and overtake us on our wanderings round the world are as follows:

To reach us before sailing: Vancouver: must be there before Sept. 6th: we are passengers on *S.S. Empress of Russia, Canadian Pacific Line, Vancouver B.C.; sailing Sept. 6th:* letters should be allowed a week full to overtake at that point.

To reach us in JAPAN: between Sept. 17 and Oct. 30: mail 4 weeks ahead of date to reach: c/o Rev. L. C. McC. Smythe: 64 Ichome, Shirakabe Cho, Nagoya, Japan.

To reach in MANILA: between Nov. 14 & Dec. 27th: allow 5 weeks; c.o American Express, MANILA, P.I.

There is no time to say much else but good-by, good luck, good hunting, and to us a sound return with the roll of time: February, 1924. In the meantime fortune favor the brave! which must include you. No more. But regards from us all as we depart upon this, to me, uncommon strange adventure. Au revoir!

The poem by Edgar Lee Masters you enclose tells the tale of Edgar Lee Masters: no wonder he found people in his world of Spoon River, a crippled, pitiful, sordid lot: men DO write much what they are, revealed in one way or another in their work.

For all you say, look at the "Abbot of Derry"! God, what a confessional of inebriety, etc., etc., etc.

Jack and I gave an enormous mouth-organ concert—that is, an enormous concert, not an enormous mouth-organ, much less an enormous mouth—the night after you were here, to speed the dull evening and cheer the depressed—we both are simply wonders on that trumpet of the poor—and I play the guitar accompanying. Jack does a wonderful obligato, coloratura second to my steady lead—we played over forty old airs; we won't play anything newer than "Casey Jones," any way.

I think Sam enjoyed the performance; so also Tom,[7] Miss Lou, Miss Loula, and the family. Sam is better than when he came; but suffers from overpreachment from an anxious and loving woman.

I gave Sam your message concerning Miss Sue Jervey; and hope H. D. will send along the Santee Jockey Club MS., to occupy Sam's tired, distressed and depressed thoughts with material so appealing to him. Young Sam once prayed, you may have heard, when a small boy: "God bless ANY good horse!"

We have written a note to Miss Webber; thanks for your kind offer. Miss FitzSimons informs me that within a short time after the operation Miss Webber had moved the fingers of her hands, and that those in attendance thought that in three days she would be able to move her feet, and that she will recover. And that extraordinary good news is good to quit on.

Good-by, Yates; again God bless you and yours! That's the message of me and mine, always. Au revoir!

Affectionately yours,
John Bennett

[*Three picture postcards sent in envelope postmarked U.S. SEAPOST TRANS-PACIFIC No. 2, EAST, 2 November 1923*]

From John Bennett,
wandering down the coast of Asia
via the Admiral Line:

1. A Temple of Pootoo.

En route, Hong-Kong: Manila:
Oct. 29th, 1923

Dear Yates:

Earthquakes to begin on, after a diet of amazing mountains; a sea-voyage more monotonous than cool, calm, sleepy death; part of Japan seen at much advantage, intimately—home-life, and the sights best chosen, the midland palaces, ancient and modern, at Kyoto, by kindness of a viscount—*we being mistaken for people of importance;* the lovely groves and temples of Nara and the huge bronze Buddha of Nara—best things we saw in Japan. Coached in our manners by Cheves & Mary Smythe *no-one suspected what common folks we were:* Shanghai distressed while interesting us: had a good hotel; but were *happy to leave the town,* and come on to *Hong-Kong,* the most picturesque & dramatic city we have seen, so strikingly heaped at the foot—and climbing the steep side of a craggy range of mountains 1500 to 2000 ft. above the harbor. The shops in Shanghai did not seem to tempt my women-folk as those in Hong-Kong did—Although 'twas Sunday, we paced the streets under the old arcades of Queen's Road, from silk shop to embroiderer's, from laces to brass-ware, shawls, and amber; and, I assure you,

2. Bingoo Pagoda.

money leaked away like the warm water out of the last hot bath on a cold night in winter. The ship was loud, last night, with embroidered shawls, mandarin coats, necklaces, pendants, ivory combs, and bracelets; and the grayer the dame the gayer the shawls, and the more glorious the trinkets; pardon the gentle irony! I admire the decorative sex. I have looked until I have cracked my scrutinizing glasses in the vain endeavor to discover for you that golden cordial you desired—in your last summer letter to me; I find it not, she said, and I am aweary; but I'm still looking. It isn't sake; I've tried that much-exploited nepenthe: It's a shrieking fraud, and has an under-taste as if the unhappy vintner had died incontinent in the vat; I wouldn't keep a Ford from freezing with sake. Found American vegetables and fruits upon this (Admiral Line) steamer; and with screams of happiness gorged on food-stuffs free from disagreeable Oriental enteric: even my novelty-loving spouse sang welcome to clean American foods once more—and, as for me, I have rejoiced my belly with two kinds of Christin pie daily. We certainly are in the Orient! Our company comprises white, yellow, cafe-au-lait, burnt Sienna brown, and every cocktail color between—Japs, Chinese, 'Pino's, mixed pickles from

3. Peak Tramway HongKong.

Singapore, brown wives, and pied children, Spanish (Jesuit?) priests with flowing gowns and exceedingly evil complexions, one prize-fighter, one Portuguese horse-jockey and diplomat, who has explained to us with great distinctness just what is the trouble with Europe, and a fine representative bunch of every-day Americans to lend an air of quality to the social chaos.

We were in wireless touch with our girl's lad before we left Japan; met him at Shanghai—whereat were two most, most happy, happy children! Then the fleet was off for sea gun-practise, Amoy, and Manila.

We after them, to meet again—to-morrow morning—Tuesday, Oct. 30th—in Manila. A wireless, this morning, has had us hurrying such preparations as could be hurried here—asking that the wedding be Thursday night—Nov. 1st, instead of Nov. 5th, as planned: So, long before you get this pitiful apology for a letter, our girl will have left young maidenhood behind and will be Mrs. F. H. Wells: "a Navy wife." This ship is full of them, going down to join their husbands. We trust that silly, asinine politico Manila will behave itself while we are there: and will let our youngsters depart in peace at the end of their station here. It is hot; and we are all out in our white ducks, including myself, looking unusually handsome, as all admit.

I wonder what has happened in Carolina since we left; little or no news has reached us.

China did not look like these pictures to me: but dingy and old & dirty.

We expect to Xmas in Japan: Susan & I; and home, via Frisco, in February.

Yrs, in transit:
J. Bennett

Just heard of DuB. Heyward's marriage. But not a breath concerning *Mabel Webber.*

ORIENTAL HOTEL
KOBE

[Undated]

Dear Yates:

There's neither nepenthe of forgetfulness; nor cordial of delight; no anodyne enabling man to forget his sorrows; nor elixir which will persuade him to murder his mother-in-law: only the juice of the nipa palm or ngkapei the bitter herb of the Chinese. I bring you, therefore, in their stead a small ivory carving of one of the small gods of merriment and happiness, and hope that he may serve a little of the purpose.

[John Bennett]

Yates Snowden. Portrait by Margaret Walker in 1934 from photographs,
Federal Art Project, South Carolina WPA. *Courtesy of the South Caroliniana
Library, University of South Carolina.*

John Bennett in the 1930s. *Courtesy of the South Caroliniana Library, University of South Carolina.*

"Woodburn", Pendleton, S.C.
October

Mr. Yates Snowden,
Charleston, S.C.

My dear Mr. Snowden:—

I owe you some coals of fire for your "In a (Charleston) Rose Garden;" so I have requested my friends of the Century Company to send to your address a copy of my forth-coming book: "Barnaby Lee." If there is interest in it for you — suppose that it entertain you in spare time — if you ever find any — remember: this is my coal of fire.

Sincerely yours,
John Bennett

Letter from John Bennett to Yates Snowden, ca. 5 October 1902.
Courtesy of the South Caroliniana Library, University of South Carolina.

Yates and Anne Warley Snowden. *Courtesy of the South Caroliniana Library, University of South Carolina.*

John Bennett when he was editor and reporter of the *Daily News*, Chillicothe, Ohio, 1885–1889. *Courtesy of the South Caroliniana Library, University of South Carolina.*

Yates Snowden in his study. *Courtesy of the South Caroliniana Library, University of South Carolina.*

John and Susan Smythe Bennett on the porch of 37 Legare Street, Charleston, ca. 1914. *Permission of John H. Bennett, Jr.*

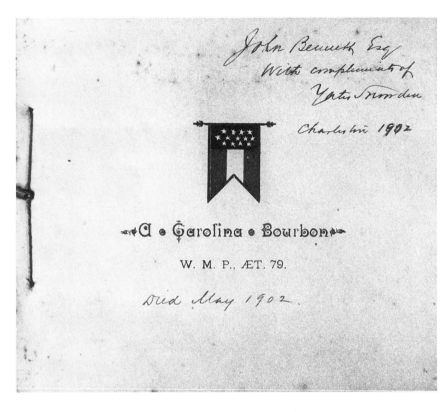

Cover of "A Carolina Bourbon," inscribed by Yates Snowden to John Bennett in 1902. *Courtesy of the South Caroliniana Library, University of South Carolina.*

Chapter 13

1924–1925

G. A. Wauchope's anthology; 1782 London account of Isaac Hayne's execution; criticism of the McCord family; Bennett's new project; Basil Gildersleeve and Charleston; F. P. Gaines's reference to Madame Margot; *Huguenot Church's Coligny medallion unveiling; tribute to Gonzales and Heyward; Southern Review authors; silhouette of flying-horse.*

IN FEBRUARY of 1924 Yates Snowden wrote of the joy that he and Mrs. Snowden were deriving from the little ivory oriental god; he critiqued Dr. G. A. Wauchope's newly published book, a copy of which he sent John Bennett; and he promised that in the near future he was going to give his friend the new *South Caroliniana in the University Library* bulletin.

In May Snowden mailed Bennett a letter to Ohio, where John had been for some time because of the death of his brother, Henry. He noted with regret that Hervey Allen was leaving Charleston.

In September Snowden was enjoying a newly purchased 1782 London volume of *The Political Magazine*, with its information about the execution of Isaac Hayne and criticism of the McCord family. He was happy to hear from Louise Jones DuBose that Bennett had begun work on a story set in Virginia and Ohio, but was sorry that John had given up his earlier plan to write a Carolina pro-Tory novel.

By the end of November Snowden had still not received a letter from Bennett, but he sent his friend a small twelfth edition of an old London book, *Selections from Physician's Prescriptions,* when he found in the *New York Times* a communication from Bennett in regard to pharmaceuticals.

Snowden quoted Basil Gildersleeve's regret that Charleston, once first in many fields, no longer continued its leadership.

At last, in December, John Bennett did write. He apologized for his lack of correspondence during the year, expressed his gratitude for Snowden's friendship, reacted to the Tory scathe on the Revolutionary War McCords, and commented on Snowden's article about dramatic possibilities of Caroliniana and on some remarks by DuBose Heyward about himself in the same paper. Bennett's absorption in the subject of old Charleston's apothecary shops, his abandonment of many writing projects, his continuing interest in the Charleston grotesque legends, his new novel about his father, his appreciation of the book on prescriptions from Yates, and his work with the Poetry Society of South Carolina were all referred to in turn.

Addressing Snowden as "Smelfungus" and using "Hannibal Crackeye" as his signature, Bennett wrote the first letter of 1925, possibly because he had been remiss in his 1924 correspondence and expected to do better in the new year, but also because Snowden had been ill with influenza. He thanked Snowden for sending him the notation from Francis Pendleton Gaines's *The Southern Plantation: A Study in the Development and Accuracy of Tradition,* in which the author referred to *Madame Margot* as an African interpretation of the Faust legend. And Bennett made a tongue-in-cheek comment on the South's debt to General Sherman in regard to plantations and megalomemory.

Bennett mentioned the joy of rereading the *Potiphar Papers* by George William Curtis, the Bennetts' Christmas, and his own recent illness. He also apologized for not having returned "The Affair of the Abduction of Sarah Hartley" and complimented Snowden on his poem "Looking Backward, 1974."

In January 1925 Snowden accepted the Bennetts' invitation to stay with them when he came to Charleston to speak in the Huguenot Church at the unveiling of the Gaspard de Coligny medallion. Bennett wrote Snowden that he and Susan had heard with regret that the pastor of the Huguenot Church, M. Florian Vurpillot, was leaving for France, for he had been a notable addition to the town. Bennett urged Snowden to have the University of South Carolina confer degrees upon Ambrose Gonzales and DuBose Heyward. He included a tribute to Gonzales and a long passage on the importance of Heyward's contribution to South Carolina.

In February Bennett received an appeal from New York for aid in identifying the authors of articles in the old *Southern Review* and turned for help to Snowden, whose printed list he had found, along with one by the Reverend Peter Shand. In one sentence Bennett referred to the biggest news story of the year, the death of Floyd Collins, trapped in a Kentucky cave.

Snowden promised assistance in tracing the *Southern Review* contributors. He also related an anecdote told about John S. Reynolds and his opinion of Spartanburg, South Carolina. In May Snowden sent notes from an 1859 New York historical magazine, and he asked Bennett to notify the Gibbes Art Gallery that their unfinished portrait of Mary Amarintha Snowden was not by Thomas Sully, but by a little-known English artist.

Addressing Snowden as Paganus Ignotus, the pseudonym with which he had signed his latest poem, "Domiduca," Bennett bewailed his lack of time in November to help his friend, being beset with requests by other writers, as well as carpenters, plumbers, and house guests. Nevertheless, he enclosed preliminary remarks on Snowden's poem. In December Bennett's Christmas present to the Snowdens was a flying-horse silhouette.

Columbia, 26th Feb'y '24

Dear John:

I send you a copy of Wauchope's *Littery* South Carolina! As you will soon see, it is fearfully & wonderfully made—utter lack of *littery* values; omissions; mistakes; shaky proof-reading, &c., &c.

Mrs. Jenny Screven Heyward[1] twice the space of Edward McCrady! James Henry Rice[2] much more than *you!* Dr. Schayer's[3] free-verse drivel several pp., & H. R. Sass *one line!* The good natured old chump, who gives *me 3 times too much space* (but makes W. P. Miles[4] instead of Mazÿck Porcher[5] the hero of my everlasting Bourbon) *asked me to write a notice* for The N. & C., which I have done & sent, & I suppose Sass will publish soon. It was a mean trick, for of course I would not *roast it* as it deserves, tho' I have put in 2 or 3 *teasers* at the end of my screed.

Wauchope is a good fellow, too good! The trouble is he wants to *puff* everything & *everybody*. What Ben Tillman said of Wilie Jones[6] applies to him: "He's too damned unanimous!"

As soon as I think you have recovered from this, I'll send you another bulletin: a *book: The South Caroliniana in the University Library;* that's "rocky" too, in spots, but infinitely better than Wauchope's.

You don't know how I enjoyed every instant of our brief interview, tho' I would have much enjoyed seeing Mrs. B. too.

Everyone admires that glorious little Jap. god of innocent merriment. My present wife shows it to nearly every visitor & offers a lens so that one can see his half-drunken jovial expression! (Much as I used to look 30+ years ago, before I was engaged to her!) Ah! How nice it is to sin, & be wicked! You should have known me in my golden (brazen) prime. It's 2:20 A.M. Adios!

Ever yours affectionately,
Yates Snowden

You saw Kenelm Digby's *reproduction* of your Xmas card from Cathay didn't you?

18th May '24

My dear John:

Many, many thanks for the copy of The Chillicothe News-Advertiser. Mack Horton told me, as I suspected, that you had gone to your old home & I was waiting for your return to Charleston to drop a line, at least, to tell you that my heart was with you.

Mac tells me now of the reason for your protracted stay at Chillicothe. But for the pitiful cause, I suppose that you are glad to linger there. I have no doubt that you love Charleston; I love Columbia in a way; but, I am sorry for the man who loves his step-mother, more than the mother who bore him, & therefore I imagine the old home town is very dear to you.

All that's trite, I know, but that's *me,* & I believe you.

As to that dear & accomplished brother of yours, my recollection of our brief but only meeting at Major Smythe's hospitable, and beautiful, "board," is vivid. I wish you had made him visit you oftener when I was at home, for I have heard you talk of him, & you have written more than once, with enthusiasm, and the warmest affection. I imagine you must have been very much "two of a kind" in taste, and sentiment, and talent, and so, ordinary filial relations aside, he must have been inexpressibly dear to you.

I hope you will be able to retain your old family nest-home! Some day, when my ship comes from sea, & I retire with more than my magnificent $1200. Carnegie annuity (unless I shall die or be "fired" meanwhile) I shall furnish the money for a little trip you & I shall take to Chillicothe. Who knows?

Years ago, before I ever knew or loved you, whether I had read something that attracted me (apart from its being the home of one of those wonderful old Grimké[7] cranks) or not—certain it is that I had a desire to visit Chillicothe! Funny? Eh. The human mind (even *mine!*) is a wonderful affair.

But, you will think that my little mind is wandering, and so I will close, with the assurance of the warmest sympathy of Annie and

Your affectionate friend,
Yates Snowden

Sorry to see that Hervey Allen is leaving Charleston. A queer, but brilliant, bird!

Hendersonville, N.C., 7th Sept. '24

My dear Jacques:

(Not "melancholy" I hope, despite the *possible* danger of that dear little woman in the far East!) It is a keen regret to the missus & me that we have not been able to get to "Many Pines" during the last four days. We leave here for Columbia tomorrow morning. Next summer (I almost write "DV," when I think of my old friend Teddy Guerard, my age 66, buried yesterday in St. Philip's ch. yard!), next summer, I say, we shall see you & yours more than once, or perish in the attempt. Indeed it was the hope of seeing you & yours that made me select Flat Rock as my "dilatory domicile" this summer, & it wasn't my fault that the bath-tubs were too small at the Stewart hostelry.

My kindest regards & Mrs. Snowden's to Mrs. Smythe, Mrs. B., Jack, Old Sam et ux, to you all and singular.

"If we do meet again,
Why then, we'll smile."

Yours aff'ly,
Yates Snowden

NB! Mrs. Snowden tried, more than once, to "ring you up," but was not successful.

Columbia, 27th Sept. '24

Dear John:

I sent a postal-order from H'nd'rsonville, for 5 shillings, for a bound vol. of *"The Political Magazine"* (London) 1782.

I "bit" at a report therein of the execution of "Col. Haynes" (*sic*).[8] It has come, & is "meaty," plenty of hot stuff, some of it new to me, as to that "ancestral rope" to which old J. B. Campbell[9] sarcastically referred, &c., &c.

What might interest *you* is a long blood-curdling story by a Tory criticising the widow McCord, who kept a tavern, & her very bad son, in the "patriot" ranks, *John McCord!*[10] Who da? Ask Mrs. Smythe, or Mrs. Jack Bennett. If you come to see me, I will show it to you; otherwise, "nothing doing"!

Yours sincerely,
Y. S.

NB! "Telfair Jr"[11] says this morning that you are writing a story about S. Eastern Ohio & Va. in Revolutionary times. Very glad; but I wish you had carried out your scheme of a pro-Tory romance, inter Charles Town & Moore's *Cr'k*, which you once had on the stocks.

28th Nov. '24

My dear John:

Frankly, I still don't understand your long protracted silence; I suppose I have "made you tired"; but, let that pass! I am under too many obligations to you, & your numerous letters in past years have brought me infinite pleasure & frequently instruction. I clipped your first-pharmaceutical-law letter from The N.Y. Times, & showed it to Mac H., who had not seen it. It will appear in Sunday's *State*. The N&C clipping man is moribund or dead! It's a Hell of a jump from the brilliant imagery of "Madame Margot" or "The Magnificat of the Hills" to pestles and pills; but, as you seem to be specializing in things pharmaceutical, I send you a funny little book, Dr. Pereira's "Selections from Physicians' Prescriptions," London, 1854 (12th edition). You couldn't understand the Latin jargon (or any one else!), but for the translation; and the whole collection of prescriptions is, in the language of Dr. Paris (p. 121) "a patchwork, not even consistent in its inconsistencies—a monster whose several parts bear no harmonious relation with each other." That "Dr. Paris" could sling English; eh?

See p. 78, for a funny footnote on *pro re nata!* &c., &c., &c.

After y'r eagle-eye has caught what little in the book will interest a modern amateur pharmacist, give it to your office cat;—or better still, send it, with your compliments, to your neighbor Dr. Wilson, or to Dr. Edw'd Parker.[12]

My regards to the mater & Mrs. Smythe!

Yours ever,
Y. S.

Grave-yard! please!

NB. *I,* parochial & provincial and unashamed, am proud of your discovery of Charleston "firsts," museum, pharmacy, &c. I was talking in that vein once to "St. Basil of Baltimore,"[13] the great Greek, who like myself was a native if not "a citizen of no mean city" and I think I told you his sadly apposite comment: "Yes, Snowden, I too am proud of those first discoveries & performances in Charleston & S.C.; *but why have we not kept it up?* It reminds me of *a foetus in a bottle!!!*

December 2nd, 1924

Dear Yates:

I suppose next you'll propose coffee and artillery for two, because, forsooth, or other reason, I have not played fair in this cross-purpose game which men call correspondence. Far from being injured, you have been—though you do not seem to know it—blessed by abstinence on my part. If challenged I shall propose exchange of daily letters, at easy mailing distance; and then may heaven have even more mercy on you than it already has evidently had! So that's that, to quote from the XIVXXXXVVVCCth Psalm, Apochryphal edition.

To put the nonsense aside and be serious and grateful—which I have been daily all summer long—I carried your beautiful, sensitive and comprehending letter of last 18th May with me all summer, meaning, and hoping, somehow, to find time properly to reply to its many-sided kindness, and to express my appreciation of your understanding of my situation, lingering there, after Henry's sudden death, in the blessed, quaint, lovely, and most loveable old town where I was not only born, but spent thirty-three odd years of my life. I did not find the time, and was ashamed to meet you face to face on Henderson streets with your letter still unanswered—no, not even acknowledged. But meet you I did; and your letter lay then on my table at Flat Rock marked at one end, SNOWDEN, for quicker recognition when the time came. And it is now December 2nd; and I have had, and acknowledge every one, at least three good letters from you since that, to none of which have I replied. I suppose I do deserve your curses, Yates.

And to read again—and again—your kind letter of last May—persuades me I do. I am sorry for it.

I know I am forgiven before I have reached this line—nor is this assumption presuming—but only confidence in a friendship and an affection which, from my earliest residence here has been and is now—and may it be for many a year!—one of the bright spots in my dwelling in the South. They have not been too many, Yates; but they have been the best man has: his wife, his home, his children, and his friends. Let it not seem flat when I say that life down here had lacked a spice without the toss of your hair, the flap of your cloak—not your inky cloak, dear Mother—and the contagion of your high spirit and your irresistible good humor. My life is memorized very faithfully, and my memory is singularly pictorial; and you are and ever will be, my dear fellow, one of the foremost and most loveable figures in the whole panorama. If my demise were the topic of the day, and you spoke with my wife, she could tell you far better what I thought of you, than I can write it: so I'll say no more, but simply thank you for all favors I have failed, somehow, to repay in sort.

"He always thought you," she would say, "a brilliant, charming, and greatly loveable man." She then might pause and say: "You were the first among his friends." She would not greatly err.

So that's that.

As to the Tory scathe on Capt. John McCord, nothing of that sort shocks my good wife: she has extraordinary breadth of mind, acquired since living with me—be gad! she had to, else it was not to be endured—and she has a sense of humor which would thoroughly appreciate a surreptitious view from the hollow rear of our heroic forebears, who on their swelly fronts so golden are! Capt. John lost too many prisoners en route, I presume, by Georgia parole. That had become quite the habit with some of the real hard-boiled whiggies of the bitter-ender breed. And, to judge by the last descendant of whom I have information, bearing that revered name, i.e., Col. D. J. McCord, of Columbia, the Captain was doubtless of a wee bit controvairsial nature! No?

Some day I must see what you have on the Captain: how many hung he?

(Y. S.: (Unlimited Creditor): in part payment of Acct.)

I must revert once more to an enclosure in one of your letters, containing one of those casual bits of commentary and suggestion of yours: "Resources in Caroliniana for Dramatic Adaptation." Over whatever signature you write, "Snarleyow," "Smelfungus," or yourself's cognomial, there is always something sprightly in your texts, beside the real meat: sometimes it's tart, and sometimes caustic; sometimes it is but a twisted grin of gentle irony: but meat always. If Dan Reed could but perceive it, there would be worse amusement, to-day, if well done—and by well-done I mean carefully caricatured and most *illy done,* should its proud first producer rise from the sands to see—in producing one of those gloriously bombastic, turgid and comic melodramas—as the Provincetown Players see 'em. But 'twould have to be extraordinarily well done, or the general audience of our acquaintance would miss the point outright.

In that same paper was marked a comment on myself, by DuBose

Heyward, in which, on what basis I know not, under the Literary Lantern head he refers to me as "distinctly Chippendale," and defines my "attitude toward life" as "quaint." What, in God's name, does the boy mean by that?

And, pray, sir, what do YOU mean by leaping upon my Museum activities with acrimony? I suppose it is, as you say, a Hell of a jump, from writing a gem like "Madame Margot" to trying to prove, for my children's sake, that South Carolina was first in something beneficial as well as a leader in a devastating rumpus which was her own undoing; but let that pass. I stirred up this question about licensing of pharmacists in investigating the early history of the Old Apothecary Shop—Billy Schwettmann's, where so often I dropped in to loaf and chatter of antiquity on my road home from the Charleston Library—and where Gude Wife never failed to locate and summon me by 'phone. And having once started it, I've got to finish it. I've begun too many noble things which Fate has well seen to it I shall never be permitted to finish, to permit such inessentials as precedence in licensing pharmacists to go to the dust undated and unproved.

That's what has happened to my dramatic Revolutionary romance of the Carolina Royalists—for one thing: and to the serious history of that war in the Carolinas, which was to make over comprehension of that struggle for the future—and, believe me, would in many things have done so for the battles and campaigns in the South. Add to these the best detective story ever written by an American author—the unfinished MS. of which I put into the fire—or I should show it to you, and prove my claim—and, anon, a picaresque romance of Charleston and the last pirate flicker in the West Indies, circa 1810; "Tales of an Innkeeper" and "The Lean Years"—tales of the wanderings of the English players when edict banished them from London stages; and the sequel to "Master Skylark," with the further adventures of that loveable rascally stage-player, Gaston Carew—who was not hanged after all, but banished. See, these are only a few, off-hand set down, of the happy things and dreams the world has missed by the perversity of Life. Believe me, these were noble books! And now they sit in memory on the shelf among the mental miscarriages, as bottled by St. Basil. Alas! Alas!

So, as a last chance to love a book and write it, I am engaging with Doubleday, Page & Co., to do one drawn from my Father's early life and singular experiences in earliest childhood in Old Virginia, and boyhood in frontier Missouri, ending with a successful youth, after hard service as furnace-store boy at old Buckhorn blast, near Hanging Rock, Ohio, and a happy outcome—ay, while it lasted—in old Chillicothe, where he achieved a position, and, permit me to say it, met and married one of the loveliest girls in that Valley of beauty, my mother.

At the same time I should like to go forward with a second one of the Charleston legends, "The Doctor to the Dead." But that I shall be allowed to finish one, or to pursue its course steadily, seems, as I regard life, to be something hardly to be hoped. Frustration is the flower which blooms most gaily in Time's garden. Nevertheless I am launched upon the story of "Buckhorn Johnny," dates 1820-'50—scenes, Virginia, Missouri, Ohio: (Southern Ohio, prythee)—Chillicothe. D. P. & Co., thought enough of it to send a representative here to see me, though I had not proposed the story to them. And their terms are so freely generous, enabling me to work almost unrestricted as to style and time taken, that I consider myself happy in this new arrangement. It may be I shall make a good yarn. I hope that I may—as Louis Stevenson said, "Just for fun!"

As to the comical "Prescriptions"—thanks, I shall *not* pass it on with my compliments to anyone—but, God willing, may yet find place for its delightful Latin in a good hearty tale—if gusto lives still under the dry hide of senectitude, which stealeth on apace—though, thank heaven, the dictionary says it's rare! If I can but pull off successfully the present adventure, it will put much new heart into the old hull. My God, Yates; it would be good to write two-three more tales!

I have been delving among the foot-notes of Pereira, those you indicated, pp. 78-79, which are almost facetious in their humor—and others, less uproarious than the antimony pill or the *pro re nata*, but not without some entertaining pith.

I am sending you enclosed one of the first licenses—in blank, of course—issued in South Carolina, in 1817-18, by the Examining Committee of the South Carolina Medical Society, to which was entrusted this duty and power, as you perceive, by act of Legislature, Dec. 18th, 1817. This form of license proved inadequate, and was superseded by a more technically precise form. I have forgot who printed it—and alas! it is too damned late in the night to hunt the fact—and, off-hand, I cannot tell what the printer's bill was for the lot; though that, too, I have. Someone should write the history of the Medical Society; but I suppose no one will. The chaps who started it were men of real stuff.

But I must end and to sleep. The affairs of the Poetry Society have descended upon my shoulders; and the rescue of more fine old apothecary-stuff from Dr. Joshua Lockwood's shop for the Museum has cut upon my time. Thanks to young Joshua L., but most to Allen Fripp, we have been enabled to preserve much antiquity. He recently brought me down a burlesque classic, which must be very like Rowland Rugeley's famous Dido and Aeneas—to extracts of which, in your possession, I have solicitously addressed A. F.—corrupt not young minds!

This is not ending, nor is it sleeping, though the night yawns behind me. Farewell; this is a broken tale; the future may repair it; but, mix well your metaphors, and quotations, and still detect the smell of the roses with which I strew it as it closes. Good-night, my dear Snarleyow! God bless and keep you ever, through the longest day! With compliments and deepest respect as well as affectionate regards, by permission, to Mrs. Snowden, I am

> With much love, yours,
> Pertinax Surly

———

January 17th, 1925

Dear Smelfungus:

We understand that you have been laid up with the Flu; for which we are cursedly sorry. We understand also that you are proposing a visit to Charleston (no matter what its extent: only the longer the better), at some time, near future, not further definitely denominated. Why the deuce cannot we also understand, dear Yates, that when you come to Charleston this time (or indeed any time that you come to Charleston), that you are going to be our cherished and welcomed guest at the big Green Barn, #37 Legaré St.?

We have rooms spoiling for occupancy, as thoughts, shut up, want air and spoil like bales unopened to the sun—ready at a postcard's notice, so that we may borrow clean sheets from the neighbors and get a cake of soap from the grocer's in anticipation of a distinguished guest. Why not, once in your career, confer the favor on a friend—on two friends—on a household—and just hang up your hat with the anomalous Bennetts?

I had missed the note of that gem MARGOT, in Gaines's[14] "The Southern Plantation," which your eagle eye detects and reports for my delight. Merci, M. Snowden!

As to *Gaines:* it was high time someone should attempt, before it is forever too late, to dam the flood of superlative nonsense being heaped by retroverted minds upon the glorious past. There's for you!

The Invaded South owes an everlasting debt to Tecumseh Sherman[15] for burning down dozens of small domiciliary structures absolutely without elegance or distinction, which, since that fortunate event, have been without exception exalted, in that strange and childlike megalomemory of the South, that sweet delusion of universal grandeur which now enshrouds the lamented past, into splendid Colonial Mansions, full of silver, jewels, costumes, tapestries, family portraits by distinguished painters, and not a damned stick of furniture short of Chippendale or Hepplewhite, nor mantel this side Adam. So, that's that for Gaines, maugre your objurgatory anent the Virginia gentleman! Scripsit damyankee: no? What!

Bless your heart, Raphael, the paintings which hung upon those walls of which we hear so much lament were for the most part commented upon in highest terms of appreciation by Mr. Halston Raycie. One of 'em has been for three weeks in the show-window of Cart's jewelry-shop, King Street, labelled "By Correggio"! Glory be to God! Back in the early years of the late lamented 19th Century, yes, enduring the roaring '40's, temporal, and not marine, taste was no more secured to the possessor of great wealth, nor culture by mastery, than by the milliards of our recent criminally rich. Go to with the glory of your old plantation! Grand-pa (*a* as in *hat*)—had one in Virginia, dubbed goldenly "White Hall," in retrospect effulgently serene; which, to-day, perhaps would serve for a fair garage for any malefactor of great wealth. Go to!

I had almost forgotten the delights of the Potiphar Papers until Christmas renewed their pleasure in Curtis's genial satire. You do not dare, being native-born, to admit just how much of that satire fits like a well-worn shoe upon the "culture of the South during the days of her glory"! I suppose you will burn this letter, lest you should mayhap be suspected of participating in heresy so profound. Go on; bring in the torch! Suppressio veri! But, remember, sir, it can never be safe to suppress what is true! (cribbed from R. L. S.)

I have been vainly endeavoring to make me a clean copy of Crossthwaite-Hartley; but they tried passionately, during the past ten days, to tear from my bleeding heart—or wherever the thing is—a pathological appendix and an accompanying ptosis; and much interrupted me. Ben Butler—and a rope to hang him? Very good, sir—had ptosis of an eye-lid; but that I had ever an eye, or an eye-lid, in my intestinal tract, or full abdominal sector, is more than I can be persuaded to believe. Still they vowed 'twas ptosis—and having no Greek I let them say; it did not make it true.

We enjoyed a hideous riot of young folks at Christmas-time, both indigines being present for their holidays; while the Dantesque maiden, as was, spent her Christmas, by greatest of luck, with her man, in Manila, not up the black, bleak, damnably terrible, mountainous coast of China. We hope her home in early summer—hooray!

Straying Columbians and pre-Columbians bring us littles from time to time appertinent to you; but little compared to a few real present hours of your godlike company—which vouchsafe to us, pray. You shall have a room with outlook, not, perhaps, upon Marion Square, or upon the Harbour, as in certain new castellated domiciles of acquisition, but on three private back-yards. There will be a desk-light in your room, so that you may indulge in your regular 3 o'clock in the morning epistolary; and breakfast easily sags after nine o'clock, and the cook makes noble waffles. All which the Chatelaine confirms.

Come, stay with us, and be our subject of all true Shakespearean song!

Yours affectionately ever:
HANNIBAL CRACKEYE.

A hasty P.S.:

My grief! I had overlooked your letter of Dec. 7th, accompanying "The Affair of the Abduction of Sarah Hartley," *You wanted it back to read at "some Kosmos Club meeting (about two weeks off),* when Bill Elliott"[16] should be present! TWO WEEKS OFF—from Dec. 7th! Oh, my King!

Whatever is necessary to be said I have said it. I repeat it twice. If not right, I amend it. If unsatisfactory then, I supplement—you dictating the terms.

My grief! and the Holy Smoke of Jove's altar!

N.B.: But if I ever get to that picaresque tale I dream of doing, shuttled between Kingston, Jamaica, and Old Charles Town, what a perfectly corking and uncorking episode!

But I can't send it back till I've copied it—I'm copying it at every spare minute—of which I have none—Margaret Widdemer[17] is our house-guest over the week-end—and I don't dare submit this rare text for copying to the Lady who does my Stenog. on acct. of ricochet verbiage.

Oh, glory! I must close.

P.S.: I have not yet put this into an envelope. But if I had I should have opened the envelope to say that I enjoyed your carsastic pome, date of Jan. 4, Biters and Rooks, entitled "Looking Backward, 1974." Gad, man; I envy that casual air without a trace of the dread nocturnal oleaginous aroma.

J. B.

21st Jan'ry '25

My dear old John:

Ha! Ha! You thought me convalescent with "flu" did you? And you spun that pretty yarn about that room all waiting for me, eh?

Well, by Heaven! I'll take you up, by coming down next Saturday on the Southern train that leaves here after dinner. I shall spend the night *chez vous,* & the next day I shall talk in the Huguenot Church, after

Father Vurpillot's sermon, apropos of Coligni & his little bronze medallion, for at least 15 minutes. Selah!

I shall dine with my poor relations; visit my sister; take a snifter with Bob Lebby[18] who married my cousin Hess Mikell; I shall then return to your shanty; talk as long as you can stand it, & take the cannonball 2 o'clock A.M. train for this benighted burg. Tell dear Mrs. Bennett that all I want Saturday night is a cup of tea; sassafras, if necessary; "sto" tea preferred. Thanks for y'r delightful letter & for the early scandal MS.

Yours till the crack of doom,
Y. S.

Have not written a line on the Admiral yet, & don't know what I shall try to say!

January 21st, 1925

Dear Yates: . . .

Come on, old chap, and stay with us this time; #37 Legaré Street will welcome you with open arms. I regret only I have no Dantesque maiden to embrace you at our door—were either here they should. Come on, and make us happy! We have waited years.

We understand that M. Vurpillot, pastor of the Church, is to depart, for France. This will be mourned by my good wife, who is intensely enjoying reading and conversation with M. Vurpillot, and has kept up her French uncommonly, thanks to his direction. With full credit to all attainment, there is none here can take his place.

And, speaking of attainment, has the University of South Carolina ever conferred a degree upon our splendidly courageous and brilliantly gifted friend, Ambrose Gonzales? If they have not, take it from me—a rank outsider, I hear you say—it is high time they did, for his service to the literature of the State, his personal contribution in the Black Border books, et al., his encouragement and fostering of literature in publication of outstanding Carolina works, as the latest, Miss W's "The Charleston Stage"; and for his unselfish labor for the adult illiterates of South Carolina—and for his unfailing and unfaltering devotion and affection for his fellowmen. A man who has embodied an era and a people in his writings should have this recognition: don't wait to put it on his tomb!

And while at that, what about the younger man who has done more to put South Carolina back on the literary consciousness of America at large than any other I can name: Heyward, who proposed and brought into being the Poetry Society of South Carolina, after which every one of the present existing Poetry Societies of the Southern States has been copied, line for line, by-law for by-law, plan for plan? Out in Texas I see that Austin College last Fall conferred a degree of Doctor of Lit. on Hilton R. Greer, specifically "for work done for literature in Texas in founding the Texas Poetry Society"—which absolutely took heart of grace from the example of the Society here, and copied its formulary item by item, sending Mrs. Therese Lindsay here to see how it was made to function, and observe its actual operation—and, though it is not to be said abroad, Mr. Greer's poetry scarce rises above mediocrity. Not only Greer was so honored; but Karle Wilson Baker, also of the Poetry Society of Texas, and a well-enough known Southwestern exemplar of verse, was given a similar degree by the Southern Methodist University, of Dallas, for her achievements in verse. (The S. M. University, by the way, has done itself no poor advertisement by it, and by making itself the center of an annual poetry contest taking in the entire country—but that's just flung in, brotus.) Then comes up North Carolina with Mrs. Olive Tilford Dargan, and confers a degree on her for her regional poetry interpreting her State. Now while we're talking about regional poetry interpreting one's native State, what is more or better so than DuBose's? Why, he is the one, present, authentic native voice—for, giving every due and courtesy to Mrs. Beatrice R. for much faithful following of her profession, hers is (with apologies) a slender inspiration indeed, though bravely and modestly followed towards the improvement of a narrowed income, as we know, and admire.

Heyward's verse is authentic poetry of unusual spirit and genuineness, in a day of manufactured stuffs of extraordinary emptiness and rotten hopes; and as Macmillan Co. says, among all the books of contemporary poetry on their lists, DuBose's "Skylines and Horizons" holds the sales record: which simply means that his is the heard and representative voice from Carolina, and is known as such across the United States. His stuff is authentic poetry; take it from me; and I know. Where the boy got his remarkable vocabulary and learned his brilliant fine-purged use of it I do not know: I leave that riddle to God in his Heaven: the high usage of English will not suffer at his hands. DuB. will be off in February for a lecture-and-reading tour of the Middle West; and in early Spring is to be among the New England colleges, to begin with Wellesley; from which institution I have a warm letter, from Katherine Lee Bates,[19] speaking in warmest praise of the work being done and inspired through the South by the Poetry Society of South Carolina— "quite putting the New England poetry societies to the blush," she concludes frankly. And this new Southern movement, so far as the now pretty widely spread action of poetry societies is concerned in the renaissance of letters with us below the Line, was fired from DuBose Heyward's conception of a Poetry Society for South Carolina.

The commentary upon his poetry throughout the sanest of the Northern reviewers is extremely favorable. And, as I said before, he is recognized as the voice of South Carolina, perhaps as no other Carolina poet has ever been recognized before—bar none; and I know them all.

I know, of course, that it is often indispensably requisite for the recipient of a scholastic degree to have accomplished a certain—or very often quite uncertain—amount of recognized academical work. If not to have done so should prevent the gift of these degrees to either Mr. Gonzales or DuBose H.—the collegiate claims of the former being not known to me—why, so much the worse for the conferrers of degrees where the wooden line of dead academics is substituted for gift and real accomplishment.

It would seem to me, Yates, that, though he may be able to present little academic, Heyward would be singularly exemplary of the long-heard claim of the South to a native refinement, culture, and high taste, supposed to be inherent in the best, and often boasted in the face of a gross and thinly-cultured Otherwhere. Isn't this so?

I recollect that during the past year—or is it two years?—the University has conferred a degree upon Rev. Wm. Way,[20] I believe for his particular instance of a history of "The New England Society" of Charleston. If I am in error, pass me up with the sparks. If right, think it over. I know Wm. Way, and appreciate him to the full.

We have now here, too, the woman of one most unexpectedly good book: Miss Willis—whose measure you will have taken more knowingly than I am able to do, being far more informed upon her theme.

But I cannot but think it a thing well and fittingly done, and a distinction well-earned indeed, and well to be still further deserved by its recipient, should your University think wisely to put this kindly distinction upon a very brave and fine young chap, a real poet from this State: namely, just DuBose Heyward, academics or no academics.

Well, perhaps that's fresh, blunt speech from Truthful James. I hope you'll perceive the merit of what I have said. And, also, Yates, we both hope, that you will, this time—and many more—accept our heart-felt invitation—which has no degrees—but is altogether whole—and just come down to the Big Green Barn, #37 Legaré St., and stop here with us while in town, this week-end, attending and addressing the gathering of the noble body of Huguenots at the Coligny affair on Sunday. Please send us a line—or COME WITHOUT: the latch-string cries for you:

Yours affectionately—
James

Charleston, February 17th, 1925

Dearest and Ablest of the Hosts of the
Unrighteous:
Greeting:
Etc. as follows:

I recently received an appeal for aid from Miss Elizabeth S. Bearden, of Columbia University, N.Y. (whom I am led to surmise has been also a correspondent of thine, also), in identifying the contributors to the old SOUTHERN REVIEW, concerning whom you printed, in The STATE, Nov. 30, last, a list of identifications, from a previous list, printed, "some time in the '40's," I believe you recklessly assigned it, in the Charleston COURIER.

Your printed list—the re-print from the COURIER of the '40's—is on file with the bound files of The REVIEW in the Charleston Library. There is also there filed a MS. list of identified authors of articles contributed to The SOUTHERN REVIEW, prepared by Rev. Peter Shand,[21] for a friend, named "Whitefoord," from entries made upon the margins of a file of The REVIEW, "in the private library of Mr. Barnwell," which entries, or checks, are supposed to have been there made by none other than Stephen Elliott, Junior,[22] who after his father's death, sometime assisted Legare[23] in the management of The REVIEW, and thus should have been with some intimacy, perhaps accuracy, informed as to the list of contributors to the magazine.

In examining this MS., having been told that it was practically only a duplicate of the list you had printed, from the Courier of the '40's, I was delighted to discover that it differs in a number of details from your re-printed list, amplifying it in some particulars, contradicting it in several, and adding, I believe, considerably to our small knowledge.

I at once transcribed this MS. list of Peter Shand's, for Miss Bearden's assistance; and have made a duplicate of that transcription for you, feeling that in your position regarding these Carolina matters you should have fullest information, and being personally very happy to add, perhaps, to your store.

I suggest that, as its publication will in no way affect Miss Bearden's application for degree, you prepare something further on this topic for The STATE, either merely an amplification of the lists, or in commentary upon the derivative information afforded by comparison of the two.

All the additional information contained in Dr. Shand's list should be given publicity, for the benefit of those who have clipped your first article, and will gladly add further information to it regarding the content of the old REVIEW—and of future students seeking further to study the character and influence of The REVIEW.

Further no more at this time, dear Lord; I should not now be engaged in so delightful a pastime as dribbling out chat to you, as I am buried under Ossa, Pelion and Chaos—in worse case, not being fortunately fatal, than poor Collins[24] in his cave!

Oh, farewell, farewell! I who am about to criticise poetry openly before its authors, to-night, salute thee! Farewell, farewell! I do not, however, care for a turtle-dove at my tomb—make it roast turkey with ground-nut inside!—and watch me rise!

Affectionately ever, yours,
Pertinax Surly

20th Febr'y '25

My dear John:

A waffles and butter letter has been long due Mrs. B. & you; but, let that pass! For 66 years I have disregarded the amenities—aye, decencies—of civilized life, and it's too late to reform. But don't think I can forget that happy day and night *chez vous*, & when I come back to town, I'll entertain Bennett *et ux* many a time, I hope, at my palatial apartments at the Enston (?) Home. My wife being a rank and obstinate American I am afraid we cannot secure a Colin McK. Grant[25] flat.

Your last letter was a *hummer!* How *can* you write your great novel and help every Tom, Dick & Harry to find anything they want about everything? I like Miss Bearden and am glad *she* got her fangs into you; but you must draw the line somewhere. Of course, you must continue the joint management with Gen'l Bragg of the Museum, & you can't overlook the Charleston Library, & you can't desert your own off-spring, the Poetry Society; and so on, & so on! But, after all, there are only 24 hours in a day, & you must sleep 4 hours. I read your fine So. Review data with infinite pleasure, and immediately carried it to Kennedy our librarian who is going to compare it with the University's *marked* Reviews, & mine (?); yours; the University's; & possibly old Aleck Salley's collection *all together* may give us a pretty correct list.

"Whitefoord" is, of course, the "great" Methodist preacher Whitefoord Smith!

Didn't you ever hear of old John S. Reynolds[26] going to *Spartanburg* to live and returning to Columbia in 4 or 5 months? When asked, "Why?" He said: "I could not live in a d——n place where you were not tolerated unless you recognised Dr. Carlisle[27] as a greater mathematician than Copernicus, and Whitefoord Smith as a greater preacher than St. Paul," &c., &c. I have forgotten the rest.

I was talking to Billiams Ball t'other day. He said he had attended some com*tee* meeting recently (not the degree committee!) and that Prexy Melton[28] had mentioned two men (outside of S.C.) he thought deserving of L.L.D. or Litt. D.; and that thereupon, he (Ball) had risen to his full height and had agreed with Prexy & had added that he had a name too, which *he* intended "to present & *push*, & that was John Bennett"!!! I then told Ball of your having strongly advocated DuBose Heyward, which Ball thought was a good idea; but persisted that Bennett was better! I don't know how it will turn out. Faculties are like juries, & you have heard of "those 11 d——n fools on the jury." Eh? But, certes, *Ball* is no fool!

My love to your wife & you,
Yours affectionately,
Y's Snowden.

4th May '25

Dear John:

I enclose you 2pp. from (Dawson's?) Historical Magazine for April 1859, pub'd in N.Y.

It may interest you a bit, that Victorian Ohio journalism, or it may be as useless as that Oregon pamphlet I slipped under your door. To the trash-box with it, then!

One word more & I am done. If you have the ear of the Gibbes Art Gallery people, please tell them that that unfinished portrait of my mother in her youth *was not by Sully*, but by an English artist named *Ray*.[29] Be with me in your prayers on Friday May 8th. It will be a horrible day!

My kindest regards to your best friend, who makes those toothsome nocturnal waffles, & to the young wife—over the water.

Yours aff'ly,
Yates Snowden

Friday 13th [Nov.], 1925:

My dear Paganus Ignotus:

I knew that some misfortune would befall upon the fatal combination of Friday and 13. It has fell. SEND BACK YOUR POEM? Why, confound it! D'you think I've no God's thing to do but mail poems to poetasters? Go To! Carpenters in the house, plumbers on their back; guests from the West; Koch[30] of North Carolina week-ending with us; Rice, and Bryan,[31] want his book reviewed; M. Whaley[32] wants *his* book reviewed—am writing—or hope someday, somehow, to begin to secure leisure to take up the idea of writing—a book—send back your poem? SEND BACK YOUR POEM? GLORY BE TO GRIEF!

I might cruelly say, "*Was* that a POEM you sent me?" But then I am of a gentle nature, more tempestuously ebullient than rough of tongue. I'll admit, for the sake of argument that the thing has merits; and—having looked it over, days ago, marked it, and thought I had returned it to you—after a wild search discover the golden prize, removed to another room by my housemaid during the incursions of the carpenter.

I have no license to keep explosives in the house—and make haste to rid us of the TNT—by this enclosure and first mail, IMMEDIATE DELIVERY—lest the Pagan perish in his pains! And there you are—and shilling to buy a rope!

The photograph, *so* gay, *so* debonair, *so* characteristic, *so* derogatory, etc., etc., gave great delight to Jane. Truly, though I hardly understand it, she was greatly pleased to be remembered, and to have that inscribed po'trait—and very justly scorns ME, who have none, but an ancient print cut from a University annual eons since—looking much like the Piltdown man. Well, so it is always: the young and fair get the golden apples from the gardens of the gods; the old, faithful, and long-snuffling are forgot! Eheu!

The silhouettes were appreciated; more the thought. Graceful little things. The reason I do not make silhouettes for Macmillan and the rest, of this sort, is that they do not pay enough for them to make it worth my time at my age—not looking forward to a life-struggle to live by art, and preferring to amuse myself and my friends with such skill as may be mine with paste and shears, and hymn-book end-papers beautifully black.

We all send affectionate regards—and more, an admiring, amused, and real devotion—heaven knows whether it be deserved or not. Only come again to see us.

Jane has improved steadily—perhaps partly through the exhilaration of your visit—or in spite of it—as you will! As to hearing some one "roast" Chillicothe: a great many have done so. What their reasons are I do not know; perhaps a plenty; when you have always loved a town, the place where you were born, and spent a happy boyhood, an austere, strenuous, yet at last successful youth and younger manhood—and see the hills and shores and woodlands ever after golden with remembrance, it makes no difference who damns a town or roasts it—dear Yates, there is one such born each moment—to perdition with the unappreciative ass—give him my compliments—he must have been there with unsalable goods, a face which convicted him, ill-introduced, or with the mob that overflowed the village like a tide of oafs during the late war—to me *which* matters not at all—nor do I mean my diatribe against the unappreciative heathen. The old town remains what it has ever been to me—and so ever will remain, though the heathen rage and skies fall—they cannot fall upon a memory of home and youth and boyhood friends—who, by some strange dispensation of providence, are my friends still—or else are—dead. God's peace be with them and the grass green over them!

I guess that's all. I truly thought I had mailed your self-addressed—and unstamped—envelope (and no glue on the flap!) days ago—I hadn't; but do now.

Farewell, God bless you; the oftener we see you the happier we all shall be, youngest and oldest!

My admiring respects to that charming and devoted wife of yours, and Mrs. Bennett's and Jane's regards therewith to her:

There's your damn ten minutes—pressed down and running over.

> Farewell!
> Affectionately yours:
> John Bennett

Dec. 23d, '25

My dear Jack:

We thank you for that brilliant flying-horse & flying dog. When my ex'or sells that series of Xmas silhouettes, he will get a fancy price, unless I generously give them to some art school before I join the angels.

I enclose $5.00 for which kindly buy *something that Jane wants,* & present it to her with my love & best wishes.

Now, I *know* (as well as you & your blessed wife!) that this proceeding is not "en règle"; "au fait"; that it is not only "bad form," but absolutely indecent; but we have known each other long enough not to be so *damned proper.*

I have had *four books* presented to me in the last four years, *which I already had in my little library!*

Nuff sed! God bless us all,

> You'uns & We'uns.
> Yours aff'ly,
> Yates Snowden

Chapter 14

1926

Revolutionary War Captain John McCord and his mother; Francis Asbury's Journal; Governor and Mrs. Thomas Worthington of Ohio; family news; Confederate General Isaac Ridgeway Trimble; Bennett's account of scene with Major Smythe at time of his request to marry Susan; "The Magnificat of the Hills"; works of Dr. Joseph B. Ladd in eighteenth century.

IN MAY of 1926 the death of Sam Stoney, Sr., was mourned by Yates Snowden and John Bennett. Snowden sent Bennett the bound volume of the 1782 London magazine mentioned the year before, which contained interesting material on South Carolinians during the Revolution, including the story about the McCords, ancestors of Susan Smythe Bennett. Snowden told of Frank Hayne's plans to mark the grave of his kinsman, Isaac Hayne, who was executed by the British during the war. In reply, Bennett mentioned that his son, Jack, and Frank Hayne's son had become friends at Yale. Later, Bennett described Jack's return home from school in June in his ancient car, by way of Shepherdstown, West Virginia.

Snowden and Bennett attempted to locate the painting of the Battle of Eutaw Springs with Laurence Manning in the forefront. Also, Snowden remarked on his purchase of an old journal of Francis Asbury that included visits to Chillicothe and notations on the Worthingtons, whom Bennett revealed in his next letter as his close relatives. John Bennett's connections with famous Confederate figures were disclosed in subsequent discussions of Asbury's *Journal*. Snowden taunted Bennett as "no more damnyankee than I." When Bennett wrote of his uncle Isaac

Ridgeway Trimble, his grandmother's brother with the squeaking "jury-foot," Snowden immediately realized that Trimble was the general called the hero of Manassas Junction by Stonewall Jackson.

On 18 July Bennett recounted the story of his conversation with Major Smythe at the time he requested Susan's hand in marriage. When asked about his family, Bennett replied that one of his father's cousins was hanged for piracy. Pressed for more information on the matter, he told the Major that the kinsman held a Confederate commission from Jefferson Davis, and that, when captured during the War Between the States, his cousin was executed by the North as a pirate and a spy.

The death of Ambrose Gonzales was commented on in July. In August the Bennetts traveled to West Virginia and Ohio. Of the return trip in the middle of September, Bennett wrote about the family's being lost in the mountains of West Virginia in the pouring rain and of their eventual return "home to Pepysian peace." Snowden took exception to his use of the phrase and Bennett countered with a discourse on Pepys.

Snowden, who regularly reprinted and distributed Bennett's "The Magnificat of the Hills" during his visits in the mountains, sent Bennett the reply he had received from Henry Bellamann about setting the poem to music. Bennett then explained that the verses were not designed to be sung; he described the inspiration for his poem in the Appalachians; and he contrasted the Blue Ridge Mountains to the Canadian Rockies. The year ended with the consideration by Snowden and Bennett of the works of Dr. Joseph B. Ladd, an eighteenth-century Charleston resident.

Columbia, 30th May '26

My dear Jack:

Only a short scrawl to you, for I must write tonight to "Miss Lou." I know what a shock Sam's death was to you *et ux;* & I turned, when I heard the news (*per* my sister May),[1] to your fine dedication to "Peyre Gaillard," every word of which you meant then, & doubly *feel* now.

Had the funeral been on *Saturday,* I would have come down. It was impossible for me to leave here Friday A.M. This afternoon I packed for express, or mail, my bound vol. of *The Political Maga* (London) for 1782.

I shall be sorry if you should have already seen (in the Gazette) Levi Smith's story of "the horrid cruelties committed by the Rebels on the King's loyal subjects of S.C."—two of the head persecutors being *the Widow McCord* & *Capt. John McCord!* If the Lady Susan Bennett thinks the article of sufficient interest, I hope she will read some of it to Mrs. Smythe—with my compliments.

Frank Hayne[2] has recently visited S.C. and went to the unmarked grave of his progenitor Isaac. (I *think* he is going to put a stone there.) I gave him Robt. Y. Hayne's[3] story of the execution of Isaac in the 1*st no.* of the Southern Review. Strange to say, he had never read it! I told him I had this "Political Magazine" with the Parliamentary proceedings on Hayne's execution, the Duke of Richmond's charges *vs* Rawdon . . . & subsequent back-down, &c., &c. Last week he wrote urging me to lend him the book. But, thinking Mrs. B., if not you, may want to read that McCord stuff, I am *sending it to you first!* I enclose mail or express charges. Will you, in a few days, forward the mag. to *Frank B. Hayne,* 225 Carondelet St., *New Orleans,* & oblige your pesky but affectionate friend,

Y. *Snowden*

NB! *By the way,* I bought *a rare bird,*[*] Francis Asbury's[4] Journal, 3 vols, unbeknownst to my wife.

Sept. 24, 1803, Asbury visits *Chillicothe,* & the neighboring country, & makes brief comments; but, "he preached in the State House which also answers for a Court House to about 500 hearers."

On Aug. 23, 1814, he is there again; one long paragraph only. Praises *Mrs. Worthington,*[5] & her children, all brought up in the fear of the Lord—but little more.

Will copy these paragraphs for you, *after exams*—if they are of any interest—I fear not.

Y. S.

Love to Jane!

[*](Asbury, not my wife!)

At P.O.

Sacre bleu! Milles tonnerres! *Decoration Day.* Sapriste! &c., &c., &c.

Stamp window closed. Can't enclose stamps until tomorrow. Will send mag. by express.

Y. S.

———————

June 2, 1926

Dear Yates:

Yours of the 30th May to hand, followed by the Political Magazine, 1782 (London), containing choice commentary on maternal ancestry of young Bennetts, Smythes, Stoneys, Wrights, et al.—our old friend Levi Smith once more to the front asking retroactive condemnation of our patriot forebears—alas! Too human, too human, all!

Well, they got even with the Widder McCord when they burnt her out; and Captain John returned the compliment when he issued Georgia paroles to prisoners consigned to his care for transfer—we understand Georgia paroles to be tolerably final!

Those were vivacious days—and even greater evidences than the vocative Levi's plaint are recorded in the hearings of the Loyalist Commission—it's God's truth, when one truly knows what has been done by those who preceded us in the world, he no longer "points with pride" (unadulterated) to "our chivalrous and noble ancestors," but, weighing both the good and bad, says with a cheerful grin, "Unchanged humanity!"

We shall make much note from Levi, that the record may be kept straight. Would to the great Jehovah those who prate so much of the keeping records straight would lie less about their grandfathers' nobility, and tell the truth more of an ancient enemy's honest aims and worth. I apply this blanket-fashion to all our wars and differences. I never knew how much the Yankees misrepresented history until I realized how terribly it was twisted from the facts by ardent advocates of that antagonistic section in which I pitched my moving tent.

When I was young I said with the great ancient, "All men are liars"; subsequently I amended it to read, "Anyone, man or woman, particularly the latter, who holds a brief for any party, to preserve its glory and obliterate its faults, and does this by diminishing the credit of its antagonist, is without doubt an unforgiveable liar."

"It must always be foul to tell what is false; and it can never be safe to suppress what is true." A better man than I said that.

But why permit myself this heat and utterly futile indignation? Yet it is one of the things which finally persuaded me to give over the writing of history: those who tell the truth are few, and those who love to hear it fewer. Let us pass on. Yet it remains true: noble souls would crucify the lie; ignoble souls preserve them.

By all means let Frank H. mark that grave: it marks a pitiful and tragic death: yet let us ask a moment what measure would Andrew Williamson[6] have received had his captors not been so swiftly and fatally made captive themselves? I own I do not know all the facts of bitter times. Out upon Rawdon and Balfour, surely!

Oddly enough, Yates, my boy, Jack, has just begun a friendly acquaintance with Frank Hayne's son, at Yale—which we are very pleased to foster.

We have also found, recently, in the story of the great firm of Alexander Brown, of Baltimore, confirmation of family tradition concerning the close business relationship existing between the house of Brown and old James Adger;[7] and of the imperative call to Langdon Cheves to rehabilitate the shaking U.S. Bank—with the evidence that he did so.

And, doubtless, both Smith and Brown are truthful.

Oh, well! I had a cousin hanged for a pirate. Let us all admit the truth.

I shall take pleasure in forwarding the Political Mag. to F. H. in a day or two, having excerpted certain vividly entertaining passages therefrom. Oh, Lord of Israel, Yates, I wish I might multiply you by several thousand, and shake the result, like a salt savor, over Dixie-land!

Or have I had the taste of Dixie—or of but a corner—a narrow corner—

I guess I am fretful of my times. All great souls have been. Yes, yes; that is it, my great soul is fretted by the times: I had not so clearly thought this out to the penultimate before. Thanks, awfly, to Levi Smith, for setting powerful ratiocinating powers in thus happily conclusive motion! Thanks, also, Y. S., for supplying the electric spark dynamic and explosive to a consoling philosophy and conclusion of my plaint!

I never have seen that rare bird, Asbury; though I have long marked him down for a spare barrel some day—which might come at last to be no day at all.

If you will indeed copy out for me Asbury's paragraphs anent the Ancient Metropolis of the Northwest Territory, I will be truly obliged.

That "State House," of which he speaks, was builded under the supervision of Maj. Edw. Rutledge, of Carolina; whom I have never been able further to identify: he died out there in Ohio, and, so far as I have been able to recover, lies in an unmarked grave.

I am pleased Asbury praises Mrs. Worthington: she was Eleanor Sweringen, of Jefferson County, Va., Shepherdstown namely, and cousin to my Father: Thomas Worthington was also a Jefferson County-an: her old home at Adena, beyond the town upon the hills, is a truly lovely place, but not now in possession of any of the family. It was the view of the rising sun beyond the eastern range of hills, from the terraced garden of Adena, gave the original idea for the great seal of the State of Ohio, the rich farm-lands in the valley below suggesting the sheaf of wheat: and recent wars and Indian troubles suggesting the emblematic strength of defense and offense in the accompanying sheaf of war-arrows. Tecumseh and Blue Jacket both were at times guests at the Worthington home,

Adena, in treaty-making conference; Tecumseh left his tomahawk-pipe there in recognition.

As to your footnote: your wife is a flower, not a bird. Where is your appreciation of loveliness? where your biology?

Of Sam Stoney's death I shall not talk. Your letter comforted his family. They are courageously and nobly meeting the great readjustment and sorrow together; Augustine providentially being resident at home, Sam coming from New York, and Louisa Popham remaining for quite a sustaining visit with her mother, who is heroic but weary and shaken. Minnie Vaux came with Sam and Louisa from Philadelphia; and Tom and his boy, David, from St. Louis: Tom is wretchedly torn; but David pretty fine, and upholding his father's intense depression of spirit by a very gentle supporting strength. They left, yesterday.

As to your stamps; shucks, lad! what's stamps among friends? My wife and children use mine as if they were communal conveniences.

And so no more at this wild writing: the house being full of pipe-fitters, plumbers, concrete-mixers, and builders, supposedly installing an oil-burning furnace against the frigidity to come; but really frightfully diverting genius from its meat! Farewell, Yates—and one more, two more, three more, four more notes: Jane is well and in Boston with Forrest; Sue will visit her a fort-night at close of school; Jack is driving home with comrades, via the Shenandoah Valley, from Yale; and Mrs. Bennett is preparing Miss Sarah Annie's house for its new purchasers, Capt. and Mrs. Traut, U.S.A, retiring; she is well & sends regards: while I, like one avoiding an old friend to whom he owes much, turn thus a sudden corner—and disappear.

> Affectionately yours,
> J. B.

[Yates:]

Feb.,   "blasphemous, drunken, insulting
1865:   bad faith..blazing houses, falling
          rafters, shrieking women and children"

("unrelieved by anything that was not
(horrible, save the kindly help of a
(sympathetic Ohio soldier"[8]

Thanks, for the one soldier.

June [16],   Yrs. faithful
1926:   et loving,
                                              D——yankee

_____

                                              18th [June] '26

Dear Jack:

I began to copy that Chillicothe item from Asbury, *in re* Worthington, when on looking at the crazy index I found that the old fellow had been to Ohio 4 or 5 times, so, I have determined to bring down the 3 vols. (tail end of next week) & let you copy the stuff for yourself. You are a great deal younger & smarter & quicker than *me!* That is, unless you are going to leave the Enchanted City *very* soon. If so, write me, & I'll copy the stuff myself.

Queer; but I sorter had a "hunch" that you were kin to the Worthingtons!

I rec'd your impudent postal card this morning; & have shown it to nine people. I hope you don't think I "imagined" that Yankee Ohioan, just to pacify *you! You* are no more of a "Yankee" than I am! I mean the genuine down East genus described by O. W. Holmes: "If the archangel offered to save him for a shilling, he would look for one with a hole in it"!!!

I have no business to pester you so often; but, *please* look at this letter of Bernard Manning[9] & *send it back to me* with the desired information!

Very late—or very early—& I'm sleepy.

                                              Adios,
                                              Y. S.

Have you sent that book to Frank Hayne yet? I heard from him Wed'y & he did not mention it.

If I sent you one of the enclosed "Master Skylark in Eng" clippings send this back. You were away when it appeared.

_____

                                              June 23rd., 1926

Dear Yates:

You did not send me one of those SKYLARK clippings, of Dec. 16, '13: and I am filing this one, which seems to have been your very generous intention—and thank you for it. You called my attention to the notice in the London TIMES, but your own expansion and improvement on it you were too modest at that time to send—it must have been modesty; for nothing in God's green world restrains your unhesitating generosity unless it be modesty.

In one of your recent vivid radio-graphs you asked me if I had forwarded the vol. of the Mag. to Hayne, in N. O. Surely—at once, insured; he should have received it very promptly. Regarding Manning's letter, I can make no reply off-hand—so hold the query until I can discover my complete ignorance or vague intuitive phantasm of facts. Will return in a day or so with honest confession of my state regarding same. Thanks for the stamped-addressed envelope for return: you are a wonderful and extravagant person.

I shall await you and Asbury. So he visited Ohio four or five times, eh? I must think better of the old duffer! I once, long ago, knew a charming lad named after Asbury. He died—and they preached a simply frightful familiar country sermon above his body which in memory grues me yet.

I shall not be leaving the Enchanted City: we have just put in a stupendous oil-burning furnace ready for July and August; so shall probably remain in town most of the summer.

As to the Worthingtons: they came from the old Shepherdstown—Charles Town neighborhood, Jefferson County, Va., where my Father was born—or did I hurl this at you before. They were consequently, in good Virginia fashion—paralleled in old South Carolina—kin to everyone in the County—but, in this instance, chanced to be near of kin. Madam Worthington may have been pious, but she had fine points—some of which I hope to elucidate in the yarn I now am desperately endeavoring to write. Latrobe designed her house, and she certainly made a lovely home on those Ohio hills. On one occasion, when my Father was desperately ill in town, the old lady rolled down from the heights in her coach, picked him up bodily—a boy of sixteen—carried him back to the hills and nursed him back to health—gave him the run of the terraced gardens and the old Governor's library—from which he sustained a lifelong fondness for Duchess pears, Milam apples, and American politics—also for the old lady's memory.

Of course, if one determines and circumscribes, one diminishes the demesne of clock-peddlers; but I thought damyankee was rather a broadly regional rather than a pinching village epithet—I'll make you a present of the extra rather. It was the boys from my home county and town held their cousins from Maryland and Virginia at the top of Cemetery Hill and debated the point with some stubbornness to mate the vivacity of their adversary kinsmen.

That is why my Uncle Isaac Trimble's[10] foot squeaked.

He was a delightful old rebel.

Some time Sunday afternoon last past an ancient and temperamental Ford car, driven by a stained and wayworn but otherwise cheery youth, pushed through the village of Columbia with a broken brake-rod dragging, one lamp out of commission, and a frozen steering-gear—homeward bound, after a delightful journey through the Shenandoah Valley, from New Haven.

He reached home, Sunday night, dodging the police adroitly, and reports a large time: two Greenville youths, and an Asheville ditto, made up the party.

When they reached Shepherdstown, Jack's cousins gave them so warm a welcome and such a hospitable reception that the boy comes home convinced that hospitality, courtesy, charming old ladies, and pretty girls are found in superior quantity in Virginia—and beyond compare. Excepting South Carolina and the Scioto Valley, Ohio, around Chillicothe, this is perhaps true.

My younger girl returns from that sink of iniquity, Massachusetts, to-morrow. The Dantesque has been giving her a huge time for ten days past, since close of school.

But name of a name! why prattle I on? This must end—I have all other earth and part of heaven to do in the fading remnant of an afternoon—farewell, farewell, farewell! (To be repeated with a dying fall—like Hamlet's ghost)—

> Adieu! adieu!
> Affectionately yours,
> John Bennett

"Margot" will not be out in Esperanto until Fall.

27th June '26

Dear Jack: . . .

Annie is still sick with neuritis or lumbago, or both! Not abed, but in great pain nearly all the time. The osteopath has given some relief & thinks she will be *o.k.* by Thursday, & that next Saturday she can go to the mts., & I to "town"—and so, I sent the books rather than delay.

. . . In Gilbert & Sullivan, *somewhere,* there is a story of two men wrecked on a desert island, Brown & Jones. There they lingered for long months, *but not having been introduced,* of course they *could not speak to each other.* At last, one day J. heard B. saying to himself: "Now, if Robinson were here, how happy I would be."

"*What!* " cried Jones rushing forward, "Do *you* know Robinson?" &c., &c., &c. And all went very well, then!!

Of course, I knew as soon as I first met you, and before you owned a house in Legare St., and before you became my friend, that you were a gentleman & a scholar, and highly respectable, &c., &c., &c.; but, your last letter was a tremendous eye-opener to me, and had the same effect as the "mutual friendship" with Robinson had on the two castaways.

And so the gallant Isaac Ridgeway Trimble was your uncle, was he? I wish he were mine; that hero of Cross Keys; the man who captured Manassas Junction at night, after marching his men 34 miles without food; "the most brilliant achievement that has come under my notice during the war," one *T. J. Jackson* said!!! I congratulate you Jacobus on that glorious old one-legged uncle! Bradley Johnson, who was no slouch himself, said that "of all Md's brave soldiers Trimble performed the most distinguished service, obtained the highest rank (Major Gen'l) and won the highest fame." Shut up, you semi-rebel, you are no more damyankee than I am, with my great grandmother Ann Lawrence of Elizabethport, N.J.

Well; here endeth the 125*th* lesson. I'm sleepy. Adios!

Yours aff'ly,
Yates Snowden

NB! Frank Hayne writes that he has rec'd, and already read much of my book. Thanks!

———————

June 28th, 1926

Dear Yates:

I'm not in the least alarmed by correspondence. Am hard-boiled.

Asbury arrived O.K. Magnum thank ye, sir.

Sorry you could not arrive also, in person: but God save the King! *It has but just let up raining* after a drowned parade—and maybe that foolish man may pull off his sham battle after all. Here's hoping—for there be a many folk come down to town.

I sincerely trust Mrs. Snowden is better. As to Brown, & Robinson— why should we be all swelled up by having decent ancestors & kinsfolk? Isn't it common down here?

Yours forever 'n ever:
J. B.

I am gratified to have your approval of a fine old fellow. He was!

Working on Asbury now.

June 29th, 1926

Dear Yates:

I am finding some excellent characteristic stuff in your friend Asbury, beyond the Chillicothe items, which are, of course, suggestive rather than expository—but the character-stuff is excellent. Thanks.

Regarding Bernard Manning: just nothing doing. I return his letter herewith. I have gone through all my own stuff, as well as is possible, and through the immediate stuff at the Library, with Miss Ellen FitzSimons' ready assistance; and find nothing there to identify or to locate the painting of which Mr. Manning speaks. It has never, *so far as I am now able to discover,* been used as an illustration, and possibly exists in private hands, whence it is to be extricated only by advertisement. Unless one fears to arouse cupidity and a high valuation by such advertising, it appears to me to be the first direct method of uncovering the location and ownership—or even the existence—of said painting.

Lossing's[11] note says that Manning[12] only *interposed* the captured British officer between himself and the enemy's fire, and has no statement as to "carrying" him off "on his back." It is the naivete and quiet humor of Manning's reply to the ornate and pompous salutation of his captive makes the point there, and not Manning's carefully covered and *heroic*—shall we say—retreat.

With regard to the play in which Manning is charactered, that is, as you know, entirely up to you, or Miss Eola Willis, since I have never ventured the plunge into the Thespian pool of researches theatricals Caroline de Sud—excusing, is it, French?

N.B.: In consideration of the several thousand good Carolinians assembled here to witness the defeat of Sir Pierre Parkerre Anglaise damnable et ses myrmidons—again excuse French, if it be French!—Pluvian Jupe held off the drench, yesterday afternoon, for about two hours, broke a slat or two of blue across the firmament in simulation of that famous standard of the crescent moon, and permitted the sham battle to move along its lines as planned, with considerable brilliance—for which I am really grateful—much preparation had been made, much careful work undertaken.

In being a Unionist to the ground, unalterably opposed to the mad doctrines of Nullification and the serious errors of Secession alike—neither of which have anything to do with the merits of the individual men who supported either, but only to their lack of ultimate judgment—I remain, as I have asserted, a damyankee—my kinsmen, God bless 'em! had similar, equal privilege of a choice, and each made it according to his vision and conscience; none did better; nor perhaps do I. Have you read

"States Rights in the Confederacy"? If not, do so. (Owsley's: a dull book, but illuminating to enthusiasts of little reflection—few of whom will read it. One cannot expect the ladies to do so—but God bless 'em!)

Sorry not to locate Manning's picture for him; but can't locate it for myself. Good-bye! and Heaven send you health and happiness, you and your blessed wife! So says my wife, and so say I:

Affectionately yours,
John Bennett.

July 18th, 1926

Dear Yates:

It is not right to make a gaillard jest of a good friend, and, for sake of a smart retort or jeer, to be cheap cavalier. My sincere apology to you for dismissal of your generous appreciation of that fine old soldier, Isaac Trimble, my grandmother's brother. Yet, ever since I came South, I have disinclined to prattle concerning the decency of my people, preferring to prove it, if I could—perhaps I was egotistical, perhaps vain—in the opinion men formed upon acquaintance—rather than to lean back upon history.

It has always seemed to me, and seems so still, that to curry approval or favor Southward by proclaiming Southern relationship, is a bit bootlicking. Particularly when, politically, or historically, speaking, one leans so strongly the other way as to make bowing painful.

Until I came South I think I had never questioned my own quality, or even entertained such thoughts as would prepare a question—yet the first time I had occasion to revert was soon enough: it was on calling upon my proposed father-in-law to suggest to him my desirability as a son-in-law. I learned afterward he felt, perhaps, almost as awkward as I—recognizing my entire outsideness, and appreciating the peculiar difficulty of his situation and mine. "Personally," he said, "I have found you unexceptionable; but our acquaintance is narrow and brief. You will pardon my solicitude for my daughter, which certainly is but natural, and understand my motive, if I ask something concerning your people. I can enquire; but perhaps," he said graciously and courteously, "You yourself can give me entirely satisfactory information regarding them?"

The fact that my people's quality was to be questioned had not until that moment occurred to me: I had rather taken my people for granted. Not a thought came into my head as personal recommendation of the distinction of my people. "Indeed, Major," said I, and was embarrassed,

"It is the truth, I can think of nothing. You are welcome to make any inquiry you will regarding me and my people. I should hardly understand, perhaps not quite pardon your not doing so at present. But, as to my family I can think of nothing to the point. My mother's brother was forty years chief counsel for the B. & O.—that's the single thing comes to me"—and then, how I do not know, and never did quite know, a second thought came into my head, and, in an habitual way I out with it, at the instant, without the least mischievous intent, but to prove my decency by at once confessing the doubt:

"It occurs to me, however," I said, "that one of my father's cousins was hanged."

The Major's kind, handsome face fell sharply. "Perhaps," he said, "It was not as bad as it sounds."

"Perhaps not; it was as bad for him; they hanged him, and the charge against him was piracy."

"Indeed?" and the Major's fine face fell further, and I could see the trouble gather in his eyes. "But that could be explained?"

"I don't know," said I, hesitatingly. "That depends on the point of view. He was hanged, surely enough, on Governor's Island, by the Government of the United States, as a warning, and one charge was piracy. His name was John Yates Beall,[13] and he held a commission from Jefferson Davis."

The Major's face changed at the instant: he half laughed—he had a delightful chuckling laugh, brief, and perfect transition—"I think that alters the case!" he said, and laughed cordially—"I thought it might," said I; "but one never can tell."

He shook my hand, laughing merrily—he had an infectious laugh—it was the one thing wholly Irish—with the twinkle in his eye—"I'll have Markley Lee write a correspondent of his in the law who resides in Chilli-co-the and tell my wife this!" And he did.

I never knew, in all the much explanation my revered Mother-in-law found it indispensable to make concerning the engagement of her daughter to a Northerner, whether the dear lady made use of that recommendation of me or not. I should like to think Yates Beall knew it; it would give him an odd new conceit of the thing, may be! It was savage, and bad—but he was the goat for the "patriots" in Canada, and damn them for trash, say I.

But that was the first inquiry into, and my own first statement of, the quality of my family, made in the horty city of Charleston.

I had never heard the praises you quote me of Gen. Trimble: I knew him only, of course, after the War, when he came to visit our people in Ohio—I think it was about 1870—circa. He went first to Hillsboro, to visit the Trimbles; Kirby Smith, my cousin, drove him through the hills to Chillicothe. "A better companion for a long drive there never was!" Kirby said to me a few months ago. He had fierce, bushy brows overhanging brilliant keen eyes, and a hooked nose like all history; he smoked a white clay by my uncle, Wm. Trimble McClintock's fire, of evenings, with a red tight-fitting, knit cap on his head; and, as I believe I remarked once before, his foot—but a jury-foot—squeaked shrill when he walked—and thrilled our young hearts with mingled ecstacy—of admiration and timidity of the fierce old Rebel kinsman, staring fixedly into the fire and puffing great clouds. That hesitating timidity vanished like mist with the first story he told us: and the laurels have never been off of his grave in our minds—let him rebel! Neither would he be first nor last who did so.

His sister, Charity Trimble, was my grandmother. His father dwelt at Kinnikinnick, died, and lies buried in the burying- ground at Crouse's Chapel near by—John Crouse's was where your esteemed friend and correspondent, Francis Asbury, put up for the night—and my Father's only brother, Tom, married lovely Mary Crouse—and their lovely old house stands among the great trees on the hill as empty as Hell—the girls, years ago, gave me his "Spectator," for remembrance—they remembered him walking the floor, reading it.

This takes a slightly melancholy turn, which I cannot help—thinking of "gentlemen unafraid"—and of Ambrose; I shall be happy to the end of my time that I had a hand with him, in doing designs for the backs of his books: 'twas pleasure to please him—and all men like him.

I have not had face yet to read your letter to the children lest they think me puffed with pride—yet I am ever tempted to do so, and probably will wear your letter out in my pocket, plucking up the egotism essential to read all you quote of my rebellious old kinsman— well, he WAS a fine fellow—and the land would be better for more of his sort.

I am filtering Asbury—he's main full of pietous dregs!

Farewell—apologia—and regard,

Always heartily yours,
John Bennett

My compliments ever to the charming woman, your wife.

We go to Virginia in August after more "atmosphere."

Sept. 17th, '26

Dear Yates:

Just returned to Paradise Perdu—find your objurgatory message of love and trust under the front port.

Grief inexpressible rending my vitals, I reply to your curse—my blessing! What plan ever worked perfectly? None of mine. Instead of newspaper files galore (and inexhaustible),[14] in Ohio, from which to gather readily material for my opusculus, found only broken, odd volumes, of wrong years, remaining from iniquitous sales by impecunious editors in bygone years, to Northwestern Historical Societies, et al., and had to extract information and data from the few remaining ancients of days residing in and about Chillicothe—much fun, but slow (work)—old ladies of 85 playing old tunes on old piano-fortes, tinkling delightfully, that I might hear just how they really went in the days of their youth. Missus, Sue, and Jack had a marvelous time in the old borough, delighting our hostess, my sister, and (in) the old house she keeps so beautifully. I worked until 11 o'clock, the last night there, and was off at seven a.m., via Charleston, W. Va., Bluefield—vile detours over thrown-out roads, of rock and mud, in furious rains—lost in the mountains—black gorges yawning, narrow roads twining round and round precipitous peaks like stripes round a barber's pole, utter darkness save for one glorious, inaccessible star far overhead in the empyrean deeps (ditched in the mire, when obliging bootlegger receiving frightage from moonshine plant, gave us brilliant illumination by his high headlights until we got chains on, crept out again and advanced in triumph gratefully)—Bluefield at 11 o'clock—night, fine hotel, wonderful bath, more wonderful beds, still more wonderful consideration and courtesy—recommend heartily the *"West Virginia"* hostelry of Bluefield; next day proceed, via Bristol (and Johnson City, over Clinch Mountain and down Elktoe), to Flat Rock (being there joined by Jane Wells, well and plumper than ever before—her husband gone to Cuba)—and thence home to Pepysian peace—where, like a bombshell at a sheriff's door, discovered your damning accusation of dereliction and your objurgatory doggone it—hence these hurrying apologies, lest you cut us out of your list of calls when next you visit the Holy City.

All pretty well—and weary.

No more at this time.

Mrs. Adger Smyth, Jr.[15]—thanks to your persistent propaganda—has discovered, to her intense surprise, that I once wrote verses: "Magnificat"—noble fellow, continue; I shall be well-known yet.

Just received: a review—referring to a *"new* child's book, "Master *Shylock,* by John Bennett." So feel humble, humble!

Good-night; God save you!

(At present I AM at home):

Ever yours utterly:
John Bennett

22d Sept. '26

Dear Jack:

Thanks for your beautiful letter, & the marvelous description of your horrendous experience, at night in the "black gorges" and "precipitous peaks," &c. I was stirred to wild excitement (imagining it a chance paragraph from your new book), until I came to "barber's pole." I tumbled out of my chair, *kerflop!*—that anti-climax was too much for me.

Another phrase startled me; you speak of returning home "to *Pepysian* peace"! The lamented Peeps did not have an ideal time, as I recall, when Mrs. Peeps accused him of little amatory indiscretions! You are as vague as the Mauve author *Beer*. "*Pepysian* peace" is a huckleberry above my persimmon.

I enclose you a letter from Bellaman,[16] poet, novelist, & *musikaner*, to whom I sent a copy of your "Magnificat" asking why it could not be appropriately set to music. As you know, I am *obsessed* by the beauty of that poem. I am curious to know how B's expert opinion strikes you, & particularly Mrs. B., who has more music in her soul than you will ever have.

Tout à vous,
Y. Snowden

Send me back Bellaman's letter. I enclose stamp; I'm rich—in Annie Snowden's love.

Sunday, Oct. 3rd, 1926

Dear Yates:

So many fine lines of correspondence are tapped by your last two letters to me, which I have just re-read, that one hardly knows where to begin a reply, a retort, or what-not, quip, query, or quandary?

To take them up one at a time: Bellaman is, unfortunately for my spreading fame and your generous enthusiasm, right about the difficulty of setting the "Magnificat" to music, or of attempting to sing it—even as a Gregorian chant. You warm my wooden heart by your enthusiastic inculcation of sound doctrine—that phrase borrowed from my good sister-in-law, Loula Stoney—in season and out, as regards the merits of my verse.

The Magnificat was written in the mountains of West Virginia, which, one may say freely, with little fear of contradiction, are part and parcel with the great blue shoulders of North Carolina and the hulking heights of eastern Tennessee. The first two lines came to me one day while riding horseback—and doing it exceeding ill, to be sure, being but a Northern mudsill, not a Cavalier—through a gap of Peters' Mountain— on the border of Old Virginia, I think I was, which may account for the inspiration.

I have thought, since seeing the Rockies on the Canadian, with their jagged terrors and prodigious cruel heights and deeps, that my lines apply, not to any such terrific stones, but peculiarly to our intimately lovely, gigantic kindly titans of the Appalachians and the Blue Ridge, and that, looking out and up to their forest fells and hog-backed heights, the emphasis should be laid strongly upon the opening word of the verse:

> THESE—THESE—are the hills the Lord hath made
> That man may fear Him unafraid—

there is no fear in them; but in the Canadian Rockies there are jagged heights meandering drunkenly about the country which should not be allowed to run loose o' nights without the police. I assure you, when I was out there, and laid me down to sleep, although, of course, I trusted the Lord my unworthy soul to keep, I shut my hotel shutters and pulled down the blinds with Scotch caution and a renewed sense of frail security before I committed myself to sleep.

But Bellaman is right: the verse won't go to music, except such music as one finds in silence. I am indebted to you just as deeply as though it were to be chorussed at Carnegie Hall by Walter Damrosch.

Sorry to have hurled you down the abrupt plunge of literal anticlimax in my description of mountain meanderings over the wet but delectable hills of our late return. Grandeur is a thing to be handled ever delicately and not too seriously in light intimate epistles; hence I got down from those heights by a sort of burlesque verbal incline.

You seem, however, to have been in captious mood: what on earth stops your gorge in my use of home and Pepysian peace? The laxed morale of the times appears to have wormed your chaste mind—was the only care Sam had at home the vapours of a suspicious and a jealous wife, poor thing? . . .

If you can find me an intimate diary anywhere with more simple home-comings, prudent, foolish, human, erring, repentant, fractious, amusing, honest after all, than our old Sam—trot 'em out! There's no such Bucephalus. I said common-place, human, vexatious, amusing, loving, forgiving, Pepysian homecoming and Pepysian peace—oft interrupted by small matters—and, though I well like a pretty face and a lovely girl, and have several to niece and friend—it has been many days since Sarah at the Swan or pretty Betty Howlett disturbed the calm waters of my heart. Home *to Pepysian peace,* I said: go, read your Pepys, man!

I enclose Bellaman's letter, for which thanks, but more for your friendship. The Dantesque maid, who is with us, while her husband is at Guantanamo, sends you her very earnest and true love; and says to tell you that her man speaks often enthusiastically of you—though, to be sure, why he should be so enthusiastic is beyond me—you flatter his little wife, but don't reprint his poems—and says that his favorite portrait is yours anathematizing His Holiness.

My boy is gone to Yale; and I feel as though some one was dead, though perhaps more subjunctive; and my youngest goes, to-morrow night: and the winter begins soon, and, perhaps, the book I am supposed to be writing, and seem to be only writing about.

I had a stamp, too: don't swank.

Tout—hoot—tout—à vous!
John

December 8th, 1926

Y. Snowden, Esq.:

Dear and Distinguished Feller-citizen!

Have you—in that wonderful bibliographical epigastrium of your domicile a neat and modest volume, published 1832, "The Literary Remains of Joseph Brown Ladd, M.D.,[17] Collected by His Sister," to which is prefixed a sketch of the Author's life by W. B. Chittendon?

Or

a still smaller volume, "Arouet's Poems," printed some time prior to 1786, and at that time said to be "in the hands of most, if not ALL, of Charleston's reading citizens"?

If so, what are said Pomes and Literary Remains—other than the Ode and Oration for Fourth of July, the mild amatives addressed to "Amanda," and the characterizations laudatory of our early Olympians, Washington, Jefferson, Adams, etc., used by Godwin[18] in his famous "lecture" on "Heads," at Harmony Hall?

There was nothing in Ladd's remains of the sort of 18th Century gaiety of Rugeley's Burlesque; yet I am curious to recover some knowledge of the Doctor's poetical cadaver—and so turn to you, as the hart to the water-brook and the traveller to the great rock.

Miss Willis refers to the use of Ladd's characterizations in the "lecture" at Harmony Hall; but gives no further information concerning the Doctor, does not even index the unfortunate young fellow, and misses one of the real episodes of the Theatre in Charleston in the 18th Century: no fault to her; one cannot recover everything.

I do not wish to filch any of dear old SMELFUNGUS'S thunder, and certainly could never presume to borrow his "damned bolt transfixing error's egregious folly"; but if you can spare a crumb or two, good Dives, of bread from this penny loaf, you will once more receive the grateful thanks of

Your poor friend
L A Z A R U S
alias
ICHABOD
alias
PERTINAX SURLEY,
J. B.

13th Dec. '26

My *dear* John:

I have not plagued you with my piffle; I have not asked you to reconstruct any rotten rhymes; indeed, I have been very considerate of your feelings for 2 or 3 months. All I have sent you was a very erudite disquisition on the movements of *squirrels*—which you gave to your office-cat; because it had some *Latin* in it—a language of which I know *little;* & you (miserable ash-cat!) know *less!*

      I. *In re* Joseph B. Ladd. (Somehow, the name seems familiar) But, let me confess, I can't give you a word of information. I know nothing about him or his "Remains." Ask Roseola!

      II. "Arouet." I have, somewhere, his real name. I thought our dear friend Aleck Salley had boasted (*I* never boast!) that he had a copy of "Arouet," while I hadn't! I was mistaken. Aleck told me yesterday that he *did not* own "Arouet." But (unless my almost septuagenarian memory

fails me!) I think you can find a copy at the corner of
Meeting St. and (late-lamented) St. Michael's Alley. Dan
Ravenel's *father* certainly had a copy of "Arouet" in his
collection; & I think Dan Jr. has swiped or heired all of
the old gentleman's books.

I am glad that Miss Willis is working these old forgotten fields; but
(in spite of Stanhope Sams' "fine Eyetalian hand" in her big book), I
think she is superficial and unreliable. Sometimes I think it an acute case
of *megalomania*. That's Latin, & means swell-head! I wish *you* had more
of it.

I turned, of course, to my bound vols. of "The 19th Century" (June
'69-Febr'y '71) and read Simms's "Early Literary Progress in S.C.,"
looking for Ladd & "Arouet," but I found nothing of either. Possibly,
if he had not died, he might have given us something; for his range of S.C.
information & his versatility were *extraordinary*—in spite of the "rot" he
sometimes published.

Wait, till I am "fired" by the new President Douglas,[19] or I gracefully
retire, and return to cranky, crazy, non-progressive, sleepy old Charleston, my heart's home! It will be a sad day for you coming all the way to
the Enston Home. (I can't bunk at the Colin McCrae Grant hospices
because my wife is a rank and virulent Episcopalian.) I'll bring all the
"bunk" I have collected for 40 years with me, & if you are ruminating
in "old-time trumpery" *you'll have to come* and see poor, but

affectionate friend,
Yates Snowden

NB! This is about the craziest letter I have written in many moons;
but, it's 2:20 A.M., & I'm not going to re-write it.

Chapter 15

1927

Vagrant Verse; *tribute to Elizabeth O'Neill Verner; Simons, Stoney, and Lapham book on Charleston architecture; W. W. Ball's move to* News & Courier; *Julien Green's* Mont-Cinère; *Salt Sulphur Springs and "Magnificat"; contemporary Charleston writers.*

AT THE beginning of 1927 Bennett thanked Snowden for the Christmas gift of a volume entitled *Vagrant Verse*, in which poems by Yates, John, and John's brother Henry Bennett appeared. Bennett also told Snowden about a new verse he had just written and sent to William Rose Benét for the *Saturday Review of Literature*, "I Want an Epitaph."

When Snowden asked Bennett's help in preparing a fitting recognition of Elizabeth O'Neill Verner to be given at an Art Association dinner, Bennett obtained the information from Alice Huger Smith and wrote a review. He was, however, taken aback by Snowden's sending his letter on to Mrs. Verner for her approval.

Annie Snowden's illness in April was mentioned in the correspondence of the next few months. And W. W. Ball's return to Charleston was both commended and regretted by Snowden and celebrated by Bennett. In one letter, Bennett told an amusing anecdote of his father's arrest for galloping a horse down city streets in 1838. Other topics were the disposition of Sam Stoney, Sr.'s estate; the book on Charleston architecture by Sam Stoney, Jr., his brother Augustine Stoney, his brother-in-law Albert Simons, and Sam Lapham, Jr.; young Jack's Easter stay in Chillicothe, Ohio; and Snowden's admiration for Bennett's and DuBose Heyward's "Epitaph" poems.

Snowden regretted that the Bennetts had not continued their work with spirituals after the article in *The Atlantic* some time earlier. During the summer, he republished, once again, his favorite poem by Bennett. Having earlier explained his inspiration for "Magnificat of the Hills," Bennett, in his 30 August 1927 letter, related the exact circumstances of its composition: his acute illness, the invitation to Salt Sulphur Springs, his recovery made possible by his hosts, lasting friendships made during those months, a horseback ride in the Appalachians, and his many rewritings of the poem until it was printed in 1892.

Bennett gave estimations of the latest works of DuBose Heyward, Hervey Allen, and Herbert Ravenel Sass. He reported that, although still "wrestling with" his main project, the book based on his father's life, he was collecting his old juvenile ballads and stories, published years earlier, to be reissued in the spring by Longmans, Green.

January 5, 1927

A HAPPY NEW YEAR!

Dear Disturbing Element:

You knew, perhaps, long ago, that verses upset me, and that the volume you sent me, i.e., Vagrant Verse, would set me out of my serene absorption in this book, and make me both sigh and laugh. I am happy to find that my brother—God rest him happy!—and you, and I, are represented in this book—and so sometime preserved together: you with your South Carolina Bourbon; he with his Flag that continually Goes By Youth's Window; I with one "immortal scrap," done for a Christmas calendar-verse, with Walter Appleton Clark's Canterbury Pilgrims, for a valiant friend of mine, who has been dying by quarter inches these fifteen years. Yates, I'm glad they have gathered us up together in print's long companionship: I shall continue to be pleased to think we shall be found together there when the house-maids of Time are sweeping us up in dust-pans. . . .

My heart has been never a high-brow; nor, before the Lord, have I: so, beginning Vagrant Verse the first night I owned it, at your hand, I went straight through it, manfully, whether it made me cry or chuckle, and chuckling, read aloud the jest to a chuckling family: the tears I kept to myself, of course.

I found many pieces in the book which, years and years ago, I myself, collated into my editorial drawer from the daily flotsam of the press, and still possess in old scrap-books full of resolution and of grief, such as all men who live might make, if in the scrap-book line. Deepest of all is the sting of memory; best of all, I now estimate, remains friendship. By which conclusion moved more than commonly, I set down the fragments of verse which rose—shall I say like the smoke of incense beside a remembered altar, at which—in one thing constant—I have truly worshipped through the years? . . .

A friend at Duke sending me The Archive Anthology for '24-'25, I found a "Requiescat" in it, by one Ronald Barr, begging his friends with subtle egotism, to cut no epitaph above him, at which I was moved enough to speak for myself on that indelicate point, lest someone make mistake—being not yet cooled down from perusing "Vagrant Verse," which brought out new perspiration on a cooled heart. . . .

> Your affectionate friend and unexpected
> bestower of "500 happy memories":
> God grant this be 501!
> [John Bennett]

A little after the New Year: 1927

The children are gone back to school; and it may be I shall progress a little bit upon my book: which, God's my judge, I have great wish—and equal need—to finish.

But, Oh! they had a Good Time—as they say—with which, being simple, I am ever made misty in the eyes, and simply pray to such, and whatever Gods there be—"Lord, give them good times, and courage—as my friends have given me!" and as I watch them out of sight—Amen, Amen, Amen—Good-night!

I owe you much.

This, though brief, is no new or sudden thought.

26th Jan'y '27

Dearly beloved John:

Exams begin on *Friday;* & yet, like a long eared-ass, I reluctantly consented to act as toast-master of an Art Ass'n "Banquet"—a role for which I am absolutely unfitted!!!!

Mrs. Verner[1] (for whom I have profound respect & admiration!) is to be there; & I am to notice, or call her out. Tom Waring[2] was to have come, but has showed his good sense by backing out, & I shall have one witness less of my asininity.

What I am pestering *you* about, Effendi, is some salient *fact* about Mrs. V. as an etcher. Has she really done *high class work;* & what is her "masterpiece," if she yet has one?

Just *one* little paragraph to add to my allusion to Mrs. Verner, & I swear I won't worry you again for 6 months, at least!

Mac Horton is off on a 15 day military jag; & Sams tries to explain away "guess" (See clipping! ["John Bennett's 'Guess' at Gullah"]). Mac wrote the original ed. I imagine.

Why *did they not elect you,* Bibliognost, -phile, -maniac; gentleman, scholar, artist, &c., &c., president of the Charleston Library?

Why does not Benét have the sense to print your charming 2 stanzas rather than the rot of the last 2 weeks?

Yours to the funeral urn,
Yates Snowden

Rush that paragraph; I spiel Monday night.

----

4 p.m., January 27th, '27

Glorious 2 a.m.

Yours recd.

"Has she really done *high class work,* and what is her masterpiece; if she yet has one?"

Miss Alice Smith, who knows more of Mrs. Verner's etchings than I do, since I have seen but one piece of her work during the past year and over, considers Mrs. Verner's place among American etchers assured, and that, within the next three years Mrs. Verner will take rank as one of the foremost etchers of this country.

In etching Mrs. Verner seems to have found her medium with extraordinary swiftness and happiness—she has exhibited, and is now exhibiting in all the largest cities of the North, West, and South: New York, Brooklyn, Philadelphia, Chicago, New Orleans and San Francisco notably among them, and her work is now found in the permanent print collections of the museums of those cities.

A swift and disciplined worker who brings rare intelligence to her work; sensitive and sympathetic, never falsely sentimental, never artificially pretty; who, loving beauty in its every shape, loves equally a severe and almost classic austerity, and draws sheer beauty from the fact, not from unsubstantial fancy.

She brings to her work a natural flair for the medium, for the actual process itself, plate, needle, the acid biting, the pulling of the print—

Her etchings show the vision of an unusually dramatic eye, a delicate austerity, a natural feeling for line and color, as it is sensed in black-and-white, for beauty devoid of sentimentality, an extreme directness of statement—and an audacity and an unfaltering courage in attacking her subject which binds the whole together.

Few who so love beauty and associated thought can so refuse the cheapening trick of sentiment—and so safely rest repute upon intrinsic honesty.

She is known throughout the South as one of the most ardent spirits in the Southern Art Association; which owes, first to last, a great debt to her zeal and tact and ability in organization.

I think it fair for you not to quote personally from Miss Alice Smith without permission—I need not tell you that, being born a gentleman— what? Yes. And you need not quote me—neither—no matter where or how I was born. Above is your thunder: it is, of course, kind, but not false. In two years of etching Beth Verner has, in heavy adversity, earned a genuine and spreading repute.

I do not say that I think as greatly of her etchings as does Miss Alice Smith—I have not seen her work on which her uncommon success is based—and therefore give the opinion of an artist who is intimately familiar with all that Mrs. V. has done and is doing. And that certainly warrants you to speak happily.

I asked Sams if authority or impudence caused the statement that I only guess the source of the title GULLAH: he cites no authority; I therefore am left thinking it impudence. Thank you for the clipping.

Please adjust the uncoordinated particles of a very hasty commentary on an artist's work—then turn loose that silvern tongue—and the little vocative gods be with you!

Good-By: POST HASTE:
[John Bennett]

March 12th, 1927

Dear Yates:

By CAREFULLEST MAIL, this day, I am forwarding to you again, with MOST ENORMOUS THANKS and DITTO GRATITUDE for perfect favor, your volumes: ASBURY'S JOURNALS, containing much stomachic reflection and pious profligacy of that SAINTED BEING—of which I have cribbed much pages of tinkling cymbals, which, twisted far indeed from their original intention, may, perhaps, reappear from the mouth of a different SAINTED BEING, if I ever complete my present monumental work.

I have not time—pardon this damnable modern discourtesy—to write more—I was flabbergasted some days since to be informed that you had sent my letter about the etchings of Mistress Elizabeth V——r direct to her! But innocent, innocent, my lord, I bore up noble, and continue, as afore, undiminished, and ever 'appy to believe myself, and confidently to assert that I am

Yours:
John Bennett

P.S.: In 1838 my Father was arrested for galloping his horse through the "streets of the city," endangering the life and limb of citizens—but incidentally and particularly splashing mud on the breeches of complainant. (He conducted his own defense.)

At trial before the Mayor's court, defendant, by testimony of acknowledged horsemen, was acquitted of riding at a gallop, the actual gait of his career having been, and so proven, a CANTER.

"Ah," says complainant, bitter: "I should have entered complaint against allowing young jackasses to run at large in the street. I made a mistake between a horse and a jackass!"

"It is evident," said my progenitor, looking his antagonist directly in the face: "That such a mistake has been made before."

Happy old days of golden repartee and rippling persiflage!

I mean to use this myself in the great BOOK:

Adieu! Adieu!
My God! how reprehensible is HASTE
AMONG FRIENDS!
Again and ever
yours,
J. B.

April 19th, 1927

Uniquely Only and Dearest Yates:

I heard, for the first time, on Sunday, at the dedication of the BACHMAN[3] room at St. John's LUTHERIAN choche, from pretty little Mrs. C. Snowden—who, I believe, is a Bachman-Chisolm child—of the serious illness of Mrs. Snowden, and have been anxious ever since. Is it possible that we cross wires, and that your yesterday's letter is in answer to our very real anxiety? It were not strange.

I am glad to hear that she is improving; glad for her sake, glad for yours; and the Dantesque Maiden, Jane Wells, and my far better half, Susan, are hardly less glad than myself—if they are less glad—and that I doubt. Pray give our most affectionate good wishes and hopes for speedy and sure recovery to Mrs. Snowden; may convalescence be swift, and health most certain!

I have been wanting, every week that slides by, to knock off a bit of resurrection stuff to the dramatic memory of the infinitesimally minor poetaster, LADD, of whom I write afore. But the demands of my own iron seem inexorable: LADD will be in SECOND CHILDHOOD before I get to him. I have been surprised that the alert EOLIAN HARP of one string had not recovered LADD's dramatic finale in her story of the STAGE. But, like the lamented McCRADY, who could not see that much of the history of early South Carolina occurred in Virginia, North Carolina, Georgia, the Floridas, and ALL POINTS WEST, and confined himself, as one hopelessly fenced-in, by the State's thin boundary-lines, The HARP which Once through TA*RA*RA's Halls did not pass the limits of her chosen Century, the 18th namely, and so missed one of the good theatrical romances of her selected age. Anon—anon—I hope to crown poor LADD with the faded remnants of dusty disaster and distinction in death.

Jane Wells is having an enormously delighted time, perusing the ancient files of the Southern Literary MESSENGER, and revelling in its excellence and hyperbole.

ARARAT plantation—Stoney holding—has been, I understand, sold by the heirs to Tom Stoney, of St. Louis; thus leaving PARNASSUS and MEDWAY in possession of the heirs, a little less encumbered by the previous triple care and costs. Louisa Stoney has bought David Dwight's[4] most pleasant house and garden, just around the corner from us, in Tradd Alley, and will remove from the great mansion in St. Philip Street about the first of May.

I am delighted to note that the handsome and excellent $20.00 volume on Charleston Architecture, produced mainly—99%—by my nephews and their partner, has sold, to date, no less than fifty-seven copies in Charleston alone, only seven of which were sold to tourists— the rest to ex- and now-resident Charlestonians: which, at $20, is a capital testimony.

But I am truly pleased to tell you, despite your complimentary hint, that the fine introduction to that volume WAS entirely the work of Sam Stoney, Jr., who must have full credit for it. I am peculiarly happy in the critical and popular success of that book, being, as it is, the product, almost in its entirety, of my own pet young fellows: "Albert Simons,

Sam Lapham, Jr.,[5] Sam. Stoney, Jr., and Gus Stoney—collaborators in text and drawings." The only intrusive burial is that of drawings by Albert Graeser, of the panelled room of old #31 Legaré Street, Mrs. Smythe's home.

Speaking of her, you will, I know be interested to know, if I had not already told you, that preliminary operations have been most satisfactorily performed upon her purblinded eyes toward ultimate relief from double cataract, by which she has been so deprived of accustomed activity: final operations probably some time in May.

My boy, Jack, spent his Easter vacation with my sister, Martha, at the old house in Ohio; and says he begins to know why I hold those hillsides in remembrance and seem in my talk to believe them somehow clothed with an other-world-like charm. I know a fine young Jew—not now young—who carried his wife from New York City to Chillicothe, simply to prove to her that what she called his pretty fairy-tales of his boyhood's environment were no word more than truth.

But, God! how the folk I know fall from the ancient trees there! Some still remain, like the sparse red apples on the bare boughs of November.

My nose is in the air, apprehensive on each mail; but not yet, not yet, the vile assault, per SKUNKUS, you have threatened. You call yourself my friend; yet send me SKUNKS—or reports of SKUNKS—and it is the REPORT of the SKUNK expires the STINK.

I welcome the advent of W. W. Ball to the News & Courier. I trust his management gives him a freer hand than the previous reign did Lathan. Now, if we could but once more call you back, it would not be so far to paradise.

And now, God grant the lady health, and soon, a physical comfort long and long, for all our happiness—but for yours, Yates, ever!

> With love to her and to you from us Three:
> Affectionately yours:
> John Bennett

H'dsonville, N.C., 16th Aug. '27

Heights by great men reached and kept
Were not attained by sudden flight;
But they, *while their companions slept,*
Were toiling upward in the night.[6]

Dear John:

All my life, as you know, I have been a toiler, and have reveled in *work* for lo, these 69 years! Indeed, the only thing that has reconciled me to this "vale of tears" has been the fear of "loafin' 'round the throne" when I reach the Presbyterian Heaven. The above verse (together with "If Anyone Can Play the Pipes") has been an inspiration to me for nearly three decades.

What, then, was my horror, when I read the ribald lines:

> He slept while his companions slept;
> He often overslept them!

Is anything safe from your polluting touch? I have not been so shocked since poor, bright, crazy Mrs. John Marshall[7] wrote me years ago: "A consecrated cross-eyed bear"!

But, jesting aside, I greatly admire your call for an epitaph. It's the best thing in mortuary *Southern* poetry I know since DuBose H. wrote the best poem in "Skylines and Horizons": "Epitaph for a Poet." . . .

There is one dept. of negro lore, the *"spirituals"* in which you and your wife were past-master & mistress, and which—barring that article in *The Atlantic*—you have both (pardonnez moi!) shamefully neglected! James Weldon Johnson (parti-colored) and half a dozen whites at Chapel Hill & elsewhere have been stealing your thunder! When I think of the "rafts" of data & ana & mem. & clippings etc., you and your *ux* have in your den upstairs (troisieme etage), unused and practically untouched *in re cuffee*, it makes me sick at heart!!! Your literary exors. (the Dantesque woman, perhaps) are going to have a Hell of a job, about the year 1945, when you join the angels—and me.

Two years I have gone to the Carnegie Library here, & copied your cussed "Magnificat" & printed it, once in *The State*, and once in circular form. The demand was so great that I have none left, & may have to copy it again, for this morning a forlorn old maid (to whom *I had read* the poem last year), accosted me, saying that I had promised her a copy! Thank Heaven, you never had but one attack of religious exaltation in the mountains!

I have done nothing—apart from desultory reading—here or at Glenn Springs this summer. I wrote a puff for Frank Stanton's[8] jingles in *The State*. I don't care what you poets think; I'm a little of a jingler myself & I love "Old St. Michael's Bells." I don't suppose you read *that*, or a long "book-review" of James Clement Furman![9] I am not a Baptist, but my grand-mother was; indeed she was one of the head "devils among the Baptists" of whom old Sam Tupper wrote his outrageous rhymes (a la "Dunciad").

Julien Green,[10] styled in the Lit'y Review, the most accomplished of modern French novelists, and who Fay said graduated at *the University of South Carolina!* has interested me somewhat, tho' A. C. Moore[11] says he is *not* one of our alumni, & Joseph Gregoire de Roulhac Hamilton does not think he belongs in Chapel Hill! Anyhow, like a long-eared-ass, I bought and read his "Mont-Cinère," and find it a chamber, or house, of horrors from start to finish. It's in French, & for fear I have not caught some psychological significance, or missed some subtle *nuances* (is that right?), I have sent it to two French scholars Graeser *et ux* at Fletcher; they'll know.

I take the *Lit. Review* and every issue *except* July 23d was forwarded to me. So I thank you ever so much for the poem & inscription. If I had dream't that you were in Charleston this summer, I would have taken at least a peep at you and yours when I ran down to poor Bob Lebby's funeral.

My dear wife has much improved, but is still far from well.

> Love to you & yours,
> Yours affectionately,
> Yates Snowden

August 30th, 1927

Dear Yates:

You are quite incurable; but without equal in the field as advertising agency par excellence and inimitable publicity-man for the verse of your not-frequently poetical friends.

I am sending you, by this same mail, perhaps to cool your kindly ardor in my behalf, official portrait, vintage, 1927: taken, not from vanity, God wot! but at request of distant cousins, one not seen for fifty years—thus made available for these intimate reprehensions of high enthusiasm.

Yet I thank you for your unparalleled devotion to the MAGNIFICAT, and persistent circulation thereof in the mountains whose northward stretch inspired the verses.

Did I ever tell you the occasion and circumstances of their writing? It is no doubt, to-day, labelled a sentimental and mauve-decade story of human friendship, kindness and encouragement to the deeply discouraged.

The latter was I. Out of a position, out of health, out of heart, and, apparently out of luck. Ill, very, in Michigan, and afraid to return; out of funds; invited, by a man I had never laid an eye on—to whom I had lent green criticism of his prose—quite in despair—and not figuratively either—accepting that blind invitation to spend what time I would as his guest, exempt from charges, at the ancient hotels of the Salt Sulphur Springs of West Virginia—I went, for the first time, to the mountains.

"Poor devil!" said observers on the hotel porch as I descended from the hack, "He has come too late!" "Old top," said my host, long afterward, "You were one of the poorest of bets, that famous day in your career of mis-spent years and profligacy—when I met you at the station and gave your frame the once-over, you may remember I urged the driver to push on nor spare the leather? Why? My dear and disreputable friend, I thought you would pass out before we reached the hotel!"

Like all discouraged young things I was a black pessimist: all the dolls were stuffed with sawdust, and earth a flop, eternity one everlasting unexplored stretch of undesirable negation, and mankind—excepting only my intimate and own—vultures, or thieves—and long-labelled and proverbial liars.

I was unutterably puzzled and suspicious of my hosts: what in heck did they expect to get out of the venture?

I found, beyond the possibility of a doubt, they expected nothing— took me, good or bad; and fed me up, lent me gay companionship, horses, amazing understanding, and corrective courage, for the unmentioned sake of a kindly and genuine humanity—I had reached my last days on the JERICHO ROAD.

One day, as on my host's own beloved horse, Don Quixote, as I rode alone on Turkey Creek, with the slopes of Peters Mountain rolling on to Old Virginia, there came into my head these lines:

> These are the hills the Lord hath made,
> That man may fear Him, unafraid.

A storm had, but a moment before, broken into blinding, thundering rage and gone booming down the ranges—and on the great blue shoulders of the mountain lay the brilliant, stormy sun, as always, strangely and almost unreally bright.

I realized that I had attained a certain measure of sound health, strength, and what was better, peace. The next lines followed with little difficulty:

> Up through the gateway of the skies
> Their purple slopes of peace arise
> Like sunlit paths to paradise.

Indeed, Yates, they then seemed so to me. Where Paradise is, or may be, or where it was then, there was no geographical knowledge. But peace at heart is near it, wherever it may be—and for those bright few months I had known peace—and made a friendship that has never changed—with the bravest, calmest people I have ever met beyond my own, and the most gallant-hearted boy I ever have known—Jack Appleton, these eight long years dying by the cruel inch, fading hopelessly, day after day, and smiling still—in Cincinnati.

The next winter my sister suggested, and I began that happy story, "Master Skylark"; the following summer a part of that tale was written at those Springs—a free and welcomed guest of generous humanity; and from that place the MS. of the unfinished book was sent for approval to Mary Mapes Dodge, of "St. Nicholas"—that I might know if it were worth my while to carry to completion a story two-thirds done—before the winter came. Through friends made there, although unknown till afterward, my sister was enabled to complete her course at Radcliffe— our own combining funds being too unsure to make it certain. My book was taken by "St. Nicholas." And at Salt Sulphur Springs I met a young girl—whom, through as unexpected turns of fate, I met again, years afterward—and married.

But the MAGNIFICAT hung unfinished in my mind, all summer, and grew by infinite re-writings and my friend's keen objurgation of ineptitudes, on rides across the ranges, and beside the big fireplace at night—I stayed, his guest, the place deserted of all summer guests, until the mountain-crests were white with snow—I had put FORTY POUNDS upon my devastated bones—but, better far—I had found unaltering friends.

Some latter stanzas stirred my laggard mind to fierce monologizing words: but the inspiration of the whole remained serene: it was no lie, and has no cheating cleverness: I re-wrote it all winter until it suited; and the "Independent" took it, and printed it, in 1892: Beer calls that decade mauve: 'tis Beer is mauve, and not the decade.

The years take toll from inspiration; the mountains now have a gravity, and a saddened memory of many departing friends, a parallel all know: but ever I am glad to know that the poem is still read, approved, and unforgotten—among the mountains.

So, too, I want my epitaph to say that I had friends—for I have had friends beyond the common run, and have loved them. See the dedication of MARGOT: brief quoted testimony.

Frances Vanderhorst stopped me, yesterday, to say she had liked my Epitaph. Thank you both. And you for your letters.

This, too, to Beer—small, flat, stale Beer—is also mauve!

As to the NEGRO: my dear chap; I long ago lost all desire to stir the earth with garnered wisdom on this subject—and now less, since the popular mob has caught it up. I was too soon; nobody northward was interested beyond polite rejection and disclaimer. One must live: and I had put already far too much upon the Negro, his music and his strange half-oriental soul and superstition; and upon the forgotten history of this State—which, for me shall remain forgotten—the endeavor to extricate and to confirm the truth being work for more than one solitary hand and less than half a life.

We have had the pleasure of guiding the scene-setter and director of Heyward's play from PORGY about Charleston, in search of locale and color—and truly hope they may among them make a successful drama:

Charleston it may never be, of course; but neither was Shakespeare's Caesar ROME.

Could Heyward's bank-account but serve to give him rest and certainty, much might be hoped of his authentic gift; but driven to produce for sustenance his physical strength ill bears the strain of unalloyed expression and true fire—which he has.

So we are hoping for success, as a play; and, if so, for successful following as a film—and of unhurried breath and life for Heyward.

Hervey Allen, with his power and breadth of comprehending ability, seems launched beyond the further need of us, is most happily married—and producing both prose and poetry.

I am wrestling with the major opus, BUCKHORN JOHNNY; but diverted by request from Longmans, Green for my collected silhouette humorous juvenile ballads and tales from St. Nicholas, which they want in hand by February, for Spring issue—and by, at this writing, consideration of a proposal—which is confidential—to film our old friend, "Master Skylark."

I have been here all the summer—with wife and girls—who send regards; the DANTESQUE sends her love—we dip in the booming salt sea at Folly Beach, frequently—and have had a happy summer, I believe. I have, surely. JACK is foresting at Yale Camp, Connecticut; JANE studies art in Boston-town this winter; her man is still in China; SUE comes home from Northern training to complete at Charleston College after this immediate year—further deponent saith not; but only adds his love and truest wishes to you and to your beloved wife whose passing illnesses we deplore with all our heart. Good-by!

Affectionately yours,
John Bennett

And Herbert Sass comes on—and his charming young wife and delightful red-headed children.

And a young fellow, Granville Paul Smith, out of long hard fortune (new English dept. at Porter's) is doing some really promissory sonneteering notes in Harper.

"Polluting touch," indeed! revivifying, you mean, for Henry W.

Chapter 16

1928

Bennett's election to Phi Beta Kappa; memories of a traveling band; Poetry Society Year Book; Dr. Robert Wilson's Half-Forgotten By-Ways; *Bennett's* Pigtail of Ah Lee Ben Loo; Romeo and Juliet *silhouette; Snowden's pamphlet jest.*

EARLY IN May of 1928 John Bennett was elected to the Phi Beta Kappa chapter at the University of South Carolina, but he was unable to receive the honor in June because of his daughter Sue's graduation in Massachusetts and his son Jack's at Yale. Bennett also had several appointments with publishers in New York.

The long-ago days of his playing a guitar with a small traveling band were humorously recounted by Bennett in May. In July while the Snowdens were at Bonclarken in the North Carolina mountains, Bennett was still in Charleston, for he and Thomas R. Waring had been toiling over the Poetry Society Year Book. A tragedy, however, had occurred. The Warings' seven-year-old son had drowned in the surf at Sullivan's Island, and his body had not yet been recovered.

In September Snowden asked Bennett's judgment on Dr. Robert Wilson's *Half-Forgotten By-Ways,* as he had promised to write a review. A few days later, with apologies for the delay caused by a severe storm and loss of electricity, Bennett replied, according the Wilson book sincere praise.

The Pigtail of Ah Lee Ben Loo, John Bennett's children's book of stories and ballads with silhouette illustrations, which was issued in late September, was selling well by the first of October. In late November the Poetry Society Year Book for 1928 appeared. In December the

Snowdens delighted in Bennett's Christmas silhouette of Romeo and Juliet, for, two years earlier, Yates had appeared in the Town Theatre's production of *Romeo and Juliet* as the Apothecary.

Snowden's Christmas present turned out to be eleven copies of a pamphlet, sent to John to distribute to family and friends. *Just Out: An Appendix to the Complete Works of John Bennett* was an alleged literary exposé, an early example of the twentieth-century roast of a friend. The outrageous jest at the expense of Bennett had been prepared by Snowden and printed by James Holmes. It received an appropriate response. As the year ended, Bennett urged Snowden to send a copy to Randell McBride, who had not read the jocular booklet and thought a rift had occurred between the two friends.

May 11th, 1928

Dear Yates:

Beloved friend: a distinction has just been conferred upon me far beyond any anticipation: Mr. Keith[1] has advised me that I have been chosen for membership in PHI BETA KAPPA. How this selection has been made I know not. I know that if there had been anything toward it in yours to give, it has been given. Whatever your friendship may have, or may not have had to do with forwarding this distinction, everywhere so greatly and rightly coveted, and by me so entirely unexpected, here are the thanks of my heart—not so much for this instant's glory, Yates, God bless you, as for the years of such friendship and friendly interchange as I have been given opportunity to know with you, since first, long since, we met, in Charleston. And for that, beyond all else, again I say, may some blessing from that heaven in which all good hearts hope, some kindliness in life, be ever yours, as is, has been, and always shall be

The love of your friend:
John Bennett

P.S.: I am driving hard to complete a volume of children's stories to be printed, my own texts and silhouette illustrations, by Longmans, Green & Co., in September; and to get away, this task done, to New England, *in June*, to attend the graduation of my two youngsters, Sue and Jack (Yale Forestry)—and to return, via highway, with Jack, in his adventurous and veteran FORD—while the Madam returns per Pullman with her daughter, like real ladies. I wish you and your beloved wife kindly health, comfort, and some of the true happiness you both have given me these years.

Ichabod

It promises a busy summer: we expect to see, in June, Harper; Doubleday, Doran; Longmans, Green on multifarious businesses of self and Smythe family letters and remembrances: hence I may not meet in Columbia, as dated, June 9th, with P. B. K.

P. Surley

It is dolorously long since a line from you: this not in chiding, but lament.

May 24th, 1928

Dear Yates:

Thanks for the "brief sketch of my notorious career." It seems to have convinced the committee that I should be dangerous running at large: hence I have been taken into that golden fold, which one so enviously eyes from the outside—and within those high delimitations the chosen bask with decent, unostentatious pride. . . .

But, alas! that said Good Wife and I shall not be in Columbia, June 9th prox., inst., or ult., and my initiation must wait a future appointment. The distinction for myself is sweet; but there is prior engagement in business northward for both myself and the Missis. I have words to change with Longmans, Green relative to their issue of my collected juvenile tales and silhouettes, come September; and Mrs. Bennett ditto with Doubleday, Doran, anent possible printing of family war-correspondence of much historical value—whether published now or not. Besides which for no distinction would I so greatly disappoint, or break long-understood agreement with, my two good children at their schools—who for years have counted on our presence on their graduations.

It will be impossible for us to reach Massachusetts in time for our girl's graduation unless we are on our way north by June first; and on that date we depart this celestial city. . . .

Already I perceive, from yours of May 12th, that you have committed some few indiscretions in revelation. What you may have uncovered beyond Ellie Smyth's[2] generous script I only dimly apprehend. Man, I NEVER blowed the B FLAT—but behind the potted palms, under the staircase, I strummed the light guitar, in many a pleasant hamlet and polonius of the fair Scioto Valley, in company with "Little Eddy" Frey and his fiddle; "Long George" his brother, and his yellow clarinet (which in the end proved his own bete noir—or do you know the legend of the yellow clarinet?); Harley Throckmorton, "the musical moke" (later of Al. G. Fields, and played Columbia many a year, on everything musical from musical-glasses to ditto beer), and Albert Griesheimer, the

only man who ever played the lead violin parts in a small orchestra—
when well-filled with sizzling quarts—on the lugubrious slide trom-
bone, to the annoy of the constituted leader. Griesy and Long George
and Throck are gone to join and to improve with infinite jest and variety
that far-famed heavenly choir of which we hear rumor beyond this
parquet row; Little Eddy is in Oklahoma City, which suits him far better
than would the Newer and more lovely Jerusalem and the serene walls
of Zion—I see him now, scuttling like a frightened cockroach down the
aisle to climb the orchestra rail and burst into "Listen to the Mocking
Bird," which, on all occasions, and invariably, he played by request
(suspected ever to have been always his own), on every occasion. Lord!
I can hear the song of the mocking-bird squealing in sixth position and
harmonics now! If there seem too many "occasions"—there truly were!

I still have the guitar, an antique Martin, its face worn by much play,
and with steel strings never quite as sweet or true as with the original old
gut; and Jack and I quite rouse the welkin with duet on mouth-organ and
guitars—else my instrument reposes, betimes, in the Charleston Museum, a cultural exhibit.

That you and George Wauchope, bless the good man! should praise
my accomplishment with preferment is generous—and appreciated to
the last penetrant period.

Well, I must end: having left unsaid many things which I started out
to say; and having said many things, as I see, which I did NOT start out
to say—like a good hereditary Episcopalian. . . .

Affectionately yours:
John Bennett

Give everybody kind a friendly greeting from me!

The Missis has taken up the Turquand matter: many thanks!

July 28th, 1928

Dear Yates: . . .

Very happy to hear that your lovely wife is doing well. I wish we
were to be at Many Pines while you both are at Bonclarken; but it is, at
present, uncertain whether we shall get to Flat Rock, unless in particles.
I discover myself suddenly loaded up—Tom Waring and I—with the
unfinished labors of the Poetry Society's Year Book—which parturition
always proves too much for our virginal editor, Miss Jo P., and is
invariably left to the efficient obstetrics of T. R. W., J. B., and a most
efficient Secretary—just now in the mountains, somewhere, on a ten

days' twilight sleep, before our last conclusive pang comes on. Mistress Ann Montague Stoney (Arthur's wife) excused herself from editorial labors, and, yesterday, gave birth to twin girls, one blonde and one brunette. I am growing a little anxious: Miss Margaret Tessier has declined further, and gone on a vacation—altogether we seem all snarled up in a shirt of eleven yards: but the Year Book will be given to an expectant world without fail, about the end of October—and will not be so ribald as my comments.

Waring has had a strange tragedy at his door-sill: his son, Edward Waties Waring, seven, ran into the surf on Sullivan's Island, yesterday, and was drowned: to plunge into deep water seems to have been an irresistible passion with the unfortunate boy. He has, as yet, not been found.

Billy Popham (Commander, U.S.N.) has been given shore-duty at Annapolis, greatly to the satisfaction of his lovely wife's good Mother, Loula Stoney; as young Louisa—said pretty wife—says that her coming child may very well be born under the aegis—whatever that may be—of the Naval Academy.

[John Bennett]

16th Sept. '28

My dear John: . . .

I want you to write, *just a postal cardful,* of what you think the fine points in Dr. Robt. Wilson's "Half-Forgotten By-Ways," &c. In a reckless moment I took the book and promised to write a "review" of it for The N. & C. Apart from being a genius, you still have *an aloofness* in judging *South Caroliniana* which I can never have. To chime in with you, in your occasional idiotic lapses, I want to know how the book strikes a Damyankee! *Comprenez?* (And *what* would Isaac R. Trimble of the Maryland Line, Major Gen'l at Gettysburg, say if you had raved that way in his presence?) I want to say in my notice: "As an eminent man of letters said to the writer"—and then I would *quote* your 2 paragraphs.

I don't want you to write, or even to "polish up" my screed, y'understand! I want my notice of the book to have at least one pregnant paragraph, though quoted.

Oh yes; I can write all 'round the subject (My father came from St. John's & St. Stephen's); and, Salley-like, I can find a wrong date, & even a name misspelled; & a *mistake* as to *what* Ravenel buried, or rather tomb-stoned Major Marshbanks, & the monstrous error as to that first (!) rice-patch in Longitude Lane, &c., &c.—but I want five lines or more from J. B. to give tone to my grind.

I know you are not as fat as you ought to be, and that you are up to neck in work. I have known that every time I have pestered you for more than a decade, & so I will make no excuses.

My affec. remembrances to Jane & her mother,

Yours always,
Yates Snowden

———————

Sept. 19th, 1928

Dear Yates:

It was so infernally dark in my study, yesterday—and, indeed, all through the house—with storm outside, shutters shut and battened down, and no electric current, gas like a yellow blight, and candles-and-eye-strain our deliverance from Egyptian gloom, that I could not reply to yours of the 16th relative to Dr. Wilson's book. First thing, this morning, however, I essay reply.

The new book has not come: a letter from Longmans, Green Friday said they were at that time shipping me the first; but to this date nothing has been heard from such alleged shipment. I hardly think 'twill off-end Charleston, being but children's ballads and tales, and presumptively amusing silhouettes—260! Count 'em! as Jack Haverley used to say of his end-men on the eight-sheet bills.

The magnum opusculus romance which has now been on the stocks in my ship-yard these three belated years will may be finished some day, the Lord of Battles and Letters willing—I hope now to be able to take it up again, since this children's story-book and my silhouettes are at long last on the market, I hope on that market to add to my unfattened income by pecuniary vitamins. . . .

As a Damyankee I have read Dr. Robt. Wilson's book with honest delectation and kindly delight—not in the historical romances, which make their appeal to a younger mind than mine; but in the charming memoirs, reminiscences, annals, or what you will, of life on old plantations, in little scattered kindly hamlets of Carolina, long ago, and yearly growing longer—of intimate particulars of life which recreate that day for me in a fascinating manner, sketches of people, sketches of field and stream, of household economies, personal idiosyncrasies, and sportsmanlike accountings of days with rod and gun. It may be, knowing Dr. Wilson as I did, a loyal friend and most charming companion, one of the first cordially to extend unquestioning welcome to a Damyankee, and never to alter his smile of greeting, or the expressive twinkle of his keen, and scrutinizing eye—with which he so graphically, so minutely, so humorously saw life—I have been prejudiced to delighting; but that delight remains beyond three readings; so that the substance must be good—and is. I can recall no book of Caroliniana with quite the same charm. It is the charm of the writer's own personality, so strongly impressed upon his intimate narratives of half-forgotten men, things, and days, as to make them as alive as he himself still is in my affectionate memory: perhaps I shall never take up the book and read but so little as a page, without seeing and hearing Dr. Robert Wilson's much-loved but shaken voice, and hearing the delightful tone of assurance in that voice, of my appreciation, as he calls my attention to some vital but unconsidered trifle in remembrance, or criticism of painting, or odd twist of personality, in memory or observation, or tradition—which we enjoyed together. I have read few books which so entertainingly return with old times in so genial, so tender, so loving, so humorous a spirit. His vivid personal interest in natural life, in humanity, in life's minute surroundings, in men, alive or dead, and in the little intimate differences of daily existence which part our times so suddenly and so far from past years. I think the book a real treasure-house in all its reminiscential parts, of half-forgotten things, noted by an extraordinary pictorial and enjoying mind wherever the writer went, in Carolina lowland or Maryland's Eastern Shore. Dr. Wilson's chapter on South Carolina Artists is a contribution deserving a careful place in the story of men who painted here: personally regret that circumstance prevented copious illustration. So far as I know he first in print called attention to Henrietta Johnson, of whom we have heard so largely of late. But the intimate, kindly, humorous, human remembrance of places and persons of the past charms me like a sort of interfusion of Elliott's[3] *Carolina Sports*, *Old Town Folk*, and *Our Village*.

There, God keep and ever bless you and your lovely wife!

Extract as you will, or need; and believe me, as you always would seem to have believed so unsuspiciously,

Your most affectionate friend,
John Bennett

How heartily I. R. Trimble detested a Yankee!

———————

2d Oct. '28

My dear John:

Just a line of congratulation on the Pig*tail* of Ah Lee Ben Loo, tho' I have not had time to look at anything yet, except the wonderful silhouettes! I know nothing of the State *book-store*— "Betsy & I are out"— but the news from Gittman's is encouraging. Mine was the 23*d* of 25 copies they had sold up to yesterday P.M.; & I saw the letter ordering 25 more! Miss Hogan said they were *keeping* the other 2 copies of the *1st Edition;* expecting a fancy rise in price!!!

So mote it be!

Tout à vous,
Y. S.

14th Dec. '28

Dear John:

Here is the brief epistle which I warned you to expect before Christmas!

I have printed (or James Holmes has) a few copies of your amazing exposé of your "little inside"; eleven of which I send to you. . . .

I think the Columbia "artist" has made a first class reproduction of your rather intelligent countenance, & I intended to keep the plate for use when you get your P. B. K., or when you are jailed for indecent publications, or for some other notable or ignotable act of your dissipated career—*in future*—But, I find, what I ought to have known, that a 133 screen, copper, half-tone can not be used on a newspaper press, and so, I *send you the plate* to use as you (or the wife, or Jane) durn please. *Comprenez?*

With Annie's & my love to you & yours, & all the best wishes of the season,

Always yours affectionately,
Yates Snowden . . .

Annie (& me) are delighted with your Romeo and Juliet (Romeo brandishing a broom!). It has the place of honor on our "drawing-room" mantelpiece, between the statuette of John C. Calhoun and the miniature of the wife's revered ancestor, "Red Paul Warley,[4] full of rum." I'm sleepy & writing on my knee. Adios! . . .

Charleston, S.C., Dec. 20, 1928
"To be opened Secretly"

Farewell! Farewell!

Mine must be God's bitter gift of exile.

But you—you shall sup the vitriolic cup of remembered treachery!

Aha!

I shall mail this somewhere on my way to unknown parts. Seek not to follow me: I return no more:

Again—bitterly—faithless yet once-trusted friend,

F A R E W E L L
forever!
[J.B.]

N.B.: I shall address you in a disguised hand.

December 29th, 1928

Dearest and confoundedest YATES:

If you have not, as you threatened, sent Randal McBryde[5] a copy of the APPENDIX, for heaven's sake employ yourself hastily in forwarding same to a disturbed mind. The good man fears a rupture between you and me because, supposing him already to be apprised of the contents of said APPENDIX pamphlet, I referred to you in the unmeasured terms of jocularity as a conscienceless villain who had stabbed me frightfully in my literary back—and, my God! he thought I was in earnest with such pyrotechnics! Certainly more than half a jest must lie in the ear of him who hears, as well as on the tongue of him who speaks.

Thus, you are apprized, I have just had to smoothe the apparently-wrinkled-front-of-war-between-you-and-me, to soothe the kindly fears of that good man; and now must in much haste write you, asking that you shall circulate still further that dastardly revelation of my errant past. One may defend himself from the assaults of his enemies; but, a Goddis name! who shall preserve him from the felonious attacks of his own dear Brutus? Alas! as Logan[6] said, "NOT ONE!"

Thus having intertwined the SAVAGE and the ROMAN, I cease my importunate clamor, being very well and my family all the same, and they, to a man, or woman, as the case may be, joining me heartily in every affectionate wish and greeting to you and to that lovely woman, Mistress Snowden, for the coming Year. May health, comfort, serenity, and the heart and mind's best prosperity of a rich peace, be yours, now and ever!

Affectionately—and in great haste—
yours—now dead at the foot of
Pompey's statue:
O O [J. B.]

N.B.: Having just returned under cover from the Orient, you will respect my incognito: Speed, speed the winged messenger of peace!

O O

Chapter 17

1929

Bennett's Northern and Southern kinsmen; Bennett's first grandchild, Anne Wells; Martha Laurens Ramsay's book; news of young Jack Bennett and friends; Eliza Crawley Murden's book; Snowden and Fitz McMaster's automobile wreck; artist Alfred Hutty.

IN FEBRUARY of 1929 Yates Snowden sent an autograph of Bennett's kinsman, the Confederate General Isaac Ridgeway Trimble, and mentioned a chapter on John Yates Beall in *The Confederate Privateers*, published by Yale University Press. In thanking Snowden, Bennett mentioned several other members of the family on both sides of the Civil War, as well as relatives who served in the Revolution.

Bennett related the story of Sam Boyer Davis, who was saved from hanging by the intervention of William Trimble McClintock and Abraham Lincoln. In addition, Bennett told an anecdote of his father's youth. In March Bennett announced with pride the birth of his first grandchild, Jane's daughter Anne Wells.

Snowden reported that *The Pigtail of Ah Lee Ben Loo* was selling well in Columbia. Near the end of April, Bennett was thankful that the Charleston tourist traffic had subsided as the garden season drew to a close, and he gave Snowden the latest news about his son Jack.

In May Bennett traveled to Columbia to be initiated into Alpha Chapter of Phi Beta Kappa. Near the end of June, the Snowdens left for a two-months stay at the Bonclarken Hotel in Flat Rock, North Carolina.

In December Snowden and Fitz Hugh McMaster were in an automo-

bile wreck on the way back to Columbia from Charleston after Thomas
Sinkler's funeral. Bennett's progress on the book about his father's life
was agonizingly slow. By the end of the year, however, he was pleased
with the last chapter he had written and planned to keep laboring on the
novel.

During 1929 the friends discussed several books. Among those
mentioned were *Mrs. Eddy: Biography of a Virginal Mind* by Edwin
Dakin, *The Generalship of Ulysses Grant* by Colonel J. F. C. Fuller, and
The Hero of Vincennes by Lowell Thomas.

5*th* Feb'y '29

My dear John:

I have not time to write even to you tonight—though *I have* finished
& sent in my exams, papers & grades. Te Deum Laudamus!!

I can only express to Mrs. B. the wife's & my keen sympathy on the
death of Mrs. Anton Pope's *14 year old* daughter![1] Oh the pity of it!—
unless she was a confirmed invalid! I hope your girls fare well—
especially *Jane!*

If you have not the brains & decency to appreciate it, give the
enclosed official autograph of your noblest relative, Trimble of Maryland! Trimble of Gettysburg!! to your son Jack with my best regards!
And further, if *you* can't appreciate such heroism, tell Jacobus Jr. to read
the chapter (pp. 221–31) on "John Y. Beall, Partisan Sea Captain" in W.
M. Robinson's[2] absorbing (it "absorbed" $4.00 of mine!) *"The Confeder-
ate Privateers"* (Yale Univ. Press). It gives details of Beall's early career
on the Chesapeake & thereabouts entirely unknown to me, and has *much*
new (old) stuff about Charleston in war time.

With my love to you'uns, severally & collectively, I am

Yours affectionately,
Yates Snowden

February 13th, 1929

Dear and Generous Old Top: . . .

I can heartily thank you in my own name and for JACK, with fullest
appreciation, for the official autograph of my grandmother's brother,
Isaac Trimble, Maj. Gen. C.S.A., and will match my own admiration of
that fine old soldier and gentleman with yours; and believe my own to
be the greater, since it travelled farther to its summit from constitu-

tional dislike and distrust of the cause to which he, and many another like him, lent its true distinction. While yours begins with a tainted predilection toward praise; which I can understand thoroughly, and pity, while declining to sympathize with its measure of human unreason, as exemplified in insane NULLIFICATION and ILL-ADVISED SECESSION.

That Isaac Trimble is, perhaps, the most gallant of my relatives, I long ago was persuaded; though my uncle's only son, JOHN McCLINTOCK,[3] as freely gave his life, and lost it, on the other side. And my cousin, JOSHUA SILL, gave his life trying to rally his men at Stone River, first day's fight: which occasion, as it may be you are informed, was a poor one for his endeavors.

Of course, as I do not confine repute to one brief generation, I consider my cousins, George Michael Bedinger[4] and Benoni Sweringen, of Virginia, entitled to mention, who decided that George Washington needed aid, and so walked from the Shenandoah to Germantown to lend theirs, and considerably distinguished themselves in subsequent controversial excursions throughout contemporary history.

Nor do I deem the performance of said Bedinger on the bloody border of Kentucky, when, left alone in the face of the enemy, with a leg broken in the wilderness, he sustained life, recovered of his wounds, hiding in the canebrakes, and there preserved and healed a companion in adversity, a parakeet with a broken wing, his sole living comrade— and this done, again safely made his way back to Virginia, to serve again whenever occasion rose.

Nor did I ever think, though in days when all fought and died as men might in trial, that my father's uncle, Joshua Bennett, of Virginia, who laid down a boy's life in defense of Boonesboro during its bitterest, long siege, was deficient in simple nobility.

Indeed, poor friend, I might go on to cite *thousands* of my kinsmen distinguished alike for those qualities you, in your simplicity, seem ever most greatly to admire and to praise; but sheer modesty restrains me: enough may have been said to persuade you that I estimate in full the valor and fineness of Isaac Trimble "of Gettysburg," or where you will, and that Jack will give to his autograph—many, many thanks, and fullest appreciation.

I have for several years been trying to obtain from my Baltimore cousins a good photograph of the gallant old fellow; but, while they accept with enthusiasm all early family history I send them, conveyed at their request, they have thus far failed to respond in kind with such portrait for our "Hall of the Ancestors."

My kinspeople of the great Valley, however, being of more generous disposition, have given me a portrait of that unfortunate fine fellow,

JOHN YATES BEALL, with whose tragic story I have been sympathetically familiar from childhood. I have not yet seen the reference you give
to Robinson's "Confederate Privateers," but shall look it up, to see if it
gives more than Judge Dan. Lucas's[5] life of his boyhood schoolmate,
Beall, has given in Virginia University annals. In recent numbers of the
Confederate Veteran—God save it!—my distant cousin—Virginia
cousinship, you understand, runs, after the fourth degree, by affection
and worth-whileness—my distant cousin, Miss Virginia Lucas, of Rion
Hall, Charles Town, W. Va., has contributed some, to me, interesting
data concerning J. Y. Beall's progenitors, illuminative of his own
character and quality. I may, through habitual garrulity and absent-
mindedness, have told you in the past that my Father, being then a little
boy and resident for the moment at "AUNT BEALL'S house," was
caught up by George Beall, on the way to his wedding, and rode behind
him to that union, first fruits of which became JOHN YATES BEALL.

I suppose, of course, in your narrow provincial position, you know
little or nothing of young Sam Boyer Davis, Lieut., C.S.A., aide to Gen.
Trimble, who was shot through the lungs in that famous charge by the
gallant men of dilatory Pickett, at Gettysburg, but escaped from Federal
hospital, made his way successfully through the lines to Richmond, and
there volunteered, at Christmastime, Dec., '64, to carry despatches
through the enemy's country to Canada, in place of Harry Brogden, of
Maryland, Confederate Signal Corps, who got cold feet in the face of
that risky errand—said despatches being JEFFERSON DAVIS'S mani-
festo, declaring JOHN Y. BEALL a duly commissioned officer in the
Confederate States Navy, and a certified copy of Lieut. Beall's Confederate commission—made his way successfully through the Northern
States, delivered his papers there, but was taken, identified, and imprisoned, on his returning trip, and sentenced to death as a SPY, by military
tribunal, in Cincinnati, Ohio, January, 1864, despite Gen. Joe Hooker's
positive and angry statement, "That man is NO SPY!"—and was permitted to lie under that death sentence, at Governor's Island, until the
middle of February—actually to see the gallows raised on which he was
told he should hang—though, already, commutation of that most unjust
sentence had been secured in Washington—maugre the vindictive opposition of Sec. Stanton, who was determined to hang Davis as he hanged
Beall—whether or no.

I suppose you do not know these small details, but take your glory
in large from your nurse's milk forward to adult confirmation in errors.
But it was ever a pleasure to me to know that my Mother's brother, Wm.
T. McClintock, of Chillicothe, was the one who recognized young
DAVIS (who was related to Mrs. Isaac Trimble—Miss Presstman), and
put those determined agencies into motion which saved the boy, in spite
of the malignant Stanton's firm intention and maneuvers to secure his

deadly end. Uncle William had by chance seen the notice in a Cincinnati paper of the identification of the Confederate officer captured in Ohio, as Lieut. Sam B. Davis, of Maryland. He found, and recognized DAVIS, although Davis did not recognize him. Davis, with his sisters, Minna and Lydia, had for some years made their home in Uncle Isaac Trimble's house, in Baltimore, and Uncle Will had known the boy there. Of this I remember nothing, being yet unborn in '64; but my cousin, Petrea McClintock, has often told of the anxiety in the house during the entire episode, until Lincoln's signature of commutation was secured—and Uncle Will's rising desperately early of a cold morning, Feb. 1st, '64, and taking the train at gray dawn for Cincinnati, to identify the boy and start measures for his rescue.

That Davis afterward subsided into nonentity, so far as the public is concerned, does not detract from his right to a place in the story of JOHN YATES BEALL—with whose trial thus, you see, my family were concerned on both sides, my father's and my Mother's. Such things give me a position in judgment of our bitter old struggle to nationality superior to yours, whose sympathies have been enlisted upon one side only, and whose errant training has, one must fancy, been ever directed toward that immaculate dream of the past so delightfully sponsored by Miss —— of Georgia, historian to the Daughters of the Confederacy— with such glorious disregard of fact.

It was "Beautiful Bedford," Shepherdstown, Va., the home of George Michael Bedinger's people, was burned to the ground by that abominable renegade Virginian, Gen. Hunter's,[6] command, by miscreant knave, Capt. Martindale, of Pennsylvania, to whose memory I will join you in contribution of obscene epithets, whenever you have a little spare time for hearty objurgation.

It was in the great cherry-trees of "Bedford" my Father ate his fill, as a small boy, with his comrades, Alex Boteler,[7] of whom you may— perhaps—know something, though I doubt such catholicity—and Henry Bedinger,[8] afterward Consul to Denmark, father of the very minor poet, Danske Dandridge;[9] these facts I state for amelioration of your ignorance—though seriously doubting the genial effect of even the most powerful nostrum on the cribbed, cabined and confined course of your Carolina training.

For your kind inquiry regarding JANE, and in recognition of your ever kind intentions toward virtue, including present generosity: viz., I. R. Trimble's official autograph—JANE herself has asked that I send you—and I enclose herewith—a silhouetted portrait of her, done not long ago—this with her love to you.

She is well, bravely cheerful in maternal discomfort now considerable as her time so closely approaches, and very happy in anticipation of her imminent motherhood—as, indeed, we are all—anxiously trusting all will go as well as all has to this time gone.

The death of Hannah Wright's only daughter, Nannie, was tragic. The course of her illness was that terrible way outlined from the same infection in poor young Lang Cheves's[10] death a few years ago. Her brave resistance to desperate disease was, when we view the inevitable end, pitifully heroic: her Mother, a noble woman, sustained her family of men; her Father, she being the apple of his eye, is heart-broken—and the three sons left without a life which to them would ever have been a central link of affection and union.

The only compensatory knowledge is that, when the disease had so run its course, had she miraculously survived, her life afterward could have been but a greater tragedy than death; so that all of us are the more willing to say, as has so often so perfunctorily been said by sense of duty, "Thy will be done!"

I congratulate you on completing your papers: through my sister's life I am familiar with papers these more than forty years. Our younger daughter, SUE, just managed to complete her mid-year exams., and to pass all with A, B, C-plus, when she went down with sharp fever and the flu, a week ago, from which she remains still in bed.

I have heard you and your lovely and beloved wife have both suffered much from the same. We all hope both are now well restored to normal health. I have had only enough of it to make me insupportable to my family and quite unendurable to myself: which may account for the scintillant brilliancy of this present epistle.

However contemning and denunciatory some passages of it may seem to your tender heart, believe me you have few more truly affectioned friends—for the number of years the opportunity has been mine to be rich with your kind regard—than

Always—yours,
John Bennett

———————

19*th* Febr'y, '29

My dear John: . . .

"*Why the Devil, then,*" I hear you *snort,* "is that pest Yates writing me a letter which he knows will provoke an answer?"

The answer is that you have insulted my intelligence, and by implication, besmirched my family-tree! i.e., you have brought this upon yourself!

Imprimis. Your smug assumption that because you had kinsmen on both sides in the great conflict for the preservation of the home market & eventually, as a war measure, for the abolition of slavery, your judgment is better than mine, is preposterous! Durn a man who can see "both sides," when there was only one side! In your Sunday-school days you possibly read of "Mr. Facing Both Ways"! &c., &c., &c.

But the meanest "dig," because it was so subtle, is vaunting yourself on your *Revolutionary ancestors* when you were fully persuaded that *I had none!* I have no doubt that you were fully aware that one Bethea[11] killed, or hanged one Snowden a notorious Tory! You will regret to hear that *that* Snowden was no relation of mine! (See Index to Gregg's[12] "Hist. of the Old Cheraws" for the melancholy story!)

All the same; I have the *original* muster-roll of the St. Helena Co., Capt. Jenkins,[13] sent to the Council of Safety, & endorsed by H. Laurens, which bears the name of *"Joshua Snowden,"* who had the honor of being my great great grandfather! (*Entre nous* that's all I know about Joshua's war record. *He* may have *turned Tory!* I'll pay you $7.25, if you find out!) . . .

My love to Jane & her mother and sister & father,

Yours affectionately,
Yates Snowden

NB! That's a *fine* silhouette of Jane; altho' it looks almost too mature! I am *lending* you a fine study of myself in black & white made by an admiring student, a nephew of Randell McBryde! Send it back!

Today Gittman thus opined: "John Bennett's first ed'n of "Pig Tail," &c. is going to increase in value by leaps & bounds, & I shall not be surprised if it gets the Nobel prize for the best children's book!" *So mote it be!!* I did not know there was a Nobel prize for that branch of literature!

The remark followed the inquiry of Miss Hogan as to the value & scarcity of the 1*st* ed'n of Skylark.

God bless us all!

February 20th, 1929

Thrice blessed and Mildly Belligerent:

Your somewhat combative and insolent epistle received.

I suppose—indeed, I perceive clearly—that there is no further use of my attempting to conceal the fact that I am just as arrogantly, just as insufferably proud of my antecedents as any South Carolina pronoun whatsoever. I have endeavored, with some success, to conceal this humiliating weakness for many years of residence among my inferiors; but now no more shall endeavor to whitewash the family sepulchre of distinction with the hypocritical kalsomine of false modesty—I admit it: my people are, and ever have been, greatly superior, and sometimes almost equal, to the world at large and the rest of mankind. I believe that it is as Zach Taylor phrased it. So, being, as I have said, modest, it will do for me.

I have for years forborne to speak of the lamented Snowden of Cheraw: but since you protest he is none of yours, hurrah for the sour-apple tree of his just but fatal ascension!

It is not that my judgment is so much better than yours, my dear fellow, but that my position, as on a peak of Darien between two oceans of obliquity, affords a sure superiority. Yet your biting retort is ingenious. I perceive that, like John C. Calhoun, you have the fatal faculty of presenting an excellent argument for everything and a substantial reason for nothing. Much may be forgiven a man of that disposition if one truly love him, as we understand his enemies sometime came to love the said John C. . . .

In vile haste, but ever affectionately:
Arrogans Ohionusis: Buffoon
[J. B.]

March 7th, 1929

My dear Yates:

After our recent furious fusillade of badinage and genial scurrility I feel that a little sense and sentiment is due you—a momentary armistice of superior intellects.

I believe you will be happy to know that our girl, Jane Wells, was safely delivered of her child, Tuesday night, March 5th, at 8:25 o'clock, Riverside hospital, and that said child is a fine girl, strong and hearty, and, as her father stoutly affirms, a most remarkable, perhaps unique example of perfect infancy. Both the baby and her mother are, thus far, progressing splendidly, to the entire approval of the attending physician, Lester Wilson, and the immense satisfaction and relief of her immediate family and intimate circle, who have with some anxious reflection unavoidably recalled the loss of her first child.

Naturally we who were nearest and most concerned breathe free and sleep sounder than we have for several weeks. I have thus far sustained the sudden increase of personal honors with humility, finding the knowledge of grandparentage a salutary offset to thoughtless exuberance. Not that my hair has suddenly grown whiter in a night, with new responsibility, but that the whiteness feels as if it had struck in, and left these busy pages blank of entertaining thought to charm the reader.

Jane says that the appearance of the child effectually proves that it is Forrest's; but that thus far no trait of charm or brilliance has exhibited itself enough to confirm the suspicion that it is hers; that she suspects it, however.

The baby is to bear the dignified name Anne, for Forrest's Mother; I think, myself, Anne Wells does excellently. Should any interstitial name be given, it is likely to be Chase, Forrest's mother being of the familiar line of Bishop Chase[14] of Ohio.

I have not yet myself recognized the phenomenal beauty so easily perceived by nurses and early parenthood: the infant, by careful examination, has a nose like its father's family—a traditional organ—long fingers like the Smythes—another tradition—and a distinct cowlick, trade-mark of the Bennett line proper: she has escaped the hereditary hammer-toe: beyond which she is ascertained to have the usual complement of arms and legs, an excellent voice of considerable sustained power, and a distinctly simian disposition to cling firmly to the branch. I have no doubt other, equally positive, details will be observed as time passes.

Meanwhile, between dizzy spells of an affectionately weak mind, I am engaged as well as may be on my book. Some times I think I come forward; sometimes am sure I have gone back; and sometimes, without a doubt, I recognize the disastrous truth that I sit upon the beach of Time, waving my hands in the futile gestures of a fiddler-crab.

Yesterday, in an hour of—was it or not—inspiration, I did a wonderfully funny chapter, which, up to 11:30 o'clock, this morning, I had not dared to inspect, knowing, by experience, how changed a funny chapter can be the morning after. My youthful hero's mother has just had a really good burial upon a Missouri hillside; and the CHOLERA is stretching out its deadly tentacles to take off his step-father, as charming a man as ever rode well or walked handsome or talked intelligently—except when he was drunk; "now go on with the story."

And that is all I shall pause to say, this morning: the only news of any consequence—I trust of interest to you—is that the child is born, and that Mother and baby are making excellent progress together—and that, God bless and keep her—my girl is for this time supremely happy—may that happiness never completely wear away!

Good-by! My compliments and regard to Mrs. Snowden, and to you my family's real affection, and mine:

> Well, Heaven keep us all!
> Affectionately yours,
> John

March 19th, 1929

Dear Yates:

I never turn over the mass of unanswered correspondence which lies heaped on my tables, chairs, desks, and floor, without discovering there some letter of yours to which I had long since meant an apt reply, in which I should

1st: confute all your arguments upon whatsoever head;

2nd: dispute brilliantly every rash statement made;

3rd: heap obloquy upon your antique line of effete State patriotism, as futile as obsolete;

4th: express in burning words my detestation of the misspent error of your ways.

Not only were such replies intended, but such were actually planned, and in pencilled scribblings, on your scanty margins and envelope-backs, were noted down the brilliant retorts, quips, jests, and masterly repartees with which said letters were to have been replete.

But there the letters lie, unanswered, and now unanswerable.

I know that you have much needed my admonitions, restraining and correcting your indiscretions; yet, though these were lacking, I rest upon the knowledge that I have wrestled often in silent prayer, hoping to draw your wandering footsteps back to Virtue's path.

Although something convinces me I have not done so, I cannot lose hope. . . .

SECONDLY: (FIRSTLY being omitted as unnecessary): Much as I have enjoyed the pieties of Mrs. Martha Laurens Ramsay, it has been perhaps in hope that her humility might in some salutary way correct your natural arrogance, that I immediately rushed to the Charleston Library and feverishly perused entire her astonishing and pitiful confessions of faith.

At first thought I had planned to gather from her pages a line of satiric hypocrisy for the portrait of a scallawag I am preserving in the amber of my genius; but, alas! the poor lady is too frightfully in earnest in her agony of soul for even me to turn her outpourings of humility and spiritual self-abasement to a light and ironic use; so I closed her book, and so home, without the sneer I seek.

What a frightful conception of Almighty God some of our worthy forebears had! . . .

What is this all about? It comes from turning up several letters of yours, in an endeavor to straighten up my tables and get on with the book under whose burden I undoubtedly bend and groan.

And with your well-known and masterly chirography upon those yellowed envelopes I have been moved to just such futile efforts as these to assure you what for years your frightful missives have meant to a missionary spirit like mine.

Still hopefully yours:
Francis Asbury D.D. . . .

P.S.: I wish I could tell you that my book flourished likewise; but although the gathering of material to be embodied in the tale amasses avalanches and mountains of quite indispensable detail, the compressed product of illustrious genius seems scarce to get on at all. Some day, I doubt not, we shall mutually be done, my book and I—at present I am swallowed up, with Korah's[15] troop, within the bowels of immense travail, and my time is not yet. Give my compliments and devoted respects to your dear and lovely wife; and do, for Heaven's sake, reform your politics and fatal prepossessions with the errors of the past!

Affectionately yours,
J B

April 22, 1929

Dear Yates:

The Spring-garden avalanche has almost thawed itself away; the Yankees and New Yorkers depart, and the peaceful voice of the turtle will, we trust, at an early date, once more be audible through the damned din of automobiles braying and snorting by the Tradd street corner of this once, long since, placid lane. . . .

You ask news of Jack. That stout-shouldered, broad-breasted, thick-thighed, long-legged son of Anak[16] is just completing his first post-graduate year in Yale Forestry school, and seems to be having a bully time. We put him into a new Ford roadster as a graduation present—in which he travels to and fro, at a somewhat high rate of speed—his latest record being 500 miles between 6:30 a.m. and 10 p.m., on returning, with two college mates, from spring vacation spent at my old home in Ohio, with my sister—and in rain all the way. I think Jack's plan is not so much to make two trees grow where one grew before, but to ensure one healthy, adequate tree to come to a fine maturity where two scrub pines or stunted oak-trees have so long disfigured the landscape of S.C. For the summer he has signed on with the U.S. Forestry Reserve force at Natural

Bridge forest, Virginia, for practical field-work and the engineering connected with the same. His Mother already is planning to drive thither to see him during July or August, with a peep at some of our relatives in the traversed or adjacent regions. I do not venture on plans; they gang too aft agley; and I grow weary of being Mousie. I shall observe a fine Lincolnian opportunism, and grab, wherever the grabbing looks good. Jack does not seem to have much taste for oats, breakfast cereal or wild; he has experimented cautiously in romance, and has but slightly burned his fingers in acquiring wisdom: his first case of hopeless devotion was to a charming girl, who, perhaps unfortunately for the two of them (they being rather fine young people), was his senior; so that (fortunately for them both, that being the fact), after a more or less stormy season of tragic delight, they agreed mutually to dissolve—age proving with increasing insistency the probable incompatibility of their lives later along. She has found another Orpheus; and Jack is fancy free, but neither down-cast nor oblivious, and from indications enjoying freedom from youth's romantic anguish, so inseparable from young heart-disease. The boy has been happier during the last two years of maturing work than ever before at school—his earlier years being embittered by uncongenial surroundings and a paucity of intelligent, purposeful companionship. His cousins, Billy and Henry Gaud,[17] are both now at Yale, and doing pretty well; so that lends something better to an outlandish world. He has found that there really are charming folk in New England, and now counts many friends in the country round, sufficient for very jolly week-ends. I do not know yet whether he will wind up in field-work or the laboratory, as the pathology of plant-disease attracts his questioning mind. He is a husky youth, heavier, taller, stronger than ever I was, and is one of the try-out boxing squad. Several years ago, last time I had on the argumentative gloves with him in our back-yard, he pelted me one on the jaw. That convinced me I had grown too old for such foolishness: I told him to go forth into the great world of men and find someone else to pelt on the jaw. I think he has done so.

Your reference to Phi Beta Kappa (my machine won't write Greek) seems obscure. I cannot make out clearly whether you say I received my P.B.K. for "destruction" or "distinction" in literature. I should like to be advised which you mean. Anxiously awaiting your reply to same, I beg to remain, quite un-bored, and ever

Affectionately yours:
John Bennett

Forget not my regards and compliments always to your blessed wife.

Uncle Tom's Cabin is showing here; come down and see it.

————————

May 21st, 1929

Dear Yates:

I have just been strewing fragrant flow'rs over Juliana's beer—Oh, I beg your pardon! I meant B I E R.

Which is to say, I have completed the Murden-Crawley[18] GEM you so generously lent me, and am perishing in a puddle of platitude.

Alackaday! I found far less fish for my nets than I had fondly hoped at first examination of these transcendental lines: the gentle poet flattens frightfully—and when she begins to print the effusions of Octavia and Victoria I gave over my hope of truly glorious banality and closed the page.

Natheless I am frightfully obliged: I found a few scraps of gush quite consonant with a proposed character in my book; and have noted these for adaptation to my own ends.

One thing I noted: the joyous frequency with which the Gentle Poet paused "to drop a tear" on the "bier."

She certainly was a WET. And appears from the text sedulously to have camped upon the trail of Murden—prolific parental, financially misfortuned, loving and beloved by that tender bosom.

I find my name in the list of subscribers to the volume: I wish to protest: this is an error: I have a perfectly wonderful alibi. I had hoped to find my great-uncle's name, Capt. Jno. Williamson—of Williamson & Stoney—but am afraid, from the date, he was dead—she did not drop any tear on his bier; which was singularly remiss—few escaped that biery tear.

But, Lord love us! how pitiful the hopes which made this book and foisted it upon one's friends—shall I add "long, long ago!" as doubtless she had done in my place?

I return the cherished volume by parcels-post, this day, insured and carefully enwrapped; wh. I trust wl. come to yr. hand in safety, Honrd. Sir. Pray make my bow to your Lady and her Sister—my book and I are in a bloody bog, progress nil, dod rot it! So no more, but hope for better days, and do remain affectionately and gratefully

Yrs.,
Affectionately,
John

To: Alex'r Findlay McClintock
Care, John Bennett Esq.
Legare St. No. 37
Charleston, S.C.

Cola, S.C., 3d Nov'r '29

Dear Mac:

I congratulate you on your noble excursion into heredity. "Seldom a Genius . . . like Me," is good![19]

Yours,
Galton[20]

December 9th, 1929

Ever God-blessedest Yates:

We hear through Miss F. Henerey[21] that on your return from Tom Sinkler's[22] funeral, last week, you and Fitz McM. smashed up by the way! We are reassured by Miss H. that though shaken and fatally disfigured—alas! that Beauty should be Marred—though seriously doubting that such Radiance as yours could ever in any way be dimmed by whatever disaster—still, as I said in beginning this last sentence, being reassured that your hurts are truly neither fatal nor great—although too much, God knows, though soever little—I venture to send enclosed a psychological plaster for your wounds, whose folly may annul some pang.

All this family rejoice that you and F. M. were not seriously injured—exact extent of accident as yet unknown—and send loving congratulations, sincere regrets, and prayers that you will never let this happen again.

Did they take away your license for driving under the influence of F. McMaster? Or versa vice?

And were you badly hurt in any way, my dear fellow?

Distressedly and affectionately yours:
John Bennett

Sympathy and rosy compliments to one of the kindest and most charming of Women: your good Wife.

A Happy New Year!

December 31st, 1929

Dearest Yates:

I am growing old and grouchy. Something acrid and crab-like is at work upon my seraphic nature.

Having some most unexpected funds put astonishingly and quite undeservedly at my disposal—and learning that the Christian Scientists of Charleston, like their brethren abroad throughout the land, have been raising very hell in the endeavor to suppress Edwin Dakin's life of "Mrs. EDDY, Biography of a Virginal Mind," Scribner's Sons, pubrs.—and that Harry Kirk, of Hammond's, was stubbornly keeping his one copy in the face of a threatened boycott—what did I do, but walk down town, seconded and abetted in iniquity by my son, Jack, and therewith purchase, buy, secure and obtain said obnoxious and suppressable life of Mary Baker Eddy, that it might not perish but have a much-extended life in a private Charleston library.

Now, so far as Mary Baker Eddy and her cult are concerned I have not the damnedest itch of interest; they may get to merry hell for all of me, along with all other sects and sectaries that have a name blown in the bottle.

But this attempt at suppression gets my most irascible goat; and I now have the balmiest, permeating sense of virtuous action merely from preventing the proposed extermination of that book in Charleston.

I must be growing old and grouchy: I never felt that way about Brigham Young and the Mormons. May be that was because I met them earliest in Artemus Ward.[23]

I never felt that way about Mahomet. Or Arius.[24] Or Calvin, or Francis Asbury, or the speculative Bishop of Virginia. I must be growing crabbed as the years creep on.

Why, I damned near went down town and bought Col. Fuller's[25] volume of horrible heresies, "The Generalship of Ulysses Grant," just because I am growing so devilish tired of never hearing the praise of anyone sung but *beaux sabreurs* and *prieux Chevaliers* of the late Confederate X-Roads. Any historian with frankness enough to dub Halleck[26] a "tactless ass" appeals to my un-balanced nervous system tremendously, and almost deserves my unquestioning trust and confidence, even though he dares peer around the enormous corners of General Robert E. Lee and see a landscape beyond.

Yes, I am growing grouchy, as time rolls on; and what is to be done to prevent the entire corruption of my sweetness baffles my conjecture.

One bright spot alone gleams through the mist and the darkness: I got me Lowell Thomas's tolerably well-done life of George Rogers Clark, "The Hero of Vincennes," with the noble and heroic story of that great campaign of audacity and brains and dauntless endurance of most desperate circumstance, and am watching with an internal smile my family read it, one by one, and for the first time, I think, become aware of what their progenitors did at the behest of old Virginia, through the noble dream and courage of that one young man—and—then—to see them each and everyone get sadly griped when they learn, at the close of a gallant story, what the grand old State of Virginia, God bless her! and the glorious United States, God help 'em! can do to one who has served them far better than well and ruined himself in that service! And how cordially one damns Patrick Henry!

Ah, I must be growing old and grouchy. But these are my books at Christmas-tide—thanks to a generous world, and others—and so "God bless us all!" said Tiny Tim—and soften the asperity of my senility!

We had a fine day, Christmas—all of us at home but my excellent son-in-law, just ordered to a new vessel, stationed at New York—and my "little sister" in Ohio. Jane Wells's baby, Anne, was a center of delight, with good-nature and smiles enough to offset my ill-natured thunders; we had the Alfred Huttys (the painter-etcher and his handsome wife, Bessie),[27] to dinner with us—and Susan gave us a glorious surfeit of edible temptations to which we fell without a struggle. Many remembrances made the day shine like the sun—among them your provocative message, the results of which I have recorded. Another was a card from a boy who, over forty years ago, was a printer and compositor in the country newspaper office where I won my first and brightest tin spurs as a journalist. I have not seen him these two generations of years, nor heard from him, nor did I expect to hear. But some remembrance from the air pressed on his medulla oblongata, and after all these years he was somehow moved, and sent me a Christmas-card. I shall not be flat enough to comment on this; but I have done some astonishing thinking.

My wife has been clambering about—oh, decorously, to be sure!—in ancient branches of my family tree, and has recently exposed my ignominy by pretending to discover my descent from a dozen or more dissolute monarchs of old empire. "Hold your hand, woman!" I cried firmly. "Crown me no crowns, and breed me no bastards; life is already enough!" We have decided to stop about two jumps this side of the crowned heads—and, with a famous young gentleman of our acquaintance, to regard all the rest as silence. She has lost me two assumptive Earls, and two pretty coats-of-arms, and has found me, instead, a poor tailor. "This," said I, firmly, "has gone far enough!"

My book comes on with frightful slowness; but my sister writes in comment on the last hasty draft of a chapter sent her for her opinion: "This is most lovely!" So I trust that, someday, somehow, I shall finish this monumental stone which grows by quarter-inches, and at far intervals. Against another scene she was pleased to write "This is all excellent fooling!" So my heart stands again and strives to simulate the face of dauntless courage—which it never had since I was born—and now I am with utmost difficulty endeavoring to visualize my conception of a lovely villain—for unless I may see with inward eyes the very features of my fancy all falls empty and is nought.

I trust with a great trust, and some genuine prayer, that you are indeed completely recovered from your reputed accident; and that Mrs. Snowden, whom the dear God ever bless! is quite herself again after her late indisposition—and that the New Year, now but a few brief hours away, may be generous of happiness and peace to you both, with bright hours, bright days, and brighter realization than ever before of the unaltering love of your many friends, one of whom I beg to write myself:

A Happy New Year—and God bless you and yours!

Affectionately yours,
John Bennett

Chapter 18

1930–1931

E. B. White and J. G. Thurber's Is Sex Necessary? *and Bennett's jest on the title; Theodore Jervey as South Carolina Historical Society president; the Appletons in the Civil War and at Salt Sulphur Springs; a parody of* Uncle Tom's Cabin; *a Revolutionary War courteous exchange; Snowden's review of* Marching with Sherman; *a double letter by David J. and Louisa Cheves McCord.*

THE LETTERS of 1930, at the beginning of the Great Depression, were few; the correspondence of 1931 was more frequent. Being asked by Dr. Robert Cathcart to read and critique the contents of a new humorous volume, as well as the remarks by others on it, John Bennett wrote instead an amusing jest on the title of the book, *Is Sex Necessary?* In January Bennett sent Yates Snowden a copy.

It was in January, also, that Snowden went to Charleston for a meeting of the South Carolina Historical Society, at which time Theodore Jervey became the new president. Later that month, Bennett mentioned Jervey, adding a short anecdote. Bennett also gleefully pointed out to Snowden the latest mistake by the *New York Times* in regard to Charleston and recalled a similar mistake made by that newspaper about DuBose Heyward. In the last letter of 1930, Bennett identified "George Taletell" for Snowden as Isaac Edward Holmes.

When asked by a student at the University of South Carolina to give a criticism on Yates Snowden for a term paper, Bennett refused to criticize his friend, but sent instead an excellent commentary, which he defended in a letter to Snowden in January of 1931. In February Bennett, saddened by the death of his friend Jack Appleton, whose father had been a Union officer of a black regiment during the Civil War, wrote of Jack's bravery during his long illness, of the generosity of the whole Appleton family to him at Salt Sulphur Springs when he was in genuine need, and of a particularly happy memory there: the presentation, with his friends, of a parody of *Uncle Tom's Cabin.*

In May, expressing appreciation for Snowden's gift to young Jack of a war-time signature of Isaac Ridgeway Trimble, Bennett told of his son's hard work on the islands and in the swamps near Charleston. He included a story of a courteous exchange between General Washington and Lord Howe during the Revolutionary War.

Bennett acknowledged receipt in September of Snowden's review of the volume *Marching with Sherman* and called the Union General's revenge on the South "a sad story of the outrage of war." Bennett regretted the misdeeds of the fanatics on both sides. He told an anecdote about an Irish patriot, adding that it was just as well he did not finish his novel of South Carolina in the Revolution, since he would have pleased no one by showing the weaknesses, as well as the strengths, of both sides.

In December Bennett extended thanks for Snowden's Christmas gift to Mrs. Bennett, a double letter written by David J. and Louisa Cheves McCord, Susan's grandparents.

January 9th, 1930

Dearest Yates:

A short time before Christmas Robt. Cathcart put into my hands that griping book, "IS SEX NECESSARY? Or Why You Feel the Way You Do," by White & Thurber,[1] Harper Bros., 1929, and asked me to read it, mark it, digest it, and write thereon a comment—which comment was to contain, also, criticism on certain remarks written on the blank fly-leaves of the book by our friends, Robert Wilson, Olin Chamberlain,[2] Ned Parker, and Sylvia Allen.

The holidays, with their confusion, being past, our boy, Jack, gone speeding back to Yale with Will Gaud's two boys and Sally Haskell Allen's Frank, I took the book in hand.

More than a desultory reading was impossible. I have no time to dwell more than in passing upon bunkum and tosh, however humorous. This book undoubtedly has its humor, and has amused many.

But, since Cathcart requested it, I asked relief from criticisms of the commentators, and produced instead a hasty disquisition of my own— one of the flatulent impromptus the intellectual cast off from time to time along the way, to relieve their minds of accumulated wind.

This, mind you carefully, is not meant for the young or virginal, but for the entertainment of the old and tough, to whom life's queer questions no more hold out enchantment or bewilderment, but Homeric laughter.

Thinking that, perhaps, as one of the Editors of the Toilet Paper Edition of the South Carolina Poets, you might find some mild amusement in this facile lucubration, I enclose a carbon-copy for your private library shelf, next to Rabelais and Rowland Rugeley, yet superior to both.

To such friends of your intimate indiscretion as you deem kind, if you think the thing provocative of laughter or of easeful mirth upon a dark, dull January day—if you have any such in Columbia, that bright City of the Sun—you may show the MS. as you will.

But, as you have loved me long, don't let it fall into the pinched hands of any Carolina Puritan, or of such as damned me long ago for an insult to the fairest daughters of Athene.

And so, farewell, and no more at this time, from

Yours indiscreetly,
John

January 14th, 1930

Dear Yates:

Thanks for the New Republic's article on Xtian Science and Free Speech. I have stuck it in my copy of Dakin, to assist in keeping that record straight. Will Ball won't print the *Carmen Triumphale;* don't expect it. I have been wanting to get that bit of history off my mind, and now have done it. Randal McBryde says he enjoyed it: I had hoped friends might.

I was completely blotto in an endeavor to write an account of a horse-race, and utterly forgot the meeting of the Historical Society, which I had firmly meant to attend. I am sorry to have missed you—if even only for a few moments exchange of noble sentiments and classic speech.

Theodore J. was the only just material; but it is a pity his sutures froze so early in life. He fined me ten dollars once for running TWENTY-SEVEN miles an hour on the far upper stretches of the Meeting street road. I have long since forgiven it in amused recollection of that meteoric and furious rate of driving!

Ned Parker, after recovering from nervous collapse resultant from reading my dissertation on SEX, told Mrs. Bennett, at Mrs. Jennie Schaeffer's tea, that he did not know where to place me, among the major or minor prophets, Hosea or Jeremiah. He may be like the Oxford man who was asked to allocate the prophets by rank, as major and minor, and replied coldly that he could not think of making such invidious distinctions.

Every now and then someone approaches me cautiously and says, "I have read your Appendix circular published by Yates Snowden"—eh, Banquo?

I suppose you have seen the delicious comment in the N.Y. TIMES, that all our forty-three Sperritual Society singers are direct descendants of the slaves of the old aristocratic families of Charleston and vicinity! God of our fathers! It was not enough to inform the world that DuBose Heyward is a Charleston negro, suppressed and neglected here, but at last come to his own glory through Northern recognition of his merits.

If you ever regard the Confederate Veteran, see the December number for a scrap of quite forgotten history—*in re* J. Y. Beall's case—contributed by myself; a family reminiscence: an account of the capture, trial, and threatened hanging of Sam Boyer Davis, of Baltimore: (not S. Davis, of Tenn.[3]).

Ever affectionately yours,
J. B.

November 23rd, 1930
Charleston, S.C.

"Lumber" of 1822 received: evident that Irving's Sketch-Book made an immediate bid for popular imitation: light-weight but interesting Christmas visit in "Country Life": thanks for opportunity to peruse. *Geo. Taletell* was Isaac E(dward) Holmes, congressman and petit maître des belles lettres, a perfect ass about States—have you his Political essays—collaborated with Robt. Turnbull?[4] *Taletell* pmpht. better claim to remembrance than dead-horse declamation. Will return *George T.,* this week: too lazy to wrap, to-day.

They are doing SKYLARK as a *marionette show* in Boston: amusing development!

"Meteoric shower" unavoidably postponed from Dec. to Jan. Date not yet definite: must first survive Christmas obsequies—pardonnez! I mean festivities—or should.

Happy to have smoothed all perturbation in re Kosmos night-blooming *serious.*

Toujours to the Nth!
J. B. Casaubon[5]
[John Bennett]

January 29th, 1931

Dear Yates:

Damn these dear women! We have been betrayed by them from the beginnings of Time! I knew in my bones that if I talked about you behind your back to Miss Emily Fowles[6] it would with the surety of the tax inquisitor get to your ears, soon or late. I see from your letter of the 25th that it has done so. Had I not known beyond a peradventure that this would be so I should and would have said much more—whether to your credit or discredit it is futile at this time to enquire. In very prosy language you have called me "one of the greatest liars in Christendom." The Pittsburgh Despatch did better than that: it said that I was "undeniably the most iridescent liar west of the Allegheny mountains," which I maintain is superior in locative vividness to your time-worn, rather pietistic reference to a non-existent kingdom of Grace.

Be that as it may, and what I said of you what it was, and your opinion of it as it is: it is true, no doubt, that, had I known you as well as did W. W. Ball in the heyday of your dissolute youth, I might have written of you more glowingly than I did. Pshaw! good-fellow; what I said was not my best, nor all that might have been. Be that too, as it may: I drew it mild, and with all modesty, in apprehension of just such event: I am sorry that it is not to be set out in print—you're welcome, fellow, to my few and weedy flowers! Do with them as your proverbially shy disposition dictates. I know profoundly well that I receive at your mad hands far more indiscreetly golden words of undeserved praise than I let drop of you; so let be; I should rejoice had I but made it fifty-fifty, as I did not, feeling in my bones that the whole thing would be betrayed. . . .

On my own part, I had not comprehended your intentions regarding the charming scape-grace of my family, Lyttleton[7] of the letters. I am truly obliged for an entertaining book—a dim-seen picture of a character. He was a distant kinsman, nephew to the Governor who came into the heritage at his death. My branch had forked from the Lyttleton tree prior to the birth of either of these—but the name was blown in the bottle of both—a synonymous elixir thrills within the veins—though thinned by years and much alloyed—of the noble and damned clever present Viscount Cobham, late Ld. Lyttleton, and your humble—but not too damned humble—servant.

Mrs. Bennett has struck up quite a friendly and pleasant correspondence—at intervals—with members of the family of these far-away kinspeople of mine—and the experience and discovery have been really a source of amusement and pleasure—as witness of her week-end at Hagley—from which fine seat the letter-writer, of your g-father's book, sought to escape into some soother solitude—and of whose little Grecian temples—misplaced, he said, upon strange hills—he exhibited such contempt and critical condemnation.

I had an uncle named Lyttleton Savage in baptism, which seemed an ill-fated essay at the continuance of the name: he did not long survive. Father was named John Briscoe, after the surgeon cousin who saw him into the world, and saved grandmother's life for far sorrier misadventures. The immediate gratitude more firmly established his constitution than the proud panoply of the past did that of my uncle—who perished, an infant in arms; while Father survived until far past eighty, hale as a hickory ax-helve.

To dig up the past disgraces of my family has been for some time my present wife's amusement and delight; but, thus far, she has turned up nothing to equal or surpass the graphic force of the story of John Yates Beall—who must have been your cousin, too—thus making us near of kin: I shall, however, demand more proof than this suspicion.

I am owing a million letters to deserving correspondents; but Rome burned while Nero fiddled. I spent the last hours of evening—last night— in trying to make clear to my enquiring son and most critical wife, the gradations of intellectual appreciation of natural beauty, from the first primitive emotional sense of external loveliness to the Wordsworthian analysis—and am, in consequence, totally unfit for coherent or comprehensible letters—hence I have written to you—who will forgive all disjointures and oblivious parentheses from a belief in the affectionate regard and well-meant essays of

> Yours most truly,
> John . . .

February 25th, 1931

Yates Snowden:
Dear old Chap: . . .

I am particularly neat with remembrance this week—wasting none idly, nor friendships, having just lost a gallant heart, for years my friend, Jack Appleton, of Cincinnati—who passed on to a long-desired and at last given, rest, after fifteen years of slow-approaching death from atrophy of the spinal cord—as gallant a soul as ever walked the ground— when last I saw him, passing through Cincinnati, last autumn, all there was left of him was a face, with a beautiful serenity in spite of great and long-endured pain, a clear brain, a stout-heart, an unchanged affection for every man who had a claim upon his friendship, a pair of eyes, deep and soft and heavy with suffering, but unafraid and quick to dance with remembrances of very happy, humorous days we spent together in the mountains of Virginia, years ago—and, on my word, Yates, that was all—there was not enough left of bones and body to wrinkle his bed-cover.

It was to him years ago I wrote the quatrain which has been often quoted in the press—and once was attributed to Berton Braley, *who did not deny it:*

> We are all but fellow-travellers
> Along life's weary way;
> If any man can play the pipes,
> In God's name, let him play!

He was a joker, a humorist, a philosopher, a good newspaper man, and a first-class advertisement-writer—and a changelessly loving friend—and had a noble wife devoted to his service, whose love eased pain, and braced his heart against the long and tortured road he came to quiet.

It was with Jo Russell Taylor, of the English Dept. O.S.U.; Billy (Tombstone) Graves, ditto, O.S.U.; my brother, Harry; Charlie Smith, of Boston; and Jack Appleton—and me—that the first—and most humorous—parody of "Uncle Tom's Cabin" as a road-show, was prepared in one afternoon, in hot collaboration, rehearsed next day, and produced with instant and tremendous success, as a divertissement during a rainy spell, at the Old Salt Sulphur Springs of Virginia—I played "Eliza"—my escape across the ice, and my topical song, with guitar accompaniment, introduced during a breathing-spell about the middle of the river, was one of the outstanding features of the entertainment; "Little Eva," six feet of "little Eva," was beautifully and tenderly played by Charlie Smith; Appleton was "Legree" the slave-driver; Taylor the most comfortable "Uncle Tom" in history.

It was these things we laughed about when I saw A. last. It was at his home I met my wife first, when she was a quite young girl and I a quite threadbare cartoonist and paragrapher.

His father, a fine man, who learned me much, had been one of the officers in the famous—or infamous, as your predilection will—negro regiment which was shot to rags in the night attack on Battery Wagner—they shot him quite to rags, also. His mother was a great and lovely woman: they gave me a hand up when I was at the very lowest ebb of physical and mental expectation of usefulness or purpose in this world—and, yet, you will pardon me, Yates, for so running on about an utter stranger—I have been rather full of remembrances since I had his wife's wire that he was gone—to rest—and I loved him very much—and found his resolute and dauntless courage a guiding star for my own vacillating soul—such have been all my friends to me: I am grateful to you all:

Affectionately yours,
Jack Bennett

Pray give my devoted compliments to your lovely and justly-beloved wife.

Some-day I mean to write an enormously successful book

THE OLD SCHOOL
ITS
SONS & STEP-SONS

———

4*th* May '31

Dearest of Damyankees:

I am enclosing for your Southern son a little mutilated document of that "wicked and causeless War of the Rebellion," which bears the signature of "I. R. Trimble," and is dated: "Hd. Q'rs, Trimble's Div. 7*th* February 1863." I would not give it even to your son, had I not a mem. of four or five lines signed officially by the old Maryland hero, in my unrivaled collection.

Thanks for your intensely interesting letter, *in re* Cooper River— read at 11:20 night before last. There are some queer paragraphs in your screed, as also in a fine letter I rec'd from little Sam *this* morning. *What* the result will be—nous verrons!

Yours *always* dear Jack,
Y. Snowden

———

May 11th, 1931

Dear Old Confirmed Rebel:

If your fine Grecian head was not firmly articulated, per vertebral hook-up, to your general anatomy, I fancy you would give it to someone as a small token of friendly regard. What they would do with such a household decoration God knows—I don't.

My Southern son—by dad! he looks it, too—was deep in muddy guts, tidal creeks and pluff-mud flats all day Saturday, putting permanent monuments to the lands of Lester Wilson; Sunday all day he was whacking brush for surveys of Johnny Muller's new purchase on James Island; to-day, from some unknown hour long before I arose, he was off to the wilds of Hell-Hole, Berkeley, on an all-day woods-cruising job. When he will get a chance to write appreciatively to you of your recent, latest, boon—Isaac Ridgeway Trimble's autograph, Hdqrs. Trimble's Division, etc., on the reverse endorsement-side of W. R. Wabsiter's draft of clothes, Camp Winder hospital—a curiously interesting scrap of paper from those bloody days of vanished heroism—I do not know. Jack means to write you, first chance, himself, to thank you. Meantime, for him, at request, I acknowledge the receipt of said signature, a valued script— which we mean to double-frame, to show both sides, better to tell the story. Thanks, my dear unreconstructed foe, for such combatant courtesy.

I have for several years tried to get out of my cousin's widow, Mrs. Ridge. Trimble, of Baltimore, a portrait of the fine old soldier; but, thus far, without avail—though I have given her two sons a devil of a lot of family history none of them possessed. I am planning to trench across *their* front, instead of hers, and see if they are more appreciative of my meaning.

Your gift—through me—to Jack, of contraband-of-war, reminds me of the exchange between Lord Howe and G. Wash., when George's letter to Martha was intercepted with other rebellious mail and taken to Howe's headquarters in New York. Howe, the story runs, sent the letter to Washington, expressing himself as happy so to return it, unopened by an enemy—to which Washington returns, with his personal regards, to Howe, a dog, picked up among American troops, having Howe's name upon its collar.

Thus courtesy between otherwise irreconcileable foes was exemplified for our emulation. Just at this writing, however, I regret, sir, to say, I cannot find, anywhere among our troops, a dog with your name on its collar. Sorry.

> Respectfully yours:
> Maj. Gen. BUMPUS, Comdg.,
> Union Troops, Charleston, S.C.
> per Orderly Sergt. and
> Secretary at Large:

Forwarded to REBEL outposts, under
FLAG, this day, May 11th, 1931,
from Hdqrs. in revolving chair
plus air-cushion.

> Yrs. affectionately, despite
> yr. regrettable recalcitrancy:
> J.B. . . . .

September 10th, 1931

Dere Confedrit & Friend:

"Marching with Sherman"[8] received. Excellently done, well-printed, shapely; a valuable contribution to the bitter story of what happens when men stoop to revenge upon an enemy's home. What an ingenuous story Hitchcock[9] tells!

I wish you had autographed it; to add real and sentimental value to it. We are indebted, truly, to E. G. S.[10] for permanency.

Well, dear Yates, it's a sad story of the outrage of war.

With my cousins—lovely people—burned out in Virginia by Hunter, and my wife's people burned out in Columbia (not Mrs. McCord, who housed Howard)[11] I suppose I should be an ardent Confederate. I suppose you must consider me (as do my childhood's beloved Roman Catholic friends who profess that I shall be saved from the final auto-da-fe, not for my stubborn unbelief and protestantism, but through my INVINCIBLE IGNORANCE of the truth proclaimed by an inerrant hierarchy) hopelessly Federal, but not incendiary.

It appears that the Iowa, Indiana, and Illinois troops, aided and abetted by a miscellany of coffee-coolers and bummers, bear the onus chiefly: the regiment of damn Yankees from my native town were provost-guard in the devastated capital; and my cousin, on the march, was quartered in the McCord house at Ft. Motte, Lang Syne, passant guardant—and *didn't burn the house.*

Did you ever read any of the war-time sermons of Thomas Smyth, D.D.?

You are a perpetual fire upon the altar, Yates; and at every adverse wind that blows upon the desolate ashes, glow like a red- hot coal. I wish I were as young as you, and could glow like a red-hot coal over the iniquities of mine enemy. But, as our old friend, Artemus Ward, said, "Alars! It cannot was!"

Isn't it a bit strange, with all the good Southern blood there is in my veins, I still remain a perennial victim of congenital historical strabismus? I do. And must forever and forever see both sides of every story. This is the reason, I suppose, that when the two winds of destiny beat upon my emotional altar, where the burned offerings of past offenses lie, they meet, balance, and raise up into the sky only gray ashes of a dispassionate regard, grown cooler as the years roll by—I bow my head with a regretful reverence for the memory of the good men who suffered for the misdeeds of fools and fanatics.

And, like the Irish patriot, under the penal act of 1798, who lay drunk in the alley, shouting, "To hell with!" "To Hell with!" and was asked by an assiduous constable, "To hell with whom?" replied genially, "Complate it for yourself, friend. It's too expensive for me!"

Perhaps it is as well I never finished, and never shall finish, my history of Revolutionary South Carolina—it is sure as the heavens are over us, I should have pleased no-one, but angered everyone, through trying the impossible feat of being just to all the combatants. This may be an arrogant belief; forgive me this conceit for the sake of the love I bear you, which is true.

Much is forgiven for honest love: I have read the war-time sermons of Thomas Smyth—and behold, have married—some time ago—his grand-daughter!

Thank you, and E. G. S., for a really valuable bit of bitter history; and believe me, ever, your damned but still devoted:

Yankee

P.S.: I sent thee late a rosy wreath—I mean a box of fruits from the GINGKO TREE—by Allen Fripp's hand—lest they be stopped in the mail as putrid. I thought you were due in Columbia, this week: but your magazine comes from Flat Rock: I do not know what has become of the fruits—but assure you, contrary to Ben Jonson, they smell only of themselves and not "of thee"; for wh. thank God!

JB

4*th* Nov. [1931]

Jacobus carus:

So sorry I missed "She who must be obeyed!" My wife, sick abed upstairs, told me she heard me slam my library door & leave, via *Green St.*, while Madame Susie Bennett rung the door-bell on *Sumter St.!*

Here is a photo, taken by a student while I sat in my fumatorium last even'g.

Adios!

Yours always,
Y. S.

December 18th, 1931

YATES, my Noble Friend:

God bless you!

What is one to do with you—but only beg on bended knees that you will take earliest opportunity to have that glorious silvery head of yours glued on afresh to your corpus, to prevent you from giving it away also to some astounded and inordinately lucky admirer and friend!

Your special-delivery bonanza received: my present—and thus far, only, wife will herself decently and properly acknowledge that marvellous double letter of D. J. and Louisa C. McCord to M. Herbemont—rich, unique and greatly valuable.

I am here deputed only to give you a reflected light of gratitude, and the desired address of our daughter,

> Mrs. F. H. Wells,
> c/o Lieut. F. H. Wells,
> U.S.S. Pecos,
> Asiatic Station,
> c/o Postmaster,
> Seattle,
> Washington.

By thus addressing her the missive or packet goes in the regular official mail to our Naval contingent in the East, ensuring delivery to Forrest, on the Pecos, and hence to Jane. All other methods of mailing are unsure—and unemployed. Mailing *via Seattle* shortens the time.

Jane is probably now in either Shanghai or Hong Kong, on her way from visiting Cheves and Mary Smythe in Nagoya, Japan—a serene and pleasant month—after leaving Che Foo, to which as yet no disturbance had approached. She and Anne will be in Manila with Forrest for Christmas; and will spend the winter there.

Mrs. Bennett, grateful and charming, the former to you for your surprising gift, and the latter ever to me, will herself see to the desired copies of the SIAMESE TWIN LETTER from the notable McCords, to be disposed of as you see fit.

With golden remembrances to you and your lovely spouse from my admirable spouse and myself, and with affectionate messages from the two wild young things, Sue and Jack, and with my own dyed-in-the-wool Yankee attachment to you and yours until the ultimate dissolution of

this astonishing universe, boundless in dimension yet somehow confined (see Einstein), may I beg ever to remain

affectionately yours,
[John Bennett] . . .

Chapter 19

1932

Snowden's first serious illness; Marie Conway Oemler's letters; news of the Wells family; Herbert Ravenel Sass's novel; Bennett's latest chapter; an acquaintance's mishap with inedible mushrooms; effects of the deepening depression; Baron and Baroness von Below in Hendersonville; growing old; sheet music of Snowden's "Carolina Hail!" and Bennett's "In a Rose Garden"; church bells for the Confederacy.

THE FINAL year of correspondence between the two friends began with a letter from John Bennett in January, acknowledging receipt of the South Carolina Agricultural Society's 1819 report that Yates had sent to Susan Bennett for use in her research. He also mentioned the mixup of tuxedo jackets among Snowden and himself and their host, Clements Ripley, when Snowden visited Charleston during the St. Cecilia festivities.

Snowden became seriously ill with heart trouble for the first time in April of 1932. Annie Snowden's sister, Pauline, who was staying with them, became ill about the same time and died. Snowden was not well enough to leave the house until June commencement at the University. When he was able to write to Bennett, Snowden noted the death of an old friend, Mrs. J. N. Oemler, and asked John to prepare a tribute to her for the newspaper.

Although greatly relieved that Snowden had recovered enough to ask a favor, Bennett declined to do an article on Mrs. Oemler, for he had met her but once. He thanked Snowden for sending him her letters and planned to copy from them for the next bulletin of the Charleston Museum.

Bennett wrote that he had some summer suits made from blue cotton coolie cloth that Jane sent from the Orient, and he told Snowden the latest news of the Wells family. Bennett, working diligently on his book, was also helping Herbert Ravenel Sass to ready a novel for publication. Other recent events were the loss of his 83-year-old kinswoman, the last of the McClintock name, and the republication in Polish of *Master Skylark*.

Bennett informed Snowden that he was keeping the most interesting Oemler letter to read to Dr. Robert Wilson, who was recuperating from an operation. He then compared a Portsmouth political orator with a character in a novel by Mrs. Oemler. He also told of the latest chapter in his book, a visit by Sam Stoney, Jr., the heat in Charleston, the weekend company, and an acquaintance's mishap with inedible mushrooms.

Snowden's and Bennett's letters continued to show the impact of the Depression, as conditions in the country worsened from month to month. Snowden's little economies stood him in good stead now. For years he had been turning manila envelopes wrongside-out for remailing or filing papers and clippings, and he saved all manner of things. In June Bennett noted some of the national and the personal problems of the times.

In September Snowden wrote from Hendersonville that his recovery was proceeding slowly, but he was enjoying the fellow visitors, including a former Columbian, now a baroness, and her husband. Bennett, working with difficulty on his novel, had not left the heat of Charleston at all during the summer. He was experiencing back trouble and commiserated with Snowden about the effects of growing old.

Back in Columbia in October, Snowden sent the sheet music of "Carolina, Hail!" and, in addition, a copy of Bennett's "In a Rose Garden," which he asked John to autograph and to add a few words explaining how he came to write it. In November Bennett replied with an account of the poem's composition, of its various publications, and of its musical renditions. He ended with a jest, warning Snowden not to try singing the Bennett song and promising in return not to perform the Snowden song in public.

Near the end of the month, Bennett requested information regarding where the bells of St. Philip's Church in Charleston were cast into cannon for the Confederacy. As the year ended, the two friends discussed the melting of church bells from both South Carolina and Georgia during the war.

January 19th, 1932

Dear Yates:

The promised pamphlet Report of the Curators of the Agricultural Society of S.C., 1819, received, and held in trust for absent idle wife—with its note of D. J. McCord's secretary-ship—of the Herbemonts, Nick and Aleck, and of my old friend, F. L'Herminier, the chemist and scientist—which latter I consider interesting, showing the interest that Gallic gentilhomme still gave So. Ca. after his misfortunes here, and his supplies to the Botanic Garden of Philadelphia and to the S.C. Ag. Socy., of SEEDS, 153 species, sent in care of M. LeSeur, "a painter in natural history, as modest as he is skilful"—extraordinary man! L'Herminier's connection with the Charleston Museum was excavated from the uninvestigated dust of the past by your correspondent—so that his further deeds after departing these shores interest me. . . .

My only wife, present, past and future, is still in Savannah shouting aloud at the rattling gossip of that town. I have advised her of the receipt of the above pamphlet. "Hold it," says she, "until I come home." She then proceeds unequivocally to show that that noblest Roman of them all, the haloed Langdon Cheves, was descended directly from the line of a Connecticut tavern-keeper! My God! This will hasten the slow senectitude of the present bearer of that hallowed name.

Who got away with whose tuxedo jacket, you, or I, or Clem Ripley?[1] I've got a pretty good one; which, however, isn't my former one. Whose have you?

Inquiringly and ever-affectionately
Thine:
Pertinax S.

My bow and best-flowered compliment to the lovely lady.

8th June '32

My dear John:

I have been very sick, & my sister-in-law died in this house since I last wrote you. I am better now, but weak physically. Yesterday I wore *shoes* for the 1st time since Apl. 19th, & today I hobbled over to "Commencement" & heard Huger Jervey's[2] fine speech. What I thought for a year was *dyspepsia*, I find was *heart* trouble, and I must be very careful of myself for my remaining years, or I shall "join the angels" much sooner than I intended. My poor wife has stood the test wonderfully, with a very sick sister *in one room,* & a very sick husband in the next!

I see by *the* "paper" this A.M. that my old friend Mrs. Oemler³ died in Charleston! I don't know of your relations with her; but if they were *at all* intimate, I am hoping you will write an *"appreciation"* of the creator of "Slippy McGee" in The N. & C. If you are *very busy;* or if you did not *know Mrs. Oemler intimately;* or if, for any reason you don't care to write about her, just *ship* these enclosures to Billy Ball with this note. I have a number of her letters, but the enclosed are all I can find tonight. I have marked some paragraphs which *may* give you a "pointer." If you use these letters at all; refer to me as a "S.C. friend," or something like, I don't care to "get my name in the paper."

My love to your wife. Mine is abed.

Always aff'ly yours,
Y. S.

Send back *my Oemler letters!*

June 10th, 1932

My dear Yates:

I can hardly tell you what a happy surprise and what a relief from anxiety it was to receive your immense mail-bag with your gallant script addressing it to me. We have been very perturbed, knowing of your recent illness, but being unable, in Miss Virginia Porcher's absence—whenever we called up her 'phone—to secure any satisfactory—or even unsatisfactory—news of your convalescence—or even of your illness—from other members of the household. The first definite tidings received came with my old friend, G. Wauchope, with whom—Ball, Cathcart included—I had the good fortune to dine as guests of Dr. and Mrs. Robt. Wilson—our next-door neighbors, a few days since. W. told me that you had weathered the confounded gale which for a time had you nigh on your beam-ends, and that you were regaining strength steadily, although slowly; and that it was confidently said that if you would take care of yourself, as all who love you beg you to do, we shall for years be glad to know that Y. S.—may God keep and bless him and his forever!—is still lending courage to the weak, new spirit to the weary, and love to the lonely hearts of his acquaintance—as he, Y. S., has ever done—brave heart! And that, although we Yankees feel assured that he is generally wrong in his major premise, he is stirring the minds of the ignorant young, who are to come after us, with some deliberate knowledge of the past, without which no conception of the present, or plan for the future, can be presumed to have a secure basis.

My dear Yates, you can have no idea—or at best but a feeble idea—of the anxiety felt by all your friends. Damn it, Yates, anything which shakes you, shakes us all—and we are many—and we love you deeply, in spite of all your faults—none of which, of course, we share. And as for your lovely wife and you, I love you and your beloved Annie as though we had been reared together and grown side by side these sixty years.

And now, God bless us, and defend us all from all untimely care, we have you restored to us, almost intact, and cautioned only to be good, that we, your many lovers, may be happy! So with light hearts again we resume the old delight—that ever-present sense of wireless communication with kindred spirits which makes this dull world a better place, and turns it far more happily around its diurnal way! Thank such Gods as may be! I have no list of them, and barely know their surnames by report—but am intensely grateful to them all for their present gift to me of a yet-unbroken friendship at least of thirty years.

Here's to your steady and long-enduring recovery, my dearly-beloved friend, and to your blessed wife days without number, and you beside her, companioning her way, and she conferring her great and golden love upon an unworthy husband—which we are, all of us abandoned males.

As to Mrs. Oemler, I have read her letters to you with kindly interest—a clean, an earnest, a busy, brave, and simple-hearted woman—a hard worker, who has had her measure of success to pay her labor: and now rests where she herself chose to sleep. But I had met her but once, and that for fifteen minutes; and save through common report open to all the world, knew no more of her personality or public repute than is found in the enclosed biographical obit. in the News & Courier, which seems to me to be very complete, and, doubtless, adequate—unless one could add some personal impressions and conclusions, out of the common knowledge; and these I cannot add to what has been said, because I have none.

I therefore am left with a quandary, Sphynx-like eyeing me, saying guess again, fellow!

P. 2, your note, says that if for any reason I should not write of Mrs. Oemler, "just ship these enclosures to Billy Ball with this note." The enclosures were Mrs. Oemler's letters to you, and two notes: of Arminius Oemler's[4] gift of German butterflies to the Elliott Society; and Mrs. O's delightful pen-picture of a Southern wind-bag blowing froth—too excellent not to be true—and probably authentic—as authentic as that lovely speech of the glowing Virginian who cried in mid-campaign: "And what shall we say of our Southern women, lovely as the Three Graces, *pure as Helen of Troy!*" that classic bitch. I have always felt grateful to that Virginia congressional district for not electing this copper-tongued wind-bag of ineptitude.

What am I to give to Billy Ball remains uncertain in my mind: for at the foot of that page—like a sober—I suppose you were sober—second thought, stands the stern admonition

"SEND BACK MY OEMLER LETTERS!"

What is there for a simple mind to do; but just to return all to the owner, for redistribution as may seem best—and this I do, regretting if I have failed to apprehend your meaning.

I have, however, taken the liberty of copying both notes: the one of Arminius Oemler for filing at the Charleston Museum, on chance of inclusion in their next-published Bulletin, in some mention there of Mrs. O's book in which the butterfly plays such a part—and of her death. The other I copy for my own refreshment and for quotation to friends.

Mrs. Bennett and I both were greatly interested in Mrs. Oemler's visit to the V.P.I., and her kind comments upon Prof. Ellison Smyth and his sister, Meta Johnson.[5]

I enclose for your interest and diversion from recent care, a letter from my son-in-law, Forrest Wells, containing a very lively account of the most important family news we have. All is going fine with the Wells triad at present; and they are to be stationed at Che Foo for the summer. Jane has sent me some dark—not so greatly dark—blue *cotton* coolie cloth; which, being public-spirited, I have had made, by a small Charleston tailor, into summer suits, and am wearing same. Jack is standing to his guns during the depression manfully, with but an occasional nervous attack of the heeby-jeebies—from watching the slow attrition of life wear down his bank-balance—yet congratulating himself on roof, board, breeches and remnant bank-balance. Sue, our tall, good-looking child, is visiting in Massachusetts with former school-mates, and attending a class reunion: she had been working hard at her music, voice, piano, and organ, and needed a respite. Mrs. Bennett, likewise, needs a respite from daily contact with the things she loves—and is to be shipped on a genealogical hunt, after Sue returns, to include, I believe, all sources in Columbia, with a flier in New York—that gorgeous Sodom and Gomorrah. I am working hard at a recalcitrant book—and move forward like the famous cat in the well—another slate and she'll be in China or Hell! I am also—darn it!—endeavoring to stiffen the creative guts of that charming young litterateur, Herbert R. Sass, and to drive him forward with a romance of the golden age of Low Country plantation-life in South Carolina, on which he is engaged for Bobbs-Merrill, but of which he is as terrified as though it were emerging, a very Frankenstein, from his trembling wits—God! and he with a free rein as to acts, scenes, and characters!—fearful to proceed as determined, and fearful not to proceed—and therefore proceeding not at all in any wise—and shaken by the present hard times until his dear long bones rattle audibly as he walks. And he still young!

I have lost many old friends of late, to North and West, including the last of my Mother's name, McClintock—she, who carried it to 83, one of the finest, sweetest, most brilliant and beautiful women I have ever known, and in the last stern asset, one of the serenest and bravest—her death leaving my one surviving sister without a soul akin by blood, nearer than a Virginia cousinship, for companioning.

But, on the other hand, we are surviving, ourselves, hard times and incidental ills with some composure, though financially cast-down—and are diverted by the entertaining news that SKYLARK has just been—the second time—translated into Polish and published at Lwow—if you know where that L'wow of a place is—for I don't. The first translation, translator and proposed publishers were wiped out by the great war as if expunged from a school-boy's slate.

N.B.—and note it well: I enclose an envelope, self-addressed, and adequately—I hope—stamped, for return of the greatly-valued letter from my son-in-law—at your peril return that letter, or—well, you remember what one king said to the other about the pig! Fail not!

Susan—that's my first wife, A-O—adds her love to you and all yours, and we join in every good wish that we who sincerely love you and Mistress Annie can devise:

Ever affectionately yours:
John Bennett

Surely your letter lightened my heart which was a bit heavy: I am grateful to God—and to you.

From the Fallen City of the Gods
Monday, June 27th, '32

Very, and again Very dear Fellawe:

I had meant to return the Oemler letters some days ago; but saved the most significantly literary letter to re-read, and to read to Dr. Robert Wilson, who has been, during the fortnight, in hospital—an operation for internal rupture, from which he is recovering most satisfactorily—and, being now home from the Riverside, is receiving ovations of flowers and admiring friends and worshipping females in his second-floor pizarro—as Col. Peter Kinney, of Portsmouth, used to say.

Alas! being only a miserable South Carolinian, you never had the felicity of knowing the Colonel! He somewhat resembled Mrs. Oemler's bag-o'-wind orator, save that he seldom essayed empyrean flight, and only wrestled at Ephesus with nice-sounding words in the wrong places.

He was the Dickensian, or Twainian, character who remarked of his daughter, just home from finishing-school in Philadelphia: "There's nothing more to be done to perfect Jenny—she is now fully manured."

I would—perhaps—have addressed you mid-week, but that I have been arguing with a recalcitrant chapter—an episode on the road from Buckhorn Furnace, La'rance County, Ohio, to the "Ancient Metropolis," of that State, viz., Chillicothe, in the days of the Murrell[6] gang and the highway bravo known in local annals as "Capt. Galilee."

Just as I had clean-drafted all my particles of accident, incident, precedent, etc., and with fine judicial care was choosing between the very best and the second-best arrangements of the said episode, in came our mutual friend, S. G. S., Jr., to discuss arrangements for issuance and equities in re "A Day on Cooper River," and to narrate certain very *ex-cathedral* anecdotes.

Subsequent to that visitation I was unable to recover my faculties and selective skill—ratiocination was fled—and I have since been, not quite successfully, endeavoring to recover that "first fine careless rapture" which makes picaresque narrative perfect.

The heated weather, the return of my lovely daughter, Sue, from a visit in Massachusetts with former school-friends—daughters of the Rose Bindery, source of beautiful tooled backs—the entertainment over the week-end of a very attractive young fellow from Savannah, great friend of the Wrights—Bob Minis—and the endeavor to exhilarate a dumb intellect to hilarious verbosity—have prevented friendly letters until Blue Monday morning.

Hence these lines of affectionate gratitude for kindnesses of Y. S., compliments, good wishes and a sweeping bow to Miss Annie S., and truly loving hope that she, and you, likewise, find steadily returning, confident and comfortable state of mind and body, after your much troubled experiences of loss and illness.

I am trying to learn the classic words of that inspiring ballad, "Let's Have Another Cup of Coffee, and Let's Have Another Piece of Pie"; but in the face of Herbert Hoover's nomination, and the appalling Democracy, I have, thus far, reached only the actual other cup of coffee—at breakfast, not in song.

My old friends are reckless: one has just lost a leg; another has been run down by a school-bus; a third has slipped away to join the majority; a beloved cousin, one of the finest and very loveliest women I have ever known, has departed, being far in her eighties and two years blind: the situation of the financial world prevents my blessed sister from visiting me, and vice versa—which is worse, as I long for sight of the charming valley where I was foaled, and the wind on the surrounding hills—and another look on earthly beauty from the top of Ginger Hill—lyric and pastoral—green woods and new pastures, l'Allegro Miltonibus molto con expressione.

Oh, let's have another cup of coffee, and let's have another piece of pie! Damn politics and the bums of the Bonus Army, Congress, nit-wits, high finance, world-trade, big business and Jeffersonian democracy alleged and unrealized—and pass on to the remembrance of friends—the only really golden thing in human association other than perfect marriage, which is almost too rarely found to be a common asset.

Ashmead Pringle grew marvellous multitudes of mushrooms in his yard; Jerry Slocum said "Are you meaning to eat them?" "I am NOT," said Ashmead. "Then I will!" said Jerry; "My sainted mother taught me mushrooms beyond error." Whereupon, gathering, he ate with shrimp, and blamed what followed on the shrimp; but Mistress Mushroom Jervey[7]—who KNOWS—says what he borrowed from Ashmead's lawn was second-worst disrupter of internal peace. The eater was ILL—in italics.

Jack has occupied the unoccupied days of depression in the forestry business building him a fine chimney and erecting a swell open fireplace, at his shack on James Island, first west of Ft. Johnson; and in getting himself dramatically turned over in a June black squall, in his small but nifty lugger, the "Fenwick K."

Did I tell you that "Skylark" is being issued in Polish. I think so; but reaffirm the fact. This is happening in Lwow—which someone informs me is in Galicia.

Otherwise no news: only the old, permanent regard for you,

> As from one friend to another: hastily
> but with love:
> Adieu—adieu!
> John Bennett

Hendersonville, N.C., 18*th* Sept. '32

My dear John:

Last year I brought to Flat Rock some of my earlier editions of "The Magnificat" but there was no special edition.

This year, by some mischance, I failed to bring either *a copy;* or your mountain photo, and story of its original composition in Va. "in time of dejection"—or words to that effect. I have read your beautiful letter (in re the origin of the Magnificat) many a time, sometimes to small boarding house audiences.

What was my surprise to be told that the little H'd'sonville wind-bag had *republished* it on Sept. 7th. I enclose a copy.

"You can't keep a squirrel on the ground"! But that's *bathos!*

I hope your *magnum opus* is at last finished; & that *"Who's Who"* says so. I saw that Herr Austin S. & family were at Flat Rock; but I have not heard of you or yours this summer, *except* that Queen Susie was *en route* to Va. with Mrs. Wright.

But I have thought of you 500 times. I eat much; *talk less; think,* ditto; & walk little, for I don't regain my physical strength as much as I hoped. I have written nothing.

We will probably remain at this attractive shanty until Oct 1st.

> In unwilling haste,
> Always aff'ly yours,
> Yates S.

NB! I read "The Magnificat" to three small batches of boarders last night; all of them were enthusiastic except, perhaps, Lieut. Gen. & Baron & the Baroness *von Below;*[8] the Baroness was once the more or less notorious "Ninna" Bryce of Columbia. She reminded me that I had once escorted her to the theatre in Charleston when her petti-coat fell down!! I told her I remembered her *beautiful* eyes; but had forgotten the petticoat incident!!!

Charleston, Sept. 20, '32

Dear Yates:

For swift procedure yours astounds me still—dated Sept. 18th, post-stamped, Sept. 18th, Hendersonville, it reached me, as by magician's flourish, by the next morning's mail—and gave me the regular thrill which accompanies the perennial republication of my verses, "The Magnificat." I realize fully that it is your own prescribed right to issue these annual editions of those famous stanzas; but I must confess it appears to me that you have hoisted your privilege (?) by your own petard, by making my nigh-forgotten verses popular through enthusiastic repetition.

Few authors have such publicity agents; and few of my verses have come to so genial a celebrity by so kindly a channel. Grateful appreciation of this fact must remain your present fee, and frank acknowledgment of the indebtedness.

I shall consider The TIMES print as the Annual Edition of 1932; and credit you with the information: I should not have known or seen this without your intervention.

That makes me realize once more how much goes on behind our backs of which we have no knowledge: Lord, grant it be always as kindly!

I had thought you back in Columbia at this time; and lately encouraged a young colored man with anticipations of meeting you and your ever-uncondescending kindness. He is from Fiske, his name, somehow, Lanier; his aim, advisory information concerning the Literature of our Tide-Water Carolina, before and since the War of the '60's—with some opinion as to the effect upon its demonstrations, of economics, the social state, and politics, prior to the War; and of the economic conditions and social revolution at present in process. A quiet, courteous, intelligent young brown man, who is to attend Harvard, this year, looking to a degree; for which I opine his enquiry provides thesis. I talked with him—exhaustingly, being tired after a long day's work of my own—and doubtless mingled much undesirable heresy with my appreciative orthodoxy as to the historic achievements of Southern literature—winding up with a curse upon Wm. Faulkner and all purveyors of fetid sewage.

He had letters to you, Wm. Gonzales, and Croft Williams.

The MAGNUM OPUS progresses as slowly as commonsense in America, or honesty in politics; but I do get on, by bits, from time to time. I had almost said from day to day; but that were too enthusiastic a statement: the book from time to time recoils upon me like the rock of Sisyphus. The hero's mother—God bless her and grant her peace!—whom we buried with tears in Columbia, two years ago (almost), has now really died—I had not finally accomplished her death when we buried her—not so horrendous as it sounds, to be sure. In reading this episode to H. R. Sass, Peter Gething, and A. Sprunt, Jr.,[9] with whom I connive in cool weather, the other two averred that the former shed tears; this he did not deny. For which excellent reason, reluctant to pain any sensitive mind with unnecessary agony, I shall not forward you any carbon copy of this really rather heart-breaking scene—saying only that it represents truth as nearly as I can find it: my Father, then but a boy of twelve, was alone with his Mother when she died, and had been almost alone, as her nurse, during her last few swiftly-declining days. Quantum suff. lachrymae.

What WHO'S WHO says of it, or of me, I do not know, beyond what we both seem to have read in the current Charleston news as rendered palatable under the aegis of T. R. W. and W. W. B. But if WHO'S WHO, by misadventure strange, announces completion of "BUCKHORN JOHNNY," it is "a typographical arror."

I have not been out of town all summer. I believe I should have done better had I gone; but there being no place to which I wished to go within the circumference of my means, I burned away strength and some courage here: with the return of cooler weather God send both once more to fair accomplishment! Susan went with Hannah Wright to Virginia, a flying drive, as much to provide a companion and to make possible a recreative holiday for Mrs. W. as to divert for herself—Mrs. W. having long sustained, in and for her family of men, the effect of the depression, which ranged like the Devil in Georgia. While in Virginia, of course, like all good Americans, Susan combined business with pleasure, and dug out genealogic data anent Langdons.

Is it possible, dear fidus, that your 500 thoughts came in as static over our radio! Believe me, well-beloved guy, I did no less; and have been constant in trust and hope for your steady recovery. It has been impossible to burn a votive candle before my special Buddha, from the excessive heat, in which my candles double down like horseshoes in the stick and puddle like all hades on my floor—or my work and you should have glimmered steadily before those kindly eyes and serene withdrawal from these mortal coils and apprehensions. The temperature is still too soft for standard candles; but, given coolth, they shall shine again for you, also for me—which is different from rotary hell's bells.

A keen attack of lumbago—or some such poisonous gripe in the rear—has crippled my progress for several days: I, too, am compelled to move more slowly: the collective assets of age, I suppose. I, also, talk less—in general—because no one will listen—and my daughter—a pretty thing!—will ever interpose with a smile and restraining finger, saying, "That's quite enough from you!" I suppose it is. When not at grips with my MSS., I, too, make every effort to think less—but plunge headlong into some frightful fiction of the lightest and maddest melodrama, to prevent cold discouragement sneaking into the gilded halls of fancy. I greatly desire the weather to be fair and tonic for you, and to pick you up before returning to Ca. My family signs round robin to that.

As to your sultry note in your N.B.: the last baroness I met brought forth the best mint-j——p ever was, tinkling through her shady house: she did not drop her petticoats; I do not recall her eyes: but, in fancy, listening, through the past, I hear that cheerful tinkle still. As to the Lt. Gen.; let me remind you

> "Man wants but little von Below,
> Nor wants that little long!"

(With my disdainful snort to the General). Pooh pooh!

Since we have not late exchanged complete gazettes, I am enclosing for your—perhaps—amusement—and some information—a carbon copy of my last Family Letter—carbons of which go weekly to Jane Wells, Cheves Smythe, and my sister, in Ohio. Having friends whom I love

with unchanging regard, yet little time to enter at length into details of
our life here, I have adopted the plan—an apology, to be sure—of now
and then enclosing, for circulation among a certain few, an extra copy
of my Sunday screed, to be passed along, per envelopes enclosed, thus to
spread the plague abroad—"just for greens"—which is remembrance.
Will you, having read at will and leisure, also forward per enclosed
envelope, my carboned budget—pray enjoy it, too!

With unaltering love to Mistress Annie and you, I am, dear Yates,

most truly yrs.—
John Bennett

Cola., 28*th* Oct. '32

Johannes Carus:

Today I mailed your *"Rose Garden"* & my *"Carolina"*: the *music!* You
will wonder *"why"*; well: to begin with, my "student song" (which is *not
the* students' song!!). I gravely doubt whether you have not lost or
discarded the copy I sent you years ago. Of this, more anon.

As to "Rose Garden," I want you to write your name on it, &
possibly a few words as to *when*, & how you came to write it; & very
possibly, *the name* of the dear girl who *inspired* it, for it *is a beautiful
inspiration!* Perhaps, too, you will tell me again, how much *you* made
from it. I think *you* got 2½ cents out of the 40¢ I paid for it today. On
Oct. 25, I had been married 38 years to my present wife and I thought
I would read it on that auspicious occasion. But the durn thing did not
arrive until today! We were lucky, for I find that the Bond-woman has
mangled (possibly for music's sake) & the original in the Library of So.
Lit. is a far nobler production, *barring* the pretty cover. I have never *yet*
heard it sung! *I* have not been "in voice," since Quattlebaum[10] pulled all
my teeth (except *one*), so I shall never sing this gem in my rich baritone
(low); but I shall get some expert to sing it for me, as soon as you send
it back. I will remember the afternoon the Timrod bust was unveiled; I
was walking away (I *think* by the side of Edward McCrady), and I passed
you and your lovely n'yung wife; & both (certainly *you*) shook your fists
at me, & I was much tickled thereby, for that day (or the Sunday before)
I had reprinted in The *N&C* your exquisite poem I gave the title "In a
Charleston Rose Garden," though I *knew* you had written it before you
met your fate!

I was a merry dog in them days!!

Now; as to *my* "pome": It has turned out "a busted flush"; no student
sings it; and damned few ever heard of it.

Leize Lockwood wrote to me for a copy of it, and I sent it to her with much of that stuff she printed. I had *no idea* she intended to print and illustrate it as she did!! I should certainly have protested, and the grand scheme to *sell it* for 25¢ a copy!! She sent my friend (then *Dean*) Baker, *stacks & stacks* (possibly 500) copies of my "pome." I knew it; Baker knows I knew it; I have never spoken to him since, about it; & I doubt if he sold a single copy to anybody!! Meanwhile Wauchope's common-place "Carolina," to the tune of "Flow Gently Sweet Afton," has been practically adopted as *the* students' song, and is sung on every public occasion & foot-ball game. The words are commonplace (much more so than mine!), and the tune is as inspiring as a funeral dirge. No wonder we lose so many foot-ball games! I can understand "the line of least resistance"; any fool from Too-ga-doo, or the dark corner of Greenville, or Hell Hole can sing "Sweet Afton"; but *"my"* tune is inspiring; it stirs the blood: a friend told me he heard 1200 German students sing it before the house of a professor who had been charged with inspiring some crazy student who had attempted to shoot the Kaiser. And those fool Germans *certainly* are *musical!* You will wonder why I overload *you* with all this *disgruntlement!* Except my wife, you are the only person in this world to whom I have spoken so freely on this matter. *So, burn this letter!!!*

I know I am no Rouget de Lisle, & this is no *Marseillaise!* But *the tune* is the thing; *damn* the words. The *words* of *Harvard Crimson* are commonplace, worse than mine; but "my" adopted tune is *"a ringer";* the best yet except Reed Smith's *"Health to King Charles,"* which *is best of all,* but has notes too high for a college song! I have lost my pen, luckily for you, & can't write any more. But, don't think that I love dear old Leize Lockwood any the less!

In haste,
Yours aff'ly always,
Y. S.

I am certain *now;* you must *burn* this scrawl!

———————

November 1st, 1932

Dear Yates:

The song, originally entitled "In a Rose Garden," but now more generally known as "A Hundred Years from Now," was written slowly, some time between 1891 and 1895. The catch-line, "A Hundred Years from Now," was taken from an older song, in which it had the phrasing "A Hundred Years Hence," a sardonic and cynical piece of verse, which, if memory serves me rightly, had wide popularity at and after the close of the 18th Century, in England and America. My Father learned it, about 1835, from a young Englishman, possibly the black sheep of his family, a foreman at Buck-Horn Furnace, Lawrence County, Ohio: I heard him quote it in moments of catastrophe, as consolatory thought, accompanied by a stanza or two of John Boyle O'Reilly's "This Too Shall Pass Away." Both lines came sharply home to me during my first real tragic experience of what life can do, when it tries, to a boy. Seven years' illusion and disillusionment brought it to the page: the first stanza was written on the back of an envelope, and carried long in my pocket; and months went by, and a year or two, before resurge brought an adequate completion of the idea, stanza by stanza, to the last. It was not meant for publication, but was simply the honest expression of a wordless emotion turned into verses. The outlook of the time was bleak, I must confess. It is not pertinent to name its object now: She was, indeed, an Experience rather than an Individual—an ideal effectually departed—a young ideal whose pedestal had crumbled into the dirt— neither more nor less. The taste was pretty bitter; and bitterness is acute in youth, as every feeling mortal knows.

About 1894, while writing book-reviews and general text, witty, and/or humorous, for the supplements, Saturday and Sunday issues, of the old Cincinnati Commercial-Gazette, I often stretched my pay-string by including bits of verse, experiments of many sorts, the most popular of which were patterned closely upon the dialect verses of James Whitcomb Riley: I did not fancy myself an Author; I was simply making a living; I sold what I wrote. The verses of "In a Rose Garden," were still almost too intimate to print; but to eke out my string I sent them to Ed Flynn, then editor of the two supplements and of the Literary Page of the Commercial-Gazette, a brilliant and generous fellow—who promptly returned them with a note: "This is too damned good for a newspaper; try it on the magazines." I took his advice: the song was as promptly rejected by every current magazine of quality in America, and most emphatically by The Century, to which, being stubborn, I sent it twice. When Stone & Kimball began publication of The CHAP-BOOK, in Chicago, I tried the verses there; they accepted them, and paid me extravagantly, $4.00. It must have made an immediate hit in popular fancy; for within the fortnight I had an urgent request from The Chap-Book to submit other verses of a like sort.

The verses then drifted from paper to paper, sometimes credited to me, sometimes to The Chap-Book, sometimes to nobody; which was where C. D. Warner found them anonymously floating, and shrined them in the Library of the World's Best Literature, to my quite astonished delight. The emotion which produced the verses was real; and the recognition pleased me: it would anyone. From that time on, under one title or other, including your own audacity, "In a Charleston Rose-

Garden," the song has been contagious to anthology, almost all of them have had it. It has been many times inadequately set to music; the best sets being those of Neal McCay, issued by Waterson, Berlin & Snyder; and of Carrie Jacobs-Bond, 1914, both under the title of "A Hundred Years from Now." The former score is most dramatic; the latter most generally known, despite the mangling of the text—a sort of musical mayhem, to make the verses fit the Procrustean staves of the musician. McCay's set was sung across the country by David Bispham; but Carrie Jacobs-Bond's "End of a Perfect Day" had achieved for her music an extensive popularity not reached by McCay's setting; so that her set for my song reached the orchestras and pianos of the moving-picture halls and had widest distribution. It was issued for piano-player by Wurlitzer; and I think was recorded for the victrola; and its issue was continued by the Jacobs-Bond Co., until their affairs were taken over by the Boston Music Co., who now handle the song. Its success with Mrs. Bond's setting was sufficient to persuade her to ask a second song, and to follow "A Hundred Years from Now" by "To-day"; which went fairly, and was recorded for the victrola, also. From Mrs. Bond's setting my royalties, while but moderate compared to the great song-hits of the day, ran well over the thousand—which may be considered a fair earning for a $4.00 song.

Mrs. Bond having mutilated the original text, I have transcribed the complete original text for you, and make bold enough to send you the McCay setting, to complete your collection of rarities; on condition that you, despite your rolling baritone and all its rotund charm, refrain from public rendition of both, or either, settings.

As you state, our acquaintance notably signalized the unveiling of Timrod's bust, immediately following your audacity of "In a Charleston Rose-Garden," the which singled you out of the mob for my permanent, and, as to date, unaltered and undiminished affection, as well as my admiration of your bold and brilliant mind, and even greater admiration for your lovely wife, to whose kindliness I owe happy memories of your home.

Remember, however, you are not to sing either of these settings; and to counter your complaint I shall promise on my crossed heart not to sing, in public, and not often in private, your Collegiate hymn, set to "Santa Lucia," though I much love that tune. There is nothing invidious in this remark; my clarion voice is much better fit to singing "Old Joe Clark" than to the rendition of psalms and hymns, collegiate or theological. But I thank you heartily for the inscribed copy you enclose so generously; making two now in my collection of genuine Caroliniana.

With best wishes ever,

Affectionately yours:
John Bennett

That signature is not notable, but this turkey quill pen is n.g.

November 28th, 1932

Y. Snowden, Esq.
Fidus achates:
   or other endearing greetings:
   Can you tell me *where* the bells of St. Philip's church were cast into cannon for the Confederacy?
   Taken down in June, 1862, they were forwarded to Columbia in response to the call of Gen. Beauregard, I believe, for such patriotic sacrifice.
   Where, at that time, was the Confederacy casting its cannon? At or in the vicinity of Charlotte? Or elsewhere?
   Some time after the check-mate battle of the Monitor and the Virginia, fearing a successful incursion at Norfolk, much of the activity of that yard was transferred to Charlotte, No. Ca.; so that as it is said "there was once a navy-yard in the inland town of Charlotte."
   The Monitor-Virginia battle took place March 9th, '62. The bells were forwarded in June.
   Were cannon cast at the Charlotte plant?
   Can you enlighten a Yankee enquirer—here undersigned as

ever affectionately yours to command,
to abuse, but, let us hope,
still, somewhat, still, to esteem:
John Bennett

   P.S.: My affectionate regard, ever, to Mistress Annie S., faithful, loving, and lovely indeed.

   N.B.: Alas! outside need and interior conditions have compelled Santa Klaus and I to announce a moratorium: hence, with deep regret we shall issue no Christmas silhouette, 1932: the rest depends on the Democratic administration.

Dec. 4, 1932

My dear Johnny:
   "Hell's Bell's"; why do you come to *me*, "gorging Jacky," for information as to St. Philip's bells in war time? I know nothing about them.

I married a St. Philip's belle; but there is no *"sounding brass"* in that angel child!

I enclose notes from the S.C. Gazette (Apl. 1744) as to a little accident to a bell-fixer, and I have copied a few lines from Dalcho[11] (*via* Courtenay's Yearbook for 1880), showing that *old* St. Philip's had bells. I have a fine picture of old St. Philip's from *The London Magazine* (?) of 1752, *extra*-illustrating my copy of Dalcho, with a sketch of the *old* church, but it is in my classroom at Davis College—lucky for you!

As to this bell business in War-times (you know all about *St. Michael's!*): I have somewhere, a letter to my mother, or an article in *The Courier,* by dear old Dick Yeadon[12] (I *knew* him!), but I can't find it, & doubt of any reference to *St. Philip's bells.*

I find this foot-note in Scharf's[13] *tremendous "History of the Confederate States' Navy,"* p. 727:

> Just previous to this time (*ca.* 1862) there had been received at the ordnance office, Richmond, a tender of the church bells at *Marietta, Georgia,* to be cast into cannon, which was accepted. The letter making the offer was signed by the Rev. E. Porter Palmer, pastor of the *Presb. Ch.;* Rev. F. B. Cooper, pastor of the *Baptist Ch.;* Rev. Samuel Benedict, rector of St. James *Prot. Epis. Ch.;* and Rev. Alex'r Graham, pastor of the *Meth. Epis. Ch.* The total weight of the bells was *1623 pounds.*

—Of course our *Charleston bells* outweighed those Jaw Jaw bells all hollow!!

And you will be wondering . . . "Why has not that ingrate Y. S. acknowledged the Rose-Garden treasures and my wonderful letter telling its history?"

And you are right. I won't write about *that,* or tell you how much I love you, until I read *and sing "Today"!* I ordered it 2 weeks ago, but it had not arrived yesterday, when I asked for it for the 9*th* time!

My love to you & yours.
Cheer up—the worst is yet to come!
Yours *always,*
Yates . . .

———————

December 14, 1932

Dearest and Most Profane:

Believe me, stout fellow, I never expected to hear a staunch Rebel, a South Carolina REBEL at that, say "Hell's Bells" when referring to the sacred tintinnabulators devoted by a patriotic bunch of Secessioniats to the blessed manufacture of cannon with which to drive back the HUNS from off our SACRED SOIL!

I am astounded and grieved.

The varied bits of local history given were already sifted from the debris of So. Ca. history to no purpose in my quest—but I am grateful for the Richmond reference, from Scharf, which I had not seen, and should certainly have missed. Some church bells went to Richmond one supposes—but, as usual, it will be left to some damned Yankee like me to dig patiently into the tons of inadequate, so-called true histories of the late unpleasantness, until the TRUTH be discovered and the Devil shamed. . . .

I still have hopes of finding some Confederate scion who knows the REAL TRUTH about church-bells, cannon and Confederate devotion. When I find the facts I will take great pleasure in communicating them to you.

> God of our Fathers, if there be
> So curious a divinity, etc.,
>   *Lest we forget*—be with us yet—etc.

I've seen that impassioned plea of R. Kipling's on so many walls down here in Dixie that I am led to suppose it to be a sort of Loisette Memory system contrived to prevent the healthful actions of the natural mind and preserve the soured antipathy of the over-heated partisan. I still believe it a great pity that we did not tow So. Ca. and Mass. somewhere far out to sea, Anno Dni., circa, 1820, and let them have it out to a finish. It would not have worried me if Mass. had been whipped—nay, nor vice versa—but it would have been a whale of a good dog-fight, and might have amused instead of seriously involving many innocent by-standers when the shooting began—my own people, for example—not a young man left in my mother's family.

But we were talking about church-bells, not about dirty rumpuses.

Your one good chance of admission at St. Peter's wicket-gate lies, as you well know, in the loveliness of that one "St. Philip's belle" whose slender finger you ringed—not rung—so many moons past.

But I shall miss you mightily, my good fellow, from the genial circle round our glowing fireside down below.

By the way, I ran across a sentence which pleased me very greatly, in comment upon great men. The writer said "Where Jackson was, there also was Trimble." I call that an accolade—aye, what!

Herbert Sass is working desperately hard upon a novel of the Golden Age of the Carolina Low-Country. If he is able to hang on like grim Death and to finish as he has begun, it promises real excellence. It is for Bobbs-Merrill Co., who sensibly are extending the contract time to give Herbert ripening opportunity.

As for me, it is snowing in Ohio, so that I am cold. Jane, her small girl, Anne, and her man, F. H. W., of the U.S.S. Pecos, are in Manila, comfortably located until the squadron goes north again in May; and, confidentially—since you were always gentle to that girl of mine—she is expecting an addition to the Wells family in March—so, if you have any kindly saint I shall ask your petition to that same.

Abusively, but ever affectionately,
your Yankee friend:
[John Bennett]

Chapter 20

The Parting

A Washington's birthday celebration at Maxcy Gregg Park, the planting of magnolia trees in memory of some of the past University of South Carolina presidents and professors, was held on 22 February 1933. At about 5 o'clock in the afternoon, after giving a speech honoring Major Benjamin Sloan,[1] the president of the University in 1905 when Snowden first came to teach there, Professor Snowden slumped forward in his chair with a massive heart attack. He was immediately attended by the two physicians on the speakers' stand, Mayor L. B. Owens[2] and Dr. Walter Bristow, but death was almost instantaneous.

On 23 February it was decided that, in memory of Yates Snowden, one more magnolia would be added to those planted the day before in the park. At the University his death was mourned by both the faculty and the students. Perhaps the professor was so greatly admired because, according to W. W. Ball in 1930, knowing the facts of South Carolina history so sympathetically, Snowden could present those facts with what "newspaper people call 'human interest' so well," for he was not only an excellent speaker, but also "a gifted writer, the possessor of an accurate and . . . delightful style."[3]

On 24 February classes at the University were suspended. That morning, the body of the beloved professor was placed in the University Library, later the South Caroliniana Library, and a student guard of honor watched over the bier. Just before eleven o'clock, the casket was carried to Trinity Episcopal Church, where Kirkman Finlay, bishop of the Upper South Carolina Diocese, and the Rev. Henry D. Phillips[4] conducted the services. Active pallbearers were the faculty of the History Department and a namesake and former president of the student body, Yates Snowden Williams. Honorary pallbearers included the governor of South Carolina, the president of the University, members of the University Board of Trustees, and members of the Kosmos Club. Many out-of-town friends were in attendance.

At three-thirty that afternoon at the Magnolia Cemetery in Charleston, the committal rites were led by the Rev. John van de Erve, pastor of the French Protestant (Huguenot) Church. He was assisted by the Rev. Alexander Sprunt of the First (Scotch) Presbyterian Church and the Rev. S. Cary Beckwith of St. Philip's Protestant Episcopal Church. A group of fifteen professors from the University traveled to Charleston for the final rites. Former Governor D. C. Heyward,[5] *The State* editor William E. Gonzales, Fitz Hugh McMaster, and A. S. Salley, Jr. also came from Columbia. About two hundred others were present—Charleston educators, newspaper men, and personal friends of many years. Mrs. Snowden, however, ill from the shock of her husband's death, was unable to attend.

Listed as survivors of Yates Snowden, besides his wife Annie, were his sister, May Snowden of Charleston; and the children of the late Robert L. and Pauline Warley Snowden: Mrs. Kirkland Trotter of Camden, and Charles J. Snowden and J. Warley Snowden, both of Charleston.

In July of 1934 the University published *In Memoriam: Yates Snowden, 1858–1933* containing articles taken from newspapers at the time of Professor Snowden's death and funeral, sketches of and tributes by members of the press and by colleagues and friends, resolutions and memorials by the South Carolina senate and house of representatives, by the faculty of the University, by his beloved Kosmos Club, and by the Columbia Art Association, of which he was the first president. The editors secured two photographs of Snowden: one for the frontispiece and one for the middle of the bulletin. The latter showed him in his library study. Both pictured the professor as most remembered him, with mustache and white hair, and wearing, as he always did, a wing collar and bow tie. The ninety-five page bulletin included a bibliography of Snowden's published works.

Favorite Snowden anecdotes have been remembered through the years, for he is vividly recalled by all who knew him.[6] One such story concerns a student who consulted the professor in regard to studying on Sunday. Snowden's reported advice was, "Do exactly as your parents told you and go to church. After Church, however, it is certainly all right to study your history. As has been well said, 'If the Lord justified the man for pulling his ass out of a ditch on Sunday, how much more would he justify the ass for pulling himself out.'"

When accused of disliking college sophomores, Snowden promptly denied the charge. His added comment was, "Sophomores are O.K. They're just a group of wise fools who have passed over the adolescence of their freshman days and have not yet reached the wisdom of juniors."

Since he kept such late hours, consistent with his earlier newspaper career, he did not greet the morning with enthusiasm. It is said that when someone brought up the subject of the beauty of dawn, Snowden liked to retort in words similar to those attributed to an old Frenchman: "I have never seen a sunrise, but it must be a horrible sight."

A lover of art, Snowden collected what he could and enjoyed discussing the topic. In regard to a French painting of a woman in tears, he was reported to have said, "A beautiful picture, but why the devil should they take off most of their clothes to cry? It's beyond me."

Snowden's aversion to college mathematics was widely known. His mention of the subject, according to tradition, was usually accompanied by colorful adjectives. His attitude was understandable, for he had struggled with math during his own undergraduate years—and had lost.

When prayers were held in Rutledge Chapel on the Horseshoe, it was Professor Snowden's habit to turn his back on the student body. His explanation was memorable: "The University building is laid out south and north, rather than the usual east and west church structure. And I pray as I was taught at the College of Charleston. We always turned south to pray, because everybody knew that God was not up north."[7]

John Bennett was profoundly saddened by Yates Snowden's death. The news reached him the same day that his friend passed away, and he immediately sent a message to Annie Snowden from the Bennett family. It was the first of the condolences from many friends to reach Snowden's widow. In extending his and Susan's sympathy, Bennett said:

> The dearest friend all South Carolina held for me is gone. That brave, true, loyal, gallant gentleman. My heart aches for you. Your immeasurable sorrow is the grief of us also who loved Yates and you, as you know I have done for thirty years and more. Love, sorrow and sympathy from us two.

After attending Snowden's funeral, Bennett wrote for his family the following comments about his friend:

> Though there were many there I knew from Columbia and around about our nearer countryside I did not stop to talk; I did not go there to chat with acquaintances or to greet strangers, but to bury a friend, the man whom, more, I guess than any other, in Carolina, I have loved most sincerely—next to the different affection I bear my son—deep—and natural.
> Well, that's that, my dears.
> For thirty years we were great friends; and we had grown very intimate—Yates, a thoroughly persuaded

Southerner, had admitted me to a singular, frank, and
delightful intimacy. How many characteristic letters I have
had from him, written at two o'clock in the morning,
when, after his old newspaper habit which he never
changed, he had come back to his books from his cup of
coffee somewhere down on Main Street—and a midnight
stop to talk of ancientry and Caroliniana with—Gittman,
the Old book dealer—or Willie Gonzales—or who you will.

He had somehow gifted me with qualities I have never
claimed and knowledge much beyond my scope, and critical
acumen entirely beyond my abilities—and would not be
persuaded by my protests to retract the most unmeasured
compliments and praises he showered on my works and me
at all times and in all places. If he did a verse—and he had
merit as a versifier, he appeared almost invariably first to
send his first clean draft to me for an opinion as to its
actual worth for printing anywhere—he did not try the
magazines—a newspaper pleased him just as much—or
begged my patching skill to mend a stanza which he could
not make come right. I had thus a share in several of his
conceits—the one I have always liked the best being Domiduca—goddess of the fireside—of which I enclose you a
copy: my tinkering has not affected its originality, nor
improved the thought—I contributed only the better meter
by playing with his own words less deftly placed—and he
too impatient to replace them and eager, having written, to
get to print—impetuous as any boy—and just as full of
youth.[8]

Bennett steadfastly refused to write an article for the South Carolina
Historical Society, or a tribute for the University of South Carolina
Bulletin, or a biography of his friend, even when requested by Annie
Snowden.

He was, nevertheless, pleased when he learned that his comments,
written in 1930 to Emily Fowles, were to be quoted at length in the
memorial tribute to be published by the University of South Carolina.
In April of 1934 Bennett expressed to Dr. Reed Smith his happiness that
the University was to issue such a memorial bulletin, and he mentioned
other matters in regard to the upcoming publication:

I cannot recollect what I wrote to Miss Fowles, but that
it was some expression of my opinion of Yates Snowden.
Whatever it was I am happy to think that you mean to
include it in the memorial bulletin. I should find it hard to
express myself as calmly and dispassionately now. Whatever
I may have said it is entirely sincere, and I fancy as clearly
expressed as anything I could set hand to. Nothing could

please me more than to know that something I have said
should be thus preserved in permanent evidence to the
friendship which existed between us, rare and delightful,
and to me always sustaining my best intentions.

Men have spoiled the word "love" with foolish misin-
terpretation: I loved Yates dearly, and shall always, here or
there.

I regret to say that, always intending some day to make
a portrait silhouette of Yates, we never came to it upon any
of his hasty and flying visits to Charleston. He was always
gone as quickly as he came, with a laugh, a gesture, and a
toss of his cloak across his shoulder—and all at once a
vacancy in the world where he had been a minute before;
an hour was suddenly empty of genuine delight. I am sorry
that I never made that silhouette, which so easily could
have been duplicated for his friends, and now employed as
you suggest. I had no decent portrait of him—but that
which vivid remembrance always held clear until Mrs.
Snowden generously sent me her own copy of an excellent
likeness after his death.

If the bulletin is to be formed like the one to Dr.
Douglas, following its plan of testimony and recorded facts,
accompanied by the portraits you cite for inclusion, there
seems nothing more to be suggested by me, unless some one
or two of his pieces of verse best representing his skill and
his personality, most excellent and most cherished by his
friends, might also be included. I can think nothing further
to amplify the issue.

John Bennett's letter of 17 December 1930, to Miss Fowles, in a more
complete form than that found in the bulletin, gave not only a tribute
to Snowden, but also an insight to Bennett's own personality:

What you ask me is not usual: to set down my opinions—criticisms, as you put it, meaning thoughts benevolent
and malevolent of the estimating kind, concerning one
whose continued friendship through thirty years has given
me one kind of intimate knowledge concerning him which
is the most difficult to express either publicly, off-hand or
in a term paper.

In the first place I do not criticise my friends any more
than I criticise the blue sky: I simply thank God for what I
have.

I knew Yates Snowden first as a journalist: a brilliant,
cultivated, perspicuous, and most entertaining writer;
everything he wrote lent character and personality to the
newspaper which printed it; his perennial and inexhaustible
humor, mellow as that of Charles Dickens, kindly as that of

Charles Lamb, caustic as that of George D. Prentiss,[9] and
his wide knowledge of human nature, of the history of his
State, and of national affairs in general, gave what he wrote,
whether as a police-court report, or a serious review of an
important book, a personality such as always marked the
work of Edgar Poe to the end of the era which bred and
sustained them. When the University coaxed him away
from journalism the newspapers, of Charleston in particular, and South Carolina in general, lost an intelligence and a
skill they could ill afford to part with: it has not been
adequately replaced to date—bright and promising as may
be some of the younger members of the craft.

When he left Charleston—for me, personally speaking—there was taken from Charleston a very definite part
of its charm, which has never been put back.

Had there been more like him in journalism and in the
community at large I should be more enthusiastic about the
present and more hopeful of the future of this State.

Without him, so far as I am concerned, life in South
Carolina would have been infinitely less worth living,
deprived of his sparkling correspondence, his conversation,
his dauntless spirit, his gallant bearing—let circumstance be
what it might—his tenderness, his cordial cheer to the
downhearted, his encouragement to the depressed and
harrassed, his unquestioning confident trust in the magna-
nimity of those whom he chose to make friends—his
unfailing gift of kindness and of generous appreciation to
those made rich and happy by that friendship.

Without him, so far as I am concerned—I repeat it
emphatically—life in South Carolina would have been
infinitely less worth while these thirty years of my citizen-
ship.

Such friends and such friendships make life tolerable
anywhere.

You ask that I write a criticism of him. I disposed of
that. That leaves his poetry and his books. He is a genuine
poet when truly moved by his emotion, tender, eloquent,
earnest, graceful, and ever intelligent and charming. His
occasional verses are full of lively and humorous fancy. I
wish there were more of his best. He excels my own great
love of books; is a discreet and wise collector; to see him
among his books is to envy him without meanness or
begrudging—and is to partake of his rare pleasure, which he
is at all times ready to share unstintedly.

To speak more intimately still, a few thin words:

In a world that is literally drab with Babbitts, Providence now and then drops a man distinguished by a difference, *pour encourager les autres.* If my French be wrong, as
it very well may be, my meaning should be clear. If it is

not, let me make it clear. Men like Yates Snowden are made
to encourage men like me.

He has done this without fail these thirty years, gilding
my days with the charm of a reckless, generous, and
delightful friendship, instilled like a Presbyterian doctrine,
in season and out.

Criticise my friends? I criticise my friends as I criticise
the blue sky above me: I look up into that infinite loveliness which shelters me like a roof, and thank God for what
I have.

About two months after Snowden's death, Bennett scribbled the
following thoughts on two small bits of paper:

YATES

That I shall never hear him laugh again, nor have from
him a merry letter breathing a manly and affectionate
regard and esteem—

I wish you knew—and I hope he did—how much these
meant to me—who all my life have much depended on the
affection of friends for confidence in my other ordinary
relations with the world.

There was something in him always made my heart
leap up, and be glad with no more or other reason than just
seeing him and hearing his ringing vibrant voice and sudden
brave gay laughter.

In Bennett's letter of 28 July 1933 to Mrs. Snowden, he explained the
impossibility of his undertaking the task of writing a life of Yates, as
follows:

Your letter came, yesterday afternoon, and for the first
time I have your present address. Had I known it before I
should have written you, certainly a few words to say what
little can be said in circumstances which were yours—the
last, great grief—and the comforting remembrance that a
gallant spirit found fitting end and rest—a noble heart—a
fine close to that unique career of selfless love for others
and for his home.

But you must believe me when I say briefly—my regret
is no aid—that it will be impossible for me to undertake the
loving labor you offer me to write of Yates. I am under
contracts for work long on the way and still incompleted;
the years are rolling fast with me, also; it becomes a real
problem to finish these things I have agreed to do in return
for a livelihood and a heritage to my children—it is impossible for me to undertake more than I am bound to at

present—I shall very probably be still completing when I myself am completed and at my ending.

I need not say how I thank you for thinking me the man to write Yates's biography: a compliment beautifully paid; and a task to stimulate one's heart. But it cannot be. I frankly think I shall not be able to complete these already promised things. But that must be as fate will—I can only continue faithfully to press on, in hopes of finishing.

The most beautiful part of my friendship for Yates I can never and could never—put on paper: I loved him as if we two had known each other for over a thousand years of confident friendship and happy esteem—and few men in a lifetime, meet or merit such deep and confident mutual regard and trust.

When he left us there went out of my life something never to be replaced—less than your loss, but great and most irreparable. I love him more than any man in Carolina, and had done so for thirty years of a unique and congenial intimacy—too close, too keen, too deep for expression in common things—too happy. J. M. Barrie made a book for sale of his Mother: I could not so use mine; nor speak so easily of Yates, my very true, most delightful, gallant friend, with whom it was a happiness even to differ in an opinion, and to whom our mutual cares were things for manly laughter together.

. . . It should, of course, be done while his memory still is fresh, to perpetuate the story of a gallant, loyal and delightful spirit, and inspiration to those who knew him, an example to all the rest. But, oh, for the State of South Carolina—how few there are who bravely follow him—and none to take his place—in that unique niche which is his in the history of the times, the State, and its people.

That he was so selfless, so genuine, so careless of his own advantage, so that friendship, affection, loyalty and his State be served, made him what I loved: it was a constant happiness to think that my regard met return in kind—my every exchange of correspondence with him, nonsense, persiflage, jest and serious, but lightly treated regard, was a constant stimulus to renewed endeavor and fresh courage in my own troubles and petty difficulties.

. . . Susy joins me in a message of deeply affectionate loving regard for you, and in remembrance of that gallant spirit—there was not one of my family but loved Yates—my oldest girl, Jane, particularly. From the Orient she wrote briefly but touchingly her grief that she should never see him again. My boy, Jack, admired and delighted in him; my younger girl held for him a youthful and delighted admiration.

And I loved him too deeply to publish my opinion in a careless and ephemeral press. . . .

When Mrs. Snowden visited her husband's grave for the first time in late October, it was the anniversary of Yates and Annie's wedding day. Having missed seeing her during the autumn trip to Charleston, Bennett wrote in November to Mrs. Snowden of his family's pleasure in learning of the scholarship given to the University in Snowden's name, including the following:

> . . . Susan and I, and the younger members of the family all cared much for Yates, particularly Jack and Jane, who better knew him than our youngest, Sue; and all were interested in your gift of a scholarship in his name to the University. That is a fine memorial to a scholarly and noble gentleman, which he was.

And he mentioned his own failing eyesight:

> . . . I speak of my failing eyes; the worst sign thus far of age and its inescapable disabilities. My sight has been hard used for fifty years; it would be a miracle if it showed no sign of wear; still good enough it yet requires careful husbanding, and that need has constricted the pleasantest of occupations, letter writing to old friends. . . .

In the final letter in the collection from John Bennett to Annie Snowden, dated 12 January 1937, almost four years after his friend's death, Bennett, now seventy-two, showed that he did not forget the past, although he was actively carrying on present work. He retold the beginning of his friendship with Yates, as follows:

> My acquaintance with Yates began in jest—which you may or may not recall:
> At about the time I appeared in Charleston, and frequently was observed to be a caller at the home of Miss Susie Smythe, there appeared a poem of mine, circulating among the newspapers, from the Chap-Book of Chicago—commonly known as "A Hundred Years from Now," but published under the title of "In a Rose Garden." It was the address of a lover to his lass.
> Yates, with characteristic love of a jest, printed it in the Sunday Courier under the pointed title of *"In a Charleston Rose-Garden."*
> I had not then met, nor seen, Yates. But, shortly thereafter, at the unveiling of the bust of Timrod in City Hall park, Susan, who was with me at that ceremony, pinched my arm, and said, "There is the man who did it—

Yates Snowden." I looked up immediately. Just opposite us
in the inner circle of attendants stood Yates, his handsome,
dashing face alight with the keen and living interest he
always showed in any tribute to the writer's achievements.
As I looked up, as if by some undercurrent of mental
telegraphy he turned his face, saw me with Susan, made a
little grimace, as if to say, "I'm caught!" and smiled, that
swift-flashing, friendly smile of his. I had been a trifle
provoked by the pointing of my poem so directly at Miss
Susy and me—but when Yates smiled and his mischievous
kindly eyes began to dance, what could any man do but feel
his heart suddenly glow with the certainty that here was a
man whose acquaintance would add to one's list of most
intimate and attached friends. So my own face cracked into
a complete smile without a reservation. Immediately after
the unveiling and the attendant speeches, we met—and from
that hour were friends—as you know, confident and
mutually affectionate beyond the common friendships of
the world.

That friendship, beginning with a jest, continued in
liking and laughter, year after year—whatever our mutual
fortunes were—and in a real love of man for man to the
end. I think I do not presume to say this: Yates's friendship
was too true, too kind, too understanding to be less than
one man's love for another.

As you have long known I loved Yates—not with a silly
sentimental caring—but fundamentally—and better than any
other man I have been privileged to know in South Carolina. There was a rare, blithe, buoyant, unconquerable
spirit of youth in him, a spirit of liking and laughter, a
radiant courageous heart which lent fresh courage to the
discouraged—and did often so to me. Naturally his memory
has not dimmed in my recollection, and cannot, however
long I stay.

Bennett also gave the latest news about *Master Skylark:*

You must have seen in the papers the announcement of
the sale of the film-rights to MASTER SKYLARK to a
producer who will star the new boy actor-singer, Bobby
Breen,[10] in that story. We have been waiting a long time for
a boy who thus could both act and sing—the singing being
indispensable to the story. I think we have found him, and
that you will like Bobby Breen as SKYLARK—when
production releases the film to the public—a year, perhaps,
from now. The producer is now in England, looking over
the scenes of the story, from Stratford down to London.
But whether the film will be produced in England or
Hollywood, I do not yet know. I shall not go to either

location; my hands are too full of my own immediate work
on two books—so that like the shoemaker of the old adage,
I shall stick to my last.

When Mrs. Snowden died in March of 1939, John Bennett was one
of the pallbearers at the funeral. Ann Eliza Warley Snowden was buried
beside Yates in Magnolia Cemetery.

In the latter part of the 1930s, John Bennett received a great deal of
attention from the press. *The Columbia Record* on 17 October 1936
reprinted a story by Bennett from the Chillicothe *News-Advertiser.* It
was a reminiscence of fifty years earlier and the newspaper headline was
"John Bennett Writes a Masterpiece, And The Hon. G. B. Shufflebottom
Is Enthroned as The Orator of the Era." At the time of the incident,
Bennett was with the Chillicothe *Daily News,* and while the rest of the
newspaper force were given a holiday, he had to cover the Memorial Day
events. The orator for the very hot May day was a particularly long-
winded politician, whose identity was covered by the alias "G. B.
Shufflebottom" for the story. As he followed at a distance the parade,
complete with brass band and two militia companies, Bennett was
stopped by a longtime friend in town for the day from Cincinnati, who
persuaded him to get into a red-wheeled buggy and go to the creek, where
the two spent the afternoon swimming and talking. After dark, the
young men returned to the newspaper office where they composed the
speech that they thought the politician must have given. Bennett wrote
two paragraphs and his pal wrote the next two, and so on until they
ended with the overwhelming applause from the audience and congratulations from the newspaper to the speaker for a "triumph of public
oratory." Leaving the copy for the typesetters and pressmen, they went
on their way. The next afternoon, less than an hour after the paper hit
the streets, the "Honorable G. B. Shufflebottom" entered the newspaper
office:

> . . . his ellipsoid face fairly beaming with gratified vanity
> and cordial emotion, and demanded a hundred copies of the
> paper to send to his constituents. "Why," said he, fanning
> himself with his panama hat, "It's the best report of a
> speech of mine that's ever been printed. By gad, sir: there
> never was a better piece of reporting—not even in the
> Congressional Globe. Gimme a hundred copies of your
> paper!" And with a grand wave of his fat hand away he
> went with his bundle of papers to spread his fame abroad.

In 1938 Bennett was still working on the novel about his father's
boyhood, which he planned to title "Buckhorn Johnny." And he was
still helping his friends, both old and new, with their writing, just as in

the past he had helped DuBose Heyward, Hervey Allen, Herbert Ravenel Sass, Alexander Sprunt, Jr., Samuel G. Stoney, Jr., and Yates Snowden.

In the May 1939 issue of the *Carolinian,* John Bennett stated that he was working on "several serious and considerable historical and fictional themes," which he hoped to finish. And he added, as follows:

> Along my wanderings I have painted scenery, stormed
> barns, stuffed animals and birds, played the guitar in a
> traveling orchestra, acted very badly in light comedy, and
> met adventures amusing and otherwise, which each in its
> own habit, enlivened a varied and often arduous career.
> I have known great kindness and met much great
> generosity; better than all I have been permitted to make
> and privileged to keep true friends.

On 21 September 1939 *The News and Courier* printed a story, written many years earlier by John Bennett, about a cow that gave black milk, as Robert Ripley's "Believe It or Not" had featured on 19 September. In the *Courier* article, "Astonishing Tale of Chillicothe, Ohio, Animal Is Recalled by Charleston Author," Bennett admitted the hoax as a "bit of wild young ribaldry, for which at the time I had some repute." Bennett's sense of fun remained with him throughout his life.

In 1946 Bennett's *The Doctor to the Dead: Grotesque Legends and Folk Tales of Old Charleston* was published by Rinehart and Company of New York. The volume included not only the title story and "Madame Margot," but also twenty-one other tales written during the years since 1916, when he first announced the project to Yates Snowden. Several of these legends had also appeared in *The Yale Review.*

In July of 1949 Bennett in a letter to Chapman Milling[11] stated that he had "been 'retired' from writing these past two years" and added:

> In plain words I was working desperately hard in weather
> just like the present—and "cracked up," with little chance
> of writing again. I regret to desist, leaving 3 books incom-
> plete; but as exhaustion was followed by influenza, dysen-
> tery and arthritis, I was compelled to admit that I was
> permanently out of the running.
> Frankly: at this time last year, my family, my friends
> and my physician were unwillingly confident that I was
> done—and would be gone before the end of autumn. But
> some hidden core of indomitable vitality remained. I was
> ready and, if need be, willing—being very tired of an
> unproductive existence, and 84 at my next anniversary. So
> instead of making a decent quiet finish I declined to go,
> grew better—to my doctor's astonishment—and am still
> here—not bed-ridden but confined to the house and looked

after by a fine nurse at night—as much for my kind family's
peace of mind as for my own comfort. I am permitted to go
up and down stairs and to spend the evening with my
indomitable wife and busy professional daughter in our
pleasant living room. My own room is cheerful and bright—
a charming garden on one side, and a beautiful crape-myrtle
in full bloom on the other. Kitty Ravenel of the *Courier's*
staff supplies me with trash to read—by the armful—and so
I pass the time. "Everybody" in Charleston is out of town
for the summer; so I am not often interrupted. My hearing
is *non est*—my eyesight grows definitely worse from week
to week; and my hands are so badly twisted by arthritis that
to write at all is a feat of notable legerdemain.

Bennett lived on for a little more than seven years. Death came on
28 December 1956, at 37 Legare Street. He was survived by Susan, his
three children, six grandchildren, two great-grandchildren, and his
sister Martha.

Saturday, 29 December, *The News and Courier* had a front-page story
and picture of John Bennett. The ninety-one-year-old author was referred to as "the Ohio native who adopted Charleston as his home more
than 50 years ago," and who had seen "his 'Master Skylark' named as one
of the '100 Best Books From All Time' less than a month ago."

According to the story in the *Charleston Evening Post* that afternoon,
"Funeral services were held at 3 p.m. today in the chapel of the Second
Presbyterian Church with the Rev. George A. Nickles officiating." The
honorary pallbearers were S. Henry Edmunds, Peter Gething, T. Marshall
Uzzell, Samuel G. Stoney, Jr., Augustine T. Smythe, Jr., Albert Simons,
and William S. Popham, now a United States admiral. The pallbearers
were Austin Smythe's three sons—Augustine T. Smythe, III, Henry Buist
Smythe, and Cheves McCord Smythe—and Albert Simons, Jr., Henry T.
Gaud, and Major I. S. H. Metcalf.

The newspaper stories noted, not only Bennett's success as an
author, but also his membership in Phi Beta Kappa, his influence on
DuBose Heyward and Hervey Allen, his ties with the Poetry Society of
South Carolina, and his skill as an illustrator, mentioning his Christmas
silhouette cards that he sent for many years. They pointed out that he
received an honorary Doctorate of Letters from the University of South
Carolina, that he was an authority on Gullah, as well as an exceptional
student of Lowcountry history, and that when writing to newspapers,
even in his later years, he always signed his articles, "Cub Reporter,
Chillicothe Daily News, 1883."

On Sunday, 30 December 1956, the following editorial appeared on
page 8-A of *The News and Courier:*

Among the many adopted sons of Charleston none was more devoted, nor contributed more to the culture of the community than John Bennett. Though he never lost his Ohio accent, he had a knowledge of the Lowcountry and its people that few if any natives could surpass in perception and affection. In a measure he helped to interpret Charleston to the Charlestonians. Through his writing, and also by means of his charming silhouettes and other illustrations, he helped to spread the fame of his adopted home throughout the world.

Mr. Bennett lived in Charleston for more than half his long lifetime. Besides his writings, he contributed generously of his time and his boundless energy to causes of a literary nature. He was one of the founders of the Poetry Society of South Carolina, which held its first meetings in his Legare Street residence. His influence, through other authors, newspaper people and admirers in many fields, was wide and sound.

Now that he is gone we shall miss his cheery company and wise counsel. His silvery hair and brisk walk, even when he was well into his 80s, were a welcome sight to countless friends on the streets of Charleston. He has left a rich heritage in his books, and in the hearts of those of us who were privileged to know him.

John Bennett, like Yates Snowden some twenty-three years earlier, was interred in Charleston's Magnolia Cemetery. The two friends, who met in 1901 at the unveiling of the Henry Timrod monument, today lie buried in the graveyard that was the scene of the first presentation of Timrod's famous "Memorial Ode."

Notes

Abbreviations for sources are listed in the bibliography.

Chapter 1: The Meeting

1. Henry Timrod (1829–1867), a Charleston and Columbia journal editor and poet, was called the Laureate of the Confederacy. Some of his best-known poems are the state song "Carolina," "Hark to the Shouting Wind," "Katie," and "Memorial Ode," his final one, which was sung 10 May 1867, in Magnolia Cemetery at the decorating of the graves of 800 Confederates who fell while defending Charleston. Thanks largely to the efforts of Yates Snowden's mother, a monument was raised at the burial site, some time later, fulfilling the prophecy contained in Timrod's lines. The memorial to the poet was dedicated on 1 May 1901. WWWH; DSCB; THT, 6–9, 126; MSC.

2. See pages e and f of Yates Snowden's biographical sketch of his mother, which may be found in handwritten form (pp. 1–30 and a–h) in the Mary Amarintha Yates Snowden Collection in the South Caroliniana Library.

3. The tablet to Yates Snowden's mother was unveiled at the S.C. capitol in November of 1917. STA, 22 Nov. 1917: 10.

4. Aaron Whitney Leland (1787–1871), a Mass. and S.C. Presbyterian minister, was pastor of the First (Scots) Presbyterian Church of Charleston (1813–1821), and then of the James Island Presbyterian Church. He was a professor at the Presbyterian Theological Seminary in Columbia (1833–1863). Leland received an honorary doctor of divinity degree from S.C. College in 1815. He was in his late seventies and quite ill at the time Sherman's Army burned Columbia. His first wife, Eliza Hibben of Mount Pleasant (1792–1856), had died some nine years earlier, and the Mrs. Leland referred to in the letter, Clara Amelia Bright of Edinburgh, Scotland (1830–1917), was his second wife. FUL, 102, 138–140.

5. One copy of the wedding invitation is in the S.C. Historical Society in Charleston, and one is in the South Caroliniana Library.

6. Many of the manuscripts of his speeches and articles are in the Snowden Collection of the South Caroliniana Library.

7. Samuel Lowry Latimer, Jr. (1891–1975), a York and Columbia newspaperman,

began work at *The State* as an office boy in 1907. After college and service
as a second lieutenant in the Field Artillery during World War I, Latimer
rose from reporter to editor-in-chief of *The State* in 1941. The advertisement here appeared in his *Story of The State,* page 342. WWW, vol. 4;
LAT.

8. The professor was Orin Faison Crow (1896–1955) of Spartanburg county,
    Hartsville, and Columbia. Married in 1919 to Innis McKewn Cuttino
    (1894–1989), Dr. Crow was a member of the University of S.C. faculty
    from 1925 until his death, being dean of the School of Education for
    almost thirty years. He left the University on three occasions to serve in
    the U.S. Army: during his student years, as a private on the Mexican
    border; just after graduation, as a lieutenant in France during World War
    I; and as a colonel during World War II, plans and training officer for the
    U.S. Field Artillery, Second Army. In 1953 he became dean of the faculty
    at the University of S.C. WWW, vol. 3; WAL, 4:896; DSCB.

9. William Watts Ball, b. 1868, a Laurens county, Columbia, and Charles-
    ton attorney and journalist, was married to Fay Witte. He was assistant
    editor of *The News and Courier* (1904–1909); managing editor (1909–1913)
    and editor-in-chief (1913–1923) of *The State;* dean of the school of
    Journalism at the University of S.C. (1923–1927); and editor-in-chief of
    The News and Courier (1927–1950). WWW, vol. 5; DSCB; CRA; WAL,
    4:685–686.

10. The colleague was Leonard Theodore Baker (1868–1955), a Charleston
    and Columbia educator, who was a professor in the school of Education,
    dean of the faculty, and acting president at the University of S.C. WWW,
    vol. 3; DSCB.

11. John Andrew Hamilton (1907–1992), Columbia and Charleston educator
    and diplomat, who taught romance languages at Harvard, Bowdoin,
    Converse, the Citadel, and the College of Charleston, and directed the
    Charleston graduate program of the University of S.C., recounted this
    story. Dr. Hamilton was a former president of Limestone College and
    served abroad as cultural and public affairs adviser for the State Depart-
    ment and the U.S. Mission to NATO. He was married to Elizabeth
    Pettigrew Verner, daughter of E. Pettigrew and Elizabeth O'Neill Verner.
    Charleston, *The Post amd Courier* 24 March 1992: 2–B.

12. The former student was Walter Derrick. This incident was related by
    Preston Musgrove, a Columbia educator.

Chapter 2: 1902–1908

1. A beautifully printed booklet copy of "A Carolina Bourbon," Yates
    Snowden's fine poetic portrait of one French Huguenot gentleman
    during Reconstruction, a tribute to William Mazÿck Porcher, accompa-
    nied the note. This reprint of the original version, and nearly all other

enclosures mentioned in the correspondence throughout the years, may be found in the Snowden-Bennett Collection in the South Caroliniana Library.

2.   Samuel Gaillard Stoney (1853–1926), the son of Samuel David and Harriet Porcher Gaillard Stoney, was a Charleston planter, stock raiser, and businessman who served as president of the Agricultural Society of S.C. He was married to Susan Smythe Bennett's sister, Louisa Cheves Smythe, the oldest daughter of Augustine T. and Louisa McCord Smythe. DSCB; CRA; SSA.

3.   William E. Barton (1861–1930) was an Ill. clergyman and author. WWW, vol. 1.

4.   Susan Bennett's father, Augustine Thomas Smythe (1842–1914), was the son of the Reverend Doctor Thomas and Margaret M. Adger Smyth and the brother of Ellison Adger Smyth and James Adger Smyth. A. T. Smythe, a Confederate sergeant major, Charleston attorney, and S.C. senator, owned one of the best libraries in S.C., containing many works from the great 24,000 volume collection of his father, as well as many from the library of his father-in-law and mother-in-law. Major Smythe was married in 1865 to Louisa Rebecca Hayne McCord (1845–1928), the daughter of the Honorable David James and Louisa Susannah Cheves McCord. WWW, vol. 1; DSCB; SSA; SMY; Yates Snowden's *Old Books and Their Lovers,* 1908.

5.   Richard Watson Gilder (1844–1909) was the N.Y. editor of the Century Company, the firm which published John Bennett's books. His younger brother, Joseph B. Gilder (1858–1936), was literary advisor to the Century Company and later editor of the *N.Y. Times Review of Books.* WWW, vol. 1.

6.   Miss Boykin, owner of the boarding house in N.Y. where the Snowdens lived while Yates was studying at Columbia University, had S.C. ties.

7.   The writer of the article was probably Henry Barton Dawson (1821–1889) who was born in England but came to N.Y. in 1834. He was the author of historical monographs, as well as editor of the *Yonkers Gazette* and of an historical magazine. WWWH.

8.   Augustine T. Smythe's sister Jane Ann Smyth, the youngest child of Thomas and Margaret M. Adger Smyth, was married to the Rev. John William Flinn, a professor and chaplain at S.C. College. Mrs. Flinn was Susan Bennett's aunt and the six Flinn children were Susan's first cousins. SSA; *Columbia Directory,* 1895–1899.

9.   Snowden here refers to Alexander Samuel Salley, Jr., b. 1871, an Orangeburg county, Charleston, and Columbia attorney and historian who was secretary of the Historical Commission of S.C. for many years. At the turn of the century, Snowden and Salley had opened an old-book store in Charleston, known as The Curio. In the summer of 1902 the

partnership was dissolved, with Snowden's buying all but one volume of the entire stock. WWW, vol. 5; DSCB; WAL, 4:611; MSC.

10.   John Bennett's *Treasure of Peyre Gaillard* (N.Y.: The Century Company, 1906) contains a list of fabricated titles and authors.

11.   Robert Wilson, D.D. (1838–1924), of Charleston, was an Episcopal priest, historian, and author. His son was also Robert Wilson (1867–1946), a Stateburg and Charleston physician and educator. Dr. Robert Wilson, Jr., was a professor of medicine at the Medical College of S.C., and later its dean; he and his wife Harriet were then next-door neighbors of the Bennetts, living at 39 Legare Street. DSCB; WWW, vol. 2; *Charleston Directory*, 1932.

12.   Daniel Ravenel (1834–1894), the son of Henry (1795–1859) and Elizabeth Peroneau Coffin Ravenel, owned a library of over 2,000 rare volumes of early Americana. His son Daniel Ravenel (1875–1947), a Charleston businessman with the Daniel Ravenel Company, Steamship and Tourist Agents, a staunch supporter of the French Protestant Church of Charleston, and a long-time secretary-treasurer of the Huguenot Society of S.C., inherited his father's extensive library which was used by many historians. His son, Daniel Ravenel (1898–1975), was Yates Snowden's godson. Daniel Ravenel (1789–1873), the brother of Henry and the uncle of the Daniel who gathered the historical collection, was chairman of the committee of twenty-five citizens who brought the body of John C. Calhoun from Washington to Charleston in April of 1850. The Ravenels were direct descendents of St. Julien de Malacare. BAI, 2:85; DSCB; MSC.

13.   Elie Prioleau, the son of Samuel Prioleau, a Huguenot pastor in France, studied theology in the Academy of Geneva and succeeded his father at the church at Pons in Saintonge before the Revocation of the Edict of Nantes. After fleeing to England, he came to S.C. and helped found the French Protestant Church in Charleston. He died in 1699. BAI, 2:43–44.

14.   Isaac Porcher, the emigré from France who died in 1727, was a St. Stephen's parish and St. George's parish planter and physician, who had studied at the University of Paris. His wife was Claude Chérigny. BAI, 2:105; DSCB.

15.   John Lawson, the surveyor general of N.C. who visited the Santee region of S.C. on a trip from Charleston begun on 28 December 1700, in his history spelled the French names as they sounded to him without regard to orthography. He was killed in 1711 by Tuscarora Indians. WWWH; LAW, 7–9.

16.   Daniel Huger, born at Loudun in Poitou, first sought refuge at La Rochelle and the Ile de Ré before coming to S.C. His son Daniel Huger, Jr. (1688–1754) was a St. John's Berkeley parish planter and S.C. representative. BAI, 2:50–51; WWWH; DSCB.

17.   Pierre Gaillard was born at Cherveux in Poitou, France, and emigrated

to S.C. in the 1680s. BAI, 2:59.

18.   Paul Hamilton Hayne (1830–1886) was a Charleston and Ga. journal editor and well-known poet. WWWH; DSCB.

19.   Because of Ben Tillman's anti-University actions, Yates Snowden considered him a political disaster. Benjamin Ryan Tillman (1847–1918) was an Edgefield county farmer, S.C. governor, and U.S. senator. And Snowden thought Ben's nephew much worse. The nephew, James H. Tillman, while lieutenant-governor, had shot the unarmed N. G. Gonzales, the editor of *The State,* on 15 January 1903, at the street corner facing the State House. Gonzales died three days later. WWW, vol. 1; DSCB; WAL, 3:412–414.

20.   Lois LeQueux, who married Charles Cantey Drake (1771–1794), was the daughter of Peter LeQueux (1742–1789) and Amelia Capers Wilkins, the daughter of William and Sarah Mathews Wilkins. Charles and Lois Drake's daughter, Maria Louisa Drake, married the Reverend Charles B. Snowden. Maria and Charles Snowden were the parents of Dr. William S. Snowden, Yates's father. MSC.

21.   George Armstrong Wauchope (1862–1943), a Va. and Columbia educator, author, and editor of many books, was a University of S.C. English professor from 1898 until his death. His wife was the former Elizabeth Bostedo. The Wauchopes lived on the University Horseshoe in the western half of the building now used as the president's home. WWW, vol. 2; DSCB; CRA.

22.   James Cosgrove (1861–1911) was a Charleston civil engineer and S.C. representative. DSCB.

23.   James Calvin Hemphill (1850–1927), Due West, Abbeville, and Charleston journalist, was editor-in-chief of *The News and Courier* (1888–1910). He was later the editor of Spartanburg, Richmond, and Charlotte papers. WWW, vol. 1.

24.   Ralph Izard, Sr. (1742–1804), a U.S. diplomat, U.S. Continental congressman, and U.S. senator, was a founder and trustee of the College of Charleston. He married Alice DeLancey on 1 May 1767. Their son, U.S.N. Lieut. Ralph Izard, Jr., wrote on 7 September 1808 from Sullivan's Island, S.C., to his mother at Clifton, near Bristol, Pa. WWWH; DSCB.

25.   John Bennett probably refers here jokingly to Yates Snowden as Mr. Pott because the character in Charles Dickens' *The Pickwick Papers* was a newspaper editor interested in politics, and, with his wife, cordially entertained Mr. Pickwick and Mr. Winkle. DICP, 168–210.

26.   Charles Woodward Hutson (1840–1936), a McPhersonville (S.C.), Miss., Tex., and La. author, artist, and college professor, wrote to Yates Snowden concerning his experiences during the War Between the States when he served in the Hampton Legion with Oscar Lieber. Lieber was

the state geologist of S.C. who fought and died as a private for the Confederacy, opposing the opinions of his father, Professor Francis Lieber, and his two Union Army brothers. Professor Hutson, after the war, taught languages at La. State University, the University of Miss., and Tex. A&M, before moving to New Orleans. WWW, vol. 1; MSC.

27.   Richard Francis Burton (1821–1890), an English explorer, writer, and linguist, is probably best known for his translation of *Arabian Nights*. COL.

28.   Paul Konewka (1841–1871) was a German artist who excelled at silhouettes. He is noted for his illustration of *Faust* and *A Midsummer Night's Dream*. G. C. Williamson, ed., *Bryan's Dictionary of Painters and Engravers*, 4th ed., 5 vols. (Port Washington, N.Y.: Kennikat Press, 1964) vol. 3.

29.   The famous inventor and artist from Charlestown (Mass.), Samuel Finley Breese Morse (1791–1872), visited and worked in Charleston (S.C.) for a time. In 1818 he married Lucretia Pickering Walker, who died in 1825. Many years later, in 1848, he married his first cousin, Sarah Elizabeth Griswold. WWWH; DSCB; DAB.

30.   Nathaniel Wright Stephenson (1867–1935), an Ohio and Charleston educator, was a professor of history at the College of Charleston (1902–1923). As acting president of the college in 1920, he asked Yates Snowden to deliver the commencement address. DSCB; WWW, vol. 1; MSC.

31.   John Blake White (1781–1859), a Eutaw Springs and Charleston attorney, artist, and dramatist, painted several historical portraits and pictures. His "Battle of Fort Moultrie" was placed in the capitol in Washington, D.C. DSCB; WWWH.

32.   David Ramsay (1749–1815), a Pa., Md., and Charleston physician and historian, was a S.C. representative, S.C. senator, and U.S. Continental congressman. He was the author of *History of the American Revolution* and *Life of Washington*. His wife was Martha Laurens (1759–1811), the daughter of Henry Laurens, and herself a writer. WWWH; DSCB.

33.   In the Bible (1 Samuel 4:21), Ichabod was the grandson of Eli and the son of Phinehas, whose mother gave him the name meaning "inglorious" when she gave birth to the child upon hearing of the death of her husband and her father-in-law and the taking of the ark of God by the Philistines. The derogatory name was used by John Greenleaf Whittier for the title of his poem condemning Daniel Webster, the great N.H. and Mass. statesman and orator, because of Webster's "Seventh of March" speech defending the view that the preservation of the Union transcended anti-slavery in importance. SMI, 261; WWWH; FOE, 715–716.

34.   The first Langdon Cheves (1776–1857), the son of Alexander and Mary Langdon Cheves, was an Abbeville county and Charleston planter, attorney, architect, S.C. representative and president of the U.S. Bank (1819–1822). He was born in a block house during an Indian uprising.

Langdon and his wife, Mary Elizabeth Dulles Cheves, were the maternal great-grandparents of Susan Smythe Bennett. DSCB; WWWH; SMY, 110–113.

35. John Randolph (1773–1833) of Roanoke was a Va. senator, U.S. congressman, and U.S. diplomat, who by his will, manumitted his slaves. WWWH; USE.

36. Tillinghast was probably Robert Lawrence Tillinghast (1817–1858), a Ga. and St. Luke's parish educator and attorney, who was a S.C. representative and S.C. senator. DSCB.

37. William G. Hinson of James Island owned a library of over 2,000 volumes, especially rich in Americana. It was included in the *List of Private Libraries in the U.S. and Canada* (1897), compiled by G. Hedeler and appearing in English, German, and French. MSC.

38. Mr. Podsnap, another memorable Dickens' character, appears in his novel, *Our Mutual Friend.* He is introduced in chapter 11, "Podsnappery." DICO.

39. John Bennett here compares the reception of his lecture to the Federated Clubs of Charleston with that accorded to the works of Giovanni Boccaccio (1313–1375); François Rabelais (ca. 1494–1553); Miguel de Cervantes Saavedra (1547–1616); Henry Fielding (1707–1754); Laurence Sterne (1713–1768); and Honoré de Balzac (1799–1850)—all considered too risque or coarse by Victorian minds. COL.

40. James Wood Davidson (1829–1905), a Newberry county (S.C.), N.Y., and Fla. educator, journalist, and author, was a U.S. Treasury Department clerk. When he first graduated from S.C. College, Davidson was engaged by Col. and Mrs. David James McCord to tutor their three children, Cheves, Hannah, and Louisa, at Lang Syne Plantation. He kept in touch with the family in later years. WWW, vol. 1; DSCB; SMY, 12.

41. George Herbert Sass (1845–1908), a Charleston lawyer, master in equity, poet, and editor of the *Sunday News and Courier,* often wrote under the pseudonym "Barton Grey." In the letters, he was sometimes referred to by his pen name alone or by his initials G. H. S. His volume of poems, including ones written in the 1870s, was published under the title *The Heart's Quest* in 1904 by G. P. Putnam's Sons. WWW, vol. 1; DSCB.

42. Charles William Kent (1860–1917) of Va. was a university professor and editor of numerous volumes, including the *Library of Southern Literature.* WWW, vol. 1.

43. Here John Bennett uses "Madame Solomon Grundy, et al." to allude to the tyranny of social opinion in matters of conventional propriety. Mrs. Grundy is an imaginary person referred to in *Speed the Plow* by the English playwright Thomas Morton (ca. 1764–1838). Charles Dickens also refers to Mrs. Grundy in *Hard Times.* OED; WBD; DICH, 15–16.

44. William Ioor (1780–1830), a St. George's parish playwright, wrote *The Battle of Eutaw Springs and Evacuation of Charleston; or The Glorious Fourteenth of December, 1782. A National Drama in Five Acts* (Charleston, 1807). The work, which was one of the volumes in the Daniel Ravenel library, included a Captain Manning, based on the American hero Laurence Manning, and M'Girt, based on the Tory Daniel McGirth. DSCB; WWWH; MSC.

45. Lieutenant-Colonel Henry Wmyss Feilden (1838–1921), the second son of Sir W. M. Feilden, Baronet, was a British officer who joined the Confederate Army. He married Julie McCord, the daughter of David J. McCord by his first wife. The couple moved to England after the War Between the States. Louisa R. McCord Smythe's half-sister, Julie Feilden, was referred to as Susan Bennett's "British aunt" in John's letter of 15 July 1920. Some of Henry Feilden's correspondence may be found at the S.C. Historical Society in Charleston. SMY, 101–103.

46. William Joseph Hardee (1815–1873), a Ga. native and a U.S. Military Academy graduate, was a lieutenant general in the Confederate Army. WWWH.

47. William Frederick Poole (1821–1894), a Mass., Ohio, and Ill. librarian and bibliographer, compiled *Poole's Index to Periodical Literature,* the first general periodical index in the U.S. Editions were issued by Poole in 1848, 1853, 1882. Afterwards, editions were issued with W. J. Fletcher. The last *Poole's Index* appeared in 1906. COL; WBD.

48. Jefferson Davis (1808–1889), a Ky. and Miss. planter, U.S. Army officer, congressman, and senator, was secretary of war under President Franklin Pierce. When Miss. seceded from the Union, Davis left the Senate, becoming president of the Confederacy in February of 1861. His grand-children gave money in his memory to the Confederate Home and School in Charleston, the institution founded by Mary Amarintha Yates Snowden for the mothers, widows, and daughters of Southern soldiers. On the back cover of the 1913 and 1931 reprints of "A Carolina Bourbon," professor Snowden included a note from Mrs. Jefferson Davis, nee Varina Howell, written to him in 1906. USE; MSC.

Chapter 3: 1909–1911

1. All the Bennett-Salley correspondence about "The Doom of Art" may be found in the Snowden-Bennett Collection of the South Caroliniana Library.

2. Fitz Hugh McMaster, b. 1867, a Winnsboro, Charleston, and Columbia attorney, newspaper editor, and S.C. representative, was the first insurance commissioner of S.C. (1908–1918), city editor and managing editor of *The State* (1917–1920), and the author of historical papers. As an

alumnus of Carolina, he was one of those who urged Yates Snowden to apply for the history position in 1904. While in Charleston, McMaster was manager of the *Evening Post,* and he married Elizabeth Sheperd Waring on 2 November 1892. WWW, vol. 5; DSCB; CRA; MSC.

3.   William Banks Dove, b. 1869, a Fairfield county and Columbia educator, was a S.C. school superintendent and served as the S.C. secretary of state. DSCB; CRA.

4.   James Abbott McNeill Whistler (1834–1903), an American artist and author, wrote *The Gentle Art of Making Enemies* in 1890. WWW, vol. 1; USE.

5.   Miles Brewton (1731–1775), a Charleston merchant, was a S.C. representative and builder of the now historic Brewton-Alston-Pringle mansion, as well as owner of extensive lands outside the city. His sister Rebecca, the widow of Jacob Motte, inherited his property when he was drowned at sea. It was on his former plantation in 1780 that the heroic incident occurred of Mrs. Motte's helping the American soldiers set the roof aflame with fire-arrows and thus forcing the British, who had seized the house, to surrender. DSCB; WAL, 2:272.

6.   Possibly Snowden was referring to Thomas Hart Benton (1782–1858), a N.C., Tenn., and Missouri statesman, who was a floor leader in the U.S. Senate until his defeat in 1850. Snowden, however, could not have met him and would have known him only through reputation. WWWH.

7.   John P. Kennedy Bryan (1852–1918), a Charleston attorney, was a leader in establishing suffrage in S.C. on a basis of property and educational qualifications. WWW, vol. 1; DSCB.

8.   The Miller of "Sans Culottes King" probably was Archibald Edward Miller (1785–1879) who lived on Tradd Street for many years. He was a Charleston printer from the early 1800s into the 1860s, as indicated in the *Charleston Directory* (1819–1868), and the *Bibliography of S.C., 1563–1950.* A. E. Miller printed John Beaufain Irving's *A Day on Cooper River* and was responsible for numerous political publications. Some years later in "A Study in Scarlet," the introduction to *The Countess Pourtales,* Yates Snowden, using the alias "Felix Old Boy," wrote about the "audacious toast offered among others in honor of Citizen-Minister Genet at Dinkins' Tavern, Camden, on 14 July 1794. 'Here's to "The fair Sans Culottes of America!"'" TUR; SEL, 13–14.

9.   "Josh Billings" was the pseudonym of Henry Wheeler Shaw (1818–1885), the Mass. and N.Y. humorist who wrote and lectured in farmer's dialect. WWWH.

10.   Maurice Augustus Moore, Sr., M.D. (1795–1871), of the Spartanburg district and Rock Hill (S.C.), was the author of an 1859 biography of Edward Lacey (1742–1813), from Pa. and Chester county, who was a Revolutionary War colonel under the command of General Thomas

Sumter, later a general, and a S.C. representative. DSCB; WAL, 2:236–238, 287; MML.

11. William Butler (1759–1821), a Va., Ninety-Six district, and Edgefield district planter and sheriff, was a Revolutionary War general, a S.C. representative, and a U.S. representative. WWWH; DSCB.

12. Andrew Pickens Butler (1796–1857), an Edgefield and Columbia attorney and judge, was a S.C. representative, a S.C. senator, and a U.S. senator. WWWH; DSCB.

13. Thomas P. Slider signed the dedication in *Memoirs of William Butler.* MWB.

14. Tarleton Brown (1757–1845), a Va., Orangeburg district, and Barnwell district planter and sheriff, was a S.C. representative and a S.C. senator. DSCB.

15. Colonel William Harden, of Beaufort district, who had fought as one of Francis Marion's men, early in 1781 raised a similar force to fight in the southeast section of S.C. and into Ga. when needed. Several months later, Governor John Rutledge of S.C. and General Nathanael Greene (1742–1786) of R.I., who became commander of the Army of the South in 1780, considered the discipline too lax in the independent bands and placed restrictions on the militia, forcing Harden from his command. His men then refused to continue service. About the same time, the new orders to fight on foot instead of on horseback, a measure taken to stop plundering, also caused General Thomas Sumter to resign, since lack of mobility for the Partisan units would make them ineffective at best and at the mercy of the British at worst. Francis Marion's group were allowed to keep their horses. WAL, 2:274, 297; WWWH.

16. Mason Locke Weems (1757–1825), an Anglican clergyman, wrote *The Life and Memorable Actions of George Washington* in 1800 and *The Life of General Francis Marion* in 1809. Both volumes contain incidents which Weems invented or unsubstantiated stories which he passed along as fact. WWWH.

17. Major Snipes was probably William Clay Snipes (1742–1806), a St. Bartholomew parish planter, who was a S.C. representative and S.C. senator. DSCB.

18. John Salley (1740–1794), an Orangeburg district planter, was a S.C. representative. DSCB.

19. William Cuningham left the Whig forces, with whom he had fought during the Cherokee War, when he found that some Whigs had treated his family roughly; and he became a Tory in 1776. A major in the Loyalist militia, he was called "Bloody Bill" because of his ruthless slaughter of captives taken in his raids. WAL, 2:313.

20. Walter Peyre Porcher (1858–1919), of St. John's Berkeley and Charleston, was a physician. At his death, he was buried at Pinopolis beside his

wife, Mary Long Porcher, who had pre-deceased him. His sister, Virginia Leigh Porcher, assumed responsibility for the children, including "Little Virginia," referred to in later letters, and Charlie, Yates Snowden's godson. DSCB; MSC; N&C, 4 Nov. 1919; STA, 5 Nov. 1919.

21. The Gourdin family, descended from the Huguenot Louis Gourdin (Gourdain), who was born at Concourt in Artois and who emigrated after the Revocation of the Edict of Nantes, became known for their success as planters and statesmen, as well as for their wine cellars. Among notable members of the family were Henry Gourdin (1804–1879) and Robert N. Gourdin (1811–1894), Charleston businessmen and members of the French Protestant (Huguenot) Church, whose wine cellar in their home at the eastern corner of Meeting and South Battery was legendary. TRA, no. 68:36; TRA, no. 93:1; MSC.

22. Edward McCrady (1833–1903), a Charleston attorney, S.C. representative, author, and historian, wrote the *History of S.C.* (4 vols., 1897–1902). WWWH; DSCB; HUN, 238–239.

23. Robert Wells (1728–1794), of Scotland and Charleston, opened a bookstore and printing shop on the bay near Tradd Street in 1758. His *Gazette* was the second paper in the colony. A staunch Loyalist, he went to England at the beginning of the Revolution, leaving his son John, an American Patriot until 1880, in charge. Robert printed and sold Rowland Rugeley's *The Story of Aeneas and Dido Burlesqued* (1774). AIK, 77, 81; TIP, 158–159, 369–170.

24. Louisa Susannah Wells Aikman (ca. 1775–1831), the daughter of Robert Wells, wrote in 1779 a journal of her 1778 voyage from Charleston to England, during the American Revolution. In 1782, Susannah married Alexander Aikman, King's printer in Jamaica. AIK, Preface, 106, 108.

25. Rowland Rugeley, of England and Charleston, was an import merchant who died in 1776. He was a S.C. representative, a Loyalist, the owner of the famous Clermont mill, and the author of burlesque translations from the classics. DSCB; WAL, 2:203, 249.

26. John Julius Pringle, Sr. (1753–1843), a Charleston lawyer, S.C. representative, and attorney-general of S.C., was the president of the Charleston Library Society (1812–1816). Joel Roberts Poinsett (1779–1851), a Charleston and Georgetown attorney and planter, was a S.C. representative, S.C. senator, U.S. representative, U.S. diplomat, and U.S. secretary of war, who developed the poinsettia from a Mexican plant. He married Mary Izard Pringle in 1833, the widow of John Julius Pringle, Jr., and the great-grandmother of Joel Roberts Poinsett Pringle (1873–1932), of Georgetown, who became a U.S. Navy rear admiral and was at one time president of the Naval War College, Newport, R.I. WWWH; DSCB; DAB.

27. Girolamo Tiraboschi (1731–1794), an Italian historian and critic, wrote a history of Italian literature that is still considered important in the twentieth century. COL.

28. Mitchell King, of Scotland and Charleston, b. 1873, was an educator and judge. DSCB.

29. "She who must be obeyed" here refers to Mrs. Bennett. Snowden alludes to Rider Haggard's Ayesha, the immortal goddess of *She, A History of Adventure* (London: Longsman, Green & Co., 1887), which had first appeared in serial form in *The Graphic* (2 October 1886 through 8 January 1887). Sir Henry Rider Haggard (1856–1925), of England and Africa, who was a novelist, colonial administrator, and agriculturist, called his awesome heroine She-Who-Must-Be-Obeyed, the name that he had, in early childhood, given to a doll which was kept in a "deep, dark cupboard" and to whom a nurse attributed occult powers. Morton Cohen, *Rider Haggard: His Life and Works* (London: Hutchinson & Co., 1960) 25, 97–118, 309; USE.

30. John Joachim Zubly (1724–1781), of Switzerland and Savannah, was a clergyman, Continental congressman, and Loyalist. WWWH; DSCB.

31. Ezra Stiles (1727–1795) was a clergyman, professor of ecclesiastical history, founder of R.I. College (now Brown University), and president of Yale University. WWWH.

32. Moses Kirkland (ca. 1725–1787), a Ninety-Six district and Jamaica planter, was a S.C. representative and Loyalist. DSCB.

33. Francis Rawdon-Hastings (1754–1826), a British soldier and governor-general of India, was the first Marquess of Hastings. Lord Rawdon, who defeated the American forces at Camden, did not assume his second surname until after his service in the Revolutionary War. COL.

34. Robert Howe (1732–1786), a N.C. congressman and major general in the Continental Army, was unlucky as a leader in the early years of the Revolutionary War. In 1778, he and Brigadier General Christopher Gadsden quarreled, and Howe challenged Gadsden to a duel. Gadsden fired in the air, and Howe missed. WWWH; WAL, 2:171–172.

35. Caroline Howard Gilman (1794–1888), a Mass., Charleston, and Wash. writer, was the wife of the Reverend Samuel Gilman (1791–1858), a Mass. and Charleston Unitarian minister and author. Caroline began the first children's paper in the country, *The Rose Bud*. WAL, 3:55; WWWH.

36. Arthur Henry Hirsch was an historian who wrote *The Huguenots of Colonial S.C.* (1928). HIR.

37. Robert MacMillan Kennedy, of Camden and Columbia, b. 1866, was the University of S.C. librarian and joint author with Thomas Jefferson Kirkland (1860–1936), a Camden lawyer, S.C. representative and senator, of *Historic Camden*. WWW, vol. 5; DSCB; CRA.

38. James Cary (or Carey) of Camden, a Loyalist, was a colonel in the Royal Militia and commanded on his plantation, Cary's Fort, a fortified redoubt that guarded Wateree Ferry. Earlier, Cary had helped build defenses at Camden for the American forces. General Sumter captured

Cary's Fort later in the war. KIR, 1:99, 104–106, 153.

39. Henry Nelson Snyder (1865–1949), a Ga. and Spartanburg educator, was a professor of English literature and president of Wofford College. WWW, vol. 2; DSCB; CRA.

40. Jabez Lamar Monroe Curry (1825–1903), a Ga. educator, U.S. congressman, Confederate congressman, Richmond College professor, and U.S. diplomat, was the author of several books, including *Civil History of the Confederate Government* (1901). WWW, vol. 1.

41. Lorenzo Sabine (1803–1877), a New England representative and U.S. representative, was a Northern historian. WWWH.

42. Mabel Louise Webber, b. 1869, was secretary-treasurer and librarian of the S.C. Historical Society. She edited the organization's quarterly magazine and, assisted by Anne King Gregorie, prepared a catalogue of the Society's holdings in the 1920s. YPS, 1928:59.

43. Daniel McGirth, of the Kershaw district, was the son of Captain, later Lieutenant-Colonel, James McGirt, who was faithful to the American forces throughout the Revolutionary War. Daniel deserted the Whig cause and became a vengeful Tory raider after being treated disgracefully while he was serving in the American Army in Ga. He was publicly whipped and imprisoned for insubordination, when he resisted an officer's attempt to take his mare Grey Goose, which he had brought from home and was using in his duties as a scout. Managing to escape and retake his horse, he vowed to avenge the ill usage. His savage retaliation as a Tory caused much suffering. JOH, 172–174; SCHM, 2(1):9; SCHM, 11(4):224; SCHM, 76(4):214.

44. Josiah Martin, who was governor of N.C. (1771–1775), fled from his post and, in the latter part of 1775, appeared with another Royal governor and three British ships in Charleston's outer harbor. WAL, 2:149; WAL, 3:551.

45. William Gilmore Simms (1806–1870), a Charleston and Barnwell county attorney and S.C. representative, was a leading novelist in the antebellum South. His library at "Woodlands" in Barnwell county, one of the finest in the state, was lost during the War Between the States. Simms's *History of S.C.* was revised and specially adapted for use in schools by his granddaughter, Mary Chevillette Simms Oliphant, in 1922. WWWH; DSCB; MSC.

Chapter 4: 1912–1913

1. At the top of John Bennett's letter, Yates Snowden wrote the following: "From John Bennett, who at my request examined, and largely recast some stanzas. Y. S."

2. States Rights Gist (1831–1864), an alumnus of S.C. College, was a general

in the Confederate Army. He was killed at the Battle of Franklin. SCA, vol. 3; WAL, 3:202.

3. Wade Hampton, III (1818–1902), a Charleston and Columbia planter, attorney, S.C. representative, S.C. senator, Confederate general, S.C. governor, and U.S. senator, was the grandson of the first Wade Hampton (ca. 1752–1835) and an alumnus of S.C. College. Confederate General Wade Hampton was a leader, not only during the War Between the States, but also afterwards in freeing S.C. from carpetbag rule. WWW, vol. 1; DSCB; SCA, vol 4; COL.

4. General Stephen Elliott (1830–1866) attended Harvard in 1846 before entering S.C. College, where he graduated in 1850. During the War Between the States, Confederate Major Elliott was placed in command of Fort Sumter on 4 September 1863. Later in the War, while serving as a brigadier-general in Va., he received a wound from which he subsequently died in 1866. His cousins who were attending Carolina at the outbreak of the war were less well known as soldiers. John Barnwell Elliott (1841–1921), a Charleston, Tenn., and La. physician and educator, left the College with the Cadet Company to help defend Fort Sumter in 1861. Robert Woodward Barnwell Elliott (1840–1887), who was also in the Cadet Company that went to the defense of Charleston, later rose to the rank of captain and served on the staffs of General Alexander Lawton, General Richard S. Ewell, and General Lafayette McLaws. R. W. B. Elliott was wounded at the Second Battle of Manassas. WWWH; WAL, 3:198; SCA, vol 3; BAR, 151–152, 188–189, 191–196, 200–205, 219, 232–233.

5. William Elliott (1838–1907), brother of General Stephen Elliott and a Beaufort attorney, attended college at Harvard and Va. He had an exceptional war record as a colonel in the Confederate Army and served as a S.C. representative and a U.S. congressman. WWW, vol. 1; DSCB; BAR, 153–154, 204–207.

6. James Henley Thornwell (1812–1862), a Marlboro district and Columbia Presbyterian minister, who graduated from S.C. College in 1831, later became a professor of logic, belle lettres, and sacred literature there. He was one of the most outstanding presidents of the institution. WWWH; DSCB; CRO, 163–165.

7. Francis Lieber (1798–1872), an educator and writer of Germany, Columbia, and N.Y., originated and edited the *Encyclopaedia Americana* (1829–1833), and taught history and political science at S.C. College (1835–1856). His mother, whose picture is mentioned in John Bennett's letter of 20 May 1912, was Mrs. Friedrich Wilhelm Lieber of Berlin, Germany. While at S.C. College, Francis and his wife, Matilda Oppenheimer Lieber, taught German to Susan Bennett's mother, Louisa Rebecca McCord. Dr. Lieber, called "Old Bruin" by the students, served as president *pro tempore* of the College. When he was not elected president by the Board of Trustees at the end of James H. Thornwell's tenure, he resigned from the faculty. Two of his most famous political works were written while

he was at S.C. College. Later he taught at Columbia University in N.Y. City. Francis and his two younger sons, Hamilton and Guido Norman, an alumnus of S.C. College, sided with the Union in the War Between the States, but the eldest son, Oscar Montgomery Lieber, as a private in the Washington Light Infantry, Hampton Legion, died fighting for the Confederacy. Oscar, educated in Berlin, Gottingen, and Frieburg, was a brilliant scientist who was the state geologist of Miss. and later of S.C. In 1860 he accompanied the American Eclipse Expedition to Labrador. WWWH; DSCB; COL; CRO, 162–163, 165–166; SMY, 8–9; DAB; MSC.

8. William Campbell Preston (1794–1860), a Pa., Va., and Columbia attorney, S.C. representative, and U.S. senator, was the first S.C. College graduate to become president of the institution. Having earned his degree in 1812, he served as president from 1845 to 1851. A great nephew of Patrick Henry, Preston was a renowned orator. WWWH; DSCB; CRO, 159–162.

9. Louisa Susannah Cheves McCord had written two songs for Carolina College before Secession. She was the daughter of Langdon and Mary Elizabeth Dulles Cheves, the wife of Col. David James McCord, and the grandmother of Susan Bennett. Mrs. McCord was a well-known author who during the War Between the States ran the Confederate hospital in the S.C. College buildings. Mary Boykin Chestnut mentions Mrs. McCord often in her diary, calling Louisa "the clearest-headed, strongest-minded woman I know, and the best and the truest." MCC, 328; SMY, 101–103.

10. Reed Smith (1881–1943), a N.C. and Columbia educator, was a professor of English at the University of S.C. for many years. He was married to Margaret Dick. WWW, vol. 2; CRA; DSCB.

11. George Peter Alexander Healy (1813–1894), a Boston painter who did portraits in Europe and America of famous political and military figures, was the first American invited to contribute a self-portrait to the Uffizi Gallery in Florence, Italy. In his *Reminiscences of a Poet and Painter* (Chicago: A. C. McClung & Co., 1894) he recalled his Charleston host hurrying him out of town at the beginning of the War Between the States. WWWH; MSC.

12. John Caldwell Calhoun (1782–1850), an Abbeville district lawyer, was one of the best-known South Carolinians. He served as a state representative, a U.S. representative, senator, secretary of war, secretary of state, and vice-president. WWWH; DSCB; WAL, 2:422, 428, 490.

13. Jared Bradley Flagg (1820–1899), a Conn. artist and clergyman, who studied painting with his brother, George Whiting Flagg, and his uncle, Washington Allston, published the life and letters of his uncle. WWW, vol. 1.

14. Washington Allston (1779–1843), a Brook Green Domain, Charleston, England, and Mass. painter and author, has been called the "American Titian." WWWH; DSCB.

15. John Stevens Cogdell (1778-1847), a Charleston lawyer, was not only a sculptor and painter, but also S.C. comptroller-general and a S.C. representative. WWWH; DSCB.

16. Edward Greene Malbone (1777-1807), of Providence (R.I.), Boston, Charleston, and Savannah, was a well-known miniature painter. WWWH.

17. Charles Fraser (1782-1860), a Charleston attorney and miniature artist, painted a number of famous people, including the Marquis de Lafayette in 1825. WWWH; DSCB.

18. According to Flagg, Mr. McMurtrie, along with Mr. Sully, raised money for the Pa. Academy of Fine Arts to buy Allston's "The Dead Man Revived" (ca. 1816). Mr. McMurtrie and Allston kept up a friendly correspondence for many years. FLA, 118-119.

19. Robert Lathan (1881-1937), a York (S.C.), Charleston, and Asheville (N.C.) editor was with *The News and Courier* in Charleston (1906-1927). WWW, vol. 1.

20. Gaston Carew is a major character in John Bennett's *Master Skylark*.

21. McDavid Horton (1884-1941), a Greenville and Columbia journalist, was first with *The Daily Record* and then joined the staff of *The State,* becoming managing editor and then editor. Horton was married to Sarah Flinn, who, as the daughter of A. T. Smythe's sister Jane Ann Smyth and the Rev. John William Flinn, was Susan Bennett's first cousin. "Ray," as Sarah was called, died in 1930. WWW, vol. 1; *Columbia Directory,* 1907-1931.

22. Samuel Chiles Mitchell (1864-1948), a Miss., Va., Del., and Columbia language and history professor, was president of the University of S.C. (1908-1913), and president of the University of Del. (1914-1920). WWW, vol. 2; CRO, 177-179.

23. Gustavus Memminger Pinckney (1873-1912), a Charleston attorney, University of S.C. graduate, classical scholar, and writer, was the author of the *Life of John C. Calhoun* (Charleston, 1903). Newspaper contributions included his severely critical review of the national government's policy of protection that exploited the Philippine natives and an unusual, perhaps unique, savagely vicious review of his own work on the life of Calhoun, which he sent to *The News and Courier* under an assumed name. It was said that he thoroughly enjoyed the letters sent in by readers that defended himself from himself. STA, 15 Dec. 1912:4; MSC.

24. Coleman Livingston Blease (1868-1942), a Newberry county and Columbia attorney, was a S.C. representative, S.C. governor, and U.S. senator. WWW, vol. 1; DSCB; CRA.

25. George Bancroft (1800-1891), a Mass. historian, U.S. secretary of the Navy, and U.S. diplomat, established the U.S. Naval Academy and wrote *History of the U.S.* (10 vols., 1834-1874). WWWH.

26. James Rivington (1714–1802), a bookseller and journalist of England and N.Y., returned to England after his printing plant was ruined by the Sons of Liberty in 1775 because of his newspaper's Loyalist policy, but he came back to N.Y. as the King's printer in 1778 and remained in newspaper publishing after the war. WWWH.

27. This Gaines was probably Edward Pendleton Gaines (1777–1849), a Virginia-born U.S. Army officer who arrested Aaron Burr. WWWH.

28. Lyman Copeland Draper (1815–1891), a N.Y. and Wis. antiquarian who collected historical papers, published *King's Mountain and Its Heroes* (1891). WWWH.

29. Peter Force (1790–1868), a Washington (D.C.) mayor, was an archivist, whose work, *American Archives* (9 vols., 1837–1853), has been considered the finest source collection on the American Revolution. WWWH.

30. Andrews was probably John Andrews (1746–1813), an Anglican clergy-man who once met Major John André (1751–1780), the British officer who was hanged as a spy for his conspiracy with Benedict Arnold in the attempt to take West Point. WWWH.

31. Wymberly Jones DeRenne published in 1902, as a contribution to the Ga. Historical Society, *Order Book of Samuel Elbert, Colonel and Brigadier General in the Continental Army, October, 1776 to November, 1778* and *Letter Book of Governor Samuel Elbert, from January, 1785 to November, 1785.* PGH.

32. Anthony Wayne (1745–1796), a Pa. representative, surveyor, and Ameri-can major general, was called "Mad Anthony" Wayne because of his daring exploits. In 1782 he occupied Charleston when the British evacu-ated the city. WWWH; COL.

33. Albert Enoch Pillsbury (1849–1930), a N.H. and Mass. lawyer who was attorney general of Mass. (1891–1894), made an address at Howard University in 1913 on the fiftieth anniversary of the Emancipation Proclamation. A. E. Pillsbury, "Introduction," *Lincoln and Slavery* (Bos-ton: Houghton Mifflin Co., 1913); WWW, vol. 1.

34. John Bennett here jokingly refers to his good friend, Dr. Thomas della Torre, b. 1860, a Charleston educator who was professor of Latin and Greek at the College of Charleston (1898–1913). He later moved to Rome, Italy. THT, 146.

35. According to notes that Snowden sent to Bennett on 4 August 1913, John H. Sargent was listed in the *Charleston City Directory* of 1809 as "Printer and Proprietor of *The Strength of the People,* 113 Queen Street." MSC.

36. Worthington Chauncey Ford (1858–1941), a Mass. editor connected with the Boston Public Library and the Library of congress, was editor of the Mass. Historical Society. WWW, vol. 1.

37.   William James Rivers (1822-1909) was a Charleston, Columbia, and Md. educator and writer. Called "the best informed man of his day on Carolina history," he was a professor of Greek at S.C. College from 1845 until 1873, when he became president of Washington College in Md. He was the author of *Historical Sketches of S.C.* (Charleston: McCarter & Co., 1857). DSCB; THT, 145; MSC.

38.   Hannah (Nancy) McCord Smythe, Augustine Thomas and Louisa Rebecca McCord Smythe's second daughter and Susan Bennett's sister, was married to Anton Pope Wright. The Wrights lived in Ga. SSA.

39.   Reuben Gold Thwaites (1853-1913), a Mass. and Wis. historian, was secretary and superintendent of the State Historical Society of Wis., a lecturer on American history at the University of Wis., and the author of many histories. WWW, vol. 1; MSC.

40.   Eliza Yonge Wilkinson, b. 1757, was a Yonge's Island diarist. DSCB.

41.   William Peterfield Trent (1862-1939), a Va. and N.Y. educator, was a University of the South and Columbia University professor, editor, and author of many literary works, including *Life of William Gilmore Simms* (1892). When he was preparing an anthology in 1905, he wanted to include Yates Snowden's "A Carolina Bourbon," which had for years been one of his favorite poems, but he disliked the phrase "pearly gates," as well as the meter of the final stanza. On 7 May 1905 reminding his friend that Wordsworth had contributed to the writing of Coleridge's *Ancient Mariner,* he sent Snowden his version of the last stanza of "A Carolina Bourbon," which kept the best lines and remained true to the thought Snowden had expressed in the earlier version, but improved some of the phrasing. Later editions of the poem omitted the fourth stanza of the original and incorporated Trent's suggestions as to the final stanza. WWW, vol. 1; MSC.

Chapter 5: 1914-1915

1.   Pauline was the daughter of Pauline Warley Snowden, Annie Warley Snowden's sister, and Robert L. Snowden, Yates's cousin. Young Pauline, sometimes referred to as "Polly," later married T. Kirkland Trotter of Camden. Annie's other sister, Lucy Lydia Warley, was married to Yates's cousin, Thomas H. Snowden. The Snowden cousins lived in Charleston before moving to Ga. Robert and Pauline Snowden, who also had two sons, J. Warley and Charles J. Snowden, moved back to Charleston in the 1920s and lived at 170 Wentworth. IMYS, 8; *Charleston Directory, 1878-1932;* STA, 27 May 1932:7.

2.   Dwight Lyman Moody (1837-1899) was a Mass. evangelist who held revival meetings all over the U.S. and Great Britain with the Pa. and N.Y.

evangelist and singer, Ira David Sankey (1840–1908), who also compiled several volumes of sacred songs, having composed many of them himself. WWW, vol. 1.

3. Henry Augustus Middleton Smith (1853–1924), of Charleston, was a U.S. District judge and historian. DSCB; MSC.

4. Langdon Cheves, IV, the son of Charles Manly and Isabella Middleton Cheves and the grandson of the first Langdon Cheves, was a Charleston attorney. He married his cousin, Sophia Lovell Haskell. Both he and his wife were first cousins of Susan Bennett's mother, Louisa McCord Smythe. SMY; SCHM, 35:79–95.

5. The home of Henry Laurens (1724–1792), a Charleston merchant and planter, who was a S.C. representative, S.C. vice-president, Continental congressman, and U.S. diplomat, was built in 1763 on the east side of Front Street (now East Bay), near Lord Anson's. WWWH; DSCB; WBD; SAH, 284–286.

6. M. Mantalini, a character in Charles Dickens' *Nicholas Nickleby*, is the husband of the London dressmaker who employs Kate Nickleby. Originally Alfred Muntle, he has changed his name to enhance his wife's establishment, but does no work at all, devoting his time to pleasure and spending her money. Near the end of the novel, when forced to labor, Mantalini refers to life as "one demd horrid grind!" DICN, 124–125, 774.

7. Sidney Jacobi Cohen (1891–1915), the son of William B. and Sarah J. Cohen, had his master's thesis, "Three Notable Ante-Bellum Magazines of S.C.," published in a University of S.C. bulletin and his "Julian the Apostate," in the *Sewanee Review*, both in 1915. His mother and his sister Helen wanted help from Snowden and Bennett in 1919 to get Sidney's poems into print. *Garnet and Black*, 1916; *Charleston Directory*, 1918–1922; MSC.

8. Albert Simons, an architect, preservationist, educator, author, b. 1890, was the son of Dr. Thomas Grange Simons (1843–1927), a Charleston physician, Confederate soldier, and educator, and Serena D. Simons. A few years after 1915 Albert married Harriet Porcher Stoney, Susan Bennett's niece. Along with Sam Stoney, Jr., Augustine Stoney, and Sam Lapham, Jr., he produced an excellent volume on Charleston architecture in 1927. SSA; *Charleston Directory*, 1914, 1916.

9. Samuel Gaillard Stoney, Jr. (1891–1968), a Charleston historian, preservationist, architect, educator, author, and raconteur, was the son of S. G. and Louisa Cheves Smythe Stoney and the nephew of Susan Bennett. A U.S. Army lieutenant in World War I, Sam, Jr., collaborated with Gertrude Mathews Shelby on *Black Genesis* (N.Y.: The Macmillan Company, 1930) and *Po' Buckra* (N.Y.: The Macmillan Company, 1930); and he wrote numerous historical papers. For thirty years, he was the Huguenot Society's vice-president for Goose Creek and president of the Society (1948–1951). TRA, no. 74:29–30; SSA; MSC.

10.   Hugh Williamson (1735–1819), a Pa. and N.C. congressman, scientist, and author, who wrote *The History of N.C.* (2 vols., 1812), began a mercantile business in Charleston before moving to Edenton, N.C. WWWH.

11.   Horatio Gates (ca. 1728–1806), of England, Va., and N.Y., who was a legislator, British officer in the French and Indian War, and American general in the Revolution, was largely responsible for the defeat at Camden in August 1780, and was relieved of his command in December 1780. WWWH.

12.   Mrs. Aymar was probably Lilly V. Aimar, the widow of George Washington Aimar, who founded G. W. Aimar and Company, a Charleston drugstore, in 1852. Captured and held in a N.C. Federal prison during the War Between the States, G. W. Aimar and several other Charleston natives donned civilian clothes and escaped. When he tried to reenlist, Aimar was asked by the Confederacy to reopen his drugstore to help furnish the army with medical supplies; he then turned the upper floors of his establishment into a Confederate hospital. "Aimar's Drugstore, A Memory," 1978 film by David Boatwright, Charleston, in his 1989 program for SCETV, produced by Charles Brown; *Charleston City Directory,* 1915.

13.   Isaac Motte (1738–1795), a Charleston and St. John's Berkeley parish planter, British officer in the French and Indian War, and American officer in the Revolutionary War, was also a S.C. representative and senator, and a Continental congressman. WWWH; DSCB.

14.   Thomas Sumter (1734–1832), a Va. and Stateburg planter, surveyor, S.C. representative and senator, Revolutionary War general, Continental congressman, and U.S. senator, was known as the "Game Cock," because of his tenacity as a fighter. WWWH; DSCB.

15.   Joseph Johnson (1776–1836), a Mount Pleasant and Charleston physician and bank president, was the author of *Traditions and Reminiscences, Chiefly of the American Revolution in the South* (1851). BAR, 397; JOH; WWWH.

16.   Elizabeth K. Shrewsbury Adger was the wife of John Bailey Adger, D.D. (1810–1899), a Pendleton and Charleston Presbyterian minister, who was Augustine T. Smythe's uncle. DSCB; SSA.

17.   Annie Raymond Stillman, b. 1855, a Charleston author, whose pen name was Grace Raymond, wrote *How They Kept the Faith: A Tale of the Huguenots of Languedoc* (1889). DSCB.

18.   Mary Elizabeth Moragné (Mrs. William Hervey Davis) of Abbeville, b. 1815, was a contemporary of William Gilmore Simms. Her short novel, *The British Partisan,* which first appeared in 1838, was set in the Abbeville district. MOR; TUR.

19.   Paul Turquand (1735–1786), a London and Georgetown Episcopal priest,

was also a S.C. representative. Annie Snowden was kin to Turquand through his daughter Anne, who married Col. Felix Warley. Susan Bennett was the great-great-granddaughter of Turquand through his daughter Hannah, who married Russell McCord. DSCB; TRA, no. 38:56–62.

20. Col. James Williams fought at Musgrove's Mill, was briefly a brigadier general before resuming his colonelcy, and was killed at the Battle of King's Mountain. WAL, 2:221–222, 235–236, 238–239.

21. Jess Willard, b. 1883, won the world heavyweight boxing title by knocking out Jack Johnson (1878–1946) in the twenty-sixth round of the championship match held in Havana, Cuba, on 5 April 1915. Johnson was the first black athlete to hold the title, having won it from Jim Jeffries in 1910. *The Schenley Sports Encyclopedia* (Toronto, Canada: A. S. Barnes and Company, 1953) 2:253–269; USE.

22. Major Hugh McGillivray, fl. 1915, was a professor at The Citadel in Charleston. *Charleston Directory*, 1916.

23. Tacitus Gaillard, fl. 1779, of St. James' Santee parish, was a planter and a S.C. representative. DSCB.

24. Thomas Smyth, D.D. (1808–1873), an Ireland and Charleston Presbyterian clergyman and philanthropist, married Margaret M. Adger, the daughter of James and Sarah Elizabeth Ellison Adger. They were the parents of A. T. Smythe, Susan Bennett's father. His *Complete Works* (10 vols., 1908–1912) were edited by Thomas's son-in-law, the Rev. J. William Flinn, D.D., and by William and Jane Ann Smyth Flinn's daughter, Jean Adger Flinn. WWWH; SSA.

25. William Charles Wells (1757–1817), of Charleston and England, was a newspaper publisher, physician, and scientist. WWWH; DSCB.

26. The Harlestons mentioned here were probably the family of John Harleston (1733–1793), a Charleston and St. John's Berkeley parish planter, Loyalist, and S.C. representative. DSCB.

27. Wilberforce Eames (1855–1937), of N.J. and N.Y., was a bibliographer and librarian at the N.Y. Public Library. MSC; WWW, vol. 1.

28. Henry Alexander White (1861–1926), a Va. and Columbia Presbyterian minister, historian, and educator, was professor of Greek at Columbia (S.C.) Theological Seminary and the author of histories, especially about the South. WWW, vol. 1; DSCB; CRA.

29. Adam Fowler Brisbane (1754–1797), a Charleston and Camden planter, judge, S.C. representative and senator, was thought to be an American patriot; while one branch of the family of William Brisbane (ca. 1710–1771), a Scotland and Charleston physician and apothecary, was thought to be Loyalist. DSCB.

30. Horatio W. (Holly) Mitchell was master in equity for Charleston county.

Charleston Directory, 1918, 1924.

31. Charles Evans (1850-1935), a Mass. and Ill. librarian and bibliographer, was the author of *American Bibliography,* a chronological dictionary of all books, pamphlets, and periodicals published in the Colonies and the States. Eleven volumes from 1639 to 1798 were completed. WWW, vol. 1.

32. Alexander Oliver Esquemeling (ca. 1645-1707), a Dutch buccaneer, traveler, and writer, was the author of *The Buccaneers of America* (1678). WBD.

33. *Recollections of the Ball Family of S.C. and the Comingtee Plantation* by Anne Simons Deas was privately published in 1909 in Summerville, S.C.

34. George Croft Williams, b. 1876, an Aiken and Columbia educator and Methodist minister, taught sociology at the University of S.C. and served as secretary of the State Board of Charities and Corrections and of Public Welfare. DSCB; CRA.

35. "Dum Vivimus Vigilemus" was written by Charles Henry Webb (1834-1905), whose pen name was "John Paul." He was a N.Y. editor and author of parodies, as well as verses. WWW, vol. 1.

36. Edith Pratt Dickins was the widow of Rear Admiral Francis William Dickins (1844-1911), of N.Y. and Washington, D.C. WWW, vol. 1.

37. John Franklin Jameson (1859-1937), of Mass., R.I., and Washington (D.C.), was a librarian and historian, who was a professor at Brown University. In 1897 and 1898, as chairman of the Historical Manuscripts Commission of the American Historical Association, he sought all Calhoun papers available and thanked Yates Snowden for helping locate them. WWW, vol. 1; MSC.

38. James Adger Smyth, Augustine T. Smythe's older brother who was a member of the company Smyth and Adger, cotton factors, was mayor of Charleston. He was married twice, first to Annie Ragin Briggs. His second wife, Ella, was the one still alive at the time of Bennett's letter. SSA; *Charleston Directories.*

39. Charles Stuart Vedder (1826-1917), a N.Y., Summerville, and Charleston newspaper editor and Presbyterian minister, served as pastor of the Huguenot Church in Charleston (1866-1914). He was president of the New England Society of Charleston, and he wrote poems, mostly occasional, such as "Commemorative Ode: 1775-1885" and "Confederate Home Song." WWW, vol. 1; DSCB; MSC.

40. Legrand Guerry (1873-1947), a Florence and Columbia surgeon, was the brother of William Alexander Guerry (1861-1928), a Clarendon county and Charleston Episcopal bishop. WWW, vols. 1, 2; DSCB.

41. John Ashe (1720-1781), a N.C. Colonial legislator and Revolutionary War general, whose wife was Rebecca Moore, had the city of Asheville named for him. WWWH; COL.

42. Alexander MacLeod was the son-in-law of Allan and Flora MacDonald and had emigrated with them, two of their sons, and his wife from Scotland to N.C. in 1775, hoping to find a better life in America. The Revolutionary War, however, was just beginning. MacLeod's mother-in-law, Flora MacDonald (1722–1790), was the Scottish Jacobite heroine who had been imprisoned in the Tower of London for helping Prince Charles Edward Stuart escape after the Battle of Culloden. MacLeod joined his father-in-law as an officer in the N.C. forces supporting the British. When the Tory troops left Fayetteville to march to Wilmington, they were ambushed and defeated at the Battle of Moore's Creek Bridge, 27 February 1776. Allan MacDonald and Alexander MacLeod were taken prisoner, along with over 800 other Tories. *The Highland Spirit*, Summer 1990:9; COL.

43. Sydney George Fisher (1856–1927), a Pa. attorney and historian, known especially for his colonial and Revolutionary War writings, was the author of *The Evolution of the Constitution of the U.S.* (1897); *Men, Women, and Manners in Colonial Times* (2 vols., 1898); and *The Struggle for American Independence* (2 vols., 1908). COL; WBD.

44. Theodore Marion DuBose, b. 1886, a Rock Hill and Columbia physician, was later an honorary pallbearer at Yates Snowden's funeral. DSCB; IMYS, 9.

45. Stewart was probably Hugh Stewart, fl. 1739, of Scotland and Charleston, a Presbyterian minister. DSCB.

46. Sir William Wallace (ca. 1272–1306), a Scottish patriot, defeated the forces of Edward I of England and unified Scotland for a time, but was in turn defeated by Edward at Falkirk in 1298. After a stay in France, Wallace was captured near Glasgow by Sir John Monteith, taken to London, and executed. COL.

47. Julian Augustus Selby (1833–1907), a Columbia publisher, was associated with both of Dr. Robert Wilson Gibbes's newspapers: *The South Carolinian,* in 1864, and, after Sherman's troops burned Columbia in 1865, *The Columbia Phoenix,* according to Dr. J. Rion McKissick (1884–1944), who was dean of the School of Journalism before becoming president of the University of S.C. *The Pheonix* was aptly named since one small part of its printing press was actually retrieved from the ashes of the building where *The South Carolinian* had been operated. Both William Gilmore Simms, the first editor of *The Phoenix,* and Henry Timrod were associated with both papers. Timrod and Selby got out the last issue of the *South Carolinian* while Sherman's shells were dropping nearby. When *The Phoenix* ceased publication during Reconstruction, Selby became affiliated with the R. L. Bryan Company. Julian and his wife Alice E. Selby's two sons Julian P. and Gilbert Augustus also worked at Bryan's. Gilbert joined the firm in 1883 at age fifteen and remained until 1948, serving as manager of the printing department for much of that time. HEN, 199–200, 232, 236–237; SJA; SGA.

Chapter 6: 1916

1. James Gadsden Holmes (1881-1942), a Charleston and Columbia merchant and business manager, was manager of sales for the State Company, as well as president and treasurer of his own business, which later became the Columbia Office Supply Company. DSCB.

2. Ker Boyce (1787-1854), of Newberry district and Charleston, was a merchant, banker, S.C. representative, and S.C. senator. DSCB.

3. Alfred Huger (1788-1872) was a Charleston planter, lawyer, and S.C. senator. DSCB; MSC.

4. Samuel DuBose (1758-1811), of St. Stephen's parish, was a S.C. representative. DSCB.

5. Fannie B. Sloan was the widow of John Trimmier Sloan (1846-1909), a Pendleton and Columbia attorney, journalist, S.C. representative, senator, and lieutenant governor. DSCB.

6. Marguerite Miller was the daughter of William Capers Miller, b. 1858, a Georgetown and Charleston attorney and president of the St. Andrew's Society. Marguerite designed her father's bookplate. DSCB; CRA; MSC.

7. Alice Ravenel Huger Smith was a well-known Charleston artist. With her father, D. E. Huger Smith, she collaborated on *The Dwelling Houses of Charleston* (1917) in which she did the paintings and Albert Simons did the architectural drawings. DSCB; MSC; SAH.

8. Edgar White Burrill was the playwright whose dramatic version of *Master Skylark* in five acts was issued by the Century Company in 1916 to mark the tercentenary of William Shakespeare's death. Bennett's Biographical Notes; The Century Company Catalogue.

9. Lancelot Minor Harris, b. 1868, a Va. and Charleston educator, was professor of English at the College of Charleston from 1898 until his death. WWW, vol. 4.

10. Thomas Janvier (1848-1913), of Philadelphia, Colo., N.M., and Mexico, was the author of many works, including *Legends of the City of Mexico* (1910). WWW, vol. 1.

11. Horace Kephart (1862-1931), a Pa., N.Y., and N.C. librarian and author, wrote *Our Southern Highlanders* (1913). WWW, vol. 1.

12. Samuel Phillips Verner, a South Carolinian and graduate of S.C. College, was a missionary and the author of *Pioneering in Central Africa*, which includes a chapter titled "Linguistic Studies—The Bakambuya." VER.

13. Thomas Hobbes (1588-1679) was an English philosopher and author, perhaps best known for *The Leviathan* and *Human Nature*. COL.

14. Sir James Augustus Henry Murray (1837-1915), a British lexicographer,

was from 1879 the editor of the *Oxford English Dictionary*. COL; USE.

15.   Lewis Parke Chamberlayne (1879–1917), a Va. and Columbia educator, became professor of ancient languages at the University of S.C. in 1910. WWW, vol. 1.

16.   Henry Campbell Davis (1879–1951) was a professor of English at the University of S.C. for many years, living on the Horseshoe in half of the building now known as the Faculty House. Davis was the author of the article, "Negro Folk-Lore in S.C.," *The Journal of American FolkLore*, 27:241–254.

17.   Walter William Skeat (1835–1912) was an English philologist, whose writings included *An Etymological Dictionary of the English Language* (4 parts, 1879–1882; 4th ed., 1910). USE; COL.

18.   Josiah Strong (1847–1916), of Ill., Ohio, and N.Y., the son of Josiah and Elizabeth Clough Webster Strong, was a minister of the Congregational Church, and an author. WWW, vol. 1.

19.   George S. Holmes, b. 1849, was a Charleston attorney who studied Greek and whose hobby was local history. Yates Snowden and H. G. Cutler, eds., *History of S.C.*, 5 vols. (New York: Lewis Publishing Co., 1920) 3:67–68; *Charleston Directory*, 1914; DSCB.

20.   T. R. Tighe wrote brief articles on Gullah for the Charleston *News and Courier*. BEN, 335.

21.   Robert Little Brodie (1829–1913) was a Charleston physician. DSCB.

22.   Elizabeth Ann Saylor Yates was the widow of Joseph Yates, a Charleston businessman (ca. 1775–1821) who died leaving her with over $100,000 and six children. Elizabeth died in her eightieth year in 1868. In a biographical sketch of his mother, Snowden wrote of his grandmother's efforts to give her children a fine education, even moving to Philadelphia for some years to put her younger children in the best schools, and of her extensive works of charity in Charleston. Referring to Elizabeth's part as "one of the leading spirits in a furious row in the First Baptist Church" at the time of the suffragette movement, Yates stated, "She made her three sons take pews so as to have the right to vote, she claimed and exercised her own right as a member and pewholder to vote, against bitter opposition, and the Rev. Dr. Brantley, her pastor, was triumphantly vindicated." Earlier minister of the Beaufort Baptist Church and founder of the Augusta, Ga., Baptist Church, the Rev. William Tomlinson Brantly, who changed his middle name to Theophilus, the *nom de plume* under which he wrote, came from the First Baptist Church of Philadelphia to the First Baptist Church of Charleston in 1837. Also president of the College of Charleston, he served in both positions until the summer of 1844, when he suffered a paralyzing stroke, from which he died the following March. H. A. Tupper, ed. *Two Centuries of the First Baptist Church of S.C., 1683–1883* (Baltimore: R. H. Woodward and Company, 1889); MSC.

23. George Hall Moffett, b. 1867, was a Charleston attorney who practiced law with Simeon Hyde, Jr., and was a S.C. representative. DSCB; MSC.

24. Thomas Wentworth Storrow Higginson (1823–1911), a Mass. Unitarian clergyman, army officer, and author, was an ardent abolitionist and became a colonel of the first black regiment in the Union Army during the War Between the States. He wrote many articles and books, including *Army Life in a Black Regiment* (1870). COL; WBD.

25. Elsie Baker, b. 1886, a Pa. and N.Y. contralto, was known for her concerts and her records. WWW, vol. 7.

26. Carrie Jacobs (Mrs. Frank L.) Bond (1862–1946), a Wis. and Calif. composer and author, was probably best known for her "Just A-wearyin' for You," "I Love You Truly," and "A Perfect Day." WWW, vol. 2.

27. Robert Spann Cathcart (1871–1949) was a Columbia and Charleston surgeon. DSCB; WWW, vol. 2.

28. Veuve Cliquot, the fine French champagne, is used here as a pun on the name of the Reverend Florian Vurpillot, the French minister at the Huguenot Church in Charleston (1913–1925), and the chaplain of the Huguenot Society of S.C. (1914–1925). During his years of ministry in Charleston, he "conducted services on three Sundays during the month in English and on the fourth Sunday in French." TRA, no. 30:43; MSC.

29. Kirkman George Finlay (1877–1938), of Greenville and Columbia, was bishop coadjutor of the Diocese of S.C. and in 1922 was consecrated bishop of the Diocese of Upper S.C. WWW, vol. 1; DSCB.

30. John Lyde (Lide) Wilson (1784–1849), a Marlboro district and Georgetown planter and attorney, was a S.C. representative, senator, and governor. DSCB.

31. Clarence Albert Graeser was a captain and a professor at the Citadel in 1916, but a few years later, became a professor at the College of Charleston. Clarence and his wife Jeanne were both referred to as French scholars by Yates Snowden in 1927. IMYS, 16; *Charleston Directory,* 1916, 1926.

32. Barnett Abraham Elzas (1867–1936), of Germany, Columbia, Charleston, and N.Y., was a rabbi and author. He served the Beth Elohim congregation in Charleston (1894–1910). WWW, vol. 1.

Chapter 7: 1917

1. Annie Elizabeth Bonham, a Columbia school mistress, was born 25 August 1857, the seventh child of Milledge Luke and Ann Patience Griffen Bonham. Her father (1813–1890), of Mass. and Edgefield district, was a planter, attorney, S.C. representative, U.S. representative, Confederate representative, Confederate General, and S.C. governor. BON; WWWH; DSCB.

2. L. A. Griffith was the mayor in 1917, having succeeded the first mayor of Columbia under the Commission form of government, Wade Hampton Gibbes, in 1914 for a term of four years. HEN, 86.

3. John Bailey Adger, II, b. 1858, a Charleston and Belton mechanical engineer, was the son of Joseph Ellison and Susan Cox Johnson Adger, and a first cousin of Augustine T. Smythe, Susan Bennett's father. John Bailey worked with the steamship firm, James Adger & Company, and with Belton Hydro-Electric Power Company. His wife was Jane A. E. Warren, also a cousin of A. T. Smythe. CRA; SSA.

4. There were two Miss Willises, Eola and her sister Azalea. Eola was probably the one to whom Snowden refers here, for she was a Charleston historian who did much research on S.C. subjects: Huguenots and early theatricals in the state, for example. She was the author of *The Charleston Stage in the XVIII Century* (1933). TRA, no. 14; MSC.

5. Louis Remy Mignot (1831–1870) was a Charleston, N.Y., and England landscape painter. S. G. W. Benjamin, *Art in America, A Critical and Historical Sketch* (N.Y.: Harper, 1880) 83; DSCB.

6. John P. Chazal (1814–1893) was a Charleston physician and educator. DSCB.

7. Rufus Fairchild Zogbaum (1849–1925), of Charleston and N.Y., was an illustrator and author. WWW, vol. 1; DSCB.

8. Samuel Greene Wheeler Benjamin (1837–1914), of Greece, N.Y., and Vt., was an artist and author who wrote numerous books, including *Art in America* (1879). WWW, vol. 1.

9. John Drayton (ca. 1713–1799) was a St. Andrew's parish planter and S.C. representative, whose home, Drayton Hall, was robbed and its residents terrorized by a band of runaway slaves led by one named Caesar from the Dorchester plantation of Daniel Drose. *S.C. & American Gazette*, 13 May 1774:2; DSCB.

10. Christie Benet (1879–1951), an Abbeville and Columbia attorney and U.S. senator, was, in the early years of the twentieth century, the coach of the University of S.C. football team. His wife, Alice Van Y. Haskell Benet, was one of the speakers for the Washington birthday celebration in Maxey Gregg Park, at which Yates Snowden died in 1933. WWW, vol. 3; DSCB; CRA.

11. Edwin Robert Anderson Seligman (1861–1939), a N.Y. economist and educator, was the author of numerous books. COL; WBD.

12. Ambrose Elliott Gonzales (1857–1926) son of Ambrosio José and Harriet Rutledge Elliott Gonzales, was a Columbia newspaper editor, student of Gullah, and author, who co-founded *The State* newspaper. WWW, vol. 1; DSCB; COL.

Chapter 8: 1918

1.   "Austin" was Augustine Thomas Smythe, Jr., Susan Bennett's brother, who married Harriott Ravenel Buist. At the time of John Bennett's death in 1956, "Austin" and Harriott's three sons were pallbearers, and "Austin" was an honorary pallbearer. SSA; CEP, 29 Dec. 1956:1B.

2.   William (Willem) Bosman, b. 1672, sailed to West Africa when he was about sixteen and remained there for fourteen years, becoming the chief factor for the Dutch West India Company at the castle of St. George of Elmina. Bosman's book, *A New and Accurate Description of the Coast of Guinea,* contains twenty-two letters written in 1701 and 1702. Translated from the Dutch, the work appeared in an English edition in 1705. The first twenty letters in his book were written by Bosman, and the last two he included were by the sea-captains David Van Nyendael and John Snoek. The remark referred to by John Bennett was made in the final letter of the volume by Captain John Snoek of the yacht *Johanna Jacoba.* BOS, v–vi, xviii–xix, 491.

3.   F. Asbury Coward, b. 1835, of Charleston, was a Citadel cadet (1851–1854), fought with the Confederate forces, and became principal of the York Military Academy. Colonel Coward served as superintendent of the S.C. Military Academy (The Citadel) for eighteen years. His son, F. Asbury Coward, Jr., b. 1877, of Charleston and Columbia, also attended The Citadel and was a physician, a lecturer in bacteriology at the University of S.C., and a World War I captain. DSCB; CRA; *The Garnet and Black,* 1917; MSC.

4.   Andrew Turnbull (ca. 1718–1792), a Scottish physician, led a group of Greeks and Minorcans to America in 1767 or 1768. They settled on land that had been granted in 1766 to Turnbull on the east coast of Fla., near the Indian River. They chose a site where there were some old Indian shell mounds, a ruined Spanish fort, and a late-seventeenth-century Spanish mission, and called their town New Smyrna. Because Turnbull supported the American Revolution, he lost his land in Fla. Moving to Charleston about 1781, he practiced medicine there until his death. One of his children, Robert James Turnbull, became a well-known political writer. COL; WWWH.

5.   Stanhope Sams, b. 1860, a Greenville and Columbia journalist, was a Spanish-American War correspondent for the *N.Y. Times* and an editor of *The State.* On the day of Yates Snowden's funeral, Sams wrote an editorial tribute to his friend. IMYS, 29–34; HEN, 202, 239; HUN, 242–243.

6.   Charles Colcock Jones, Jr., of Ga., wrote a book of folk stories in Gullah, *Negro Myths from the Ga. Coast* (Boston: Houghton Mifflin & Company, 1888). When it was reprinted by the State Company in 1925, Ambrose Gonzales wrote a review of the volume. BEN, 335.

7.   Francis Marion (1732–1795), a St. John's Berkeley parish and Georgetown planter, S.C. representative and senator, and Revolutionary War general,

was known as the "Swamp Fox." After the war, in 1786, he married Mary Esther Videau, who died in 1815 and was buried beside General Marion at Belle Isle Plantation in St. Stephen's parish. WWWH; MSC.

8. Edward Porter Alexander (1835–1910), of Ga., Columbia, and Georgetown, was an engineer, educator, businessman, planter, and Confederate general. WWW, vol. 1; DSCB.

9. John Leighton Wilson (1809–1886), a Salem (S.C.) editor, author, and translator, was a Presbyterian missionary to West Africa. WWWH.

10. Uncle William was William Trimble McClintock, the brother of John Bennett's mother. See Bennett's letter of 6 July 1926.

11. John Addington Symonds (1840–1893), an English author and translator, wrote several volumes of travel essays, biographies, and verses. COL.

12. John Stuart Mill (1806–1873), an English philosopher, was an economist and author. COL.

13. Herbert Ravenel Sass (1884–1958), the son of George Herbert and Anna Ravenel Sass, was a Charleston author who wrote novels and collaborated with Alice R. Huger Smith on *A Carolina Rice Plantation of the Fifties* (1937) and with DuBose Heyward on *Fort Sumter* (1938). He lived at 23 Legare Street, near John Bennett. WWW, vol. 3.

14. John Bennett enclosed his latest poem, "The Abbot of Derry."

15. Walter Eichelberger of Charleston was a state constable. *Charleston Directory,* 1918.

Chapter 9: 1919–1920

1. Charlotte Reynolds McCord, "Totty," was the daughter of the Rev. Dr. James Lawrence Reynolds (1814–1877), a professor of Belles Lettres and Elocution, then of Sacred Literature, and later of Philosophy at S.C. College; Charlotte was the widow of Langdon Cheves McCord, Mrs. A. T. Smythe's brother, who died of wounds in Richmond during the War Between the States. Langdon Cheves McCord Smythe, "Chimpy," born in 1883 in Charleston, was a Presbyterian missionary in Japan; he and his wife, Mary Fletcher of Va., helped entertain the Bennetts when John and Susan, Cheves's sister, went to the Far East for Jane Bennett's wedding. Augustine Thomas Smythe, Jr., Susan Bennett's brother, was known as "Austin" or "Ocky." David McCord Wright, "Cordite," was the son of Hannah McCord Smythe Wright. Louisa McCord Stoney, "Gary Evans," was Susan Bennett's niece, later referred to as a Navy wife married to William S. Popham, an ensign who rose to the rank of admiral. Louisa Cheves Smythe Stoney, "Loula" or "The Old Woman," was Susan Bennett's sister. And Miss Sarah Ann Smyth, "Taddy," was Susan Bennett's aunt, who lived at 35 Legare Street. DSCB; SSA; SMY; MSC.

2. As Yates Snowden once explained when asked about the poem's title, "Okrantomottis" was the Charleston black street vendor's cry when selling fresh tomatoes and okra from door to door. MSC.

3. Henry Romeike (1855–1903) was the Russian originator of the press clipping bureau, first in Paris, then in London, and later in N.Y. WBD.

4. Charles Coker Wilson, b. 1864, of Hartsville and Columbia, was an architect who designed plans for many large buildings. DSCB.

5. Marcus Antokolski (1843–1902) was a daring and independent Russian sculptor. COL.

6. The three referred to by Bennett are H. A. M. Smith, of Charleston, a U.S. District Judge; John H. Marshall, of Va. and Charleston, a dignified newspaper editor and stock broker; and probably Edward McCreight Moreland, a Charleston stock broker and father of the Episcopal Bishop William Hall Moreland (1861–1946); although, since Bennett sometimes spelled names just as they sounded, Old Moreland might be George Morland (1763–1804), a brilliant English painter who led a dissipated life. COL; *Charleston Directory,* 1878–1913; USE; MSC.

7. Dr. John Johnson, engineer officer of Fort Sumter, wrote *The Defense of Charleston Harbor, 1863–1865,* published in 1890 and often quoted by historians. WAL, 3:163–166; BAR, 400.

8. Charles E. O'Connor was a lawyer in Charleston in 1882, the year that Yates Snowden was admitted to the bar. John Palmer Lockwood, of Charleston, was a phosphate company salesman who wrote *The Gospel in Gullah* under the alias "Rebren Isrel Manigo." When the Gullah sermons were republished by the State Company in 1925, Yates Snowden wrote the introduction. Lockwood's widow, Leize F. B. Lockwood, in 1925 published the musical arrangements of Snowden's "Carolina, Hail!" in two keys. Hartwell M. Ayer was the editor of the Charleston *Evening Post* in 1895. BEN, 335; *Carolina, Hail!* sheet music; *Charleston Directory,* 1882–1913; MSC; IMYS, 45.

9. James Crichton (1560–1582) was a Scottish adventurer who was called "the admirable Crichton" because of his many accomplishments. The use of the term "admirable" in regard to Crichton first occurred in 1603 in *Heroes Scoti* by John Johnston. Stories grew around the legendary figure: a novel about him was written by W. Harrison Ainsworth, and in 1902 Sir James Matthew Barrie used the epithet for the title of one of his plays, *The Admirable Crichton,* to refer to his main character, the butler. EBR, 690; COL, 144, 443.

10. Theodore Dehon Jervey, a Charleston judge and historian who died in 1947, was president of the S.C. Historical Society and the author of historical articles. For thirty-six years, he served as Charleston police recorder. WAL, 1:222; WAL, 2:452; MSC.

11. Sir Fretful Plagiary is the delightful character in Richard Brinsley Sheridan's *The Critic,* who says that he welcomes criticism, but he is greatly offended by it when given, and he accepts none. SHE.

12. Mrs. Thomas Taylor was Sally Cantey Elmore Taylor (1829–1919) who, with Mrs. A. T. Smythe and several other Daughters of the Confederacy, edited and published *S.C. Women in the Confederacy* (Columbia: The State Company, 1903). Yates Snowden wrote the introduction for the book. MSC.

13. Isabella D. Martin, a Columbia teacher and author, kept a school at 1702 Blanding Street, was secretary of the S.C. Monument Association of Columbia, and wrote historical articles. MSC.

14. Beatrice Witte Ravenel (1870–1956), the wife of S. Prioleau Ravenel, was a Charleston writer of poetry, fiction, and criticism. WWW, vol. 3; HUN, 242.

15. Thomas E. Watson (1856–1922), a Ga. attorney, was a U.S. senator. WWW, vol. 1.

16. Richard Smith Whaley (1874–1951), a Charleston attorney, was a S.C. representative and speaker of the House, a U.S. congressman, and chief justice of the U.S. Court of Claims. WWW, vol. 3; DSCB; CRA.

17. William Turner Logan, b. 1874, a Summerville and Charleston attorney, was a S.C. representative and a U.S. representative. WWW, vol. 5; DSCB; CRA.

18. Arthur Hugh Clough (1816–1861), an English poet, was born in Liverpool but spent his early childhood in Charleston, returning to England in 1828. COL; USE.

19. The elder Robert Withers Memminger was the son of Christopher Gustavus Memminger (1803–1888), the secretary of the Confederate treasury, and Mary Withers Wilkinson Memminger. He married Susan Mazÿck, and one of their sons, Robert Withers Memminger, the younger (b. 1867), was a Charleston judge. WWWH; WWW, vol. 1; DSCB.

20. Referring to himself as one who was sullenly obstinate or severely fault-finding, John Bennett sometimes signed his letters with the soubriquet "Sir Pertinax Surly." Pertinax Surly, a character in Ben Jonson's *The Alchemist* (1610), was a sour skeptic who thought he was too astute to be tricked. CYC.

21. James FitzJames Caldwell, b. 1837, a Newberry attorney, author, and aide-de-camp to General Samuel McGowan in the Confederate Army, was married to Rebecca Capers Connor and wrote *History of a Brigade of South Carolinians* (1922), as well as poems. DSCB; CRA; MSC.

22. Edwin DuBose Heyward (1885–1940), a Charleston poet, novelist, and dramatist, probably best known for *Porgy* (1925), was a member of a large

insurance firm and organized the Poetry Society of S.C. with John
Bennett and others. He and his wife, Dorothy Hartzell Kuhns, whom he
married in 1923, collaborated on the dramatization of *Porgy*, which was
produced in 1927 by the Theatre Guild and received the Pulitzer Prize
before being made into the opera *Porgy and Bess*, with music by George
Gershwin. WWW, vol. 1; USE; COL; HUN, 236; DUR, 1, 42.

23. William Stanley Beaumont Braithwaite (1878–1962), a Boston and N.Y.
author, was a poet who compiled and edited anthologies of verse. WWW,
vol. 4.

24. Reginald Bathurst Birch (1856–1943), of England and N.Y., an artist with
St. Nicholas, Harper's, Century, and other publishers, illustrated Frances
Hodgson Burnett's *Little Lord Fauntleroy* and many other works of
fiction, as well as John Bennett's *Master Skylark.* WWW, vol. 2.

25. Josephine Lyons Scott Pinckney (1895–1957), a Charleston writer and
one of the founders of the Poetry Society of S.C., is perhaps best known
for her book of poems, *Sea-Drinking Cities* (1927) and the novel, *Three
O'Clock Dinner* (1945). WWW, vol. 3; DSCB.

26. Frank Ravenel Frost, b. 1863, a Society Hill and Charleston attorney and
businessman, once practiced law with Augustine T. Smythe and A.
Markley Lee in the firm of Smythe, Lee, and Frost. He owned one of the
finest libraries in the state, having inherited over two thousand volumes
from his father, E. Horry Frost. Frank Frost was the first president of the
Poetry Society of S.C. and served as secretary-treasurer and librarian of
the S.C. Historical Society. DSCB; *Charleston Directory,* 1900; MSC.

27. Abraham Ben Meir ibn Ezra (1092–1167) was a Spanish poet, philoso-
pher, physician, astronomer, and traveler, who by the shortened name of
Rabbi Ben Ezra spoke as the old master to a younger person in Robert
Browning's dramatic monologue of the same name. WBD; COL.

28. William Hervey Allen, b. 1889, a Pa. novelist and poet, taught English in
Charleston in the 1920s, collaborated with DuBose Heyward on *Carolina
Chansons* in 1922, had *Israfel,* his biography of Edgar Allan Poe, pub-
lished in 1926, and became widely known for his historical novel,
Anthony Adverse, in 1933. COL; WBD.

Chapter 10: 1921

1. John Beaufain Irving (1825–1877) was a Charleston artist of historical
scenes and portraits. John Beaufain Irving, the elder (1800–1881), was a
Charleston physician who wrote *A Day on Cooper River,* which was
published by A. E. Miller in 1842, and later edited and enlarged by Louisa
Cheves Smythe Stoney and published under the auspices of St. John's
Hunting Club by the R. L. Bryan Company in 1932. WWWH; DSCB;
MSC.

2. Edwin Luther Green (1870–1948) was a professor of Ancient Languages, who wrote *A History of the University of S.C.,* and was with the University Press in 1921. Green helped write the faculty memorial to Yates Snowden (5 April 1933) with R. L. Meriwether and Reed Smith. IMYS, 59–64.

3. Dr. Samuel W. Woodhouse, Jr., was curator of the Pa. Museum. MSC.

4. William Henry Trescot (1822–1898), a Charleston historian, lawyer, orator, and diplomat, served as a S.C. representative, a Confederate negotiator with Britain, and from 1877 to 1889 as a U.S. special envoy in transactions with Canada, China, Central America, and South America. WWWH; N&C, 22 May 1921:2.

5. James Dunwoody Brownson DeBow (1820–1867), a Charleston, La., and N.J. journal editor and statistician, was editor of the *Southern Quarterly Review* (1844–1845), and founder of the *Commercial Review of the South and Southwest,* later known as *DeBow's Review* (1846–1867). In the 1850s DeBow was director of the National Census. WWWH; DSCB; N&C, 22 May 1921:2.

6. John McCrady (1831–1881), a Charleston, Boston, and Tenn. naturalist and military engineer, served as a major with the Confederate engineers and taught mathematics at the College of Charleston, zoology at Harvard with the Swiss naturalist Louis Agassiz, and biology at the University of the South. DSCB; N&C, 22 May 1921:8.

7. John Howard Payne (1792–1852), a N.Y. actor, playwright, and diplomat, was appointed American consul at Tunis in 1841. Payne, perhaps best known as the author of "Home, Sweet Home," died in Africa, far from home, almost seventy years before John Bennett's feigned meeting with the writer in the whimsical exile letter. USE.

8. Joseph Walker Barnwell (1846–1930), of Charleston and Beaufort, was an attorney, historian, S.C. representative, and S.C. senator. He fought in the War Between the States as a Citadel Cadet and, in later years, served as an officer of the Charleston Library Society and of the St. Cecilia Society. He wrote articles for the *S.C. Historical and Genealogical Magazine* and was president of the S.C. Historical Society (1903–1930). DSCB; CRA; BAR, 268, 272–275.

9. Ferdinand Foch (1851–1929) was the marshal of France who was made commander-in-chief of the British, French, and American armies in 1918, and was responsible for the final Allied victory. COL; WBD; USE.

Chapter 11: 1922

1. James Otey Reed (1846–1922), a Beaufort district and St. George educator and businessman, served as private secretary to C. G. Memminger, treasurer of the Confederacy, and later as a volunteer with the Hampton Legion. After the war, he held several public offices, among them mayor

of St. George. Reed's daughter, Lucy, was married to Kirkman Finlay. WAL, 4:278–279; MSC.

2.   "Angus McGlockity Fergus McKlintock" is a teasing reference to the pseudonym, "Alexander Findlay McClintock," used by John Bennett in writing verses for the Sunday *State.* In his 23 June 1922 reply, Bennett jokingly alludes to the sobriquet as "Alexander Fergus Aeneas MacGillicuddy of that ilk."

3.   Forrest Hampton Wells, son of Mr. and Mrs. George T. Wells of Booneville, Ind., graduated from the U.S. Naval Academy in 1921. He was an ensign when he and Jane Bennett became engaged. They were married in Manila on 1 November 1923, at the Cathedral of St. Mary and St. John. Manila, P.I., *Sunday Times,* 4 Nov. 1923.

4.   Charles Graham Dunlap, professor of English at Kans. State University, was born in 1858 in Chillicothe, Ohio. WWW, vol. 1.

5.   Henry Ravenel Dwight, of Pinopolis, a cousin and close friend of Yates Snowden, was well-known for his interest in history and his participation in the Huguenot Society of S.C. He was secretary of the St. John's Hunting Club when the members decided to republish J. B. Irving's *A Day on Cooper River.* In 1933 he attended Snowden's funeral. TRA, no. 38:8; IMYS, 16; MSC.

6.   Isaac de Chérigny Porcher, who died in 1933 at age 74, was a direct descendant of the Huguenot emigrés Isaac and Claude Chérigny Porcher. I. deC. Porcher lived in Pinopolis and was the Berkeley county superintendent of schools. Of unmixed Huguenot blood, he portrayed his ancestor, the emigré, in Danny Reed's *Hail, S.C.,* the state historical pageant in which Snowden appeared as History. BAI, 2:105; MSC.

7.   Ludwig Lewisohn (1883–1955), of Germany, Charleston, Ohio, and N.Y., an educator, editor, and author who received his undergraduate and graduate degrees from the College of Charleston, deprecated most Southerners, especially writers. W. W. Ball said of Lewisohn's article, "S.C.: A Lingering Fragrance," that it was "exquisitely written—rot." Later, in *Cities and Men* (N.Y.: Harper & Brothers Publishers, 1927, p. 86), Lewisohn referred to Snowden: "Dear Yates Snowden, antiquary, poet, scholar, used to tell the most amazing anecdotes of Simms and of the old Carolinian gentry and in the same breath and with equal sincerity utter the sentiments of a schoolgirl. . . . Everyone was seemly and noble and loyal. . . . an unreconstructed Confederate . . . ." On another occasion, in an article that appeared in the *Nation,* Lewisohn called Snowden "the last gentleman in S.C." WWW, vol. 3; MSC.

8.   Charles Wesley Bain (1864–1915), a Va., Ky., Tenn., S.C., and N.C. college professor, received an L.L.D. degree in 1913 from the University of S.C., where he had taught ancient languages (1898–1910) prior to becoming professor of Greek at the University of N.C. He married Isabel Plummer in 1891. WWW, vol. 1; MSC.

9. Isaac Edward Holmes (1796–1867), a Charleston and Calif. attorney, who wrote under the pseudonym "George Taletell," was a S.C. representative and a U.S. congressman. WWWH; DSCB.

10. William Crofts, Henry T. Farmer, and Edwin C. Holland were the authors of *Omnium Botherum,* an answer to Thomas Bee's *Omnium Gatherum.* Thomas Bee (1725–1812), a Charleston lawyer, Continental congressman, S.C. representative, member of the Revolutionary War Council of Safety, and a U.S. District judge, was educated in his native city and at Oxford. William Bee, also of Charleston, was the schoolmaster of the S.C. Society. In his 31 July 1922 letter, Snowden confuses Thomas with William. WWWH; *Charleston Directory,* 1819.

11. Ambrose Elliott Gonzales, with his two sisters and three brothers (Narciso Gener [1858–1903], of Edisto Island and Columbia, who was editor of *The State* when he was killed by Ben Tillman's nephew; William Elliott [1866–1937], of Charleston and Columbia, who was editor of *The State* and the first U.S. ambassador to Peru; and Alphonso Beauregard, an accomplished raconteur to whom Ambrose dedicated *Laguerre*), was reared at Oak Lawn plantation by maiden aunts—Anne, and Emily Elliott. Although the home, with its fine library and famous experimental gardens, had been destroyed during the War Between the States, Ambrosio José Gonzales brought his children to Oak Lawn after his wife, Harriet Rutledge Elliott, died of yellow fever in Cuba in 1870. WWW, vol. 1; DSCB; CRA; WAL, 3:412–414; BAR, 147–148; LAT, 64, 138, 394.

12. This "Old Bee" was William Bee, fl. 1819, the S.C. Society schoolmaster in Charleston. *Charleston Directory,* 1819.

13. "Smelfungus" was the pseudonym that Yates Snowden often used in writing letters to newspapers. It was the name that Laurence Sterne, the British priest and author, called George Tobias Smollett, the Scottish novelist and surgeon, because of Smollett's captious and faultfinding criticism in *Travels Through France and Italy* (1766). OED.

14. Charles Wilson Kollock (1857–1931), a Cheraw and Charleston surgeon and educator, was a professor at the S.C. Medical College. WWW, vol. 1; DSCB; CRA.

15. Harriet Horry Rutledge Ravenel (1832–1912), whose *Charleston, the Place and the People* was published in 1906, was the wife of St. Julien Ravenel (1819–1882), a Charleston physician and agricultural chemist. WWWH.

16. Francis Kinloch (1755–1826), of Charleston and Prince George's parish, was an attorney, planter, Revolutionary War officer, S.C. representative, and U.S. Continental congressman. WWWH; DSCB.

17. Dr. James Killpatrick, who lived in the eighteenth century, introduced into S.C. inoculation for smallpox after a son died of the disease raging

in Charles Town in 1738. According to A. S. Salley, Jr., Killpatrick changed his name to Kirkpatrick when he went to England. MSC; WAL, 1:408.

18.   John Lining (1708-1760), of Scotland and Charleston, was a physician and a judge. WWWH; DSCB.

19.   Henry Augustus Middleton (1770-1887), of Charleston and Prince George's parish, was an attorney and planter. DSCB.

20.   William Henry Timrod (1792-1838), of Germany and Charleston, was the father of the Poet Laureate Henry Timrod, and an editor and a poet himself. WWWH.

21.   Henry Holcomb Bennett (1863-1924), John Bennett's brother, two years his senior, was a Chillicothe (Ohio) writer and artist. WWW, vol. 1.

22.   Henry Clarence Pitz (1895-1976), a Philadelphia artist, was the illustrator of over 160 books and numerous magazine stories, earning many awards. WWW, vol. 7.

Chapter 12: 1923

1.   William Ashley Sunday (1863-1935), the flamboyant Iowa evangelist, was a professional baseball player and assistant secretary of the Chicago Y.M.C.A. before he began preaching sermons in 1896. He became a Presbyterian minister in 1903. USE.

2.   Alfred Moore Rhett (1829-1889), a Beaufort and Charleston planter and Confederate officer, was publicly insulted in 1861, when he was a first lieutenant at Fort Moultrie, by his commanding officer of the First S.C. Artillery, Captain W. Ransom Calhoun. Rhett invited a challenge, but Calhoun refused to call Rhett out until September 1862, after his friend Arnoldus Vander Horst, a month earlier, lavishly praised Calhoun, now a colonel, in the presence of Rhett, now a major in command of Fort Sumter. Vander Horst himself challenged Rhett. The outcome was bloodless, because Rhett refused to kill Vander Horst, aiming his second shot into the air. Calhoun's challenge stated that their duel must be to the finish. When Rhett killed Calhoun, he was cleared of blame by a Court of Inquiry and, shortly thereafter, promoted to colonel. BAR, 171; WAL, 3:95-97.

3.   Danny Reed (fl. 1920s), who was stationed at Camp Jackson at the close of World War I, founded the Town Theatre on Sumter Street in Columbia and was its first director. MSC.

4.   Elizabeth W. (Mrs. Arthur L.) Jones, as president of the Pen Club, wrote Professor Snowden requesting him to speak to her group when he came to Charleston. He graciously accepted the invitation. MSC.

5.   Dr. Christian Frederick Schwettmann (1828-1894), of Germany and Charleston, served as an apothecary in the Confederate Army and, after

the war, operated the Charleston pharmacy that had first opened in 1780. He filled prescriptions with precision and skill for many years and in 1872 he helped organize the S.C. Pharmaceutical Association. His son, Dr. Frederick William Schwettmann, graduated from the Medical College of S.C. and took over the shop after his father's death. With the same scrupulous thoroughness as his father, William continued the business until he died in 1915. WAL, 4:624–625.

6. Laura Mary Bragg (1881–1978) was director of the Charleston Museum (1920–1931) and of the Bershire (Mass.) Museum (1931–1939). S.C. Historical Society, Charleston, S.C.

7. Thomas Porcher Stoney, a cotton merchant of St. Louis, Missouri, was the son of Samuel David and Harriet Porcher Gaillard Stoney and the brother of Samuel Gaillard Stoney, Sr. SSA; Huguenot Society of S.C. records.

Chapter 13: 1924–1925

1. Janie Screven DuBose (Mrs. Edwin Watkins) Heyward, b. 1864, mother of DuBose Heyward, was the author of poems and of a book of Gullah stories, *Brown Jackets* (1923). DUR, 3–4, 59.

2. James Henry Rice, Jr. (1868–1935), of Abbeville county and Wiggins (S.C.), was a naturalist, editor, author, and translator. He wrote many articles for magazines and newspapers and served as president and treasurer of the Conservation Society of S.C. WWW, vol. 1; MSC.

3. Isadore Schayer was a Columbia physician for many years and a member of the University faculty. A major, he was a regimental surgeon in the S.C. National Guard. STA: 23 July 1922; IMYS, 15.

4. William Porcher Miles (1822–1899), of Walterboro, Charleston, Va., and La., was an attorney, planter, president of the University of N.C., C.S.A. representative, and U.S. representative. W. P. Miles owned an extensive library of over 3,000 volumes. WWW, vol. 1; DSCB; MSC.

5. William Mazÿck Porcher (1812–1902), a St. Stephen's parish planter and a S.C. representative, was the model for Snowden's Huguenot gentleman, who espoused the Southern cause from first to last. His motto as stated in "A Carolina Bourbon," first published in 1886 in *The Southern Bivouac*, was "Loyal je serai durant ma vie." In January 1890, about a month after the death of Jefferson Davis, a prose tribute by Snowden to W. M. Porcher, "The Dirge in the Pines," appeared in *The News and Courier*. Having been forced by Union soldiers with fixed bayonets to watch while others, under orders, burned his ancestral home, Mazyck Porcher never forgot. His hopes for a fair Constitutional government were gone forever, and, over twenty-four years later, on 11 December 1889, the day of the funeral of the president of the Confederacy, the old man in his late seventies paid the lost cause a final tribute by tolling the bells of the little,

old Episcopal church in Pineville. DSCB; MSC.

6. Wilie Jones, b. 1850, was a N.C. and Columbia banker and planter. WWW, vol. 4; DSCB; CRA.

7. The daughters of Judge John Faucheraud Grimké, Sarah Moore Grimké (1792–1873) and Angelina Emily Grimké (1805–1879) of Charleston, were noted abolitionists and reformers who moved to the North. Angelina married Theodore Dwight Weld, an abolitionist and schoolmaster. WWWH; DSCB; COL; WAL, 2:496.

8. Colonel Isaac Hayne (1745–1781), a Colleton district planter, S.C. representative and senator, and Revolutionary War officer, was hanged by the British. After being ordered to join the British Army, in violation of the terms of the oath of allegiance he had sworn to the Crown after the fall of Charles Town, he rejoined the S.C. Militia. When captured in July, Hayne was imprisoned. In August, he was executed. WWWH; DSCB; WAL, 2:283–286.

9. James Butler Campbell (1808–1883), of Maine, Charleston, and Edisto Island, was an educator, attorney, S.C. representative and senator, and U.S. senator. DSCB.

10. Sophianisba Russell McCord, who died in 1784, was the widow of John McCord, who died in 1768. Her oldest living son was John (1757–1785), a captain in the American forces led by Thomas Sumter. Her youngest son was Russell (born ca. 1765), who married Hannah Turquand. Russell and Hannah were the parents of David James McCord and Susan Bennett's great-grandparents. SCHM, 34:177–193.

11. "Telfair, Jr." was Louise Jones (Mrs. W. Howard) DuBose (1901–1989), a Ga. and Columbia editor and author, who wrote under the pen name "Nancy Telfair." DSCB.

12. Edward Frost Parker (1867–1938), a Charleston physician and educator, was a professor at the S.C. Medical College. WWW, vol. 1; DSCB; CRA.

13. Basil Lanneau Gildersleeve (1831–1924), a Charleston, Va., and Md. classical scholar, served in the Confederate Cavalry, founded and edited the *American Journal of Philology*, was a professor of Greek at the University of Va. for twenty years and at Johns Hopkins University for thirty-two years, and wrote numerous Latin and Greek texts. COL; WBD; HUN, 37–41, 232.

14. Francis Pendleton Gaines (1892–1963), of Due West (S.C.), N.C., and Va., was president of Wake Forest (1927–1930), president of Washington and Lee University (1930–1959), and then chancellor (1959–1963), as well as the author of several books. WWW, vol. 4.

15. William Tecumseh Sherman (1820–1891), a Union Army general, who devastated much of Ga. and S.C. in his march through the South, including the burning of Columbia, was stationed before the War Be-

tween the States at Fort Moultrie, Charleston, and did not include in his personal vendetta the city where the first shot of the conflict was fired. WWWH; WAL, 3:202–215; MSC.

16. William Elliott (1872–1943), of Beaufort and Columbia, son of the congressman Colonel William Elliott and Sarah Means Stuart Elliott, was an attorney, president of the State Company, and publisher of *The State*. He was married to Leila G. Sams. WWW, vol. 2; DSCB; CRA.

17. Margaret Widdemer, of Pa. and N.Y., who died in 1978, was an award-winning author, who wrote poetry, short stories, and essays, as well as many books. WWW, vol. 7.

18. Robert Bee Lebby (1865–1927), a Charleston businessman married to Snowden's cousin, Hess Waring Mikell, was vice-president and treasurer of Bailey-Lebby, a machinery and supplies company. DSCB; CRA.

19. Katherine Lee Bates (1859–1929), a Mass. college professor of literature, who taught at Dana Hall and at Wellesley College, wrote "America the Beautiful." WWW, vol. 1.

20. The Reverend William Way, b. 1876, a N.C. and Charleston Episcopal clergyman, was rector of Grace Episcopal Church, Charleston. During 1919 and 1920, Way wrote a centennial history of the New England Society of Charleston, of which he was president. WWW, vol. 5; DSCB; CRA; MSC.

21. The Reverend Peter J. Shand, of Charleston and Columbia, who was rector of Trinity Episcopal Church for 54 years, died in 1886. Although the church was not destroyed during the War Between the States, a trunk containing the communion silver was forcibly taken from Mr. Shand by General Sherman's soldiers; and the parsonage and the Sunday-school building were burned to the ground. The silver was never recovered. THO, 538–540.

22. Stephen Elliott, Jr. (1804–1866), of Beaufort, Charleston, Columbia, and Ga., was an attorney, planter, college professor, and Episcopal Bishop. His father, Stephen Elliott, Sr. (1771–1830), a Beaufort and Charleston botanist, author, and S.C. representative and senator, was the founder and editor of *The Southern Quarterly Review*. Elliott College, built in 1838 on the University of S.C. Horseshoe, is named for the senior Elliott. DSCB; BAR, 50–51, 64–67.

23. Hugh Swinton Legaré (1797–1843), of Charleston and John's Island, was an attorney, journal editor, S.C. representative, U.S. representative, and U.S. official and diplomat. DSCB; HUN, 237; BAR, 64, 129, 156.

24. Floyd Collins (1887–1925), a Ky. farmer, onyx miner, and cave explorer, who discovered Crystal Cave in 1917, was looking for a new entrance and tunnels joining the Flint Ridge System with Mammoth Cave when he was trapped in Sand Cave on 30 January 1925. He was found, but amid much confusion, along with dissension over rescue methods, misinformation in

the press, government intervention, and even a court of inquiry, no one was able to get him out. Collins remained alive for over a week; a collapse of the passageway ended direct communication with him. When reached through a parallel shaft on 16 February, he was found dead. The shaft was filled in, and it was April before his body was removed. The entrapment was followed avidly by all the media, and "The Death of Floyd Collins" became a well-known ballad. Not until 1972 was the interconnection of the caves proved. MUR; NEB, 4:835.

25. Colin McCrae Grant, fl. 1745, of Scotland and Charleston, was a Presbyterian minister. DSCB.

26. John Schreiner Reynolds (1848–1909) was the author of *Reconstruction in S.C., 1865–1877* (Columbia, S.C.: The State Company, 1905).

27. James Henry Carlisle (1825–1909), a Winnsboro and Spartanburg educator, was a mathematician and president of Wofford College. WWW, vol. 1; DSCB.

28. William Davis Melton (1868–1926), a Chester and Columbia attorney, was president of the University of S.C. WWW, vol. 1.

29. John Ray, b. 1815, was an English artist of Sunderland, county Durham, who painted portraits. HAL, 54; WOO, 387.

30. Frederick Henry Koch (1877–1944), of Ky., Ill., N.D., and N.C., was a professor of dramatics who organized the theater group Sock and Buskin at the University of N.D. and the Carolina Playmakers at the University of N.C., where he taught from 1918 until his death. Koch influenced the development of outdoor historical plays. WWW, vol. 2; DABS.

31. Thomas Smith Bryan, b. 1856, a Charleston and Columbia businessman, succeeded his uncle as president of R. L. Bryan Company. DSCB; CRA.

32. Marcellus Seabrook Whaley, b. 1855, a Charleston and Columbia lawyer, was a Richland county court judge and president of the Columbia Art Association. His book, *The Old Types Pass: Gullah Sketches of the Carolina Sea Islands,* was published in 1925 in Boston by the Christopher Publishing House. DSCB.

Chapter 14: 1926

1. May Snowden, Yates Snowden's sister, was also known as Maria L. Snowden, the secretary and later chairman of the board of the Confederate Home. May's legal name, according to her mother's will, was Amarintha Lois Snowden. She was unmarried and still lived in Charleston at the time of her brother's death. *Charleston Directory,* 1900, 1932; IMYS, 8; MSC.

2. Franklin Brevard Hayne, b. 1858, of Charleston and La., was a cotton broker and businessman. DSCB.

3. Robert Young Hayne (1791–1839), of Charleston and St. Paul's parish,

was an attorney, S.C. representative, S.C. governor, and U.S. senator. WWWH; DSCB.

4. Francis Asbury (1745–1816), of England and America, the first Methodist Episcopal bishop consecrated in the U.S., established the Circuit Rider system and personally supervised the work of the church throughout the original thirteen states and in the West, travelling over 5,000 miles every year and keeping a journal of his life, as well as a valuable account of contemporary society. COL.

5. Eleanor Van Sweringen Worthington, who was a kinswoman of John Bennett, was the wife of Thomas Worthington (1773–1827), a surveyor, governor of Ohio, and U.S. senator. WWWH.

6. Andrew Williamson (ca. 1730–1786), of Scotland, Ninety-Six district, and St. Paul's parish, was a planter, merchant, S.C. representative, and Revolutionary War brigadier general in the S.C. Militia. Accused of treason after the fall of Charleston to the British, he was captured by Isaac Hayne, but the charge was not proved, and he was not harmed. WWWH; DSCB; WAL, 2:284–285.

7. James Adger (1777–1858), of Ireland and Charleston, came to America in 1793. He first established a hardware store; then the James Adger and Company, Charleston agents for the world bankers; and later Adger Warves and a steamship line between N.Y. and Charleston. His daughter Margaret married Thomas Smyth, D.D.; they were the parents of Augustine T. Smythe, Susan Bennett's father. SSA; Richard Wright Simpson, *History of Old Pendleton District* (Anderson, S.C.: Oulla Printing & Binding Company, 1913), 123–124.

8. During the night of the torching of Columbia by Sherman's forces in February 1865, when the Leland home on Gervais Street where the Snowdens were staying was on fire, Snowden's mother sent him, along with his little sister, his aunt, and his aged grandmother to the home of Dr. John Fisher and his wife, Jane Tucker Fisher, thinking they would be safer there. As they tried to make their way through the streets where Union Army men were setting fires, one soldier from Ohio came to their aid, escorting them the rest of the way to the Fishers' house at the corner of Henderson and Plain (renamed Hampton Street in the early 1900s). Snowden related this personal experience when speaking in June of 1926, at the Ursuline graduation exercises. Most of his speech concerned the well-documented account of the burning of the Ursuline Convent that night in spite of pleas to General Sherman. STA: 13 June 1926; *Columbia Directory,* 1859–1910; MSC.

9. Bernard Manning, fl. 1920, of Sumter county and Spartanburg, was a stock broker. DSCB.

10. Isaac Ridgeway Trimble (1802–1888), of Va. and Md., was an engineer, U.S. Army officer, and Confederate Army general. His first wife was Maria Presstman, and his second, her sister Ann. He was the brother of

John Bennett's grandmother, Charity Trimble McClintock. Wounded so severely at Gettysburg that his leg had to be amputated, Trimble could not be removed with the Confederate forces and had to be left in the hands of the enemy, by whom he was imprisoned. FRE, 3:195; WWWH.

11. Benson John Lossing (1813–1891), of N.Y., was a wood engraver, an editor, and the author of *Pictorial Files Book of the Revolution* (2 vols., 1850–52). WWWH.

12. Laurence Manning (ca. 1756–1804), of Pa. and Claremont, was a Revolutionary War soldier, planter, and S.C. representative. DSCB.

13. John Yates Beall (1835–1865), of Va., was a Confederate Army and Navy officer who was hanged at Fort Lafayette, N.Y., on charges of espionage, in spite of requests for clemency from Governor John Albion Andrew of Mass. and Thaddeus Stevens of Pa. WWWH.

14. Parentheses here and in the rest of this letter show changes and additions made by Bennett in another copy in the collection. MSC.

15. Mary Hutchinson Smyth was the wife of James Adger Smyth, II, son of Ellison Adger and Julia Gambrill Smyth. Adger was Susan Bennett's first cousin. SSA.

16. Henry Bellamann (1882–1945), a Missouri, Columbia, and N.Y. author and musician, was dean of the School of Fine Arts at Chicora College for Women in Columbia (1907–1924), chairman of the Examining Board of the Julliard Music Foundation (1924–1926), with Vassar College (1928–1929), and dean of the Curtis Institute of Music (1931–1932). In July of 1921 he won *The State's* short-story contest, in which Yates Snowden was one of the judges. Bellamann later served as literary editor of *The State* (1923–1933). WWW, vol. 2; MSC.

17. Joseph Brown Ladd (1764–1786), a R.I. and Charleston physician and the author of *The Poems of Arouet* (1786), used the surname of Voltaire (François Marie Arouet) in writing his works. The young doctor gave the 1785 Fourth of July oration in Charleston at the invitation of Governor William Moultrie. At age 22, Ladd was killed in a duel. *The Literary Remains of Joseph Brown Ladd*, collected by Elizabeth Ladd Haskins. Introduction by W. B. Chittenden (N.Y.: H. C. Sleight, Clinton Hall, 1832); WWWH.

18. Mr. Godwin was a comedian who came from Jamaica to America in 1779 to join an acting company. With another member of the troupe, he built Savannah, Ga.'s first theatre, and then moved on to Charleston, where he erected just beyond the city wall a small playhouse, which he named Harmony Hall. Charleston's new, and its first post-Revolutionary, theatre opened 11 July 1786, with a program that included the exhibition of paintings of ancient and modern heads, with an accompanying lecture by Mr. Godwin between the acts of a musical concert. WIL, 84, 103, 107–110.

19. Davidson McDowell Douglas (1869–1931), of Fairfield county, N.C.,

Md., Clinton, and Columbia, was a Presbyterian minister, president of Presbyterian College, and president of the University of S.C. WWW, vol. 1; DSCB; CRA.

Chapter 15: 1927

1. Elizabeth O'Neill (Mrs. E. Pettigrew) Verner (1883–1979), a Charleston artist, author, and lecturer, was known especially for her etchings and pastels of Lowcountry life. Snowden's remarks at the opening of Art Week in Columbia on both Elizabeth Verner and Alice Huger Smith were noted in the *Charleston Evening Post* on 26 February 1927. WWW, vol. 7; DSCB; MSC.

2. Thomas Richard Waring (1871–1935), a Charleston newspaperman, was the long-time editor of the *Evening Post,* as well as president of the Poetry Society of S.C. His wife was Laura Campbell Witte. WWW, vol. 1; DSCB; CRA; MSC.

3. John Bachman (1790–1874), a N.Y. and Charleston Lutheran minister and naturalist, founded S.C.'s Lutheran Theological Seminary and collaborated with Audubon in his volumes of birds and animals. Dr. Bachman's fine library was lost during the War Between the States. WWWH; DSCB; MSC.

4. David G. Dwight, b. 1871, a Winnsboro and Charleston educator and manufacturer, married to Susan Chisolm, was manager and treasurer of McCabe Fertilizer Company and was commandant of Porter Military Academy. DSCB; CRA.

5. Samuel Lapham, Jr. (1892–1972), a Charleston architect, collaborated with Albert Simons on several other books and contributed articles to architectural and historical journals. WWW, vol. 5.

6. These lines are from Henry Wadsworth Longfellow's "The Ladder of Saint Augustine."

7. The Mrs. John Marshall referred to by Yates Snowden was probably Mildred R. Marshall, the wife of John H. Marshall (b. 1865), a Va. and Charleston newspaper editor and stock broker, who was the city editor of *The News and Courier* in the 1890s and early 1900s. DSCB; *Charleston Directory,* 1898–1903.

8. Frank Lebby Stanton (1857–1927), a Charleston and Atlanta journalist and poet, was on the staff of the *Atlanta Constitution.* Stanton was Ga.'s Poet Laureate and the author of "Mighty Lak a Rose" and "Just A-wearying for You, " as well as Snowden's favorite, "St. Michael's Bells." WWW, vol. 1; DSCB; MSC.

9. James Clement Furman (1809–1891), of Charleston and Greenville, was a Baptist minister and the president of Furman University. He was the son of Richard Furman (1755–1825), a N.Y. and Charleston Baptist

minister and educator, who founded the college in Greenville and was also a founder of George Washington University. WWWH; DSCB.

10. Julien Green, born in 1900 in Paris of American parents, served in World War I, first as a Red Cross ambulance driver and later as a French soldier. After the war he attended the University of Va. In 1922 Green returned to Paris, where he became a painter before publishing his first novel in 1924. When France was occupied during World War II, he came to America, where he remained until the Germans surrendered in 1945. He served in the American Army before being transferred to the Office of War Information. The celebrated author of more than forty books, Julien Green was elected to the Académie Française in 1971, the only American ever to be so honored. USE; Book Cover of *God's Fool: The Life and Times of Francis of Assisi* (San Francisco: Harper & Row, 1987); Julien Green, *Oeuvres Complètes,* Vols. 1-6 (Gallimard, 1972-1990).

11. Andrew Charles Moore, b. 1866, a Spartanburg county and Columbia biologist, was a University of S.C. professor, dean, and acting president. He compiled a list of the college alumni in seven volumes in 1905. CRA; SCA.

Chapter 16: 1928

1. Oscar Lovell Keith was a professor of Romance languages at the University of S.C. and a Phi Beta Kappa officer. He was married to Frances Guignard Gibbes, an author of plays and poems. HUN, 231.

2. Ellison Adger Smyth, II (1863-1941) was the son of James Adger and Annie Briggs Smyth and was married to Grace C. Allan. A biologist and educator, he taught at the University of S.C. and Va. Polytechnic Institute. He wrote a biographical sketch and an estimate of the works of John Bennett for the *Library of Southern Literature.* WWW, vol. 1; SSA; HUN, 228.

3. William Elliott (1788-1863), of Beaufort, who wrote *Carolina Sports by Land and Water* (Charleston, 1846), was the father of four sons and five daughters, including Harriet Rutledge Elliott Gonzales. In addition to being an author, this William Elliott was the mayor of Beaufort, entertained LaFayette, and was a Unionist. BAR, 59-60, 68, 145-146; HUN, 21-24, 231; MSC.

4. Paul Warley (1751-1807), of St. Matthew's parish and St. John's Berkeley parish, a kinsman of Annie Snowden, was a planter and a S.C. representative. DSCB.

5. Randell W. McBryde, of the Chattanooga (Tenn.) real-estate firm of McBryde & Reeder, was an old friend of Yates Snowden and often corresponded with both Snowden and John Bennett. Some of the letters are to be found in the South Caroliniana Library.

6. Logan, called John or James (ca. 1725-1780), was a Mingo chief whose

Indian name was Tah-gah-jute. He supported the whites until his family
was massacred by settlers on the banks of the Ohio in 1774, at which time
he began his vengeful raids. His refusal to sign a treaty at the end of Lord
Dunmore's War or to attend a council was delivered in an eloquent
speech. WWWH; COL.

Chapter 17: 1929

1. Hannah (Nannie) Turquand Wright, the daughter of Anton Pope and
   Hannah McCord Smythe Wright, was Susan Bennett's niece. SSA.

2. William Morrison Robinson, Jr. (1891–1965), a Ga. and Fla. historian,
   wrote several military and religious works including *The Confederate
   Privateers*. WWW, vol. 4.

3. John McClintock, a Northern soldier, was the son of John Bennett's
   Uncle William, his mother's brother, and also the great-nephew of Isaac
   Ridgeway Trimble, the gallant Confederate general. MSC.

4. George Michael Bedinger (1756–1843), a Va. and Ky. army officer in the
   Revolution, represented Bourbon county in the Ky. legislature and his
   state in the U.S. congress. WWWH.

5. Daniel Bedinger Lucas (1836–1909), a Va. and W.V. judge and Confederate Army officer, wrote several books, including *Memoir of John Yates
   Beall* (1865). WWW, vol. 1.

6. David Hunter (1802–1886), a Union Army general, commanded the
   Department of the South in 1862 and later was president of the military
   commission that tried those accused of conspiracy in the assassination of
   Abraham Lincoln. COL; WBD.

7. Alexander Robinson Boteler (1815–1892), of Shepherdstown (W.V.), was
   a U.S. representative, C.S.A. congressman, and U.S. Department of
   Justice assistant attorney. WWWH.

8. Henry Bedinger (1812–1858), of Shepherdstown (W.V.), was a U.S.
   congressman and Charge d'Affaires to Denmark. WWWH.

9. Danske Bedinger Dandridge, b. 1858, a Denmark, N.Y., and
   Shepherdstown (W.V.) author, was the daughter of Henry and Caroline
   Lawrence Bedinger. She wrote both poetry and historical accounts.
   WWW, vol. 4.

10. Langdon Cheves, V, to whom Bennett refers here was the son of Henry
    Charles and Langdon Cheves McCord Cheves. He was Susan Bennett's
    first cousin. Langdon, who died in 1923, was an ensign in the U.S. Navy
    during World War I. SSA; SMY; SCHM, 34:190; SCHM, 35:79–95.

11. John Bethea, called Devil John or Sweat Swamp John, was the one
    credited with killing the Tory Snowden during the Revolutionary War.

Other Betheas who fought as Patriots were William Bethea and Buck Swamp John Bethea. Philip Y. Bethea and Power W. Bethea's *Genealogy of the Bethea Family of the South* (Columbia: The State Company, 1926) 6–8; GRE, 393–394.

12. The Right Reverend Alexander Gregg (1819–1893), of Society Hill, Cheraw, and Tex., was an attorney, an Episcopal priest and bishop, and an author. WWWH; DSCB.

13. Captain Jenkins probably was John Jenkins (1750–1814), of St. Helena's parish, who was a S.C. representative. DSCB.

14. Philander Chase (1775–1852), a native of N.H., became the first Episcopal bishop of Ohio and was later the bishop of Ill. and the presiding bishop of the Episcopal Church. In addition, he was president of Cincinnati College and of Kenyon College, which he founded. WWWH.

15. Korah, the son of Izhar and great-grandson of Levi, who along with his company of Levites, had been excluded from the office of priesthood, nursed his grievance until he finally led an unsuccessful rebellion against Moses and Aaron in the Wilderness. SMI.

16. Anak was a race of giants mentioned in the Old Testament (Joshua 14:15). SMI.

17. William Steen Gaud, Jr. (1907–1977), a N.Y. City and Charleston lawyer and association executive, and his brother Henry, who both attended Yale at the same time as Jack Bennett, were the sons of William S. and Isabel Cleland Gaud. WWW, vol. 7.

18. Eliza Crawley Murden, a Charleston housewife, was the author of *Miscellaneous Poems* (Charleston, S.C.: Philip Hoff, 1826), which contained a poem on the death of Juliana Mayer. Eliza also included in her book verses about and by her daughters, Victoria and Octavia. Victoria Murden was the author of a children's book, *Little Dora* (George S. Appleton, 1848), written for her nephew, George Herbert Sass. South Caroliniana Library.

19. Yates Snowden here refers to John Bennett's poem that had just appeared in *The State* under his alias "Alexander Findlay McClintock" and entitled "Thoughts on Climbing My Family Tree."

20. In keeping with Bennett's humorous verse on heredity, Snowden signs his postcard Galton for Sir Francis Galton (1822–1911), cousin of Charles Darwin. Galton was an English scientist best known for his work in anthropology and heredity. He founded the science of eugenics and devised the system of fingerprint identification. COL; WBD.

21. Florence Maria Henerey, the daughter of William S. Henerey, attended the Confederate Home College as a young woman. She was a close friend of the Snowdens, to whom she wrote letters recalling many vivid memories of the latter part of the nineteenth century. One reminiscence was of

the first Memorial Day celebration held at Magnolia Cemetery. Timrod's "Memorial Ode" was sung by the Confederate Home girls to the tune of "The Reaper," under the direction of Thomas O'Neale, who hired a small organ and carried it to the cemetery on a wagon. When the Yankees in command at Charleston objected to the ode's being used, the officers' wives who studied music under O'Neale used their influence to let it be sung. MSC.

22. Thomas S. Sinkler (1861-1929), a Berkeley county and Charleston businessman, was a banker and a member of the wholesale coal company of Johnson, Sinkler & Stone. DSCB; CRA.

23. "Artemus Ward" was the pseudonym of Charles Farrar Browne (1834–1867), the New England humorist who contributed to various American and English periodicals. WWWH.

24. Arius, who died in A.D. 336, was the Greek theologian whose views were repudiated at the Council of Nicaea in A.D. 325. WBD.

25. John Frederick Charles Fuller, b. 1878, a British soldier and author, served in the Boer War and World War II and became an authority on tank warfare. He wrote several histories, including *The Generalship of Ulysses S. Grant* (1929). COL; WBD.

26. Henry Wager Halleck (1815-1872), a N.Y. army officer and businessman, was made general-in-chief of the U.S. Army and military adviser to President Abraham Lincoln in 1862. In 1864 he was superseded by Ulysses Grant, whose chief of staff he became. WWWH.

27. Alfred Hutty (1877-1954), a Mich., N.Y., and Charleston artist, was a designer and fabricator of stained-glass windows, who was invited by the Carolina Art Association to start an art school at the Gibbes Museum in Charleston in 1919. His career as an etcher began in 1921, first of architecture and then of trees and people. He also used the media of pencil drawing and drypoint. Alfred and his wife, Bessie, were friends of John and Susan Bennett. Columbia Art Museum Exhibition folder, February 1990: "Alfred Hutty and the Charleston Renaissance."

Chapter 18: 1930–1931

1. White and Thurber, who wrote the humorous book *Is Sex Necessary?* in 1929, were Elwyn Brooks White, b. 1899, a N.Y. author and magazine editor, and James Grover Thurber (1894-1961), an Ohio and N.Y. cartoonist and author. Both men worked on *The New Yorker*. USE; WWW, vol. 4.

2. Olin Burnham Chamberlain (1892-1968) was a Charleston physician and educator. DSCB.

3. Sam Davis (1842-1863), of Tenn., was a Confederate Army scout, who

was captured by Union forces and hanged 27 November 1863. WWWH.

4. Robert James Turnbull (1775–1833), the son of the colonizer and physician Andrew Turnbull, of Fla. and Charleston, was an attorney, an advocate of nullification, and a political writer, who used the pseudonym "Brutus." He was the author of *The Crisis,* published by A. E. Miller. WWWH; DSCB; WBD.

5. In his signature, Bennett uses his own initials and the surname "Casaubon" for Isaac Casaubon (1559–1614), of Geneva, France, and England, who was a French Huguenot classical scholar, theologian, and author. For a time, he was Henri IV's royal librarian in Paris. After the murder of the French king, he went to England, became an Anglican, and was made a prebendary of Canterbury and Westminster. He was buried in Westminster Abbey. COL; WBD.

6. The correspondence between Emily H. Fowles and John Bennett is in the South Caroliniana Library. In a tribute to Snowden in the University bulletin, *In Memorium: Yates Snowden, 1858–1933,* Emily Fowles included a large part of Bennett's comments. IMYS, 49–51.

7. John Bennett's branch of the family spelled their name Lyttelton most of the time, except for his father's brother, Lyttleton Savage Bennett, who died in childhood. John Bennett was distantly related to Viscount Cobham, formerly Lord Lyttleton, who was alive in 1931. William Henry Lyttleton (1724–1808), of England, Charleston, Jamaica, and Portugal, was a member of Parliament, governor of S.C., governor of Jamaica, and British ambassador to Portugal. WWWH.

8. Yates Snowden's review of *Marching with Sherman: Passages from the Letters and Diaries of Henry Hitchcock, 1864–1865,* edited by M. A. DeWolfe Howe (N.Y.: Yale University Press, 1927), first appeared in *The State* in 1929. Consisting of 58 pages, it was reprinted in booklet form in 1931. The inaccurate statements made by Major Hitchcock in regard to events that took place in Columbia were refuted by Snowden with citations from more reputable sources: other Federal officers, particularly General W. B. Hazen, U.S.A.; Southerners of highest integrity; and various historical documents. MSC.

9. Henry Hitchcock (1829–1902), an Ala., Mass., and Missouri teacher, lawyer, and editor, served as judge advocate on General Sherman's staff during the March to the Sea. WWW, vol. 1.

10. Edwin Grenville Seibels (1866–1954), a Columbia insurance executive and S.C. representative, had Yates Snowden's review of *Marching With Sherman,* which first appeared in *The State* in 1929, reprinted in booklet form. The data gathered by Professor Snowden clearly revealed errors in Hitchcock's story by using historical documentation. In the foreword, Seibels stated: "Broadly paraphrasing the words of Abraham Lincoln—it is published 'with malice toward none, with charity for all';—'that truth and justice shall not perish from the land.'" WWW, vol. 3; CRA; DSCB; MSC.

11. Oliver Otis Howard (1830–1909), a Maine Union Army officer, served in many campaigns with distinguished bravery. General Howard commanded the right wing of General Sherman's army on the March to the Sea. WWW, vol. 1; COL.

Chapter 19: 1932

1. Clements Ripley (1892–1954), a Tacoma, Los Angeles, and Charleston author and peach grower, wrote short stories, novels, and motion picture scripts. He was married to Katharine Ball, an author in her own right. Katharine was the daughter of William Watts and Fay Witte Ball, whose house in Charleston was less than one hundred yards away from the Ripleys' home. WWW, vol. 3; MSC.

2. Huger Wilkinson Jervey (1878–1949), a Charleston and N.Y. lawyer and educator, was a professor of Greek at the University of the South and dean of Columbia University Law School. WWW, vol. 2.

3. Marie Conway Oemler (1879–1932), a Savannah author married to John Norton Oemler, was a member of the Poetry Society of S.C., as well as the Poetry Society of Ga., and wrote several books, including *Slippy McGee* and an historical novel about John Wesley, *The Holy Lover.* WWW, vol. 1; MSC.

4. Arminius Oemler (1827–1897), of Savannah, was an agriculturist and a Confederate Army officer. WWWH.

5. Meta Johnson was Margaret M. A. Smyth, who was married to J. S. A. Johnson. She was the daughter of James Adger and Annie Briggs Smyth and the younger sister of Ellison. Meta and Ellison were Susan Bennett's first cousins. SSA.

6. John A. Murrell (1804–ca. 1846), a Tenn. outlaw and leader of a large band that terrorized the Southwest territories, was the subject of a biography written by his captor, Virgil A. Stewart. WWWH.

7. Ida Morris Jervey (1861–1939), the wife of Francis Jervey, was an authority on mushrooms. She painted them and also ate them to test whether they were poison. According to her grandson, Edward Ball of Charleston, the National Geographic Society had her edit an article they published on mushrooms. Thirty-two of her watercolors are in the Charleston Museum. Anne W. Rutledge and Edward Ball, personal communication, Charleston, May, 1990.

8. Baron Otto von Below, b. 1857, was a Prussian general, who commanded the 8th Army at Tannenberg and Masurian Lakes (1915–1916), the 6th Army and the 14th Army against Italy, and the new 1st Army (1918). The Baroness von Below was the former Ninna Bryce of Columbia. WBD.

9. Alexander Sprunt, Jr. (1898–1973), a Rock Hill and Charleston ornithologist and author, was the son of the Rev. Alexander Sprunt, Sr.,

pastor of the First (Scotch) Presbyterian Church of Charleston, who helped conduct the final rites for Yates Snowden at Magnolia Cemetery in 1933. Alexander, Jr., was ornithology curator of the Charleston Museum and wrote scientific articles and nature stories for magazines, as well as *Birds of S.C.* (1949), and other books on Southern birdlife. WWW, vol. 5; IMYS, 15.

10. Edwin G. Quattlebaum, b. 1864, of Fairfield county and Columbia, was a dentist. DSCB.

11. Frederick Dalcho (1770–1836), of England, Md., and Charleston, was an Episcopal priest, physician, church historian, and the author of *History of the Protestant Episcopal Church in S.C.* DSCB.

12. Richard Yeadon (1802–1870), of Charleston, was an attorney, a newspaper editor, and a S.C. representative. DSCB.

13. John Thomas Scharf (1843–1898), of Md. and N.Y., was an historian and an officer in both the Confederate Army and the Confederate Navy. WWWH.

Chapter 20: The Parting

1. Major Benjamin Sloan (1836–1923), of Pendleton, was an officer in the Confederate Army, a school principal, the superintendent of the Greenville and Columbia Railroad, a college professor, and the president of the University of S.C. (1902–1908). CRO, 134.

2. Lawrence Beacham Owens, b. 1869, of La. and Columbia, was a practicing physician for many years, a S.C. representative, and the mayor of Columbia (1926–1941). WAL, 4:878–879; HEN, 86, 452.

3. William Watts Ball's comments were written on 17 December 1930, to Emily H. Fowles, in response to her request for information about Snowden for her term paper. MSC.

4. Henry Disbrow Phillips (1882–1955), of Columbia and Va., was rector of Trinity Episcopal Church (1921–1938) and bishop of Southwestern Va. (1938–1954). HEN, 146; Tombstone in Trinity Cathedral Churchyard, Columbia, S.C.

5. Duncan Clinch Heyward (1864–1943), of Richland county, Colleton county, Charleston, and Columbia, was a rice planter for twenty-five years, then a businessman and banker. He was governor of S.C. for two terms (1903–1907) and the author of *Seed from Madagascar* (Chapel Hill: University of N.C. Press, 1937). WAL, 4:587–588; WWW, vol. 2.

6. Several of these stories appeared in *In Memorium,* in an article by LeRoy Want, first written for *The News and Courier* (27 February 1933). The others were told by Orin and Innis Crow, who were friends of the Snowdens. IMYS, 21–25.

7. Interestingly enough, the English of ancient days believed that the devil lived up north, just as ardently as did the Southerners of the nineteenth century. It was the custom to leave the door in the north transept open during baptism, so that when the evil spirit came out of the child during the ceremony, it would not stay inside the church but depart for the northern regions.

8. These comments come from the S.C. Historical Society, Charleston, S.C.

9. Prentiss was probably George Denison Prentice (1802–1870), a Conn. and Ky. journalist, who was an ardent Unionist, although both his sons fought for the Confederacy. He was the first editor of the *New England Review* (1828); founded the Louisville *Daily Journal* (1830); and wrote a column for the N.Y. *Ledger,* "Wit and Humor." COL.

10. Robert Breen in 1937 was a young Hollywood actor with a fine soprano voice. In 1944 and 1945 Breen was a U.S. soldier with a fine tenor voice, who served in Jeep Shows, the first troop entertainment outfit of World War II in Europe, which abandoned stage presentations to fight alongside other troops during the Battle of the Bulge. The Special Services unit, manned by musicians and actors such as Hollywood's Bobby Breen and Mickey Rooney and Broadway's Laurence Hugo, was led by Captain James R. D. Anderson, of Ga. and Columbia, a University of S.C. graduate.

11. Chapman James Milling, b. 1901, a Darlington and Columbia psychiatrist, was the author of *Red Carolinians, Singing Arrows,* and *Exiles Without End.* He also collaborated with Carl Julien on *Beneath So Kind a Sky* and wrote numerous poems and scientific papers. SCL.

Select Bibliography

AIK   Aikman, Louisa Susannah Wells. *The Journey of a Voyage From Charlestown, S.C., to London, Undertaken During the American Revolution By a Daughter of an Eminent American Loyalist in the Year 1778 And Written From Memory Only in 1779.* New York: The New York Historical Society, 1906.

BAI   Baird, Charles W. *History of the Huguenot Emigration to America.* 2 vols. New York: Dodd, Mead and Co., 1885.

BAR   Barnwell, Stephen B. *The Story of an American Family.* Marquette, Mich.: 1969.

BEN   Bennett, John. "Gullah: A Negro Patois," *The South Atlantic Quarterly* 7 (1907): 332–47 and 8 (1909): 39–52.

BON   Bonham Family Manuscripts, 1765–1961, in the South Caroliniana Library.

BOS   Bosman, William (Willem). *A New and Accurate Description of the Coast of Guinea.* A Facsimile of the 1705 English Edition, with New Introduction by John Ralph Willis. London: Frank Cass & Co., Ltd., 1967.

CEP   *The Charleston Evening Post,* Charleston, S.C.

COL   *The Columbia Encyclopedia.* Edited by Clarke F. Ansley. New York: Columbia University Press, 1940.

CRA   Crawford, Geddings Hardy, ed. *Who's Who in South Carolina: A Dictionary of Contemporaries, Containing Biographical Notices of Eminent Men of South Carolina.* Columbia: McCaw, 1921.

CRO   Crow, Orin Faison. "The Control of the University of South Carolina, 1801–1926: A Case Study of State University Control." Doctoral diss., George Peabody College for Teachers, 1931.

CYC   *Cyclopedia of Literary Characters.* Edited by Frank N. Magill. New York: Harper and Row, 1963.

DICH Dickens, Charles. *Hard Times for These Times.* New York: The Heritage Press, 1966.

DICN Dickens, Charles. *The Life and Adventures of Nicholas Nickleby.* New York: The Heritage Press, 1940.

DICO Dickens, Charles. *Our Mutual Friend.* New York: The Heritage Press, 1957.

DICP Dickens, Charles. *The Posthumous Papers of the Pickwick Club.* New York: The Heritage Press, 1938.

DAB *Dictionary of American Biography.* Edited by Dumas Malone. 20 vols. New York: Charles Scribner's Sons, 1933.

DABS *Dictionary of American Biography, Supplement 3 (1941–1945).* Edited by Edward T. James. New York: Charles Scribner's Sons, 1973.

DSCB *Dictionary of South Carolina Biography.* Edited by Richard N. Côté and Patricia H. Williams. Easley, S.C.: Southern Historical Press, 1985.

DUR Durham, Frank. *DuBose Heyward: The Man Who Wrote Porgy.* Port Washington, N.Y.: Kennikat Press, Inc., 1965.

EBR *Encyclopaedia Britannica.* Edited by Walter Yust. Chicago: 1952.

FLA Flagg, Jared Bradley. *Life and Letters of Washington Allston.* New York: 1892.

FOE Foerster, Norman, ed. *American Poetry and Prose.* 3d ed. Boston: Houghton Mifflin Co., 1947.

FRE Freeman, Douglas Southall. *Lee's Lieutenants: A Study in Command.* 3 vols. New York: Charles Scribner's Sons, 1944.

FUL Fulmer, Henry Griffin. "The Civil War Diary of Samuel Wells Leland, M.D., 1861–1865." Master of Arts Thesis, University of S.C., 1985.

GRE Gregg, Alexander. *History of the Old Cheraws.* New York: Richardson and Co., 1867.

HAL Hall, Marshall. *The Artists of Northumbria.* Newcastle upon Tyne, England: Marshall Hall Assoc., 1973.

HEN Hennig, Helen Kohn, ed. *Columbia: Capital City of South Carolina, 1786–1936.* Columbia: The R. L. Bryan Co., 1936.

HIR Hirsch, Arthur Henry. *The Huguenots of Colonial South Carolina.* Durham, N.C.: Duke University Press, 1928.

HUN Hungerpiller, J. C., ed. *South Carolina Literature.* Columbia: The R. L. Bryan Co., 1931.

IMYS *In Memoriam: Yates Snowden, 1858–1933.* Columbia: University of S.C., July 1934.

JOH Johnson, Joseph. *Traditions and Reminiscences, Chiefly of the American Revolution in the South.* Charleston: Walker & James, 1851.

KIR Kirkland, Thomas J., and Robert M. Kennedy. *Historic Camden.* 2 vols. Columbia: The State Co., 1905.

LAT Latimer, Samuel L., Jr. *The Story of the State, 1891–1969, and the Gonzales Brothers.* Columbia: The State Printing Co., 1970.

LAW Lawson, John. *History of North Carolina: A Journal of a Thousand Miles Travel Among the Indians from South to North Carolina.* Edited by Frances Latham Harriss. Richmond: Garrett and Massie, 1961.

MSC Manuscript Collections of the South Caroliniana Library, Columbia, S.C.

MCC *Mary Chestnut's Civil War.* Edited by C. Vann Woodward. New Haven: Yale University Press, 1981.

MWB *Memoirs of William Butler.* Atlanta: James P. Harrison & Co., 1885.

MML Moore, M. A., Sr., M.D. *Life of General Edward Lacey.* Spartanburg, S.C.: Douglass, Evins & Company, 1859. Reprint. Greenville, S.C.: A Press, Inc., 1981.

MOR Moragné, Mary Elizabeth. *The British Partisan.* Macon, Ga.: Burke, Boykin, and Co., 1864.

MUR Murray, Robert K., and Roger W. Brucker. *Trapped.* New York: G. P. Putnam's Sons, 1979.

NEB *The New Encyclopaedia Britannica.* 15th ed. Edited by Philip W. Goetz. 1989.

N&C *The News and Courier.* Charleston, S.C.

OED *The Compact Edition of the Oxford English Dictionary.* Edited by James Murray, et al. New York: Oxford University Press, 1971.

PGH Publications List of the Georgia Historical Society, 1989.

SGA Selby, Gilbert Augustus. *Anthology of Poetry and Prose.* Introduction by A. S. Salley, Jr. Columbia: The R. L. Bryan Co., 1953.

SEL   [Selby, Julian Augustus]. *The Countess Pourtales.* A Reprint of the 1878 *A Checkered Life* by "One Who Knows," with New Introduction by Felix Old Boy [Yates Snowden]. Columbia: S. & H. Publishing Co., 1915.

SJA   Selby, Julian Augustus. *Memorabilia and Anecdotal Reminiscences of Columbia, S.C., and Incidents Connected Therewith.* Columbia: The R. L. Bryan Co., 1905.

SHE   Sheridan, Richard Brinsley. *The Critic, or A Tragedy Rehearsed,* in *British Dramatists from Dryden to Sheridan.* Edited by George H. Nettleton and Arthur E. Case. Boston: Houghton Mifflin Co., 1939.

SAH   Smith, Alice Ravenel Huger, and D. E. Huger Smith. *The Dwelling Houses of Charleston, South Carolina.* New York: J. B. Lippincott Co., 1917.

SMI   Smith, William. *A Dictionary of the Bible.* Revised and edited by F. N. and M. A. Peloubet. Chicago: The John C. Winston Co., 1884.

SMY   Smythe, Louisa Rebecca McCord. "Recollections." Typed manuscript copies in the South Carolina Historical Society, Charleston, and the South Caroliniana Library, Columbia.

SSA   Smythe-Stoney-Adger Papers. South Carolina Historical Society, Charleston.

SCA   "South Carolina College Alumni Records." Collected by Andrew Charles Moore. 7 typed vols., 1905. South Caroliniana Library, Columbia.

SCHM   *South Carolina Historical and Genealogical Magazine.* Vols. 2 (1901), 11 (1910), 34 (1933), 35 (1934), and 76 (1975).

SCL   *South Carolina Lives: The Palmetto Who's Who.* Edited by Louise Jones DuBose. Hopkinsville, Ky.: Historical Record Association, 1963.

STA   *The State,* Columbia, S.C.

THO   Thomas, Albert Sidney. *A Historical Account of the Protestant Episcopal Church in South Carolina, 1820-1957.* Columbia: The R. L. Bryan Co., 1957.

TIP   Thomas, Isaiah. *The History of Printing in America.* 2 vols. Worcester, Mass.: Isaiah Thomas, 1810.

THT   Thompson, Henry T. *Henry Timrod: Laureate of the Confederacy.* Columbia: The State Co., 1928.

TRA   *Transactions of the Huguenot Society of South Carolina.* Charleston, S.C., 1889-1989, 1-94.

TUR   Turnbull, Robert J. *Bibliography of South Carolina, 1563–1950.* Charlottesville: University of Virginia Press, 1956.

USE   *The Universal Standard Encyclopedia: An Abridgement of The New Funk & Wagnalls Encyclopedia.* Edited by Joseph Laffan Morse. New York: Unicorn, 1955.

VER   Verner, Samuel Phillips. *Pioneering in Central Africa.* Richmond: Presbyterian Committee of Publication, 1903.

WAL   Wallace, David Duncan. *The History of South Carolina,* 4 vols. New York: The American Historical Society, 1934.

WBD   *Webster's Biographical Dictionary.* Edited by William Allan Neilson. Springfield, Mass.: G. & C. Merriam, 1943.

WWW   *Who Was Who in America.* 7 vols. (1897–1981). Chicago: Marquis, 1943–1981.

WWWH   *Who Was Who in America.* Historical Volume (1607–1896). Chicago: Marquis, 1963.

WIL   Willis, Eola. *The Charleston Stage in the XVIII Century, With Social Settings of the Time.* Columbia: The State Co., 1924.

WOO   Wood, Christopher. *The Dictionary of Victorian Painters.* 2d ed. Woodbridge, England: Antique Collectors' Club, 1978.

YPS   *The Yearbook of the Poetry Society of South Carolina.* Charleston, S.C., 1921–1928.

Index

All individuals are included, except for Yates Snowden, Ann Warley Snowden, John Bennett, and Susan Smythe Bennett, whose names appear in almost every letter.